SOVIET–BRITISH RELATIONS
SINCE THE 1970s

Soviet–British Relations
since the 1970s

Edited by
ALEX PRAVDA and PETER J. S. DUNCAN

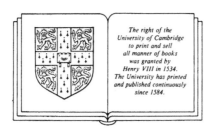

*The right of the
University of Cambridge
to print and sell
all manner of books
was granted by
Henry VIII in 1534.
The University has printed
and published continuously
since 1584.*

PUBLISHED IN ASSOCIATION WITH

THE ROYAL INSTITUTE OF
INTERNATIONAL AFFAIRS

CAMBRIDGE UNIVERSITY PRESS

CAMBRIDGE
LONDON   NEW YORK   PORT CHESTER
MELBOURNE   SYDNEY

CAMBRIDGE UNIVERSITY PRESS
Cambridge, New York, Melbourne, Madrid, Cape Town, Singapore, São Paulo

Cambridge University Press
The Edinburgh Building, Cambridge CB2 8RU, UK

Published in the United States of America by Cambridge University Press, New York

www.cambridge.org
Information on this title: www.cambridge.org/9780521374941

First published 1990
This digitally printed version 2008

A catalogue record for this publication is available from the British Library

Library of Congress Cataloguing in Publication data
Soviet–British relations / edited by Alex Pravda and Peter J.S. Duncan
        p.   cm.
Published in association with the Royal Institute of International Affairs.
ISBN 0-521-37494-4
1. Great Britain – Foreign relations – Soviet Union. 2. Soviet
Union – Foreign relations – Great Britain. I. Pravda, Alex, 1947–
II. Duncan, Peter J.S., 1953–   III. Royal Institute of
International Affairs.
DA47.65.S64 1990
327.41047–dc20 89–36868 CIP

ISBN 978-0-521-37494-1 hardback
ISBN 978-0-521-05497-3 paperback

Dedicated to Joseph Frankel

Contents

Contributors

Christoph Bluth, Research Associate, Department of War Studies, King's College, London

Michael Bowker, Lecturer, Department of Linguistic and International Studies, University of Surrey

Michael Clarke, Lecturer in Politics, University of Newcastle-upon-Tyne

Peter J.S. Duncan, Research Associate, Soviet Foreign Policy Programme, Royal Institute of International Affairs, 1986–8; Lecturer at the School of Slavonic and East European Studies, University of London

Anna Dyer, Executive Director, Trade Advisory Service, Glasgow, on secondment from Glasgow College

Michael Kaser, Professorial Fellow in Soviet Economics, St Antony's College, Oxford

Sir Curtis Keeble, GCMG, HM Ambassador to Moscow (1978–82)

Margot Light, Senior Lecturer, Department of International Relations, London School of Economics

John D. Morison, Senior Lecturer, Department of Russian Studies, University of Leeds

Alex Pravda, Director, Soviet Foreign Policy Programme, Royal Institute of International Affairs, 1986–9; Fellow of St Antony's College, Oxford, and Lecturer in Soviet and East European Politics at Oxford University

Peter J. Shearman, Lecturer in Soviet Foreign Policy, Department of Government, University of Essex

Acknowledgments

The idea for a volume on Soviet–British relations grew out of the process of formulating research projects for the new Soviet foreign policy programme at Chatham House. The establishment of this core programme at the Royal Institute of International Affairs was made possible by a grant (No. E00 22 2011) from the Economic and Social Research Council. We would like to take this opportunity to express our gratitude to the ESRC for its financial support for the programme in general and for this project in particular.

Contributors to the volume benefited greatly from their draft chapters being exposed to vigorous and critical discussions at a series of study groups held at Chatham House. These proved an invaluable source of correction, fresh information and new insights. Participants in the study groups included David Wedgwood Benn, John Berryman, Lord Brimelow, Robin Edmonds, Admiral Sir James Eberle, Joseph Frankel, Lawrence Freedman, Mike Gapes, Sir John Killick, Ralph Land, Neil Malcolm, Monty Johnstone, Malcolm Mackintosh, James McNeish, Edwina Moreton, Sir Frank Roberts, George Robertson, John Roper, John Harvey Samuel, Sir Howard Smith, Alan Brooke-Turner, Audrey Wells and William Wallace. The groups were also attended by officials from the British Council, the Department of Trade and Industry, the Foreign and Commonwealth Office and the Ministry of Defence. We are grateful to them all for giving so generously of their time and helping to make the study groups not merely useful but stimulating and enjoyable occasions.

Within the RIIA, our particular thanks go to William Wallace who provided advice and support throughout the project. It would have been impossible to produce the volume without the help of other members of the team at Chatham House. The Library and Press Library staff, notably Mary Bone, Jenny Foreman, Lesley Pitman (now at the School of Slavonic and East European Studies, University of London) gave generously of their expert knowledge. Our thanks also go to Pauline Wickham, head of publications, for her encouragement and patience. Last but not least we should like to take this opportunity to record our gratitude to Shyama Iyer, the Soviet foreign policy programme secretary, without whose efficiency and organisational talents the production of this study, as of other programme publications, would not have been possible.

While credit for the volume thus belongs to a large number of people, responsibility for its contents rests, of course, with the contributors and editors.

A.P.
P.J.S.D.

I   Introduction: pre-*perestroika* patterns

ALEX PRAVDA

The Soviet Union is central to British defence policy and Moscow considers London to be a pivotal member of the Western alliance. Yet relations between the Soviet Union and Britain have attracted little attention and less analysis. The Soviet literature is smaller than that on relations with France or West Germany and consists largely of descriptive historical surveys.[1] What analysis exists is confined mostly to studies of Britain and British politics which pay scant attention to relations with the USSR. On the Western side there is remarkably little on contemporary relations between the two countries. We have a number of good historical studies, concentrating mostly on the pre- and immediate post-war periods.[2] The sparseness of the literature on the last twenty years is highlighted by the fact that two reports of the House of Commons Foreign Affairs Committee provide perhaps the fullest information and comment on the recent period.[3] Britain hardly figures in the relatively small body of literature on Soviet relations with Western Europe and what treatment it attracts is typically couched in security terms.[4]

The thin coverage of Soviet–British relations in the academic literature is a product of both scholarly focus and the nature of the subject. British foreign policy questions, outside the defence and security areas, have until very recently attracted surprisingly little academic interest. Analysts working in the Soviet foreign policy field have long neglected relations with the states of Western Europe by comparison with their extensive concern towards relations with the US and the Third World. The relative neglect of British–Soviet relations in the literature reflects not just the vagaries of academic fashion but the nature of the relations themselves. For thirty and arguably forty years after the revolution of 1917, Moscow's relations with London were critical to Soviet foreign policy and figured centrally on the international stage. Since then the decline of British power and the rise of superpower dominance have combined to overshadow Soviet–UK relations. Even within the superpower shadow Soviet relations with Britain have had a less discernible profile than those with West Germany or

1

France. Elusiveness has compounded this decline in salience. Soviet bilateral relations with Britain have appeared to be less active than those with other major West European states. Paris, Rome and Bonn have conducted quite vigorous bilateral relations while London has preferred to deal with Moscow through multilateral fora, the CSCE and most notably NATO. Similarly, the Soviet Union has conducted its British policy as part of a wider strategy towards Western Europe and the Atlantic alliance. Soviet relations with Britain depend more than do relations with France or West Germany on movements in larger East–West contexts. Relations between the Soviet Union and Britain are thus particularly difficult to disentangle from the skein of broader multilateral interactions.

The fact that the strands of the relationship are woven closely into the larger pattern of Soviet relations with the United States and Western Europe does not diminish their significance or interest. Indeed, the very diffusion of British–Soviet relations makes their study as rewarding as it is difficult. While West German relations with the Soviet Union constitute the central focus of the triangular European–Atlantic–Soviet relationship, looking at this through the prism of Soviet–British relations yields a revealing perspective that sets into sharp relief the Atlanticist/European problems of managing change in East–West relations.

Soviet–British relations are significant not simply for the insights they can provide into these wider sets of relationships. Though very much a part of East–West relations, the bilateral relationship between the Soviet Union and Britain does have a life of its own, distinct though not autonomous. A degree of distinctiveness emerges, for instance, if we compare the patterns of Soviet–British and more general East–West relations over the years. While the cycles in bilateral relations have followed the overall East–West pattern, the exact contours differ significantly. A graph plotting the course of development of the two sets of relations would show the Soviet–British curve declining earlier and often more sharply at times of general decline in East–West relations but also rising earlier from the low points in the broader relationship. As Curtis Keeble chronicles in chapter 2, active hostility in relations between Britain and the fledgling Bolshevik regime in the civil war period was followed by the early establishment of formal contact. Similarly, after the Second World War relations between Britain and the Soviet Union were among the first to cool and the first to start showing signs of warming in the mid-1950s. Over twenty years later, events in Afghanistan and Poland affected Soviet relations with Britain more adversely than they did with France, Italy and West Germany. Yet it was Soviet–British relations which were among the first to show some recovery in the post-Brezhnev period. The historical record thus delineates a relationship between the two countries that has oscillated with a slightly different rhythm and within a somewhat narrower band at the lower end of the spectrum of variation in East–West relations.

Two sets of features of the relationship have helped to account for this distinctive pattern of oscillation. One is the low intensity, the 'thinness' of bilateral contacts. Attitudes on both sides have tended towards cool wariness. Cultural affinities and non-governmental as well as economic ties have been weaker than those linking the Soviet Union with France, Italy or West Germany. This has made the relationship vulnerable to its other distinctive feature: ill-aligned national interests. Not only have British and Soviet interests intersected at few points; their compatibility has also been complicated by dependence on the development of broader East–West and West–West relationships. The first two sections that follow review the nature of mutual perceptions and the 'thinness' of contacts; the last briefly considers the configuration of interests that have shaped relations. This introductory chapter thus seeks to sketch the *established* features and patterns of the relationship before *perestroika*.

IMAGES AND PERCEPTIONS

Notoriously slippery as objects of analysis, national images and perceptions merit the careful attention they receive in chapters 3 and 4 since they affect the mutual assessment of behaviour and shape the climate in which Soviet–British relations are conducted. Through the decades the prevailing climate has been one of mutual mistrust based on distant wariness. This contrasts with the mixture of more intense emotions linking the Soviet Union with countries such as France or Germany, both countries with histories of far greater and more direct involvement with Russia and the USSR. History also affects, if to a lesser degree, mutual national images in Britain and the Soviet Union. For the British, the Soviet system still bears the imprint of imperial Russia, a regime combining the worst features of continental authoritarianism. The more recent history of the Soviet Union reinforces such negative images with Marxism–Leninism and totalitarianism. The image of the Soviet system as totalitarian, as a regime suppressing individual rights and values has, as Michael Clarke shows in chapter 4, long prevailed among the British public, officials and politicians alike, largely regardless of party affiliations. Alien in its domestic absolutism and ideology, the Soviet system also appears objectionable and threatening by virtue of an imperial expansionism often perceived to be inherent in national ambition and compounded by Marxist–Leninist messianism. For many British politicians and officials, then, the Soviet Union has seemed a threat on at least two scores: as an alien system of government and as an insecure and ambitious international power. Shaping their image of the Soviet Threat is a mixture of instinctive antipathy to Marxism–Leninism and pragmatic mistrust of historical Russian security concerns and imperial ambitions.[5]

Given the huge disparities in power and influence between the two countries, it is hardly surprising that Britain figures far less prominently in Soviet public and elite consciousness. The Soviet picture of the West is dominated by the United States, and in the European context, France and the Federal Republic of Germany. Soviet public attitudes towards Britain may be described as ones of detached respect rather than the admiration for cultural achievement which still attaches to France or the curious blend of awe and anxiety that surrounds Germany. Britain is seen as a rather distant, old-fashioned and conservative society, nostalgic about its historical greatness rather than optimistic about its future. Among the Soviet elite these general images are amplified by assessments of Britain found in the specialist literature which here, as in other areas, reflects as well as refracts opinion within policy circles. As Peter Duncan shows in chapter 3, Soviet specialists have tended to highlight the economic ills and social injustices of a divided society ruled by an entrenched elite serving the interests of 'monopoly capital'. British ruling circles have appeared to their Soviet counterparts as old-fashioned, formal and aloof if polite in manner. Andrei Gromyko, who once served as Ambassador to London, recalls in his memoirs how Anthony Eden conformed to his picture of a typical Englishman: 'Tall, gaunt, slightly phlegmatic and almost always smartly dressed in black.'[6] Another former Ambassador to London, Ivan Maisky, recalls his Minister, Litvinov, telling him of the existence within the British elite of class-based hostility towards socialism and *realpolitik* inclination towards co-operation with the Soviet Union.[7] Soviet commentators and officials still tend to see these two tendencies as creating a duality, a certain ambivalence in British elite attitudes towards the Soviet Union that makes them unpredictable and unreliable as a partner. A mix of instinctive antipathy and pragmatic wariness on the British side has thus reinforced Soviet uncertainty and detached suspicion.

CONTACTS AND TIES

Distance and wary detachment in mutual images and perceptions correspond to a pattern of contacts and ties that may be described as low in intensity.

Cultural contacts have run at a relatively low and fluctuating level. The regular educational, scientific and artistic exchanges which began in earnest thirty years ago have remained hostage to the vicissitudes of the overall political relationship. As John Morison points out in chapter 8, cultural relations are a sensitive barometer of political relations and have usually been the first to reflect a downturn in the general climate, as happened, for instance, in the aftermath of the invasion of Afghanistan and the imposition of martial law in Poland. Slow to build up, cultural relations have failed generally to realise the full potential of

British interest in Russian culture and, more markedly, have fallen short in capitalising on the popularity in the Soviet Union of English literature and especially language. In part this reflects the difficulties of working with the Soviet bureaucratic machine which, until Gorbachev, had regarded with suspicion attempts to spread Western values. In part, too, the failure to take full advantage of Soviet public interest in things English stems from the low priority London has typically accorded cultural diplomacy, an activity promoted far more vigorously by Italy, West Germany and France. The Continental intellectual tradition that helps to explain the differences between British and other West European states' cultural relations with the Soviet Union also partly accounts for distinctions in non-governmental political contacts.

The presence on the Continental political scene of large Marxist parties and trade union movements has meant that their contacts with Moscow have traditionally formed an important element in overall national relations with the Soviet Union. Differing attitudes to the USSR have often figured significantly in domestic politics, making relations with the Soviet Union a salient if divisive issue. In Britain the question of contacts with the Soviet Union has been neither as prominent nor as controversial. One obvious reason lies in the very different composition, political orientation and influence of the Left in the United Kingdom. The most evident disparity in the configuration of the Left in many Continental countries and the United Kingdom is that between communist parties. By comparison with France or Italy Britain has scarcely had a serious communist movement. This has clearly affected Moscow's conduct of relations with British communists. Coming on top of the usual problems posed by political disagreements, the derisory electoral performance of the British party has prompted Moscow, at least over the last thirty years, to keep relations at a low level.

The Soviet Union has paid far more attention to fostering ties with two components of the broad Left exercising far greater influence on society and policy: the peace movements and the trade unions. The Soviet Union has consistently given declaratory though not material support to the various peace groups, notably CND, not so much for their leftist political tendencies as for their influence on public opinion on defence issues. Potential policy utility rather than political affinity has also shaped Soviet attitudes towards the trade union movement. As Mike Bowker and Peter Shearman stress in chapter 7, when choosing partners, whether within the trade union movement or elsewhere in Britain, Moscow has typically made attitudes and benefit to the Soviet Union and its foreign policy the most important criteria.

Pragmatism and regard for Soviet foreign policy interests have also shaped Moscow's relations with the most important organised force within the Left in Britain, the Labour Party. While evincing public preference, albeit mixed with critical comment, for Labour's policies over those of the Tories, Soviet

5

commentators have often found it difficult to distinguish Socialist from Conservative foreign policies. In Moscow's eyes Labour's international stance has suffered from two disabilities which have tended to complicate relations. First, those on the British Left often feel even more strongly about the Soviet pursuit of coercive policies at home and, particularly in Eastern Europe, than do their Tory counterparts. Secondly, in order to deflect criticism from strongly patriotic opinion within the party, the trade unions and the electorate, Labour pledges on foreign and especially defence policy have often undergone substantial trimming in their translation into policy once the party is in government.[8] Such pragmatic shifts, as well as the perennial divisions within the Labour Party, have often created the impression in Moscow of a lack of trustworthiness and principle. Gromyko, for instance, writes derisively of the Labour Party's ideological foundation under Gaitskell as that of 'the ruling class, the bourgeoisie, plus some petty bourgeois admixtures'.[9] As the Soviet Union sets great store by predictability and policy consistency, Moscow may well prefer dealing with Conservative rather than Labour governments.[10]

The low level of Soviet contacts with the Left in Britain and the adjustment of these contacts to pragmatic foreign policy utility considerations has meant that non-governmental political ties have had little direct apparent impact on overall Soviet–British relations. The same pragmatic factors have shaped a far thicker relationship with the Left in Germany, particularly with the SPD, and have significantly affected Soviet relations with the FRG. The absence of a strong non-governmental strand has had mixed indirect effects on Soviet–British relations. On the one hand relations have developed in a less politically and ideologically contentious domestic atmosphere than is the case with France, Italy or West Germany; on the other, the relationship has not had the important political constituency and lobby it enjoys where ties with the Left are far stronger.

The area usually expected to provide non-contentious and stable support for strengthening bilateral relations is trade. Commercial relations formed the earliest links between Britain and Soviet Russia and have since proved a resilient if slender bilateral connection. The 1921 trade agreement marked a pioneering move to recognise the new Bolshevik regime. Britain was the first Western ally to try and normalise relations and considered trade the most appropriate instrument. As Lloyd George told the House of Commons in February 1920: 'We have failed to restore Russia to sanity by force. I believe we can save her by trade. Commerce has a sobering influence in its operations.'[11]

The extent to which trade proved able to help relations was conditioned, as Michael Kaser chronicles in chapter 9, by disruptive changes in Soviet policy. Commercial contacts did little to cushion these. Still, the United Kingdom remained the Soviet Union's leading Western trading partner until the mid-

1960s when the expanding volume of exchanges quickly dwarfed Britain's sluggish share. Over the last ten years Britain has ranked between sixth and ninth in OECD exports to the Soviet Union, coming well below all major competitors. France and Italy have stayed comfortably in the top half dozen, a group headed of course by the FRG.[12] The reasons for the slow growth in trade that underlies Britain's slippage in the league table of Soviet Western partners are both political and commercial. The general climate of political relations has on occasion affected the development of trade. The series of expulsions of Soviet representatives from London in 1971 and the freeze in political and diplomatic relations between 1979 and 1983 may well have impeded the success of British companies in securing contracts.[13] On the British side, political tensions can foster an impression in business circles that the government disapproves of trade with the USSR.[14] A more specific source of difficulty has been the constraints that COCOM restrictions place on British sales of high technology, a field which figures importantly in UK exports to the Soviet Union.[15] COCOM therefore attracts occasional complaints from British businessmen as well as perennial criticism from Moscow. In general, however, the range of potential exports covered is relatively small and Michael Kaser suggests that the hampering effect on British exports has not been particularly great. Nor indeed has the impact of the overall changes in political relations: the analysis of data in chapter 9 shows that the historical pattern of Soviet trade with Britain seems to be freer of fluctuation than that with other major Western partners.

Stability at low levels of trade seems, therefore, largely to be the result of a range of economic and commercial factors. The 'fit' between the Soviet and British economies is less good than that between the USSR and other West European trading partners. Industrial structures are less compatible and patterns of exchange less conducive to expansion of trade.[16] The high expectations set by agreements reached in 1975 when Mr Wilson extended a £950 million credit were disappointed when the Soviet Union failed to take advantage of the facility offered.[17] More recently, British exporters have suffered from the fact that the United Kingdom, unlike its European competitors, does not import large quantities of energy from the Soviet Union. Since Moscow has traditionally sought to balance trade where possible with individual hard currency countries, Britain has been at a disadvantage. West European states such as West Germany, France and Italy, which import large quantities of Soviet natural gas, have been better placed to make counter-trade arrangements.

Furthermore, as Mr Gorbachev told Mrs Thatcher in December 1987, British companies are seen as less competitive than those from other West European states.[18] It does seem that even in some traditionally strong export sectors British companies perform less well than their West German, French or Italian counterparts. This may be linked to issues of British business approach and

7

culture. As Anna Dyer suggests in chapter 10, British companies tend to be less interested in penetrating the bureaucracy that surrounds the Soviet market, a tendency noted by the 1986 Foreign Affairs Committee report on UK–Soviet relations which described British businessmen as often lacking in the 'persistence, tolerance, flexibility and patience required'.[19] While Italian, French and particularly West German firms are prepared to invest steady effort over a period of several years and ultimately reap the benefits of a lasting relationship, the horizons of most British companies are limited to the short term. Only a handful of the 1,200 that do business with the Soviet Union have the commitment or the facilities to compete effectively on the Soviet market. Of the 600 members of the Soviet–British Chamber of Commerce, a mere ten large companies account for approximately one-quarter of all exports to the Soviet Union.[20] This narrow base of British business interests in the Soviet Union has policy as well as commercial dimensions. The low level of overall Soviet trade – running at something like 1 per cent of British foreign trade, approximately on a par with Turkey – means that commercial support for better relations with the Soviet Union is relatively weak. Soviet commentators tend to exaggerate the interest of British business circles in Soviet trade as well as their efforts to influence government.[21] Soviet–British relations have typically lacked a powerful lobby capable not only of cushioning disruptions in ties but, more importantly, of promoting a thicker and more stable relationship.

POLITICAL AND SECURITY RELATIONS AND INTERESTS

The climate of political, diplomatic and security relations has clearly set the dominant tone of the overall relationship between the two countries. This dimension of relations, particularly in the security sphere, presents a pattern of contact that is stronger and more extensive than in other areas. Nevertheless, political relations are still low in intensity when compared to Soviet contacts with other major West European states. Symptomatic of this is the relative infrequency of high-level political contact between London and Moscow when compared to substantial periods of near-institutionalised summitry between Soviet leaders and their American, German and French counterparts. As in other spheres of the Soviet–British relationship, bilateral relations have been confined to a narrow band of issues. The low level of bilateral contact reflects the paucity of direct interests linking the two countries, interests that they can both best deal with on a bilateral rather than multilateral basis. Neither country has vital interests of a political rather than security nature that directly involve the other.[22] This contrasts starkly with Soviet relations with the Federal Republic of Germany insofar as they share direct interests particularly vital for the FRG, including the issue of ethnic Germans resident in the USSR as well as the obvious question of the development of relations with the GDR and its East European neighbours, issues over which the Soviet Union has exercised a dominant sway. Where British and Soviet interests intersect they form part of wider sets of issues which involve multilateral structures on the British side. Neither human rights questions nor matters of Third World conflict, let alone British and European security issues, lend themselves easily to bilateral negotiations.

While the agenda for bilateral negotiations has remained very restricted, the spectrum of issues for dialogue between Moscow and London has typically ranged more broadly than is the case in Moscow's relations with Bonn or Paris. The Soviet–British pool of issues suitable for useful discussion is wider if less deep. The 'wide and shallow' nature of the agenda mirrors the breadth and diffuseness of British international experience, interests and to some extent influence. Soviet estimates of Britain's international status have tended to highlight its global as well as Euro-Atlantic standing. While Soviet analysts stress the international decline of the United Kingdom and the tendency of London to entertain unrealistic ambitions,[23] based on past rather than present capabilities, they give more credence to British than to French claims to global interests. Britain is still often described as a major factor in world politics,[24] as a 'second-rank leading power', and is valued for its Third World experience. Permanent membership of the United Nations Security Council and the respect London commands in other international organisations reinforces Britain's global status in Soviet eyes. Moscow has often found it useful to consult London on regional issues, particularly in those areas where Soviet involvement exceeds knowledge and experience.[25]

Two factors have coloured Soviet–British exchanges on Third World issues as on other questions: a high degree of friction and the United States connection. Precisely because Britain retains interests in the Third World and still aspires to global influence, London is sensitive to signs of Soviet expansion and reacts more critically than do other major West European states. At the same time, the British tend to take a somewhat less automatically ideological view than do the Americans of the Soviet pursuit of regional influence. Exchanges with London, therefore, provide Moscow with an informed, critical yet less emotionally charged view of Third World issues than they get from Washington. In substantive terms, however, Britain's political proximity to the United States and its very limited global capabilities confine exchanges to consultation rather than anything approaching negotiation. Britain may adopt a somewhat more detached stance than the United States, yet, in Soviet eyes, almost invariably supports American policy.

The United States connection also bears centrally on Britain's relations with the Soviet Union in the European arena. Soviet assessments have generally depicted Britain's European affiliation as lacking in the strong commitment evident among its major European Community partners; Britain has appeared as a rather reluctant European in Moscow as well as elsewhere.[26] Undoubtedly a major force within the Community, Britain is seen as adopting an Atlanticist rather than European stance on many critical policy issues. The basis on which the UK qualifies as a 'medium power of the first rank' in Soviet eyes, remains predominantly Atlantic rather than European. Its Atlantic approach to Europe means that London takes a rather broader view of most European issues and considers that key European questions fall within the ambit of multi- rather than bilateral political discussion with the Soviet Union. For instance, Britain has generally displayed less interest than has France, Italy or Germany in Eastern Europe *per se*, except in the wider context of human rights issues. Britain's concern with Soviet and East European human rights records is inherent in the emphasis placed on the objectionable moral nature of the Soviet system, the totalitarian dimension of the Soviet threat. Characteristically, it was on Basket Three of the Helsinki process that Britain played an active and at times leading critical CSCE role.[27]

The broader processes of European political détente associated with Helsinki have figured less prominently in British–Soviet exchanges on European issues. Paris, Rome and Bonn have provided more fruitful and important partners for Moscow on the mainstream agenda of East–West political relations within Europe because they have a strong commitment to the notion of détente as a process of change. They have therefore ranked far higher in Soviet estimates as European interlocutors.[28] Britain, by contrast, has shown itself chary of détente as a process of changing East–West relations in Europe since the shifts involved have appeared to threaten or at least weaken Atlantic links which are essential to NATO, European security and, perhaps most important from London's standpoint, Britain's Euro-Atlantic standing and role.

At the core of post-war anxiety about the Soviet threat lies traditional British concern about the emergence of a hegemonic power on the European continent exercising political domination rather than simply military primacy. Actual fears of the Soviet Union posing a military threat to Western Europe have long receded; over thirty years ago Anthony Eden minuted to Cabinet that he did not believe the Russians had any plans for military aggression in the West.[29] However, Eden's apprehension about the potential danger and challenge to Europe represented by Soviet economic and political influence, backed by military power, has remained at the forefront of British thinking about the Soviet threat. London has tended to place far more consistent emphasis than Rome, Paris or Bonn on Soviet determination to drive wedges in the Western Alliance. Its stress on Moscow's 'splitting' strategy stems not so much from a more percipient or even different understanding of Soviet objectives as from a greater concern that *any* loosening of Atlantic ties represents a particular threat to British interests. After all, it was London which played the key role in initially inducing the United States to make a firm commitment to Europe on the basis of a Soviet threat to West European democracy. The American commitment and its associated NATO–Atlantic linkages clearly remain the keystone of the arch spanning Britain's Atlantic influence and its standing in Europe. Not unnaturally, Soviet moves to thicken bilateral political relations with Western European states, especially the FRG, raise a spectre of wedge–driving and decoupling. London is therefore peculiarly reluctant to engage with the Soviet Union on a bilateral basis on political issues of a European nature. As Margot Light notes in chapter 6, Britain has kept bilateral political relations, as distinct from multilateral relations, to a minimum. Moscow fully appreciates London's position and has therefore concentrated European diplomatic efforts on France – which is inherently inclined to assert national independence of the United States – and in particular on the FRG, which has the greatest national interest in long-term political rapprochement in Europe.

Soviet analysts see Britain's standing in Europe as determined by its Atlantic links. They view London as Washington's most loyal European ally and in turn see Britain's influence in Europe hinging on its special relationship with the US. As seen by Moscow, the strongest element of that relationship and indeed the firmest basis for British influence in Europe lies in the military sphere. Britain qualifies militarily as the most important European member of NATO [30] in as much as it alone possesses a strategic and nuclear deterrent, deploys considerable forces on the central front and plays a full role in the integrated military structure of NATO. British interests and opinion thus bear importantly on all NATO questions, particularly those involving the nature of transatlantic links. The security standing of Britain and its key involvement in European and also out-of-area NATO activity makes London both an important yet difficult interlocutor for Moscow.

Military issues make up a thicker strand of common concern shared by the two countries yet they also present the most intractable conflicts of interest as they are all inherently adversarial. Moreover, security issues overwhelmingly, of course, form part of a multilateral rather than bilateral agenda. British policy towards the Soviet Union is shaped in security matters, to an even greater extent than in other areas, by Alliance considerations. For instance, as Christoph Bluth notes in chapter 5, British concern to pre-empt unilateral moves to reduce forces on the central front prompted London to play an active role in promoting MBFR talks. The fact that Moscow has not been able to deal with London on security matters as a French-style independent actor does not, however, negate the considerable importance of the security dimension of the relationship. In some circumstances Britain's very embeddedness in NATO, as well as its own military capability, have enhanced the salience of London for Moscow and vice versa. On strategic nuclear issues, Britain's national capability and its integration in NATO have enlarged areas of common concern and potential interaction. The fact that Britain's deterrent is targeted against Moscow (the 'Moscow criterion') increases the importance for the Soviet Union of British nuclear forces beyond their numbers. As Christoph Bluth notes, Soviet analysts do not rule out the possibility that in a crisis Britain could assert national targeting priorities. Possession of a nuclear deterrent force gives Britain an interest in preventing nuclear proliferation, seeking to limit testing to some extent and halt the spread of chemical weapons. All these are areas in which London has played an important part in multilateral negotiations involving Moscow.[31]

Generally, however, Moscow sees Britain's 'independent' nuclear deterrent as highly dependent on the United States both in a strategic and technical sense. Security links with the US in Soviet eyes give London the kind of access to Washington not shared by other NATO members. Such access, and the special relationship of which it forms part, have considerably raised the status and value of Britain in Soviet eyes as an interlocutor on security as well as regional and other political issues. The value of the special relationship has of course declined since the 1950s and early 1960s when Britain could still perform some mediating or at least communication role between the United States and the Soviet Union. As direct superpower relations developed, the scope for any such role narrowed. The value of Britain's special relationship has also to some extent been reduced by the rise of West Germany to prominence as the United States' key European ally, at least in political regional terms. Still, there is no zero-sum relationship between West German and British ties and influence with the United States. London's close links with Washington have continued to provide a basis for British involvement, albeit increasingly an indirect one, in superpower relations.

Looking not merely at the security strand of Soviet–British relations but at the relationship as a whole, it is clear that the circumscribed agenda of common concerns and directly negotiable issues limits both the stake and the leverage on either side. The highly asymmetrical nature of the relationship means that the Soviet Union should possess potentially far greater leverage, in the form of sanctions. Yet moves such as political and military pressure on NATO which might operate as sanctions have in fact only helped to further objectives to maintain firm Atlantic links. The incentives that Moscow can offer London are also few since Britain has remained wary of rapprochement, again for reasons of Atlantic solidity. On the British side, leverage has been limited to trade, which has generally run at low levels, and co-operation or opposition in various multilateral fora on political and security issues. In none of the above areas have considerations of British policy movement constituted a sufficiently important factor for Moscow to act as effective leverage. The Soviet Union has long considered relations with London as important but less likely to yield as high a return on the same investment as relations with Paris or Bonn. For the last thirty years Britain has figured importantly for the role it plays and the returns it may yield in larger sets of relations with the West in general and the United States in particular. For Britain the larger structural dimension of the relationship has also proved decisive. Relations clearly figure more prominently in calculations in London than in Moscow. But they figure as part of a more complex equation that also involves Washington and Bonn. Considerations bearing on the Western Alliance and British domestic politics, rather than changes in the nature of the Soviet Union and threat, have tended to shape British policy towards Moscow. London has tended to view rapid changes in East–West relations as likely to disturb the stability of the framework which largely defines Britain's established international position and role. Hence, while remaining wary of Soviet expansionism, London has tried on occasion to correct destabilising tension as well as to warn against excessive détente in relations between Moscow and major Western capitals. British policy, as Margot Light notes, has typically been a dual one of armed vigilance coupled with a search for agreements.

It is largely British concern to be both vigilant and prudent, to help temper the extremes of East–West relations, that accounts for the distinctive historical pattern of relations between the two countries noted earlier. In both the 'first' and 'second' Cold Wars, it was British policy moves which initiated shifts in the bilateral relationship. Soon after the end of World War II the United Kingdom took a key role in alerting the West to the dangers of the Soviet threat; by the mid-1950s London was trying to play an active part in seeking to engage the USSR politically and relieve some of the Cold War tension. Similarly, Mrs Thatcher, after taking a harder stance than most of her allies towards the Soviet Union in 1979–83 – perhaps uncharacteristically doctrinaire by standards of traditional British pragmatism – sought to improve dialogue with Moscow at a time when general East–West tensions remained high. Soviet–British relations during the first three years of the Gorbachev leadership generally ran ahead of those between the Soviet Union and other West European states. In line with traditional British concern to strike a balance and avoid extremes, as East–West relations have improved apace since 1987, so unease seems to have grown about the destabilising effects of such a rapid new détente and London has played a prominent role in cautioning against premature changes in Western security policy.

To a marked extent, then, the contours of the last decade and indeed of current British policy and Soviet–British relations seem to conform to the historical pattern: oscillation between distant coolness, friction and some degree of warmth. At the same time, the last four or five years have seen the political relationship reach a level of dialogue and contact higher than at any period since the war. While many elements of the historical relationship remain in place, structural factors that have long shaped the cyclical path of the relationship now themselves appear to be changing. Since Mr Gorbachev came to power Moscow has radically altered its foreign policy thinking and strategy in an effort to reduce the salience of the military factor and ideological conflict in Soviet relations with the outside world and instead emphasise the importance of co-operation. Gorbachev is clearly seeking to increase Soviet international influence by working through and with rather than against the international system. His moves in the military sphere as well as on regional problems suggest that this strategic shift from conflict towards co-operation is serious rather than rhetorical.

In the West European context the new Soviet strategy has taken the form of far greater willingness to upgrade political and economic relations. This, plus apparent Soviet readiness to eliminate the conventional superiority of Warsaw Pact forces, may help reduce the basic tensions that have traditionally plagued relations between Moscow and London. At the same time, renewed détente between Moscow and Bonn may arouse traditional anxieties in London. Whatever the eventual effect of these changes on the historical cyclical pattern of Soviet–British relations, the impact of shifts in the international environment is readily apparent in all dimensions of the relationship. It is perhaps too soon to judge whether that impact is moving the relationship away from its historical pattern. It is a major objective of this study to offer some basis for the consideration of this question by examining the nature and development of the relationship, particularly over the last decade. The opening chapter by Curtis Keeble sets this decade into historical context and those that follow examine the main facets of recent and current bilateral relations. By covering policy perspectives, cultural and non-governmental contacts as well as more traditional areas such as economic, security and diplomatic and political ties, the volume seeks to provide a fully rounded picture of recent relations between the two countries.

NOTES

1. V. G. Trukhanovsky and N. K. Kapitonova, *Sovetsko-angliiskie otnosheniia 1945–1978* (Mezhdunarodnye otnosheniia, 1979); and V. A. Ryzhikov, *Sovetsko-angliiskie otnosheniia. Osnovnye etapy istorii* (Mezhdunarodnye otnosheniia, 1987).
2. For instance, F. S. Northedge and A. Wells, *Britain and Soviet Communism* (Macmillan, 1982); S. White, *Britain and the Bolshevik Revolution: A Study in the Politics of Diplomacy, 1920–24* (Macmillan, 1979); G. Gorodetsky, *The Precarious Truce: Anglo–Soviet Relations 1924–27* (Cambridge University Press, 1977); and R.

H. Ullman, *Anglo–Soviet Relations 1917–21*, 3 vols. (Princeton University Press 1961–72). An exception is Curtis Keeble's excellent history of Anglo–Soviet relations (Macmillan forthcoming) which, while concentrating on the first forty years, does cover more recent developments.

3. House of Commons Foreign Affairs Committee, Second Report, Session 1985–86, *UK–Soviet Relations*, 2 vols. (HMSO, 1986); and First Report Session 1988–89, *Eastern Europe and the Soviet Union* (HMSO, 1989).

4. See, for example, E. Young, 'Britain: lowered guard' in G. Ginsburg and A. Z. Rubinstein, eds., *Soviet Foreign Policy towards Western Europe* (Praeger, 1978), pp. 134–50.

5. See, for instance, Raymond Smith, 'A climate of opinion: British officials and the development of British–Soviet policy 1945–47', *International Affairs*, 64: 4 (Autumn 1988), pp. 631–47.

6. Andrei Gromyko, *Memories* (Hutchinson, 1989), p. 155.

7. I. M. Maisky, *Vospominaniia sovetskogo posla* (1964), Vol. 2, p. 35 quoted in A. Lebedev, *Ocherki britanskoi vneshnei politiki* (Mezhdunarodyne otnosheniia, 1988), p. 188.

8. Trukhanovsky and Kapitonova, *Sovetsko-angliiski otnosheniia*, pp. 243–6.

9. Andrei Gromyko, *Memories*, p. 160.

10. For a clear statement to this effect, see *Khrushchev Remembers* (Sphere Books, 1971), p. 375.

11. *Parliamentary Debates*, 5th Series, vol. 125, p. 44.

12. Foreign Affairs Committee, *UK–Soviet Relations* (1986), vol. 2, p. 342; Foreign Affairs Committee, *Eastern Europe and the Soviet Union* (1989), p. 190.

13. *UK–Soviet Relations*, vol. 2, pp. 14–15.

14. *Ibid.*, p. 258.

15. Foreign Affairs Committee, *Eastern Europe and the Soviet Union*, p. 190.

16. See 'UK trade with the Soviet Union', Memorandum submitted by the Department of Trade and Industry, Foreign Affairs Committee, *Eastern Europe and the Soviet Union*, p. 183; Kestor George of the DTI, *ibid.*, p. 194.

17. *Financial Times*, 20 September 1975.

18. *Soviet News*, 9 December 1987, p. 437.

19. Foreign Affairs Committee Report, 1986, p. 265.

20. Kestor George in evidence to the Foreign Affairs Committee, *Eastern Europe and the Soviet Union*, p. 201.

21. V. A. Ryzhikov, *Sovetsko-angliiskie otnosheniia*, pp. 222–5.

22. See J. Frankel, *British Foreign Policy 1945–73* (Oxford University Press, 1975), p. 190.

23. Trukhanovsky and Kapitonova, *Sovetsko-angliiski otnosheniia*, p. 10.

24. S. Volodin, 'Britain in today's world politics', *International Affairs* (Moscow), 7 (1984), p. 73; Ryzhikov, *Sovetsko-angliiskie otnosheniia*, p. 258.

25. For instance, see the accounts of David Owen's talks in Moscow, *Pravda*, 12 October 1977, p. 4; *The Observer*, 9 October 1977; Trukhanovsky and Kapitonova, *Sovetsko-angliiskie otnosheniia*, p. 236.

26. See V. G. Baranovsky, *Evropeiskoe soobshchestvo v sisteme mezhdunarodnykh otnoshenii* (Nauka, 1986); and N. S. Kishilov, ed., *Zapadno–Evropeiskaia integratsiia: politicheskie aspekty* (Nauka, 1985).

27. Michael Clarke, 'The implementation of Britain's CSCE policy 1975–85', in S.

Smith and M. Clarke, eds., *Foreign Policy Implementation* (Allen and Unwin, 1985), p. 145; Golubev, 'Sovetsko-angliiskie otnoshennia na rubezhe 70–80-kh godov', *Voprosy Istorii*, 7 (1984), p. 52; and Trukhanovsky and Kapitonova, *Sovetsko–angliiskie otnosheniia*, p. 240.

28. See James Callaghan's reference to Britain being lower down in the 'batting order', Foreign Affairs Committee, *UK–Soviet Relations* (1986), vol. 2, p. 60.

29. A. Eden, *Full Circle. The Memoirs of Sir Anthony Eden* (Cassell, 1960), p. 363.

30. G. V. Kolosov, *Voenno–politicheskii kurs Anglii v Evrope* (Nauka, 1984), p. 28.

31. David Owen in evidence to the House of Commons Foreign Affairs Committee, *UK–Soviet Relations* (1986), vol. 2, pp. 369–71.

2 The historical perspective

CURTIS KEEBLE

In December 1917 the British War Cabinet confronted the problem raised by the October Revolution in Russia: whether to come out in open opposition to the Bolsheviks or to make the best deal possible with them. Balfour summed up his policy in the memorable phrase: 'If this be drifting, then I am a drifter by deliberate policy'[1] – and his colleagues were content to leave the dilemma unresolved. Over the next seventy years, and frequently in the most critical international situations, successive British Governments were to be confronted by the same problem. They did not always drift. From David Lloyd George to Margaret Thatcher, Prime Ministers placed their personal imprint upon policy. Trade agreements were made, unmade and remade. Diplomatic relations were established, broken and re-established. Political dialogue was initiated, interrupted and restarted. Policies were pursued which at one extreme brought Britain and the Soviet Union into open military conflict and at the other into formal military alliance. The relationship was rarely symmetrical. By the time the revolutionaries of 1917 had created the world's second superpower, Britain had declined from the zenith of imperial power and, within the context of this evolving power ratio, the problem of achieving a stable and satisfactory British–Soviet relationship remained unsolved.

Now with a new Soviet leadership pursuing a policy of 'reconstruction' and exercising a more flexible and sophisticated diplomacy, a new phase in the relationship may be opening. The purpose of the present chapter is to set that phase in the context of earlier phases in British–Soviet relations as they have developed since 1917. It is written from a British standpoint. It is an attempt to explain how successive British Governments have viewed the Soviet Union, how they have responded to the evolution of Soviet policy and how, as a result, the British–Soviet relationship itself has evolved. To condense the diplomatic history of these seventy years into a single chapter has required a degree of simplification, compression and omission which, I am conscious, does less than justice to many facets of a complex relationship and to the personalities who have done much to shape its evolution. Alongside the direct inter-governmental relationship lies the whole range of non-governmental and quasi-governmental relationships. Below it lies the web of covert and semi-covert activity ranging from the manipulation of public opinion to the classic intelligence and counter–intelligence operations. Relevant though all this has been to the totality of the relationship, space does not permit more than the briefest mention in this chapter. Moreover to present the British–Soviet relationship as a specific relationship in its own right is to underrate the complexity of the Alliance relationships and the interaction of the two Governments in the United Nations and other multilateral negotiating bodies, for instance in the area of arms control, where the wider East–West relationship has been developed, in the context of which British policy has had to be formulated and implemented. I hope nevertheless that some recital of the main events may serve, even for those familiar with the period, as a convenient reminder of a well-trodden path, an inducement to re-examine some of the scenery along the way and a guide to what may lie around the next corner.

The year 1917 makes a convenient starting point, but diplomacy does not start with a clean sheet. Neither the Soviet Government nor those who had to deal with it could escape the geo-political realities of Europe or the legacy, part substantive, part emotional, part instinctive, of the policies of pre-revolutionary Russia. The year 1917 brought a new ideological confrontation, but problems such as Russia's frontier with the states of Eastern and South-eastern Europe, the conflict with Britain over Afghanistan and the whole triangular British–German–Russian relationship were deep rooted.

REACTION TO REVOLUTION

The prospect that the February Revolution might lead to a more democratic system of government in Russia had been generally welcomed in Britain, but Kerensky had proved a disappointment. His overthrow by the Bolsheviks might not, it seemed, make matters much worse, but there were few people in Britain in 1917 – or, for that matter, in Russia – who expected a Bolshevik Government to last for long. There was already concern enough about the potentially disruptive effect of Karl Marx's teachings, but ideology had little to do with the initial British reaction to the October Revolution and the potential impact of Russian power harnessed to Communist doctrine was not a factor in British calculations. At that time Russia mattered to the British Government in one respect only. The war against Germany was at a critical stage. The dissolution of the Eastern front and the transfer of German and Austrian forces to the West might suffice to ensure a German victory. The British Government cared little who ruled Russia, so long as the Eastern front could be held open. For the Bolshevik leadership, however, the ending of hostilities with Germany was a primary requirement if they were to establish their own control over as much as possible of the territory of Imperial Russia. In this their interest was directly counter to that of Great Britain. In a revolutionary situation, it is always tempting for a foreign government, uncertain of the outcome, to seek to safeguard its position with both camps. This the British Government did, allowing Litvinov to stay in London and despatching Robert Bruce Lockhart to try to secure the co-operation of the Bolsheviks, while giving financial support to those anti-Bolshevik elements of the Imperial Army which might be prepared to continue the war against Germany. At some point, however, as the internal conflict is resolved, a dual policy of this type must become untenable. The failure of British policy was that, as the Bolsheviks strengthened their grip on Russia, so the British and French Governments increased their commitment to the anti-Bolshevik forces.

The ratification of the Treaty of Brest-Litovsk effectively marked the point at which the policy of seeking Bolshevik co-operation in the war against Germany had to end. Ignoring the fact that the anti-Bolshevik forces were concerned only with the pursuit of the civil war, the British Government saw them as the only potential allies. Allied supply bases for the Imperial Army still existed in Archangel and Vladivostok; from the beginning of 1918 Allied strategists had been tempted by the idea of landing a primarily Japanese force which could link up with the 70,000 Czech forces stranded in Siberia and form a common front against the Germans with a much smaller British force driving south from Archangel. British policy was formulated in the context of Alliance policy for the war against Germany. With France urging belligerence, the United States hesitant and Japan pursuing its own interests in the East, the process of Allied consultation dragged on through 1918. Repugnance at Bolshevik excesses turned the British mood progressively against the Bolsheviks. In Moscow Lockhart was arrested on suspicion of plotting against the regime and Litvinov was imprisoned in London. Eventually, in August 1918, an operation conceived as a means of pursuing the war against Germany with Bolshevik assistance, or at least Bolshevik acquiescence, was set in train, almost at the moment of victory over Germany, as a joint operation by Allied and anti-Bolshevik forces against the Bolsheviks.

With the defeat of Germany, the cause for the conflict of interest between Britain and Russia was removed. There was no longer any need for an Eastern front or for any British involvement in Russia. Opposition to the Bolsheviks had, however, continued to mount in Britain and, within the Cabinet, Churchill sought to convert the military operation in Russia into a campaign openly designed to unseat them. There was never any real possibility that a war-weary Britain would engage in such an enterprise and it took the Cabinet little time to decide that the British forces should be withdrawn. At the same time, rather than abandon their erstwhile friends, they decided to continue the flow of supplies to the White forces and thus once again to pursue simultaneously two incompatible policies. The momentum of earlier commitments and the difficulty of extricating the British forces were such that the two years following the defeat of Germany brought the only significant involvement of these forces in operations against the Bolsheviks. They brought also a decision that a state of war existed in practice, although, since the Bolsheviks had never been recognised, it could not be declared. A policy which saw Russia only as a factor in the war against Germany had failed because it ignored the realities of the Russian political scene and, in failing, it had, in practice, if not in intention, involved the British Government in an unsuccessful attempt to unseat those who were to determine Russia's future. It could scarcely fail to be seen as such by the Bolshevik leadership. Nevertheless, political and economic self-interest required the establishment of relations with the Allied Governments and, deep though the trauma of the intervention was, once power had been secured this became a primary objective of Soviet foreign policy.

RELATIONS ESTABLISHED, BROKEN AND RE-ESTABLISHED

For the Allied Governments, the consolidation of Bolshevik power in Russia presented a peculiarly intractable problem. Should they wait for this new Russia to crumble under the burden of its malign administration and its abhorrent doctrines and, while waiting, content themselves with walling off Europe – and above all a potentially Communist Germany – against the danger of infection? Or was there the possibility that, by the establishment of working relations and the development of common interests, the new leaders of Russia could be persuaded to forget their doctrine and act as responsible members of the international community? While they pondered, Russia, hitherto the object of others' policies, erupted on to the European scene. When the Red Army repulsed the Polish invasion in 1919 and took its counter-offensive to the suburbs of Warsaw, Lloyd George himself proclaimed British policy as being 'to arrest the flow of lava . . . to prevent the forcible eruption of Bolshevism into Allied lands'[2] and committed the British Government, very much as Chamberlain was to do in different circumstances twenty years later, to use 'all the means at their disposal' in assisting the Polish nation to defend its independence. On this occasion, however, Poland saved herself largely by her own efforts and, apart from the supply of some material, the British guarantee was not invoked.

It was Lloyd George who personally drove forward British policy towards the new Russia and the essence of that policy was less to contain Russia than to draw her into the international community. In this, he began to establish a community of interest, if only temporarily, with the Russian leadership. His first efforts to bring about a political settlement, made in the margins of the Peace Conference in Paris, were frustrated in part by the obduracy of the French Government and in part by the intractable political problem of Russia itself. However, he was able to secure the concurrence of the Allied Governments in establishing trade contacts and in consequence it was the British Government which, having led in the intervention, led the way in the establishment of relations by the negotiation of the 1921 Trade Agreement,[3] the *de facto* recognition of the Soviet Government and the setting up of Trade Missions in London and Moscow. The agreement in fact went well beyond the normal scope of a trade agreement. It was seen as preliminary to a formal treaty of peace and was accompanied by mutual commitments to refrain from 'hostile actions or undertakings' and the conduct of hostile 'official propaganda'. The Soviet Government, for its part, agreed to refrain from 'any attempt by military or diplomatic or any other form of action or propaganda to encourage any of the peoples of Asia in any form of hostile action against British interests or the British Empire, especially in India and in the Independent State of Afghanistan'. The agreement represented, for both parties, a remarkable success. For the Soviet Union, it marked the ending not only of the economic blockade, but, even more important, the breaking of the political blockade. For Britain, there was not only the prospect of the reopening of the Russian market, but the securing of guarantees against the disruptive effects of the dreaded Bolshevik propaganda. However, it was an agreement which, in a sense, went beyond the underlying political realities and in large measure its implementation was to be frustrated by both parties.

The setbacks followed quickly. For a time, though, the initiative rested with Britain. Seeking to broaden out his initiative into a major multilateral settlement with Russia, Lloyd George initiated the Genoa Conference of 1922. The invitation itself was seen in Moscow as 'confirming the recognition of Russia as a power whose participation in European affairs would be indispensable in the future'. Soviet policy was proclaimed as one of peaceful coexistence, although the Soviet tactic was 'without concealing our communist views, [to] confine ourselves to a brief and passing mention of them' and to 'do everything possible . . . to disunite the bourgeois countries that will be united against us'.[4] Allied claims for a settlement of pre-revolutionary Russian debts were countered by a Soviet demand for compensation in respect of losses sustained during the Allied intervention. The resulting deadlock was not broken by the follow-up meeting at The Hague. Indeed, the main – and for Britain highly unwelcome – outcome of Genoa came through a Soviet initiative in the form of the signature by the Soviet Union and Germany of the Treaty of Rapallo, an engagement, described by Lloyd George as an 'act of base treachery and perfidy'. It raised the spectre of Soviet–German rapprochement which was to haunt British policy makers throughout the subsequent years. As for the British claim in respect of pre-revolution debts, the effective writing off of claims and counter-claims, which could have been achieved in 1922, eluded generations of negotiators until it was eventually accepted in 1986.

With the fall of Lloyd George, the primary impulse for the development of British–Soviet relations was lost. Throughout the 1920s and 1930s, British policy varied according to the fluctuations of political power in Britain and the varying perceptions of Soviet policy. For its part, the Soviet Union, having achieved international recognition, sought with little success to derive economic and political benefit from it. In 1923, in the 'Curzon ultimatum', the British Government formally gave notice that they would consider themselves free from the obligations of the trade agreement unless, within a period of ten days, satisfactory assurances were received on various issues. These ranged from the continuation of Soviet propaganda in Persia, Afghanistan and India to the seizure of British trawlers and crews, proceedings against British subjects charged with espionage in Russia and, as the 'human rights' strand was woven into the relationship, the persecution of Russian priests. The crisis was resolved on the basis of Soviet assurances and, with the formation of Ramsay MacDonald's Labour Government, Britain proceeded in February 1924 to formal *de jure* recognition. From MacDonald's point of view, recognition was in part a political response to Labour Party opinion, in part a practical move designed to secure increased trade. For the Soviet Union, it represented a major diplomatic achievement and there was hope that it might lead to the grant of new British credit for the re-equipment of Soviet industry. In this expectation, definitive treaties on trade and financial questions were negotiated and initialled, but were set aside by the Conservative Government which took office in November 1924 after the incident of the Zinoviev letter. The letter (widely and probably correctly believed to be a forgery) allegedly contained instructions from Zinoviev as President of the Comintern to the British Communist Party concerning, *inter alia*, the formation of cells within the armed forces. Policy towards the Soviet Union was already a major election issue and the letter must have helped to seal MacDonald's fate. The downward slide in relations gathered force and in 1927 the Home Secretary authorised a police raid on the London offices of the Soviet trading company Arcos and the Soviet Trade Delegation. The raid failed to bring to light any convincing evidence of improper activities, but, relying largely on the evidence of intercepted Soviet cypher traffic, the British Government formally terminated the 1921 Trade Agreement and the Chargés d'Affaires in Moscow and London were withdrawn. The first decade had seen the whole cycle, from active military conflict between the forces of the two countries to the establishment of commercial and diplomatic relations and then to their breach.

In these early years, it was Britain which to the Soviet leaders seemed the effective bastion of imperialist power and the City of London the key to its finance. The bilateral relationship was therefore of special importance to them and they made some efforts to cultivate it. The tone of the relationship was, however, set largely by Britain and its oscillating pattern stemmed primarily from the oscillation of political power in Britain. Nevertheless, the evolution of the Soviet Union was also relevant. In the immediate post-revolution years the Bolshevik leaders had been concerned to establish their own power within Russia and then to secure their international recognition. To the extent that this was contrary to British objectives – first in relation to the pursuit of the war against Germany and then in relation to the independence of Poland – it had led to direct conflict. The military or economic power which the Bolsheviks could subsequently deploy outside their own borders was, however, negligible; it was the ideological threat to the British imperial structure which was the principal cause of concern to the British Government and it was against this that Lloyd George had sought and obtained assurances in the 1921 Trade Agreement. With the introduction of the New Economic Policy by Lenin, it had begun to seem that Lloyd George's dream of the evolution of the Soviet Union away from extreme socialism might be realised. Thus the advent to power of the Labour Party in Britain came at a moment when, despite the accession of Stalin and the waning of NEP, the Soviet Union was still showing its less menacing face to the world. To many in Britain the great socialist experiment, for all its tragedies, was a source of hope and admiration. In these circumstances, progression from the intervention of 1918 to the establishment of trade relations in 1921 and diplomatic relations in 1924 represented not merely the trend of political power in Britain, but a realistic reaction to the apparent trend of the Soviet Union itself. The subsequent trend of policy – the rejection of the 1924 Treaties, the Arcos raid and the breach of relations – reflected the Conservative election victory in 1924 and the ascendant influence of the Diehards. But again the underlying circumstances were changing. Within the Soviet Union the Stalin years were beginning to take shape. Few resources were available for the support of external subversion, but doctrinally it was important. It was barely necessary to forge the Zinoviev letter: the Comintern was in practice an instrument of the Soviet state and the contents of the letter were not out of line with Comintern policy. The provision of Soviet funds to back the miners in the General Strike of 1926, albeit under the guise of voluntary contributions by the Soviet miners to their fellow workers, fell into place as part of this policy. The Soviet threat perceived by the Diehards was not wholly imaginary. What they could not (or would not) understand was that the ideological and practical gulf between the British trade union movement and the exponents of Soviet Communism made it a hollow one.

The next cycle in the relationship, from 1927 to 1935, again corresponded in part to the evolution of political power in Britain. It was the declared policy of the Labour Party to resume full diplomatic relations with the Soviet Union and, despite Ramsay MacDonald's well-established dislike of the Bolsheviks, an emotion which they fully reciprocated, Ambassadors were exchanged within a few months of the Labour victory in 1929 and a new Temporary Commercial Agreement was negotiated. Again, a reversal of political fortune brought a reversal of the British–Soviet relationship, but again the deterioration was provoked in part by external circumstances. The international economic crisis and the introduction of Imperial preference provided a motive for denunciation of the trade agreement and in 1933 the arrest, trial and sentencing of the British engineers employed by Metropolitan-Vickers in Moscow precipitated a major political crisis, with the imposition of trade embargoes by both the British and Soviet Governments.

THE SEARCH FOR SECURITY

The Metropolitan-Vickers trial was the last major crisis in British–Soviet relations during the pre-war years and the years 1934 and 1935 were marked by a brief and superficially promising revival. For the early years of the Stalin regime, the Soviet Union had been turned very much inward. In its external policy it had opposed the post–Versailles structure and it had done much to create the political circumstances which destroyed the Weimar Republic and made possible the rise of the Nazis. Now, as the Nazi threat began to develop, Soviet policy appeared to change. The Soviet Government seemed ready to accept at least the possibility of ranging itself alongside the defenders of the status quo in Europe. The first overtures met with an encouraging, if less than enthusiastic, British response. In February 1934 a new, temporary Commercial Agreement was concluded; in July the first serious political discussions were initiated between Sir Robert (later Lord) Vansittart, Permanent Under-Secretary at the Foreign Office and Ivan Maisky, the Soviet Ambassador; and in September the Soviet Union, with support from Britain and France, took the momentous step of joining the League of Nations, an organisation which it had, until then, consistently denounced. In the following year, the visit of Anthony Eden as Lord Privy Seal to Moscow and Litvinov's visit to London for the funeral of King George V seemed to demonstrate that the policy of collective security might indeed provide the framework within which, irrespective of the doctrinal gulf between the two countries, a new and constructive alignment of British and Soviet foreign policy might take place. The reversal of Soviet policy which had opened up this prospect was remarkable, but it is legitimate to question whether, had it been put to the test, the policy would have survived. Would the Soviet Union have been prepared to hazard its own security in order to frustrate German expansion before a direct attack on its own territory? In 1939 it was certainly not prepared to do so, but by then Litvinov, the would-be architect of collective security, had gone and four more years of mistrust had accumulated.

As it was, the British Government saw the route to security in the consolidation of Western Europe and the appeasement of Germany. In such a situation, the development of a closer relationship with the Soviet Union seemed to them more likely to endanger than to promote the security of the United Kingdom. As Europe moved through the crisis years of the Spanish Civil War, the *Anschluss* with Austria and the annexation of Czechoslovakia, relations between Britain and the Soviet Union became gradually more tenuous. In the case of Spain, special factors came into play and emotions in Britain were aroused to an intensity which left its mark upon a generation – the generation to which Maclean and Burgess belonged – then growing into political awareness. In the early stages of the Civil War, the Soviet Union joined under British chairmanship in the work of the Non-Intervention Committee and some alignment of policy seemed possible, but as the inefficacy of the Committee became increasingly apparent the Soviet Union turned first to a policy of intervention in support of the Republican forces and then, for its own political reasons, began to distance itself from them. There was no identity of purpose between Britain and the Soviet Union at this time, but the Chiefs of Staff Sub-Committee noted in a Review of Imperial Defence in February 1937[5] that, although the Soviet Union would have no objection to a war between the capitalist powers, for the next few years 'the British Empire and the Soviet Union are likely to have two common enemies in Germany and Japan as well as a common desire for peace'. That the logic of this analysis did not carry over into the formation of policy is scarcely surprising when one remembers that this was a time when Stalin was largely occupied with the violent disposal of much of the top political and military leadership of the country. When the Spanish crisis was overtaken by the threat to Austria's independence, there was no disposition on the part of the British Government to consult the Soviet Union. The Soviet Government's proposal of March 1938 for measures of collective security either within or outside the League of Nations was met with a reply from the British Government indicating that a conference 'designed less to secure the settlement of outstanding problems than to organise concerted action against aggression' would not necessarily have a favourable effect.[6] Throughout the Czech crisis the Soviet Union, despite its interlocking treaty obligations to France and Czechoslovakia, was held at arm's length and its assertion of readiness to honour its obligations was never put to the test. After Munich, when the question of Soviet participation in a guarantee to the rump of the remaining Czech state was mooted, Chamberlain remarked that it would be 'much easier for everyone' if the Czechs decided they did not want this.[7]

Soviet historians allege that the objective of British policy at this time was to divert the thrust of German aggression away from Western Europe by turning it against the Soviet Union. Baldwin certainly once remarked that his heart would not be broken if Hitler turned eastward and that if there were to be any fighting in Europe he would as soon see it done between the Nazis and the Bolsheviks.[8] Yet there was no active policy to this effect and on at least one occasion, far from conniving in a move against the Soviet Union, the British Government stated specifically to the German Government that they could not compromise in respect of the German desire to isolate the Soviet Union and would not refuse co-operation with the latter solely on account of Soviet political views.[9] A more accurate charge would be that throughout the appeasement years the Soviet Union was seen as no more than a distasteful, potentially disruptive, but fortunately peripheral factor in British policy making. For its part, the Soviet Government doubtless hoped to stand aside and profit from any inter–imperialist war.

THE 1939 NEGOTIATIONS

It was only after the seizure by Germany of the rump of Czechoslovakia in March 1939 that the British Government began to consider some co-ordination of policy with the Soviet Union. A first anxious enquiry about possible Soviet aid to Romania brought a positive, but qualified, response. When the threat to Poland became more acute, the British Government, having given a unilateral guarantee, sought to reinsure with the Soviet Union. The British–French–Soviet negotiations, conducted on the Soviet side by Molotov and on the British by Sir William Seeds, HM Ambassador in Moscow, and William (later Lord) Strang, were the first substantial experience which the British Government had had of negotiating with the Soviet Union on a major politico-strategic issue. The mutual suspicion was intense. Chamberlain wrote to his sister on 26 March: 'I must confess to the most profound distrust of Russia'.[10] Stalin, for his part, had proclaimed on 10 March that the Soviet Union would not be drawn into conflicts by warmongers who were accustomed to have others pull their chestnuts out of the fire. After beginning the tripartite negotiation, he gave practical effect to his new policy by dismissing Litvinov and replacing him with Molotov. The British objective at the start of negotiations was to secure, at no cost in terms of new British commitments, a Soviet guarantee to Poland which could be called in at Polish discretion. The Soviet counter-offer was a formal tripartite treaty and to this, after much procrastination, the British Government agreed. The refusal of the Polish Government to accept a Soviet guarantee was a major problem, but step by step the British and French negotiators conceded virtually every Soviet requirement in relation to the main treaty, preserving only a thin cover against a Soviet right of intervention to prevent 'indirect aggression' through any of the border states, a right which in effect would have authorised the Soviet Union to move forces into those states at its own discretion and regardless of the wishes of their Governments. The Soviet requirement then turned to the parallel conclusion of a detailed agreement on the military measures to give effect to the political commitment, but while negotiations were in train, the Molotov–Ribbentrop Agreement was concluded, the British and French negotiators were left to pack their bags and the way was clear for the German–Soviet partition of Poland. The negotiations left a legacy of deepened mistrust. On the British side, the recollection of Rapallo could scarcely be avoided, the worst suspicion of Soviet double-dealing seemed confirmed and the doctrine of collective security exposed as a sham. On the Soviet side it was alleged that the British and French objective was essentially to divert the German drive eastward and embroil the Soviet Union in war; that the conduct of negotiations had never been serious; and that the Soviet Union had no option but to safeguard its own security. It is idle now to speculate whether, even as late as March 1939, a swift and positive acceptance of the Soviet proposal for a treaty might have brought success in the negotiations and what the consequences might then have been. As it was, there seemed little to choose between the Nazi and Soviet governments and British policy was formed accordingly.

After the declaration of war on Germany, the British Government had neither the time nor the inclination to devote much thought to relations with the Soviet Union. The conduct of Soviet policy confirmed their fears. After the partition of Poland came the move of Soviet forces into the Baltic States, the seizure of Bessarabia and Northern Bukovina from Romania, the attack on Finland and finally the formal incorporation of the Baltic States into the Soviet Union. A Soviet suggestion that Britain might mediate in the conflict with Finland brought an uneasy recollection of the fate of Czechoslovakia. Complicity in the dismemberment of yet another small country was rejected and, by the time the fighting ended, preparations for the despatch of a British force to Finland and an air attack on the Baku oil fields were well in hand. Had the Finnish–Soviet war been prolonged, British and Soviet forces might once again have been directly engaged on opposing sides.

A desultory effort was made to wean the Soviet Union into a neutrality less favourable to the German cause, but Britain had little to offer by way of inducement and as the German forces overran Europe there was less and less reason for the Soviet Government to compromise their relationship with a victorious Germany for the sake of an apparently defeated Britain. It was immediately after the fall of Paris that Stafford Cripps was appointed

Ambassador to Moscow and delivered to Stalin a letter in which Churchill pointed out bluntly: 'Germany became your friend almost at the same moment as she became our enemy.'[11] Nevertheless, Churchill expressed British readiness to discuss 'any of the vast problems created by Germany's present attempt to pursue in Europe a methodical process by successive stages of conquest and absorption'. The attempt to build a closer relationship at this stage of the war was fruitless. What it produced was the first indication of the coming confrontation over the political shape of Europe. 'If the Prime Minister wishes to restore the old equilibrium', replied Stalin, 'we cannot agree with him'.[12] Throughout 1940 and 1941 mutual suspicion grew. Molotov's visit to Berlin was seen in London as confirmation of the identity of view of Germany and the Soviet Union, while, in Moscow, Hess's flight to Britain seemed to confirm that a British–German peace was about to be concluded in preparation for an attack on the Soviet Union. Stalin was, however, in no mood to heed warnings of the imminence of a German attack and even less inclined to do so when they emanated from Britain.

THE WARTIME ALLIANCE

In his broadcast on the occasion of the German attack on the Soviet Union on 21 June 1941, Churchill proclaimed the policy of aid to Russia. No one, he said, had been a more persistent opponent of Communism than he and he would unsay no word he had spoken. But: 'The past with its crimes, its follies and its tragedies flashes away . . . We shall give whatever help we can to Russia and the Russian people.'[13] In formal terms British–Soviet relations were transformed. But the past could not be so easily dismissed. Britain and the Soviet Union had indeed a common interest in bringing about the defeat of Germany. So long as for each country the pursuit of the war was of supreme importance, that common interest could override the fundamental divergence in other respects. Once victory was assured, the bond was too weak to hold.

It was not easy to give immediate effect to the offer of aid. Influenced by the poor Soviet performance against Finland, the British Chiefs of Staff predicted that Soviet resistance would be a matter only of weeks. Even in his speech, Churchill had described the invasion of Russia as 'no more than a prelude to an attempted invasion of the British Isles'. It was thought to be relevant to the British war effort only in that, by delaying the invasion, it would allow more time for the re-equipment of the British forces. There was little incentive to sustain an apparently forlorn Soviet resistance if the price were to prejudice the defence of Britain by the diversion of essential American supplies. As Churchill expressed it: 'In the early days of our alliance there was little we could do, and I tried to fill the void by civilities.'[14] The wartime relationship was, however, quickly placed on a formal basis by the Anglo–Soviet Agreement of 12 July 1941[15] in which the two governments undertook to render each other 'assistance and support of all kinds' and not to conclude any armistice or peace treaty except by mutual agreement. Early in September the British Government agreed to provide, from British production, half the monthly Soviet requirement of 400 aircraft and 500 tanks and shortly afterwards a formal protocol on supplies was agreed at a tripartite meeting in Moscow. The visit to Moscow by Eden in December 1941 for discussion of questions relating to the post-war reconstruction of Europe was marked by a sharp conflict of views over the Soviet demand, as a condition for the conclusion of a formal Treaty of Alliance, for the recognition of the inclusion of the Baltic States in the Soviet Union and the restoration of the 1941 Finnish–Soviet frontier. The Soviet demand was refused, and the Treaty[16] concluded in the following year, when Molotov visited Britain, contained no territorial provisions. Part I provided for co-operation in the war against Germany and was valid for the duration of the war. Part II, valid for a period of twenty years, provided for common action to preserve peace and resist aggression in the post-war period, as well as for collaboration in the organisation of security and economic prosperity in Europe.

The wartime relationship presented certain clear features:

1   In the military field, the principal Soviet demand was for the opening of a Second Front in the West in order to relieve the pressure on the Soviet armies. It was first made in a message from Stalin to Churchill in July 1941 and was reiterated throughout the war. The communiqué issued on the signature of the Treaty of Alliance in May 1942 recorded 'full understanding' on 'the urgent task of creating a Second Front in Europe in 1942',[17] but the British Government were not prepared to accept a formal commitment and the communiqué was qualified both orally and by a confidential aide-mémoire. The definitive agreement on the launching of 'Overlord' in the summer of 1944 was not reached until the Teheran Conference in November 1943 and the delay was a constant source of recrimination. Such has been the depth of mistrust that, forty years later, Soviet historians have claimed that the delay was part of a 'policy designed to weaken the USSR to the maximum extent'.[18]

2   Although the volume of war material eventually delivered by Britain to the Soviet Union (including some 5,000 tanks and 7,000 aircraft) was substantial and the losses sustained in the Arctic convoys were very heavy, recrimination was constant. Soviet co-operation in the supply

arrangements was minimal and so too was the provision of operational intelligence.

3 Soviet political objectives had become apparent in the 1939 negotiations and were confirmed in 1940, when Stalin refused to accept the 'old equilibrium' in Europe. Disagreement over the future of Poland began as early as 30 July 1941, when the Foreign Secretary stated that the British Government did not recognise any territorial changes effected in Poland since August 1939. Soviet determination to retain the territorial gains of 1939–41 was made clear when Eden first discussed post-war questions in Moscow in December 1941 and on every subsequent opportunity, but the British Government, although it had not guaranteed the Polish frontier, was mindful of the Polish relationship. More significantly, committed by the Atlantic Charter and dependent upon American support, it would not enter into bilateral commitments regarding post-war territorial adjustments. The closer victory came, the more apparent became the threat of Soviet domination of Eastern Europe and the less the Allied power to prevent it.

4 Even prior to entry of the United States into the war, American assistance was of critical importance to the British war effort and prior consultation was therefore essential in respect of British policy on all major questions concerning relations with the Soviet Union. The pattern of American influence was inconsistent. At one extreme, it hardened British opposition to recognition of the integration of the Baltic States into the Soviet Union. At the other, Roosevelt was less squeamish than Churchill about accepting the Soviet Union as an ally of Britain in 1941 and subsequently less concerned about Soviet control of Eastern Europe.

5 The bilateral British–Soviet relationship was significant during the war years. Churchill's visit to Moscow in 1942 was the first East–West summit and the British record combined with his personality to enable Britain to play a role disproportionate to the underlying military and economic resources which it could deploy. The tripartite relationship developed in the wartime conferences represented a unique attempt at the co-ordination of policy, in relation not merely to the conduct of the war, but also to the post-war political reconstruction. The political agreements reached at these conferences proved valid only in so far as they first reflected and could later be secured by the military power of the parties. Militarily unenforceable policy declarations proved ephemeral.

6 Respect for the Soviet war effort and sympathy with the suffering of the

Soviet people, symbolised by the presentation by King George VI of a Sword of Honour to commemorate the defence of Stalingrad and given practical effect by Mrs Churchill's Aid to Russia campaign, brought a tendency towards more sympathetic interpretation of the Soviet political scene. The Soviet Union, for its part, officially regarded the Alliance as proving the possibility of effective political and military co-operation between states with differing social systems.[19] Yet mutual suspicion remained the essence of the inter-governmental relationship and with growing experience it tended to deepen. Churchill subsequently commented: 'We had always hated their wicked regime.'[20]

THE POST-WAR CONFRONTATION

The confrontation with Soviet military power in Europe and the threat of its projection worldwide has become such an accustomed feature of political-strategic analysis that it is necessary to make the effort to recognise its newness in 1945. Throughout the twenties and thirties the ideological challenge and the subversive application of Marxist doctrine as espoused by the Soviet leaders had been a potent factor in British politics – a promise to some and a threat to others. So too had been Soviet economic policies. As a military force, the Soviet Union had seemed largely irrelevant and certainly no cause for concern. The intergovernmental relationship had been characterised on the British side by bursts of enthusiasm from the Left and somewhat contemptuous hostility from the Right. On the Soviet side, Britain was seen as the leading imperial power and potential common interests in trade and security were outweighed by an instinctive and doctrinally motivated blend of confrontation and suspicion. Despite substantial diplomatic activity, both positive and negative, the actual content of relations had remained thin and the points of contact limited. There had been no common policy on European security and only an insignificant volume of trade. To describe it as a relationship of mutual irrelevance would be an exaggeration, but not wholly unmerited. After 1945 there was no question of irrelevance. The domination of Eastern and Central Europe by the Soviet armed forces introduced the relationship of armed hostility which was to dominate the British–Soviet relationship throughout most of four decades and to give the Soviet Union a substantial, sometimes dominant, place in the formation of British foreign and defence policy.

It is tempting, but in some respects misleading, to see a consistent evolution of policy from the end of the war, through the crises of the Cold War years to the Helsinki agreement in 1975. Within that period, the threat of Soviet expansion into Western Europe can arguably be regarded as a relatively short and distinct phase, beginning in 1944 and ending with the defeat of the Berlin blockade, while the European crises of subsequent years were caused more by Soviet determination to hold on to their wartime gains than by attempts to extend them. Throughout the whole period, Germany (and especially Berlin) remained a focal point of the confrontation and it was through the German agreements that the route to Helsinki was opened. Thus the old triangular British–German–Russian relationship remained valid and the residual quadripartite responsibility for Germany was of particular relevance to the conduct of British–Soviet affairs. From a different and wider perspective, however, there is a case for marking the transition to a new phase with the later years of the Khrushchev era, when the Cuban crisis and the subsequent concentration on the Soviet–American bilateral relationship brought a new dimension into the conduct of relations with the Soviet Union.

The first steps in the contest to determine the post-war political structure of Europe had been taken with the Soviet annexations of 1939–41 and the political skirmishing had begun in the wartime conferences. As early as 14 May 1942 Sir William Strang was minuting: 'I do not think we can counter the establishment of Russian predominance in Eastern Europe if Germany is crushed and disarmed and Russia participates in the final victory.'[21] By the time of the Teheran conference of November 1943 the shape of Soviet pressure could be seen, but Churchill commented: 'It would not have been right at Teheran for the Western democracies to found their plans upon suspicions of the Russian attitude in the hour of triumph and when all her dangers were removed.'[22] In April 1944 he was still disposed to 'let matters drift a little longer before considering a show-down'.[23] From mid–1944 the advance of Soviet forces into Eastern Europe and the destruction of the Polish resistance in Warsaw demonstrated the reality of Soviet power and the political ambitions of the Soviet leadership. At the bilateral British–Soviet summit in Moscow in October 1944, percentage figures for the British and Soviet interest in Romania, Greece, Yugoslavia, Hungary and Bulgaria were discussed, but by the time of the Yalta Conference in February 1945 Soviet forces were already in occupation of the greater part of Eastern Europe. It was against this background that the Yalta decisions, in particular about the future of Poland, were taken. Foreign Office planning for the post-war years recognised the prospect of a direct clash of interest with the Soviet Union in Europe and the Middle East and the Chiefs of Staff were already contemplating the need to organise resistance to the Soviet armed expansion, but priority was still given to the search for 'full and friendly co-operation' in a new system for world security.[24] On his return from Yalta, Churchill warned against the risk of 'some awful schism' and refused to question the good faith of the Soviet leadership who 'wished to live in honourable friendship and equality' with the West.[25] On 12 May, four days after the German surrender, he recognised the fact of the schism in a telegram to President

Truman about his anxiety over the Soviet domination of Eastern Europe behind the 'iron curtain': 'This issue of a settlement with Russia before our strength has gone seems to me to dwarf all others.'[26] As seen by Soviet historians, it was at this point that the Allied policy 'to weaken the position of the USSR at all costs, to harness German militarism and try once again to use it against the forces of peace, socialism and democracy' clearly emerged.[27]

The public mood in Britain did not change overnight and continued for some time to reflect the wartime alliance, but the negative factors in Soviet policy soon came into focus. Heir to the imperial ambitions of Tsarist Russia, the Soviet Union seemed ready to back a doctrine of ideological confrontation with massive armed force. The thought that a Labour Government in Britain might find common ground with the Soviet Government, voiced in the 1945 election, was soon dispelled. Successive British Governments, both Labour and Conservative, were forced to give priority to the wholly new fact of Soviet military power, first in the form of conventional forces in Europe and then in the development by the Soviet Union of the full military capability and global ambitions of a nuclear superpower within the European continent. In 1945, continental Europe was close to becoming a power vacuum, in which, with Britain exhausted by the war and the United States preparing to withdraw, the total dominance of Soviet power seemed a real prospect. Nevertheless, it was more than two years before defence policy became the primary factor in British policy towards the Soviet Union. When it was, it had to be formulated in terms of the consolidation of Western Europe and alliance with the United States. The scope for an independent British policy was correspondingly reduced and a line of development began which can be traced through to the present situation in which the twin elements of the Soviet–American nuclear balance and the balance of conventional forces in Europe still dominate a British–Soviet relationship subsumed in the post-1945 concept of an East–West relationship.

The oscillation of the relationship continued, but it stemmed now more from the fluctuating manifestations of Soviet policy than from the fluctuation of political power in Britain, where a degree of bipartisan support gradually developed in favour of policies designed first to resist the Soviet threat and then, to the extent permitted by Soviet policy, to work towards a sounder, more positive, relationship. In practice it fell to the post-war British Labour Government to initiate policies which reflected the assessment made by Winston Churchill in his 'iron curtain' speech at Fulton, Missouri in March 1946. They did not do so lightly. The sterile meetings of the Council of Foreign Ministers in the immediate post-war years gave little ground for optimism and Bevin was clear from the outset about the need for firmness in resisting Soviet expansion. In December 1945, he warned Stalin that there was a 'limit beyond which we could not tolerate continued Soviet infiltration and undermining of our position'.[28] He was, however, conscious of the danger of a total rift between the major powers and, although less inclined than Attlee to place full reliance upon the United Nations, he was concerned to avoid what he called an 'anti-attitude' towards the Soviet Union. In 1946, in an attempt to break down the tension, the British Government offered a thirty-year extension of the Treaty of Alliance. The offer was not taken up and the Treaty remained a dead letter, but as late as the spring of 1947 Bevin was able to derive some reassurance from a talk with Stalin. The hardening of American policy now began to exercise a certain influence and the deterioration in relations accelerated after the final failure of the Council of Foreign Ministers in December 1947. On 3 January 1948, after the exclusion of Eastern Europe from the Marshall Plan on Soviet dictation and the suppression of democratic rights supposedly guaranteed by Yalta, Attlee summed up the new threat in terms which were to become a standard description of Soviet policy: 'Soviet Communism pursues a policy of imperialism in a new form – ideological, economic and strategic – which threatens the welfare and the way of life of the other nations of Europe.'[29]

Against the background of this assessment, the relationship fell into a pattern which, throughout the remainder of the Stalin period and also in the fluctuations of the Khrushchev and Brezhnev years, showed a certain consistency in its main features. Britain no longer had the military or economic capacity to play a dominant role in the formulation of policy towards the Soviet Union, but the British role in the formulation of a collective response was important and it was seen as such in Moscow. Moreover, in a period when the European confrontation found its sharpest focus in the division of Germany, the British share in the post-war quadripartite arrangements, backed by the presence of British forces in Berlin and in West Germany, gave Britain a major role in the European component of East–West relations. What was at stake for Britain, as for the Soviet Union, was the central strategic issue of the control of continental Europe and there was little room for compromise.

In the immediate post-war years, Soviet policy in Eastern Europe had aggravated the deterioration in relations, and with the Czechoslovak coup of February 1948 Attlee's assessment of Soviet imperialism was swiftly confirmed. Less than ten years had passed since the trauma of Munich and the emotional effect of this new crisis provided a new impulse to the British initiative to develop a military and political consolidation of Western Europe. It was the Berlin blockade of 1948–49, however, which brought the open recognition by Bevin that the British Government could no longer exclude the use of force against the Soviet Union. He put the issue bluntly to Cabinet. To yield over Berlin would lead to further withdrawals and in the end to war. With firmness 'we might reckon on ten years of peace during which the defence of Western Europe might be consolidated'.[30] For the Conservatives, R. A. Butler, no scaremonger, commented in Parliament that war was 'not immediately inevitable'. The crisis was sufficient to provide the final spur for the formation of NATO in April 1949 and hence to set the parameters of the British–Soviet relationship for the next four decades. It may be noted that not only were British forces in direct confrontation with Soviet forces during the crisis, but that British diplomacy in Moscow played a significant part in its resolution. Indeed, in the combination of firm resistance and constructive negotiation it served as an object lesson in the handling of the relationship during this stage. With the defeat of the Berlin blockade and the formation of NATO the balance had been stabilised, but it was the stability of opposing tensions. They were tensions stemming not so much from misunderstanding or uncertainty, though neither had been obviated, but rather from a clear clash of interest. In the successive crises of the fifties and sixties, the Soviet Union did not again seek, by direct action, to bring further areas of Western Europe under its control. For both parties, change could be dangerous and initiatives were likely to prove unprofitable.

The years between the Berlin blockade and the death of Stalin offered little opportunity for development of the British–Soviet relationship. The East–West conflicts were spreading beyond Europe. The Korean War and the movement in the United States towards more aggressively anti–Soviet policies compelled a certain reorientation of policy. The consequences of the re–appraisal in Britain of the European, Commonwealth and American relationships do not belong in this study, but they could not fail to be reflected in some measure in the relationship with the Soviet Union. There was in fact little concern with the Soviet Union in the British general elections of 1950 and 1951. A Churchill proposal, made in 1950 and repeated in 1951, for a new meeting at Head of Government level was dismissed by the Soviet Union as an electioneering stunt. The defection of Burgess and Maclean reintroduced in heightened form the concern with Soviet subversion and espionage which had been a significant factor throughout the whole bilateral relationship and was to continue through all the post–war years.

THE KHRUSHCHEV YEARS

Only with the death of Stalin did there seem to be the opportunity for a new impulse to the bilateral relationship. Because the Khrushchev years were ones of activity, albeit of a highly erratic kind, in Soviet foreign policy, they offered the potential for a more meaningful British–Soviet relationship, in the context of which British diplomacy might have its effect on matters which were not, of themselves, susceptible to bilateral resolution. Even in the perspective of seventy chequered years of British–Soviet relations, this was a tumultuous period, with swift and repeated alternations between the prospect of understanding and the threat of nuclear war.

The British response to the change of leadership on the death of Stalin was quick and positive. In the attitude if not yet in the actions of the Soviet Union, a change was apparent. In power again, Churchill saw it as a 'supreme event'. Citing the telegram of 29 April 1945 in which he had warned Stalin not to underrate the divergences which were opening up, he recalled Locarno and sought to assure the Soviet Union that 'so far as human arrangements can run, the terrible events of the Hitler invasion will never be repeated and that Poland will remain a friendly power and a buffer, though not a puppet state'.[31]

Against this background, the British reaction to the Soviet suppression of the East German disturbances of 17 June 1953 was restrained and government policy was directed towards resolution of the major issues of tension in the East–West relationship. Substantive progress was slight. After the 1954 quadripartite Conference of Foreign Ministers in Berlin the Foreign Secretary noted the 'extreme rigidity' of the Soviet attitude on European questions.[32] Shortly afterwards, Churchill provoked a substantial tiff in Cabinet by telegraphing to propose a bilateral meeting with Malenkov. His colleagues, who had not been consulted, thought it a poor idea and the Soviet proposal for an all-European security conference provided the opportunity to drop it.[33] No progress was made towards quadripartite agreement on the German problem as a whole and in May 1955 the Soviet Union annulled the 1942 Treaty of Alliance with Britain on the ground that the British Government had inspired the restoration of German militarism by promoting German membership of NATO. Yet, a week later, the conclusion of the Austrian State Treaty seemed to indicate the prospect of a relaxation of the Soviet grip on central Europe, and July saw British participation for the last time in a quadripartite conference of Heads of Government. In February 1956 the Twentieth Party Congress marked the formal breach with the Stalin era and offered the establishment of 'firm, friendly relations' with Western powers. The dissolution of Cominform seemed to symbolise the potential new relationship and in May 1956, accepting the Charlemagne prize, Winston Churchill spoke of 'a new Russia' which, if the repudiation of Stalin were sincere, must have its part in a true unity of Europe.

The symbolic culmination of the bilateral relationship was the visit to Britain by Khrushchev and Bulganin in April 1956. This was the first and, until 1987, the only visit to Britain by the leader of the Communist Party of the Soviet Union while in office. Ministers seriously considered withdrawing the invitation in response to hostile Soviet statements about Britain, but the visit went ahead and the joint British–Soviet declaration of 26 April[34] seemed to inaugurate a new tone and content to the relationship, in which increased technical, scientific and cultural exchanges would be accompanied by both a substantial increase in bilateral trade and increased co-operation on the major current international problems, in particular the Middle East and disarmament. In the United States, there were even murmurings about the risk of British 'neutralism' and *The Times* commented that the task of handling the relationship was far more complex than it had been when the Soviet Union presented 'a simple military threat or simple subversion'. Prime Minister Eden, commenting that 'in the long history of diplomacy, suspicion has done more harm than confidence', saw in it the 'beginning of the beginning'.

In fact, if anything was beginning, it was the era in which superpower nuclear rivalry, symbolised by the launch of Sputnik in October 1957, was to dominate the structure of East–West relations. The Suez fiasco revealed the scraggy nakedness of British imperial power and prompted a graphic illustration of the changing power ratio when, in November 1956, Bulganin warned Eden of the threat that 'stronger states' might use rocket weapons against Britain. At the same time, the use of the Soviet army to crush Hungary dispelled any thought that the Austrian Treaty might presage an easing of the Soviet grip on Central Europe. The Soviet leaders, six months after their reception by Queen Elizabeth II, were described by the Archbishop of Canterbury as 'instruments and slaves of the devil'. The Labour Party denounced this reversion to the worst practices of the Stalinist period and a number of people resigned from the British Communist Party. In 1958 the Khrushchev ultimatum on Berlin brought the European tension back almost to the level of the immediate post-war years. British bilateral diplomacy played its part in the resolution of that crisis and the opening of the tripartite test ban treaty negotiations. Prime Minister Macmillan's visit to the Soviet Union in 1959 set the scene for a further revival of bilateral relations in the form of new trade and cultural agreements, the formation of an Anglo–Soviet Parliamentary Group and a visit to Britain by a Supreme Soviet delegation.

The limitations upon British bilateral diplomacy became apparent as the early 1960s saw the transition to a new stage in the British–Soviet relationship. It was almost by chance, but was symbolic nonetheless, that the collapse of the 1963 Paris summit, for which Macmillan had worked so hard, should have been brought about by the shooting down of the American U2 aircraft over the Soviet Union. The events of these years demonstrated above all the problems of a relationship which had to be conducted at two quite different levels. At the one level was the routine bilateral exchange of delegations and the development of political, cultural and commercial contacts which had been a feature of the late fifties and was continued with the exchange of major industrial exhibitions in London and Moscow in 1961. The building of the Berlin Wall had little effect on this process. At the other level, the Cuban crisis in the autumn of 1962 demonstrated the unique potential of the American–Soviet relationship both for good and for ill and inaugurated a period in which the agenda of East–West relations was to be dominated by the military security requirements of the two nuclear superpowers. The principal problem for British diplomacy was to bring the two levels of activity together, using the network of bilateral contacts not merely for its own value, but also as a means of generating an influence which might be effective in terms of the wider issues of East–West relations. In itself, even the Cuban crisis had remarkably little effect on the course of Soviet–British relations. Soviet action was condemned by Macmillan as a 'deliberate adventure', but within months the normal bilateral activities were resumed. That they were not wholly irrelevant to the superpower relationship was indicated by the successful culmination of Macmillan's efforts in the conclusion of the Partial Test Ban Treaty in August 1963. The co-chairmanship of the Geneva Conferences on Indo-China and on Laos had also left Britain with some basis for continuing the bilateral dialogue with the Soviet Union on the problems of this area. Nevertheless, the British role was now significantly reduced. The Sino–Soviet rupture introduced a new element into the pattern of East–West relations and in the succeeding years it was the Nixon–Kissinger diplomacy centred on the strategic defence relationship which inevitably occupied the centre of the stage.

DÉTENTE AND ITS FAILURE

Against the background of the gradual evolution of the broader East–West relationship, the movement of power between the Conservative and Labour parties did not, of itself, substantially change the pattern of British–Soviet bilateral relations in the sixties. The failure of the first attempt to join the European Community left a major hole in British policy, but the search for a more constructive relationship with the Soviet Union continued to be balanced by policies designed to promote the political, economic and strategic consolidation of Western Europe within the Atlantic Alliance. As President of the Board of Trade and later as Prime Minister, Harold Wilson consistently sought to maximise the relationship, but when he visited Moscow in 1966, he was treading a path not dissimilar to that taken by Macmillan and the subsequent development of scientific, technological and cultural contacts was built on an already established basis. On a return visit to London in 1967, Kosygin proposed a Treaty of Friendship. There was no indication of any reduction in Soviet ideological hostility, subversive activity or pressure on the Third World, but at least the fall of Khrushchev might, it seemed, lead to a more sober and predictable Soviet foreign policy, offering a possible basis for a more productive relationship.

The reality of Soviet power and Soviet policy in Eastern and Central Europe was, however, unchanged. In 1968 the Soviet and Warsaw Pact forces entered Czechoslovakia and, as in 1956, a promising trend towards better relations was abruptly broken. In 1956 the events in Hungary had, for Britain, taken second place to the Suez crisis. In 1968, without this complicating factor, the reaction was stronger. The example of 1938 was compelling. Parliament was recalled and Wilson spoke of 'flagrant aggression', but the burden of the Prime Minister's argument was that, while the West must look to its own defences, there must be no relapse into the 'frozen immobilism of the cold war'.[35] The cancellation of an exhibition of Anglo–Russian relations since the Middle Ages and a visit by the Red Army Choir constituted a less than dramatic response. The mood was one of anger and frustration. Once again Soviet action had caused international outrage, but it was action taken within an established sphere of Soviet interest and there were no options for effective counter-action by the West. In the Soviet Union Britain was seen as 'among the most active proponents of a policy of gradually separating individual European socialist countries from the socialist community' and was charged with deliberately provoking a deterioration in the climate of relations.[36] Even by the following year, however, Gromyko was in London, calling for an expansion and improvement in relations; by 1970, with the Soviet position in Czechoslovakia firmly re-established, bilateral British–Soviet relations were beginning to revert to normal. The European divide had been intensified and the wide gap between the content of the normal bilateral relationship and the major issues of European security had been graphically illustrated. It was the continuing Soviet covert activity in Britain which precipitated the next deterioration of the bilateral relationship in 1971, when the British Government ejected 105 Soviet intelligence agents. By this time, however, events on the wider scene were maturing to bring about the first major trend towards détente in East–West relations.

The détente of the early and mid-seventies appeared to offer a striking opportunity for qualitative change, comparable perhaps to that offered some forty years earlier by Litvinov's policy of collective security. The power relationships were, however, radically different. It was a decade in which, with the United States weakened by the Vietnam war, the Soviet Union could claim that the correlation of forces was moving steadily in favour of socialism. In nuclear weaponry the Soviet Union had attained a broad strategic parity with the United States and *Pravda* was able to proclaim that the authority of the homeland had never been higher.[37] In Europe, the key to the relationship with the Soviet Union still lay through Germany and the residual quadripartite responsibility gave Britain a direct role. Now, however, instead of Britain seeking security against a German threat, the German Ostpolitik seemed to open the way for a significant easing of European tensions and a reduction in the Soviet threat. The Nixon–Brezhnev summit, the negotiation of the SALT I agreement and the move towards SALT II set a tone which was matched in Europe by the German–Soviet and quadripartite agreements leading to the recognition of the German Democratic Republic and the Helsinki agreements. The Soviet Union could feel that it had at last obtained effective Western acceptance of the key element in its European security perimeter. The West could see in the Helsinki agreements of 1975 a recognition of the community of interest of the nations of Eastern and Western Europe, a route to freer interchange between them and even the prospect of some modification of the more oppressive features of the Soviet regime.

With the US–Soviet relationship active and apparently fruitful, with Germany in the centre of the European stage and France pursuing an active policy towards the Soviet Union, the place of Britain in Soviet foreign policy was reduced. Nevertheless, in the Helsinki climate, with arms control negotiations proceeding at the superpower level and parallel negotiations in train on the balanced reduction of conventional forces in Europe, there seemed to be the potential for the development of a positive British–Soviet bilateral relationship and a more effective linkage between bilateral and multilateral policies. In 1975 the Labour Government under Wilson concluded yet another package of bilateral agreements covering in substantial detail the familiar ground of economic, industrial, scientific and technological co-operation and providing not only for the development of Parliamentary and other exchanges, but also for regular bilateral political consultation between Ministers of Foreign Affairs or their representatives. The two Governments committed themselves to ensuring that 'favourable changes in the international situation become irreversible and that détente is extended to all areas of the world'.[38]

For two or three years, the progress in British–Soviet relations was maintained, but by the end of the seventies the mood had changed profoundly. The collapse of détente was marked by the repression of the Helsinki monitoring groups in the Soviet Union; the tension over Soviet policy in Angola, Mozambique, Ethiopia and South Yemen; the Soviet occupation of Afghanistan; the repression – albeit significantly without the use of the Soviet forces – of the Solidarity movement in Poland; and the installation of new Soviet weaponry in Europe.

An analysis of the failure of the détente of the seventies would require consideration not merely of these external manifestations of Soviet policy but also of several other areas: the longer term development of Soviet military power; the sluggish evolution of the Soviet state as well as the post-Vietnam recovery of the United States; the peculiar inability of President Carter to command Soviet respect; and the movement to the Right both in the United States and more widely in the politics of the Western democracies. It would take us far beyond the bounds of this chapter. In the perspective of British–Soviet relations, it was, however, not wholly coincidental that the critical point in the breakdown of détente should have been Soviet action in Afghanistan and Poland, areas of such concern to Britain in the 1920–21 negotiations. The use of the Soviet Army in Afghanistan was an attempt to hold by force a territory which, by revolution, had fallen within the socialist community but might not of itself remain there. Doctrinally, the Soviet Union claimed not to export revolution, but regarded itself as entitled to prevent by force the counter-revolutionary process. The Soviet action seemed only too clear a demonstration of the continuing force of Marxist-Leninist doctrine and old-style imperialism as the twin powers behind Soviet foreign policy. The threat to Western interests posed by the Soviet action in Afghanistan was not such as to justify direct use of armed force against the Soviet forces, but it was seen by the British Government as justifying bilateral and multilateral measures which would demonstrate effectively to the Soviet Union that the forcible extension of the territories under Soviet control was incompatible with the maintenance of normal relations with the Western democracies. It was clear that, if such measures were to have any effect, they would need co-ordination between the Western democracies and the moral support of the United Nations. Despite open and protracted dissension, both internationally and within Britain, over the precise nature of the response, measures were adopted, the net effect of which, so far as Britain was concerned, was to reduce relations with the Soviet Union, sixty years after they had first been established, to no more than minimal diplomatic contact.

A NEW START?

When considering the prospect for relations after 1979, the new Conservative Government faced a dilemma which, while the parameters of possible action were radically different, presented a depressing similarity to that of 1917. The policy choice still lay between open opposition and making the best deal possible. The precedents for both courses were unpromising and the consequences of failure were high. Soviet global policy still seemed to be based upon the presumption of an irreconcilable conflict leading to the eventual victory of Soviet socialism, while Soviet internal policy violated the principles which Western Governments believed they had secured at Helsinki. Soviet disarmament initiatives seemed designed primarily to play upon European nuclear anxieties while safeguarding and possibly enhancing the effectiveness of the superior Soviet conventional forces in Europe. The countering of Soviet military force by equivalent force on the part of NATO could ensure the physical security of the West, yet the need for something beyond a policy of endless armed confrontation was clear. There was, however, no clear route to it. Beyond the need to avoid a nuclear war, there was no solid community of interest. The mutual mistrust was

41

as profound as it had ever been and its potential consequences were substantially more alarming. The gradual development of a comprehensive network of contacts, the provision of credits, the access to Western technology, the encouragement of political dialogue – the whole process of seeking to build upon common interests rather than conflicting ideologies – had, it seemed, proved futile.

Nevertheless, unpromising though the prospects were, the need for resumption of the political dialogue was clear and it was perceived rather sooner in Britain than in the United States. In her speech to the Conservative Party Conference of 14 October 1983, Mrs Thatcher spoke of the need, when circumstances were right, to talk to the Soviet leadership. A month later, at the Lord Mayor's Banquet – the forum chosen by Lloyd George in 1919 for the initiation of his Russian policy – she set out the aim of reaching a 'broad understanding' on the 'common interest in peace and security at a lower level of weapons'. The British Government's policy was supported in the following year by other NATO governments and the alliance committed itself formally to the pursuit of a more stable relationship through dialogue and co-operation and to the search for a genuine long-term détente.[39]

The chance to give practical effect to this policy came with the accession of Mr Gorbachev to the leadership of the Soviet Union. A successful visit to Britain shortly before he assumed power had led to the establishment of a useful relationship with the Prime Minister. In his earliest policy statements he spoke of a period of 'abrupt change' and the development of the 'restructuring' process demonstrated his intention to effect it. The main thrust was the reform of the economy, but a 'new political thinking' was proclaimed in which a doctrine of interdependence replaced the traditional doctrine of irreconcilable conflict in foreign policy, and security was to be sought by political rather than military means. The substantive effects of the new doctrine were quickly apparent in the withdrawal from Afghanistan, the readiness for greater co-operation in the handling of regional disputes and the conclusion of the INF treaty.

The opportunity for a productive dialogue was obvious and in the establishment of that dialogue it was possible for the United Kingdom to put the 1983 policy into practice. The bilateral agreements concluded during the visit of Mrs Thatcher to Moscow in 1987 followed a well-established pattern, but in the opportunity for serious discussion with the leadership and direct access to the Soviet people the visit broke new ground. The subsequent extension of the dialogue to cover co-operation on problems such as drug trafficking, AIDS and terrorism opened up the possibility of finding new areas of common interest and the personal authority of the Prime Minister added to the impact of British policy. By comparison with the 1971 experience, the expulsion of Soviet intelligence officers by the British government in 1985 and again in 1989 did not prove a substantial set-back to relations, although Soviet counter-moves did adversely affect the normal conduct of diplomatic business.

The question which must now arise is whether the current upturn in relations represents just one more cycle in the fluctuating relationship in which the pursuit of common interests will take precedence over the clash of ideology and power. The historical perspective is chastening. The prospect of co-operation which Lloyd George glimpsed was to prove largely illusory. The mood of optimism when Eden visited Moscow in 1935, Churchill in 1942, Macmillan in 1959 and Wilson in 1975 was short lived. The dominant theme of seventy years has been one of mutual mistrust and basic antagonism. The ideological confrontation of two fundamentally opposed systems of political thought has waxed and waned and its impact has varied with changes in the political balance in Britain as well as in the leadership of the Soviet Union. Policy may have had its origin more in perceived national interest than in ideology, but the ideology has itself coloured the perception and heightened the mistrust. Covert activity, some proven and some suspected, has enhanced its effect. When objective consider-ations of national interest demanded co-operation, mistrust frustrated it. When national interests conflicted, mistrust aggravated the conflict. In part the mistrust stemmed from misunderstanding, but too often it was justified by experience. The nature and scale of the confrontation have changed over the years. The development of the ideological confrontation into a confrontation of military power, both nuclear and conventional, changed the nature of the bilateral British–Soviet relationship and contributed to its subordination to the superpower reationship, while the maintenance of Soviet armed power in Central Europe heightened the implications of that relationship for the European nations. Within Europe, British membership of the Community gave an impulse to the European co-ordination of East-West policy although, to some extent, it constrained British ability to use an independent commercial policy as an element in the bilateral political relationship with the Soviet Union. British preoccupation with the defence of imperial possessions broadened into a wider contest for power and influence in the Third World. For its part, the Soviet Union had by 1985 largely lost the initiative in Europe and found itself fully occupied with the ills of its own economy and the defence of its existing positions. New focal points of conflict had arisen, but in Europe the old ones remained. The nature of the tensions on the Western borders of the Soviet Union had changed radically from the time of the Polish–Soviet war of 1920 to the Polish–Soviet crisis of 1980, but the potential for prejudice to European stability and security was no less. With the Soviet imperial frontier running through Germany, the German–British–Russian policy nexus remained.

Looking to the future, it is reasonable to expect that the fluctuating pattern of tension and crisis will be smoothed. The confrontation of ideology and power, if not active, remains latent. New tensions may arise at the familiar focal points as the Soviet leadership resist the gradual disintegration of the periphery of their empire and this will militate against the swift reduction of forces within Europe. Even in the worst periods, there was, however, on both sides a sufficient degree of realism for the tensions to be contained. This is likely to continue and economic pressures will for many years provide a powerful impulse for the Soviet Union to seek to maintain military parity with the United States at a lower absolute level. The constraint upon the use of force between nuclear powers will continue to enhance the role of diplomacy and, even against a background of strategic confrontation, the potential area of common interest may broaden. In a more productive relationship, levels of weaponry need not be the determining factor. None of this, however, provides any certainty that the old cyclical pattern will not continue.

What remains to be seen is whether the process of reform in Soviet domestic and foreign policy will acquire such a momentum that the mould of old attitudes will be broken, the deeper roots of conflict will begin to wither and a more profound change in the relationship with the Soviet Union can be envisaged. My own view is that we are at one of those moments of flux in history – and they do not occur very often – when the old alignments begin to shift and new patterns are formed. We have already seen a swifter and more far-reaching change in the internal political evolution of the Soviet Union than seemed conceivable even two years ago. Its permanence cannot be guaranteed, but the objective factors which have produced it are strong. There must now be a real possibility that, by harnessing popular support and Party power, Gorbachev will so transform the very nature of the Soviet Union as to require a reassessment of its whole position within the community of nations and hence of the traditional concept of the East–West relationship. The nature of that relationship will depend not only on developments within the Soviet Union, but also on the Western perceptions of those developments and the ability to respond to them.

Where, in this process, is the role for Britain? The points of intersection of direct British and Soviet interests are still relatively few, but so, too, are the direct and necessary sources of conflict. The British–Soviet relationship lacks some of the special factors of other bilateral relationships with the Soviet Union. A nuclear weapons power, Britain does not have the superpower role of the United States. Directly and vitally concerned with European security, Britain confronts Soviet forces in Europe, but on German, not on British, soil. Britain has a negligible Communist Party and no dependence upon Soviet energy supplies. A measure of detachment can lead – and on occasion has led – to an infirmity of policy. But it need not do so. Recent experience has shown that it can equally give an independence of judgment and consistency of purpose which can command respect in the Soviet Union.

The bilateral British–Soviet relationship may not in the future be a determining factor in the pattern of East–West relations, but the British and the Soviet interests in European security and prosperity are such that it must continue to constitute a major element in British foreign policy. Britain in turn remains well placed to integrate the bilateral relationship into the Atlantic, European and Third World context and thus to play in the development of a new and more constructive relationship with the Soviet Union as significant a role as, in the years after 1945, it played in the containment of Soviet expansion.

NOTES

This chapter is drawn largely from the author's book, *Britain and the Soviet Union* (Macmillan, 1990).

The historical development of British–Soviet relations is dealt with in a number of general works, but the range of those devoted specifically to it is relatively small. The two-volume *History of Anglo–Soviet Relations* by W. P. and Z. K. Coates (Lawrence and Wishart, 1943 and 1956) contains much useful material, but its value is limited by the consistent pro-Soviet bias. *Britain and Soviet Communism* by F. S. Northedge and Audrey Wells (Macmillan, 1982) is a comprehensive and authoritative review. Among the works which are of particular value on the political relationship at specific periods are the three-volume study by Robert Ullman *Anglo–Soviet Relations 1917–1921* (Princeton, 1972); *The Precarious Truce: Anglo–Soviet Relations 1924–1927* by G. Gorodetsky (Cambridge University Press, 1977); *British Foreign Policy in the Second World War*, by Sir Llewellyn Woodward (HMSO, 1976); *Stafford Cripps' Mission to Moscow 1940–1942* also by G. Gorodetsky (Cambridge University Press, 1984); *Britain and the Cold War 1941–47* by V. R. Rothwell (Jonathan Cape, 1982) and *The British Between the Superpowers 1945–50* by E. Barker (Macmillan, 1983). A convenient guide to Soviet thinking in the Brezhnev years – but not to current policy – is contained in *Soviet Foreign Policy* edited by A. A. Gromyko and B. N. Ponomarev (English edition, Progress Publishers, 1981).

References, unless otherwise indicated, are to Foreign Office and Cabinet documents in the Public Record Office.

1. Memorandum GT 2392 of 9 December 1917 annexed to W.C. 295 of 10 December 1917.
2. 131 HC Debates, col. 519.
3. Anglo-Russian Trade Agreement, Cmd 1207, 1921.
4. A. Gromyko and B. Ponomarev, *Soviet Foreign Policy 1917–1945* (Progress Publishers, 1981), vol. I, p. 165.
5. Appendix I to *Documents on British Foreign Policy (DBFP)*, 2nd Series, vol. XVIII.
6. *DBFP*, 3rd Series, vol. I, Nos. 90 and 116.
7. *DBFP*, 3rd Series, vol. III, No. 325.
8. Meeting at 10 Downing Street 28–29 July 1936, quoted in Keith Middlemas and John Barnes, *Baldwin: A Biography* (Weidenfeld and Nicolson, 1969), p. 947.
9. Despatch of 15 July 1937 from Foreign Secretary to HM Ambassador, Berlin.

10. Quoted in Keith Feiling, *The Life of Neville Chamberlain* (Macmillan, 1946), p. 403.
11. FO 371 24844 N5853/30/28.
12. FO 371 24844 N5937/30/38.
13. Churchill, *The Grand Alliance* (Cassell, 1951), p. 300.
14. *Ibid.*, p. 312.
15. Treaty Series No. 15 (1941) Cmd 6304.
16. Treaty for an Alliance in the War against Hitlerite Germany and her Associates in Europe and Providing also for Collaboration and Mutual Assistance Thereafter, Cmd 6368, 1942.
17. Churchill, *The Second World War*, vol. 4, *The Hinge of Fate* (Cassell, 1951), p. 388.
18. A. Gromyko and B. Ponomarev, *Soviet Foreign Policy 1917–1945*, vol. I, p. 432.
19. *Kommunist*, 3 (1975), p. 7.
20. Churchill, *The Hinge of Fate*, p. 388.
21. FO 371/30834.
22. Churchill, *The Second World War*, vol. 5. *Closing the Ring* (Cassell, 1952), p. 318.
23. FO 371 43304/2128 of 5 April 1944.
24. CAB 80/84 COS (44) 527 (O)PHP 15 June 1944. For a fuller discussion see V. Rothwell, *Britain and the Cold War 1941–47* (Jonathan Cape, 1982).
25. *Hansard*, 27 February 1945.
26. Churchill, *The Second World War*, vol. 6. *Triumph and Tragedy* (Cassell, 1954), p. 458.
27. *Soviet Foreign Policy*, vol. 2, p. 477.
28. FO 371 56763/4065. For a discussion of the role of Bevin and Attlee see *inter alia* Smith and Zametica, 'The Cold Warrior: Clement Attlee reconsidered', *International Affairs*, 61:2 (Spring 1985), pp. 237–52.
29. *Hansard*, 3 January 1948.
30. CAB 54 (48).
31. *Hansard*, 11 May 1953.
32. CC 10 (54).
33. CC 48 (54).
34. Statement on the Discussions of the Prime Minister of the United Kingdom, Sir Anthony Eden, with the Chairman of the Council of Ministers of the Soviet Socialist Republics, Mr. N. A. Bulganin, and Member of the Praesidium of the Supreme Soviet of the Soviet Socialist Republics, Mr. N. S. Khrushchev, Cmd 9753, 1956.
35. *Hansard*, 26 August 1968.
36. *Soviet Foreign Policy*, vol. 2, p. 425.
37. *Pravda*, 2 January 1972.
38. Cmd 3924, 1975.
39. NATO Council statement, 31 May 1984.

3 Soviet perspectives on Britain and British foreign policy

PETER J. S. DUNCAN

In this chapter I shall attempt to describe how Soviet policy makers view Britain and British foreign policy. Since direct information about this is scarce, it is necessary to examine the views expressed by Soviet journalists and academic specialists. While these cannot be considered official statements on a par with those of Party or foreign ministry representatives, they may reflect the views of the leadership or of informed policy opinion.

THE CREATION OF SOVIET PERCEPTIONS

Attitudes to Britain in the Soviet Union are conditioned by a number of factors: the historical experience and memory of British–Russian and British–Soviet relations; official Marxist–Leninist ideological doctrines; and personal experiences which Soviet citizens have of visits to the United Kingdom or of dealings with British people. The continuing (and much resented) restrictions on travel to the West limit access to Britain for Soviet people. Not only teachers of English but even many specialist analysts of British affairs have never visited the UK. The expansion of tourism to the Soviet Union and of cultural links has not made acquaintance with Britons an easy affair for ordinary Soviet citizens. Although English, in its British form, is still the most widespread foreign language taught in schools and universities, perceptions of Britain are influenced by the writings of such authors as John Galsworthy and Charles Dickens (who still seems to be the Russians' favourite British writer). For a younger generation, Britain is remarkable above all for its rock musicians.

In spite of the Crimean War and the Anglo–Russian rivalry in South-West Asia, relations between Tsarist Russia and Britain were often friendly. British investment flowed into St Petersburg, British ideas about representative government were widely known, and the last Tsar preferred to use English in his family correspondence. At the same time Russian socialists from Herzen to Lenin used London as a base from which to organise anti–Tsarist activities.

Britain occupies a special place in the history of Marxist–Leninist ideology; not only did Marx and Engels live and produce their major works there but London was the final location of the Second Congress of the Russian Social Democratic Workers' Party (RSDRP) in 1903, where Lenin split the party and Bolshevism was born.

According to Soviet writers, the British intervention in Russia after the October Revolution was intended to strangle Bolshevism in its cradle. It led to a division in British ruling circles between those like Winston Churchill who wished to carry the fight to the finish and those realistic elements of the ruling class such as David Lloyd George who were prepared to develop economic links with the Bolsheviks. British workers helped to stop the intervention in 1920, and then demanded trade with Soviet Russia.[1] It was a Labour Government which gave *de jure* recognition to the Soviet Government in 1924. Histories of the Second World War portrayed the British as an ally of the Soviet people against Hitler, although Churchill and other British politicians are sometimes accused of trying to weaken the Soviet Union in the course of the war.[2] Positive feelings towards the British, as wartime allies, seem to have survived the Cold War among many older people.

The experience of the Cold War undoubtedly clouded mass and elite perceptions of the Soviet Union in the West. The official requirement to portray Britain in all published work in a way that is compatible with the ruling ideology has to a still greater degree affected Soviet perceptions of Britain.[3] If Soviet journalists were required to depict a Britain bedevilled by unemployment and racism, even if they were themselves aware of more positive aspects, then such a view of Britain had an effect on mass perceptions. Admittedly, part of the Soviet population seems in the 1970s to have become so cynical about communism that they refused to believe anything in the mass media, and developed an idealised image of the West, but the reappearance of mass unemployment in the main Western countries in the 1980s seems to have diminished the attractions of capitalism. It should be remembered that in the nineteenth century rejection of bourgeois society was characteristic not only of Russian socialists but of Slavophiles like Aleksei Khomiakov and reactionaries like Konstantin Leont'ev. Disillusionment with communism by no means leads to enthusiasm for capitalism.

The aims of the Soviet media, in reporting foreign affairs, are related to external and internal audiences. The Soviet population must be reassured that life is bad under capitalism, with poverty, violence and racial oppression. At the same time, the media must serve the aims of foreign policy. They must denounce foreign nuclear weapons, but also encourage foreign countries to develop trade and co-operation with the Soviet Union, which may require them to produce a favourable image of certain foreign governments. All these objectives are not necessarily easy to combine. The function of informing the population is not as important as in the West; more sensitive information can be given at closed lectures, or to those who need to know through 'White Tass', and the still more restricted 'Red Tass'.[4]

For the mass of the Soviet population, television is the most powerful medium for creating their perception of Britain. Film sequences of police fighting trade union pickets are much more persuasive than newspaper reports. Naturally, the image of Britain does not loom as large in the Soviet Union as the image of Russia does in Britain; there is much more about the United States, both positive and negative, than about the United Kingdom. Until the rise of Gorbachev, Soviet news programmes were typically dull and stereotyped. For example, British foreign policy was regularly presented as following a Washington line whereas coverage of domestic issues focused on unemployment, strikes, racism and Northern Ireland. Trade and cultural exchanges, however, were always dealt with in a positive manner. Following the shake–up within Soviet TV which reflected the policy of *glasnost'*, the routine harping about Britain's social ills has been reduced. The tone of the coverage, and the expressions used, have become less denunciatory, more sophisticated, and generally more responsive to events. It would be going too far to say that the changes generally were very dramatic; an exception to this would be Mrs Thatcher's visit of March 1987 and the interview she gave then. But the treatment of Britain seems to have become more objective. While the Thatcher Government has not been portrayed as an economic success, the Prime Minister has on occasions been shown in a favourable light (for example, visiting Hungerford to offer condolences to the victims of a major shooting incident).

While the impact of Soviet television has probably made Radio Moscow less important in creating Soviet perceptions of Britain, the same cannot be said of the influence of broadcasts from the West. An estimated 20 million Soviet citizens listen to the BBC Russian Service every week. Soviet citizens are not discouraged from listening to the BBC World Service, which broadcasts regular news features about Britain. The Russian Service, which concentrates more on Soviet affairs, is not so acceptable; it has frequently been subject to jamming (almost continuously from 1980–86) which makes it difficult to be heard in the cities (see chapter 8).

Turning to the print media, it is necessary to distinguish between those books, journals and newspapers intended for mass Soviet audiences, published in large numbers of copies, and the books and periodicals intended for small specialist audiences. The former, at any rate before the January 1987 Central Committee Plenum, had been more stereotyped; books such as *Apartheid – British Style*, in the series 'Imperialism', emphasised the negative sides of life in the capitalist world.[5]

Of the specialist journals, some are directed mainly at foreign audiences and published in foreign languages as well as Russian. Those dealing with Britain include the weekly *New Times*, and the monthly of the Knowledge Society, *International Affairs*. The latter, which has a Russian-language circulation of 68,000, took a hard line until 1987 when the Ministry of Foreign Affairs became a co-publisher. Others are published in Russian alone and are presumably directed primarily at internal specialist and policy making audiences. Among these, the most important journal to deal with Britain is *Mirovaia ekonomika i mezhdunarodnye otnosheniia* (World Economics and International Relations – hereafter *MEMO*), published by the Institute of World Economics and International Relations (IMEMO) of the USSR Academy of Sciences. *MEMO* had in 1987 a circulation of 26,000 copies (much more than the monographs designed for specialists) a circulation which had been reduced from the 1975 figure of 46,900, supposedly owing to the shortage of paper. IMEMO includes within it a section dealing with British Studies, where the former British diplomat Donald Maclean worked until his death in 1983. Owing to his British education and experience in Government service, Maclean seems to have had an important influence in shaping the image of Britain held by Soviet specialists.[6]

These specialists have access to the British press and official documents and cite these sources freely, as well as the *Morning Star* and *Marxism Today*. The functions of these specialists have changed since the death of Stalin. Whereas under Stalin their main job was to produce evidence to back up the resolutions already passed by the leading bodies of the Party, the institutes have been converted into think-tanks for the Ministry of Foreign Affairs and the International Department of the Central Committee. Debate occurs which may later influence policy making. Even in 1987, however, works which purport to be academic and have small print-runs sometimes had little more than propaganda value. Those which make useful scholarly contributions to the Soviet debate were still required to include paragraphs or whole sections explaining the peace-loving nature of Soviet policy, as well as a sprinkling of citations from Marx, Engels or Lenin, in order to give legitimacy to the rest of what they were saying.

BRITISH SOCIETY

The accounts by Soviet correspondents in London of their experiences in Britain are useful sources. Vsevolod Ovchinnikov was *Pravda* correspondent for five years in the latter part of the 1970s. He found it difficult to acclimatise to Britain: 'English life was certainly no more, and perhaps far less, comprehensible than Japanese life'. It was 'inappropriate' to converse with a stranger, unless one needed directions.[7] Discussing Britain's social structure, he referred to

Benjamin Disraeli's comment about there being 'two nations' in Britain, a comment which has been axiomatic for Soviet accounts of Britain. He admitted that a great deal had changed since Disraeli's time, with the enormous growth of the middle classes. Yet 'class distinctions and social divisions are, to this day, far more typical of Britain than of any other Western nation'.[8]

A more systematic discussion of the British social structure was conducted by V. Peschansky in *MEMO* in 1981. He divided society into the proletariat, the middle strata and the bourgeoisie. He estimated that the 'proletariat', comprising manual and ordinary white-collar workers, formed nearly 80 per cent of the working population by the beginning of the 1980s. The proportion of the proletariat which he called the 'industrial proletariat', engaged in industry, transport and construction, was, however, falling. He complained that a large part of this proletariat nevertheless voted for the 'bourgeois parties'. This label, incidentally, in contemporary usage excludes the Labour Party, in spite of Lenin's characterisation of the latter as 'a thoroughly bourgeois party'.[9] Turning to the middle strata, Peschansky noted that it was smaller than in other capitalist countries. Small business people had maintained their share of the population since the early 1970s. The managerial strata were growing rapidly, and owing to dissatisfaction with their pay and fear of unemployment were turning to the unions.[10]

BRITISH DOMESTIC TRENDS

Against the background of this social structure, I shall now consider Soviet specialist attempts to explain the phenomenon of Thatcherite conservatism. In an authoritative *MEMO* article of 1984, entitled 'England: Keynesianism to Monetarism', Efim Khesin (head of the British sector) and V. Studentsov point out that Britain in 1979 was the first major Western country to move from the post-war welfare state consensus to the bundle of policies known as monetarism, or what they termed the 'neo-conservative variant of state-monopoly regulation'. Thatcherism preceded 'Reaganomics' by nearly two years. Since the war, Britain had lost an empire, the system of imperial preferences, and the sterling area. The role of the London commodity markets as centres of world trade declined. Britain had fallen from second to sixth place in the capitalist world in industrial production. The contradictions between the demands of the 'scientific and technical revolution' and the British socio-economic structure, exacerbated by the high level of defence spending, were nowhere else so deep, and the general crisis affecting the whole capitalist world struck Britain more strongly than the other leading countries.

The crisis of the mid-1970s led to the acceptance of the view that the priority given to the short-term over the long-term was 'breaking the process of the reconstruction (*perestroika*) of the economy'. By the late 1970s, the export of North Sea oil was hastening the deindustrialisation of Britain. The fall in the rate of profit and investment within Britain had encouraged the export of capital, weakening the domestic productive base. The 'monopolies' now lost faith in Keynesian techniques and in the possibility of maintaining full employment, and promoted anti-state feeling. They decided to try to solve their problems at the expense of medium-size and small businesses, and of the wage earners. With the Labour movement also moving leftwards, there was a 'sharp polarisation of political forces'. But 'big capital' succeeded in bringing the Conservatives to power in the 1979 election, under the leadership of the Thatcherite right wing.[11]

Khesin and Studentsov claimed that the monetarist economic policy which was implemented by the Thatcher Government included 'attacks on trade unions' and cuts in social benefits. The employment acts attacked picketing, solidarity action and the closed shop. Proposals to 'democratise' the unions were really attempts to split them from within and weaken their fighting ability, and also to inhibit the spending of union resources for political purposes. Particular compromises made by the government did not represent the abandonment of monetarism, which had succeeded in changing relations between wage labour and profit to the benefit of profit. They also claimed that the 'growth rate of the real income of workers has fallen sharply'. They further noted that the combativeness of the workers was rising (in fact the miners' strike had just begun).[12]

By 1987, A. Timokhin could question the commitment to monetarism: 'in economic policy, the Tories show a pragmatic approach and remember monetarist dogmas only when they have to'. He added that with general elections approaching, and with their popularity having fallen, the government was considering raising its spending. Between 1979 and 1986 employment in engineering had fallen by one-third. But Timokhin acknowledged that there had been some economic success. In 1986 real incomes had risen 4.2 per cent, consumer expenditure by 4.7 per cent (which was the highest increase since 1972), while inflation had fallen to 3.4 per cent (the lowest figure for nineteen years).[13] Irina Strizhova, writing in *International Affairs* about the same time, was less generous about the results of Mrs Thatcher's policies. 'A slight drop in inflation, a rise of the annual GDP growth and the volume of industrial output should not be interpreted as signs of the country's economic recovery ... but even this slight advance has been achieved at an exorbitant social price and has caused a notable drop in the living standards in Britain.'[14]

How did Mrs Thatcher nevertheless manage her remarkable feat of winning three elections in a row? Soviet analyses published between the elections of 1979 and 1983, and also between those of 1983 and 1987, tended to focus on the unpopularity of the measures taken by the Conservative Government, both in its domestic, economic and social policies and in its policy towards the Soviet Union.[15] Sergei Peregudov's *MEMO* article of November 1983 sought to explain the sweeping Conservative victory of June that year. He pointed out that the Conservative vote had actually fallen in comparison with 1979, but the split in the opposition caused by the emergence of the Social Democratic Party (SDP) and the formation of the alliance with the Liberals, together with the functioning of the voting system enabled the Tories to win nearly two-thirds of the seats. Peregudov used this fact to argue for the introduction of proportional representation.[16]

Peregudov's explanation for the degree of support enjoyed by the Conservatives showed the clear influence of the 'Euro-Communist' wing of the CPGB, around the journal *Marxism Today* rather than the more traditional, pro-Moscow line of the *Morning Star* which by then was in a minority within the CPGB. The new conservatism was 'authoritarian populism', of which the most important element was the 'Falklands factor'.

In the conditions where the opinion that 'Great Britannia' had changed into 'little England' was becoming more and more widely held, the Falklands crisis served in its way as a catalyst of national feelings, and also of imperial moods and ambitions which, it seemed, had long since disappeared into the past. The nationalist and chauvinist hullabaloo was taken up by a significant proportion of English people, many of whom did not adhere to Conservative beliefs at all.[17]

The level of support for the Conservatives had shot up from 30 per cent to over 50 per cent after the decision to send the fleet was taken. Further, Mrs Thatcher's firm line in economic policy, in comparison with the compromises and lack of principle of her predecessors, corresponded to the spirit of the times. The Tories' attack on the welfare state struck a chord with a public dissatisfied with bureaucracy in the social security system, increase in state interference, and high taxation, and Labour had passively ignored these moods. The whole British Establishment had opposed a Labour victory, and had given the Conservatives £10 million for the election. At the same time, the Labour Party had been divided over policy. (Peregudov did not specify defence policy as a source of division.) But the volatility of the electorate made it necessary to rebut the view that the 'new conservatism' would be confirmed as the 'dominating political tendency'.[18]

By the time of the June 1987 election, Mrs Thatcher had become better known to the Soviet public through her visit to Moscow in March of that year. It is normal when foreign Heads of State or Government visit the Soviet Union for the media to present a courteous if not positive image of the guest, and the treatment of Mrs Thatcher was no exception. The weekly *Literaturnaia gazeta* carried a four-column biographical article about her, containing several images which seemed to have been designed to have a favourable response from the Soviet reader: a father who lacked money but loved books; a family where persistent work was highly valued; as Prime Minister, sleeping only four or five hours a day, but always preparing breakfast for her husband; a target, in the Brighton bombing, of the 'IRA terrorists'; the tears when her son seemed lost in the Sahara, and how she then understood (according to her own account) how the mothers of the Falklands combatants had felt. On the negative side, it was she who had ordered the sinking of the Argentinian cruiser *General Belgrano*, with the loss of 368 men; she was the proponent of monetarism and 'popular capitalism', and the opponent of the trade unions, who enjoyed 'the unconditional respect of the voters' but not their love.[19]

The same newspaper provided its readers with a full page account of a round-table discussion of the elections, with Sir Anthony Kershaw, Michael Meacher, Roy Jenkins and Alan Beith, outlining the domestic and foreign policy approaches of the four major parties.[20] Soviet coverage of the elections, like coverage of foreign affairs generally, was dominated by nuclear weapons issues. Soviet journalists reported that the government was concentrating on attacking Labour's non-nuclear defence policy in order to 'distract voters' attention from the discussion of social problems'.[21] The television spoke of the Tories' intention of cutting social programmes and privatising industries, and deploying the Trident nuclear missile, while Labour wished to cut unemployment and improve health, social security and education. As far as the Alliance was concerned, Vsevolod Shishkovsky claimed that domestically 'its programme is reminiscent of the Labour programme, with some deviations', whereas in defence it was 'almost identical to the Conservatives".[22]

The reaction of *Pravda*'s correspondent Arkady Maslennikov to the election results was to note the improved position of the Labour Party and the 'serious defeat' for the Alliance. It blamed the Conservative victory on 'selling on the cheap around two-and-a-half million houses', and performing 'the same operation with shares'. Further, the government had played on 'patriotic feelings' accusing Labour of 'dooming the country to capitulation' by its rejection of nuclear weapons. Like Peregudov in 1983, Maslennikov referred to the 'split' in the opposition, and attacked the electoral system for allowing the Conservatives to have a majority of seats with a minority of the vote.[23] The *New Times* analysis of the result by Aleksandr Pumpiansky claimed that Mrs Thatcher's Moscow visit had helped her in the election. Labour was split, 'with the moderates frantically silencing the hard Left', and 'not once during the campaign did Kinnock pronounce the word "socialism"'. Labour's focus on unemployment was successfully countered by the Tories' emphasis on the spread of home ownership and by rising living standards. In defence policy, the government 'in the spirit of panic-stricken McCarthyism' had warned that a

Labour victory would make Britain 'completely defenseless in the face of Soviet intimidation, which would mean that an invasion was inevitable'. A notable feature of Pumpiansky's analysis was the absence of any reference to the CPGB.[24]

As Bowker and Shearman show in chapter 7, Soviet attitudes to the Labour Party have become more favourable since 1979, and not only because of the adoption of the non-nuclear defence policy. Peregudov after the 1983 general election and the election of Neil Kinnock as Labour leader warned that the soft Left, now in the ascendant, were inclined to compromise with the Right, but the party conference had confirmed left-wing policies.[25] From then until the 1987 election, however, Soviet commentators had little to complain about. Maslennikov's *Pravda* reports of the 1985 and 1986 Labour Party conferences conveyed sympathetically and uncritically Labour's domestic policies and welcomed the confirmation of the non-nuclear defence policy.[26] Peregudov in an 1986 *MEMO* article said that the Labour Party was strengthening its links with the workers, the trade unions, and the 'new social movements', singling out the peace and ecology movements (but not mentioning the women's movement). After the 1987 election, *New Times* published an article which seemed to support Kinnock against both the Left and the Right within the party. It said that the leaders were now concerned 'to unite the two conflicting wings of the party around the organising centre [and] strengthen discipline within the party and democracy'. The writer considered that 'the Labour leadership has no intention of retreating from the main points of its programme including its defence policy'.[27]

There is no space here to deal with other important aspects of the Soviet perception of British politics and society under Mrs Thatcher. The major themes included the resistance of the trade unions to Conservative economic and social policies, and the use of the police force against strikers (the miners' strike of 1984–85 attracting particular attention, as Bowker and Shearman show in chapter 7);[28] the unsuccessful efforts of the British Government to solve the problems of Northern Ireland, and the continuing existence there of discrimination against Catholics;[29] the activities of the British secret service, plotting not only against communists, the peace movement, trade unionists and the Wilson government but also against Conservatives of the Heath variety;[30] Government censorship of the media;[31] and examples of racial discrimination or physical abuse of racial minorities.[32]

SOVIET PERCEPTIONS OF BRITAIN'S WORLD ROLE

Donald Maclean claimed in his seminal book on British foreign policy that while the Foreign Office 'had considerable influence on policy', it could not 'despite

55

popular legend, pursue its own way regardless of which Government is in power or of what the Prime Minister, the Foreign Secretary and the Cabinet want'. There were 'tactical' (although 'not strategic') differences between the Labour and Conservative leaderships.[33] Trukhanovsky and Kapitonova put forward a cruder analysis. The leaders of both parties recognised foreign policy continuity. 'English foreign policy is dictated by the monopoly capital of the country.' This control was assured by staffing the senior posts in the FCO by permanent officials who were 'products of the milieu of the big and middle bourgeoisie'. Moveover, 'the reactionary nature of the English state apparatus is common knowledge', and post-war attempts to reform the Diplomatic Service had failed.[34] The 1980s seemed, however, to bear out Maclean's analysis. S. Volodin said in 1984 that British foreign policy was 'largely shaped by Prime Minister Mrs Margaret Thatcher personally in collaboration with the right-wing of the Conservative Party close to her'.[35]

Soviet analysts do not consider Britain to be of little importance on the world stage. After Prime Minister Aleksei Kosygin's meeting with Harold Wilson in London in 1967 *International Affairs* rejected the view of 'certain circles' in the USA and FRG that 'Britain's time has passed'.[36] Trukhanovsky and Kapitonova twelve years later noted that in some countries, 'even in England itself', it had become fashionable to minimise Britain's world role. They considered that Britain's role in the world economy was much greater than its share of production or exports would suggest, because of the large amount of investment abroad and because of the size of British-owned transnational corporations. Further, Britain derived advantages from being the 'economic centre of the Commonwealth'.[37] The pound still played an important role in international finance, and the 'powerful' British banking system enmeshed the globe.[38] Vikenty Matveev claimed in 1986 that, despite decolonisation, 'British big capital, far from reducing its expansion, has increased it'. This overseas investment was accompanied by declines in domestic production and continuing high military expenditure needed to defend British assets around the world. Foreign investment flowing into Britain, especially from the United States, FRG and Japan, had 'invaded' not only industry but also the City of London.[39]

Despite Britain's position as a major exporter of capital, Soviet analysts have continued to emphasise Britain's decline on the world stage. The words of Trukhanovsky and Kapitonova represent a typical formulation of the Soviet line on Britain's foreign policy. Britain, they said, had not been able to find the 'correct, optimal relationship between foreign policy aims and the material position of the country'. The decision to try to enter the EEC, taken in the early 1960s, represented a realisation of the need to limit Britain's world role, but the ruling circles still wished to play a 'leading role' in Western Europe.[40] Volodin wrote in 1984 that Britain was 'still capable of influencing many international processes, especially in Europe . . . Britain remains a major factor in inter-national politics.'[41] An IMEMO volume of 1985 argued that the British establishment had stuck to the European course persistently. Even though the Thatcher Government had had sharp confrontations with the other members over the Community budget, it was committed to membership. Indeed, it was Britain which had played perhaps the most active part in promoting foreign policy co-ordination within the Community structures. 'Many important joint initiatives, undertaken by the member states of the Community, especially relating to the Middle Eastern and Southern African conflicts, bear on them the imprint of British diplomacy.'[42] The EEC has been seen by Soviet analysts as one of the three 'power centres' of imperialism, together with the United States and Japan. The EEC was unpopular, however, with the British public, as was shown by the fact that Labour Party policy for the 1983 election was to bring Britain out of the EEC, and this position was also held by the left wing of the trade unions and by the CPGB.[43] Maclean, writing in the late 1960s, did not seem to have a negative view of the EEC, and implied that Britain's decline might be reversed in the 1970s and 1980s if it joined, and if it also cut defence spending and ended sterling's role as a reserve currency.[44] Subsequent Soviet comment has been divided over whether Britain has had any real benefits from membership.[45]

In Soviet discussions of British foreign policy, the dominant theme over the period 1979–87 has been to present the British Government as almost always following Washington's policies. Soviet commentators protray Britain as being more willing than the other West European countries to back the White House line, in the hope of maintaining or re-creating the 'special relationship'. 'Acting in line with the fixed idea of a "crusade" against communism, it has backed every attempt of the Reagan Administration to impose its will on the USSR or to exhaust it by the arms race.'[46] On the other hand, Britain is not seen as having follow the United States has been linked to the British decision to rely on the American-built Trident missile system as the successor to Polaris. The Soviet analysis has emphasised the Thatcher Government's unwillingness to impose sanctions on South Africa (a stance it shared with the Reagan Administration) and its isolation in the Commonwealth on the issue, whereas it has minimised differences between the United States and Britain on the Middle East. *Izvestiia* noted that the government's decision to follow the US out of UNESCO was taken despite the urgings of the nations of the Commonwealth and Western Europe, and against the advice of the House of Commons Foreign Affairs Committee.[47] Britain's membership of the EEC is seen as likely to tend to weaken the 'special relationship' in the long run even where defence is concerned. In economic matters Britain's orientation is already seen as European rather than trans–Atlantic.

While it is true that Britain and the United States usually vote the same way at the United Nations, this is as likely to follow from a coincidence of interests or ideology as from the exercise of influence by Washington on London. It has suited Soviet propaganda to suggest that Britain is acting against its own interests and in deference to Washington, whereas in fact the stimulus to British policy may be mainly internal. A 1987 IMEMO volume illustrated the concessions made by scholarship to propaganda. It claimed that the British government in the early 1980s followed Washington in adopting a policy of 'anti–Sovietism'.[48] A few pages further on, however, it shows that Britain's cooling towards the Soviet Union came in the late 1970s. In this more scholarly discussion, the British change in attitude is not attributed to Washington but is linked with Soviet policy in Africa and the trials of dissidents in the USSR.[49] The image of a subservient British government has on occasion been grossly exaggerated. *International Affairs* claimed, for example, that the American-led invasion of the Commonwealth state of Grenada took place, 'without a murmur of protest from London', although in fact the Prime Minister and Foreign Secretary made public their opposition to the invasion.[50] On the issue of the American bombing of Libya from British bases in May 1986, the Soviet position would appear more justified.[51] The IMEMO defence specialist Gennady Kolosov even claimed that the British government supported President Reagan's view that nuclear war might be limited to Europe, but this was rejected by A. Likhotal'.[52]

Soviet commentators claim to believe that the reason Britain has maintained relatively high defence spending and its own strategic nuclear deterrent is to compensate for the loss of influence caused by relative economic decline. Kolosov has stated that military strength has not translated into influence for Britain in non-military fields but this did not prevent him writing: 'England became the third great power [*derzhava*] when it made its own nuclear weapons in the 1950s'.[53] Not all Soviet analysts make such a direct link between great power status and the possession of nuclear weapons. Trukhanovsky in his 1985 volume on the British nuclear deterrent refers to Britain as being one of the imperialist great powers at the end of the war, but sees the decision to construct the British A-bomb in the late 1940s as intended to preserve its status as a 'top rank great power [*velikaia derzhava*]'. 'London considered that only its own atomic bomb would raise England's prestige in its relations with the USA.' It would also place Britain in a 'superior position' in relation to all the other West European states.[54] Here Trukhanovsky follows Maclean's view that the British independent nuclear force had more to do with British policy towards the United States than with policy towards the Soviet Union. In evidence Maclean quoted Harold Macmillan's statement that an independent nuclear force 'gives us a better position . . . with respect to the United States. It puts us where we ought to be, in the position of a great power.'[55] British Governments had stated that Polaris was assigned to NATO and required a NATO decision to be used, but had insisted on the right to withdraw it from NATO under extreme circumstances.[56]

Kolosov observes that NATO is the centre of Britain's defence policy. 'In this bloc England has occupied from the time of its creation a privileged position, and plays the second role, after the USA, in the activity of the military organisation.'[57] This influence depended on Britain's contribution of arms and personnel. Britain's policy depended on close co-operation with its NATO allies. Many British leaders expected that entry into the EEC would lead to increased defence co-operation with the other EEC members, and a reduction in collaboration with the Americans. According to Kolosov, while British defence co-operation with Western Europe (in the non-nuclear sphere) did increase, British military dependence on the United States in fact grew especially in respect of the plans to replace Polaris with Trident. The British concentration on Europe reduced its privileged position within NATO but Britain still remained more privileged than other member states with respect to consultations with Washington. Both Conservative and Labour leaders desired to participate in Western European co-operation with the aim of taking a 'leading role' for Britain, to make it possible 'to speak to the USA not only in its own name, but to some extent, on behalf of all the West European allies'.[58] Kolosov claims that Whitehall evaluates plans for Western European defence systems according to whether they secure the leading role for Britain. London seeks to strengthen the role of the Western European Union, and of the Eurogroup of NATO. Talk in the early 1970s of strengthening the 'European pillar' of NATO based on the UK and the FRG did not, according to Kolosov, lead to major change, because it was impossible to avoid reliance on the US nuclear guarantee and on immediate American assistance in a conflict. This meant that it was undesirable to reduce the American role in NATO. The Heath Government had gone so far as to propose nuclear weapon co-operation with France, but had refused to review US–British nuclear co-operation, and this position had been upheld by the subsequent Labour Governments. The Thatcher Government was more concerned with developing links with the United States than with Western Europe.[59]

BRITAIN IN EAST–WEST RELATIONS

Discussion of Britain's defence policy is linked closely with British policy towards the USSR, and both are heavily influenced by the overall state of relations between NATO and the Warsaw Treaty Organisation countries. Even under Gorbachev, policy makers and analysts alike tend to see bilateral relations between the USSR and West European countries more as a sideshow in the Soviet–American game than as having particular importance in their own right. Trukhanovsky and Kapitonova claimed that 'on all important international questions England either follows the United States or adheres to the line defined by the NATO military bloc'.[60] More recent Soviet analyses distinguish between Atlanticist trends and those favouring a more integrated West European approach. But, more importantly, what has hardly changed since 1917 is the Soviet claim that British policy makers are divided into two groups: those who are implacably hostile to the USSR, and those more realistic and pragmatic elements who see the benefits of economic and political co-operation with Moscow. These divisions cut across the main political parties. The Soviet leaders always sought peaceful coexistence with Britain: according to Ryzhikov the Soviet Union 'has always regarded and regards Britain as a big power [*krupnaia derzhava*], exerting significant influence in world and European affairs, and as an important and long-term partner in trade, economic, scientific-technical and other areas of co-operation'. The state of Soviet–British relations depends, therefore, on the outcome of the struggle between the 'hardliners' and 'realists' in London.[61]

The Heath Government was unenthusiastic about the negotiations which led to the Helsinki Conference on Security and Co-operation in Europe (CSCE) in 1975, but the Labour Government was warmer towards the process of détente. This was linked with the move to the left in the Labour Party while in opposition; in 1973 it had lifted the ban on its members participating in societies for friendship with the USSR and the following year the National Executive Committee had come out for direct party to party contacts with the CPSU. This sentiment facilitated the success of the 1975 Wilson–Brezhnev summit in Moscow, where important bilateral agreements were signed.[62] *Kommunist* quoted the *Financial Times* as saying that the long-term plans for economic co-operation showed Britain's willingness to adapt its economy to Soviet needs.[63]

Mrs Thatcher's election as Leader of the Opposition in 1975 was followed by an anti-Soviet campaign by the right, alleging Soviet military superiority and calling for higher defence spending while opposing the expansion of Soviet–British trade.[64] In January 1976 *Krasnaia zvezda* dubbed her the 'iron lady' after a speech which was highly critical of Soviet policy.[65] In 1978–79, however, according to contemporary Soviet writings, Callaghan's Labour Government itself took a harder line. It approved Operation Chevaline, modernising the Polaris system by increasing its ability to penetrate the Moscow ABM defences. It supported President Carter's stance on human rights in the Soviet Union, at the Belgrade conference held to review progress since the CSCE; it supported the American proposal to NATO members to increase their contribution by 3 per cent per annum in real terms; and it was ready to accept the neutron bomb. 'For some reason', said Volodin, the British leaders forgot the words they had spoken in 1975.[66] Soviet commentators drew particular attention to British–Chinese military co-operation. The Chief of the Defence Staff, Air Marshal Neil Cameron, had told the Chinese in 1978 that they and the British shared a common enemy in Russia, and he had not been disavowed. Moreover, Britain was trying to sell Harrier jump–jets to Beijing.[67]

Moscow reacted cautiously to the advent of power of Mrs Thatcher. *International Affairs* pointed out that the Queen's speech opening the 1979–80 session of Parliament expressed the desire for greater stability in East–West relations, but it also claimed that there was worry within the Carter Administration that the Conservatives might impede the improvement of relations between the USA and the Soviet Union.[68] Less than a year later, any caution was abandoned. The Thatcher Government was being described as the most diligent of America's allies following Carter's anti–Soviet swing.[69] At the same time it was recognised that the British Government has refused to allow American pressure to damage Britain's trading interests (except as far as COCOM categories are concerned), although it was claimed in 1984 that the poor state of political relations between London and Moscow and the lack of British Government encouragement had held back the level of trade.[70]

On the question of the Strategic Defense Initiative, it was recognised that London (like Paris and Bonn) had major 'concern' about both the feasibility and the desirability of President Reagan's vision. In particular if the Soviet Union followed the United States in building a ballistic missile defence system (BMD), this would undermine deterrence, and furthermore would render obsolete Britain's own strategic weapon.[71] Britain's decision in 1985 to sign the Memorandum of Understanding with the Pentagon on British participation in SDI led to repeated criticism from Moscow.[72] In the Soviet view, the SDI is not only part of the anti-communist crusade. It is also a means whereby the United States is seeking to exert its control over the two other 'imperialist power centres', Western Europe and Japan, by increasing their defence dependence on Washington, and by procuring the most advanced technological resources from them for the benefit of the American economy. Likhotal' noted in a 1987 *MEMO* article that Sir Geoffrey Howe, the British Foreign Secretary, backed the 'narrow' interpretation of the ABM treaty, which would restrict the possibility for SDI research, but had refused the Soviet proposal to put this in writing.[73]

Signs of a more positive Soviet evaluation of Britain came in 1984. *International Affairs* in July that year welcomed British proposals to improve economic and other bilateral relations.[74] With the General Election behind it, and following a policy review, the British Government had taken a decision to seek to raise the level of relations with Moscow (see chapters 1 and 6).[75] Gorbachev's parliamentary visit to London of December 1984 (three months before becoming General Secretary) had a 'wide positive resonance'.[76] By late 1986 the improvements in Soviet–British relations were being overtaken by the new warmth between Gorbachev and Reagan. Soviet commentators became aware of concerns in European NATO circles that the superpowers might strike a deal on nuclear weapons which would sacrifice the interests of Western Europe. *New Times* reported in January 1987: 'London, Paris and Bonn are anxious to warn Washington (much, one suspects, to its pleasure) not to be carried away by an accommodation with Moscow.'[77]

Mrs Thatcher's visit to Moscow took place in the aftermath of the Reykjavik summit between Reagan and Gorbachev, which had fed the suspicion of Western European Governments. Her visit had a major impact on the Soviet public. Wherever she travelled she was greeted enthusiastically and warmly. Gorbachev's willingness to spend nine hours in discussion with her was an indication of the seniority achieved by the Prime Minister as the longest serving head of a Western Government, and of Britain's importance in the relations between the Soviet Union and the United States. Before, during and after the visit, the Soviet media attacked Thatcher's view that nuclear weapons had helped to keep the peace in Europe.[78] Her television interview with three Soviet journalists gave an unprecedented opportunity for a Western leader to explain and defend her views to a Soviet audience.[79] In some respects the Soviet leaders probably hoped to encourage Britain to use its influence in Washington and Western Europe (for example, over SDI and the interpretation of the ABM treaty). On the question of the desirability of nuclear weapons, however, Reagan personally was described as being closer than Thatcher to Moscow's thinking. It would seem that a major Soviet objective was to overcome Britain's objections to possible superpower disarmament agreements.[80]

Soviet treatment of Soviet–British relations normally includes sections dealing with opposition to British defence policy from the Labour Left, the peace movement and the CPGB. The Soviet media informed the public about the Greenham Common women and the mass demonstrations organised by the Campaign for Nuclear Disarmament.[81] Close attention was given to the adoption by the Labour Party of a non-nuclear defence policy, to be implemented within NATO. Statements critical of American or British policy, are widely and approvingly reported.[82] At the same time, before the 1987 elections, there was scepticism as to whether a Labour Government would actually implement such a policy.[83] Soviet analysts feared that the British military establishment, acting together with the United States and NATO, would succeed in preventing it. Even so, it must be asked why the Soviet Government felt the need to give the Conservative election campaign such a boost as the Thatcher summit. (The Conservative election manifesto contained a picture of Mrs Thatcher with Mr Gorbachev, and several election broadcasts featured footage of the summit.) The Soviet explanation was that Moscow had to be concerned with the actual policies pursued in government, rather than with ideology.[84] One must assume that by March 1987, the Soviet leadership had concluded from the opinion polls that there was little chance of a Labour Government being elected, and that they had better make the most of the government which was about to be reelected.

CONCLUSION

It is not always easy to separate out the real perceptions of Britain held by Soviet specialists and policy makers from the propaganda statements that they are required to make. It is probably somewhat of an exaggeration to say that there are 'debates' in the Soviet specialist press about British affairs. It is true, however, that some analysts are looking out for new explanations for the changes in the British political climate, and are combing British indigenous accounts rather than seeking to impose models based on past experience. Despite Britain's economic decline, it seems that Soviet specialists still recognise Britain to be of major importance in the world economy. Mrs Thatcher's domestic strategy is seen, after three elections, as having been an ideological, political and, to some extent, even an economic success. None the less, Moscow would prefer to have a Labour Government in London in the future. Even if it did not have a completely non-nuclear defence policy, it would be favourably inclined towards Soviet proposals for nuclear and conventional disarmament measures and would have a positive attitude towards agreements between the superpowers. A Labour-led coalition would be preferable to a Conservative Government. But while the Conservatives are in power in London, the present Soviet leaders will seek to achieve the maximum co-operation with them, for they have seen little chance of a government more sympathetic to Soviet policy aims coming to power in the near future.

While remaining staunchly allied to the USA, Britain is considered as having economic and strategic interests which sometimes diverge from those of the Americans, but do not necessarily thereby converge with Soviet interests. It is not only Mrs Thatcher's status as the longest serving Western leader which gives Britain a special status. Britain has preserved its position as the most influential power in NATO after the United States, being the only European member of the integrated military structure with its own nuclear weapons, and making a major conventional contribution in Europe and the Atlantic as well. Although it is not clear from the published Soviet literature, one can assume that the Falklands victory gave a favourable impression of British military preparedness. Moreover, as a permanent member of the UN Security Council, as the centre of the Commonwealth, and as perhaps the driving force behind European Community foreign policy co–ordination, Britain is seen as having an influence in world affairs which is not likely to diminish.

NOTES

I gratefully acknowledge the substantial help of Lesley Pitman and the other staff of Chatham House Library and Chatham House Press Library, and also of Shyama Iyer and Robert Sasson. I am solely and fully responsible for the content.

Abbreviations

IAM	*International Affairs (Moscow)*
Izv	*Izvestiia*
LG	*Literaturnaia gazeta*
MEMO	*Mirovaia ekonomika i mezhdunarodnye otnosheniia*
MO	*Mezhdunarodnye otnosheniia*
NT	*New Times*
Pr	*Pravda*
SWB	*BBC Summary of World Broadcasts*

1. For example, V. Matveev, 'Krupnyi shag na put' pretvoreniia v zhizn' programmy mira. K itogam sovetsko–angliiskoi vstrechi na vysshem urovne', *Kommunist*, 4 (March 1975), pp. 46–7.
2. *Sovetsko–angliiskie otnosheniia vo vremia velikoi otechestvennoi voiny, 1941–1945. Dokumenty i materialy*, 2 vols. (Politizdat, 1983); V. Kelin, 'SSSR – Angliia: opyt sotrudnichestva v bor'be protiv obshchei opasnosti', *MEMO*, 8 (1984), pp. 105–12.
3. For discussions of the impact of Soviet ideology on perceptions and policy, see Stephen White, *Political Culture and Soviet Politics* (Macmillan, 1979); *Ideology and Soviet Politics*, ed. Stephen White and Alex Pravda (Macmillan, 1988).
4. See Hedrick Smith, *The Russians* (Sphere, 1976), pp. 433–5.
5. Vladimir A. Zhitomirsky, *Aparteid po–britanski* (Mysl', 1985).
6. Vladimir A. Ryzhikov, *Sovetsko–angliiskie otnosheniia. Osnovnye etapy istorii* (MO, 1987), refers to Maclean as the 'very important specialist [*krupneishii spetsialist*]' (p. 127). His publications included *British Foreign Policy since Suez 1956–1968* (Hodder and Stoughton, 1970), translated as *Vneshniaia politika Anglii posle Suetsa* (Progress, 1972); *Velikobritaniia*, ed. S.P. Madzoevsky (pseud. Maclean) and Efim S. Khesin (Mysl', 1981); and a large number of articles and chapters. See 'Pamiati Donal'da Donal'dovicha MAKLEINA', *MEMO*, 5 (1983), 157.
7. Vsevolod V. Ovchinnikov, *Britain Observed: A Russian's View*, trans. Michael Barker (Pergamon, 1981), pp. 6, 8; translation of *Korni duba. Vpechatleniia i razmyshleniia ob Anglii i anglichanakh* (Mysl', 1980). Other journalistic accounts of British life are V. Larin, *Londonskii dnevnik* (Izdatel'stvo politicheskoi literatury, 1983); Vladimir Osipov, *Britaniia glazami russkogo* (Novosti, 1976). The word *Angliia* is often understood in Russian to include Scotland and Wales.
8. Ovchinnikov, *Britain*, pp. 100–1.
9. V. Peschansky, 'Sdvigi v klassovoi strukture britanskogo obshchestva', *MEMO*, 8 (1981), pp. 109–13. Lenin, *On Britain* (Foreign Language Publishing House, n. d.), p. 541.

10. Peschansky, 'Sdvigi', pp. 113–16.
11. Efim S. Khesin and V. Studentsov, 'Angliia: ot keinsianstva k monetarizmu', *MEMO*, 6 (1984), pp. 66–70. Similar points on the economy were made in the Aleksandr Naumenkov, 'V labirinte problem', *MEMO*, 10 (1986), pp. 135–7. Thatcherism is placed in a West European context in O. Timashkova, K. Voronov and G. Ponedelko, 'Politicheskaia bor'ba i regulirovanie ekonomiki v Zapadnoi Evrope', *MEMO*, 5 (1986), pp. 58–71, where it is described as an extreme example (p. 64).
12. Khesin and Studentsov, 'Angliia', pp. 70–8.
13. A. Timokhin, 'Velikobritaniia', *MEMO*, 3 (1987), pp. 108–10.
14. Irina Strizhova, 'The consequences of the Tory's [*sic*] tough policy', *IAM*, 4 (1987), p. 46.
15. Sergei Peregudov, S. Efimov and S. Madzoevsky, 'Angliiskie konservatory u vlasti', *MEMO*, 11 (1979), pp. 114–21; S. Madzoevsky, Sergei Peregudov and Efim Khesin, 'Pravye konservatory u vlasti', *MEMO*, 6 (1981), pp. 73–85; Y. Ustimenko, 'Hard Times for Britain', *IAM*, 5 (1982), 120–2; V. Raznitsyn, 'Britons' Worries', *IAM*, 2 (1984); Krivopalov, *Izv*, 11 May 1986; Vasilets, *Pr*, 5 September 1985; Arkady Maslennikov, 'Izbytie priem', *Pr*, 7 June 1987.
16. Sergei Peregudov, 'Velikobritaniia: vybory pozadi, sopernichestvo prodolzhaetsia', *MEMO*, 11 (1983), pp. 108–10.
17. *Ibid.*, p. 110, cited in *The Politics of Thatcherism*, ed. Stuart Hall and Martin Jacques (Lawrence and Wishart in association with *Marxism Today*, 1983), which was based mainly on articles in *Marxism Today*. The Soviet mass media treatment of the Falklands War is discussed in Howard M. Hensel, 'The Soviet perspective on the Falklands War', *The Round Table*, 288 (October 1983), pp. 395–432. He found the coverage during the crisis to be uniformly hostile to Britain, with the exception of a television broadcast by Aleksandr Bovin. See also G.G. Grigoreva, 'Britanskii shovinizm i folklendskii krizis', *Vestnik Moskovskogo universiteta*, Series 8, *Istoriia*, 2 (1986), pp. 40–52, on the impact of the crisis on British public opinion; and Iu. Barsegov and L. Imnadze, 'Folklendskie (Mal'vinskie) ostrova: staryi spor v novykh usloviiakh', *MEMO*, 6 (1982), pp. 129–34, calling for negotiations between Britain and Argentina, leading to 'decolonisation'.
18. Peregudov, 'Velikobritaniia: vybory', pp. 110–14.
19. Dmitry Voskoboinikov, 'Portret s sinimi gvozdikami', *LG*, 25 March 1987.
20. O. Prudkov, 'I vishnevyi sad srubit' ne grekh', *LG*, 29 April 1987.
21. Maslennikov, 'Izbytie'.
22. 'International Panorama', Soviet TV 1400 GMT 7 June 1987, in SWB/ SU/8589/A1/2 (quotation; see pp. 1–5 of this for further coverage).
23. Arkady Maslennikov, 'Pochemu tori pobedili', *Pr*, 13 June 1987.
24. Aleksandr Pumpiansky, 'How to win an election', *NT*, 29 June 1987, pp. 6–8.
25. Peregudov, 'Velikobritaniia: vybory', p. 112.
26. Maslennikov, *Pr*, 6 October 1985; *Pr*, 6 October 1986.
27. Sergei Peregudov, 'Sotsial-demokratiia pered litsom novykh problem', *MEMO*, 6 (1986), pp. 16–30; Iury Kudimov, 'Plans of the Opposition', *NT*, 17 August 1987, pp. 6–7.
28. Raznitsyn, 'Britons' worries', pp. 129–33; Strizhova, 'The consequences', pp. 46–52, 65; Arkady Maslennikov, 'Rabochie zanimaiut zavod', *Pr*, 2 May 1987; Edgar Cheporov, 'Chem bol'na Angliia?', *Nash sovremennik*, (1984), pp. 146–63.

29. Kh. Zagladin, 'Ol'ster – novaia faza konflikta?', *MEMO*, 4 (1987), pp. 83–6; Igor D. Biriukov, *Ol'ster. Krizis britanskoi imperialisticheskoi politiki (1968–1984 gg)* (Mysl', 1985); Elena Iu. Poliakova, *Ol'ster. Istoki tragedii* (Nauka, 1982).
30. Arkady Maslennikov, 'Chego oni boiatsia?', *Pr*, 27 July 1987; V. Kalashniko, 'The "cradle of democracy" under watchful eyes of the Special Service', *IAM*, 11 (1985) pp. 113–26.
31. Krivopalov, *Izv*, 4 August 1985.
32. Zhitomirsky, *Aparteid po-britanski*, Y. Ustimenko, 'Street clashes in Britain', *IAM*, 10 (1981), pp. 142–3.
33. Maclean, *British Foreign Policy*, p. 287.
34. Vladimir G. Trukhanovsky and Natalia K. Kapitonova, *Sovetsko–angliiskie otnosheniia 1945–1978* (MO, 1979), pp. 14–16.
35. S. Volodin, 'Britain in today's world politics', *IAM*, 7 (1984) p. 73.
36. P. Kriukov, 'The Soviet Union and Britain', *IAM*, 3 (1967), p. 41.
37. Trukhanovsky and Kapitonova, *Sovetsko–angliiskie otnosheniia*, p. 9. The view that Britain gained economically from the existence of the Commonwealth was shared by I. Lebedev and Efim S. Khesin, '"Sodruzhestvo natsii" – problemy i perspektivy', *MEMO*, 1 (1983), pp. 32–50.
38. Trukhanovsky and Kapitonova, *Sovetsko–angliiskie otnosheniia*, p. 9.
39. Vikenty Matveev, 'Britain and the world', *IAM*, 11 (1986) pp. 93–5. Also N. Gnatovskaia, 'Angliiskii kapital za rubezhom', *MEMO*, 5 (1984), pp. 136–42. The success of Japanese firms in securing high productivity in Britain is discussed in M. Beliaev, 'Iaponskii kapital v Anglii', *MEMO*, 7 (1985), p. 133–7.
40. Trukhanovsky and Kapitonova, *Sovetsko–angliiskie otnosheniia*, pp. 6–10 (quotation p. 10).
41. Volodin, 'Britain', p. 73.
42. *Zapadno-evropeiskaia integratsiia. Politicheskie aspekty*, ed. N.S. Kishilov (IMEMO) (Nauka, 1985), pp. 69–70, 74–5 (quotation p. 75).
43. *Ibid.*, pp. 70, 76–7.
44. Maclean, *British Foreign Policy*, pp. 327–9.
45. S. Volodin, 'Political zigzags in Britain', *IAM*, 6 (1979), pp. 32–3; cf. Vladimir Zuev, 'Angliia v obshchem rynke', *MEMO*, 5 (1983), pp. 84–9.
46. S. Volodin, 'USSR–Britain: 60 years of diplomatic relations', *IAM*, 4 (1984), p. 63.
47. *Izv*, 7 December 1985.
48. *Razriadka i konfrontatsiia: dve linii v sovremennykh mezhdunarodnykh otnosheniiakh*, ed. V. I. Gantman (Nauka, 1987), pp. 246–7.
49. *Ibid.*, pp. 256–7.
50. Volodin, 'Britain', p. 79.
51. TASS described Britain as a 'direct accomplice' of the United States. *Pr*, 17 April 1986.
52. Gennady V. Kolosov, *Voenno-politicheskii kurs Anglii v Evrope* (Nauka, 1984) pp. 22–3; A. Likhotal', 'Velikobritaniia v evropeiskoi politike', *MEMO*, 9 (1985), p. 144.
53. Kolosov, *Voenno–politicheskii*, pp. 10, 49.
54. Vladimir G. Trukhanovsky, *Angliiskoe iadernoe oruzhie. Istoriko-politicheskii aspekt* (MO, 1985), pp. 35, 48–50 (quotation p. 49).
55. *The Times*, 24 February 1958, cited in Maclean, *British Foreign Policy*, p. 285.
56. Kolosov, *Voenno–politicheskii*, pp. 64–5; Trukhanovsky, *Angliiskoe iadernoe oruzhie*, p. 182.

57. Kolosov, *Voenno-politicheskii*, p. 28.
58. *Ibid.*, pp. 9, 38–42 (quotation p. 42).
59. *Ibid.*, pp. 44–7, 170–200.
60. Trukhanovsky and Kapitonova, *Sovetsko-angliiskie otnosheniia*, p. 284.
61. Ryzhikov, *Sovetsko-angliiskie*, pp. 258–9.
62. Trukhanovsky and Kapitonova, *Sovetsko-angliiskie otnosheniia*, pp. 226–34, 246–7.
63. Matveev, 'Krupnyi', pp. 47–51.
64. Kolosov, *Voenno-politicheskii*, pp. 11–20; Trukhanovsky and Kapitonova, *Sovetsko-angliiskie otnosheniia*, pp. 218, 234, 252, 275.
65. Iu. Gavrilov, ' "Zhelezanaia dama" strashchaet', *Krasnaia zvezda*, 24 January 1976.
66. Volodin, 'Political zigzags', pp. 35–7.
67. *Ibid.*, pp. 27–9; Trukhanovsky and Kapitonova, *Sovetsko-anglisskie otnosheniia*, p. 239–40, 276–9; Trukhanovsky, *Angliiskoe iadernoe oruzhie*, p. 159; Kolosov, *Voenno-politicheskii*, p. 84–5.
68. Y. Ustimenko, 'Great Britain's new government', *IAM*, 8 (1979), pp. 123–5.
69. S. Volodin, 'Britain's policies under the Conservatives', *IAM*, 4 (1980), pp. 38–47.
70. Volodin, 'USSR–Britain', p. 63.
71. Aleksandr Bovin, 'Western Europe: "strategic concerns"', *IAM*, 12 (1985), pp. 94–103; Maslennikov, *Pr*, 17 March 1985.
72. Maslennikov, *Pr*, 10 December 1985.
73. A. Likhotal', 'Na evropeiskom napravlenii', *MEMO*, 7 (1987), p. 15.
74. Volodin, 'Britain', p. 80.
75. House of Commons, Second Report from the Foreign Affairs Committee, Session 1985–86, *UK–Soviet Relations*, HC 28–I and HC 28–II(HMSO, 1986), Vol. I, p. xxii, Vol. II, pp. 295–6.
76. Ryzhikov, *Sovetsko-angliiskie*, p. 12.
77. Aleksandr Lebedev, 'Bomb for Europe? The British and French nuclear arsenals', *NT*, 26 January 1987, pp. 20–3. See also Likhotal', 'Na evropeiskom', pp. 8–12.
78. See, e.g., Aleksandr Maslennikov, 'Zavisit ot Londona', *Pr*, 24 March 1987; the speeches of Gorbachev and Thatcher in *Pr*, 31 March 1987, and the reports in *Pr*, 1 and 2 April 1987; 'Summit Meeting', *NT*, 13 April 1986, pp. 3–4; SWB SU/8529/A1/1–10 (30 March 1987).
79. Vladimir Simonov, 'How the rose was repainted: a postmortem of the TV Interview with Mrs Margaret Thatcher', *Moscow News*, 12 April 1987.
80. At the XXVII Party Congress, Gorbachev expressed concern at the stand by Britain and France over the role of their own nuclear forces in disarmament negotiations. M.S. Gorbachev, 'Politicheskii doklad . . .', *Materialy XXVII s"ezda Kommunisticheskoi partii Sovetskogo Soiuza* (Politizdat, 1986), p. 69.
81. E. Silin, 'Antivoennoe dvizhenie na sovremennom etape', *MEMO*, 6 (1985); pp. 21–32; and I. Aliev, 'The Tories vs. the peace campaigners', *IAM*, 11 (1985), pp. 117–23.
82. G. Vorontsov, 'SShA, NATO i evrorakety', *MEMO*, 11 (1984), p. 17.
83. Trukhanovsky, *Angliiskoe iadernoe oruzhie*, p. 191.
84. Aleksandr Lebedev and Vladimir Orel, 'The other Britain', *NT*, 20 April 1987, p. 5.

4 British perspectives on the Soviet Union

MICHAEL CLARKE

A NATIONAL PERSPECTIVE

The concept of a national perspective on another country is at once important and elusive. National perspectives set the context within which policy choices are made; they encompass what is deemed to be possible and they condition policy makers' and the public's views of how another society will respond to its policies. Yet it is almost impossible to offer a precise analysis of what constitutes a national perspective, for it is made up of a series of historical, social and political factors, interacting and constantly changing to produce a series of images, stereotypes and expectations, that must somehow offer a guide to action.

Any analysis of British perspectives on the Soviet Union, therefore, must take account of some obvious methodological problems. To begin with, there is no way in which British and Soviet perspectives of each other can be seen as mirror images. Both societies are too different. It is difficult to measure British public opinion with great precision, and the relationships between public opinion and official opinion, or between public attitudes and policy, have to be stated very tentatively. In the case of the Soviet Union, notwithstanding the fact that one or two public opinion polls now exist, there is nevertheless no accumulation of such data over time and its relationship to policy and officialdom would have to be approached in a completely different way.[1] As in so many other respects, Britain and the Soviet Union are asymmetrical societies and assumptions we make about our own society – so often the prism through which we form our expectations of other societies – cannot easily be transferred to the Soviet Union.

More particularly, when we try to analyse 'British' perspectives, it is necessary to distinguish what might be seen as a spectrum that runs from official opinion – as defined by key bureaucrats – to public opinion – as expressed in the grossest form by general opinion polls. Within this spectrum various shades and categories of opinion can be discerned. There may be differences within the collective view of officials over a period; there is frequently a difference of emphasis between the opinion of officials and that of their political superiors; and shading into the governmental/official opinion will be that of key interest groups involved in Anglo–Soviet relations. Further along the spectrum we might place informed and interested opinion, followed by party political attitudes, the opinions expressed in the mass media, and then, finally, the broad trends of opinion expressed by the general public. Having defined such a spectrum, however, it is also necessary to distinguish a little more closely what such opinions are about. There is a clear distinction between perspectives focused on Soviet society and those focused more specifically on Soviet policy. We might also conceive of further distinctions between attitudes to Eastern Europe as opposed to the Soviet Union, and attitudes to Communist ideology as opposed to Soviet society. Clearly such distinctions highlight certain shades of opinion, though for the purposes of this analysis we can accept that officials generally assume that East European and Soviet policies are effectively one; and that, for all but the most specialist observers, 'Soviet society' is synonymous with communism both in theory and in action.

Acknowledging the obvious imprecisions which even these essential distinctions create and with all the appropriate caveats, it is possible to describe British perspectives as existing within a simple matrix: official opinion and public opinion on one axis; attitudes to Soviet foreign policy and more general attitudes to Soviet society on the other. On the basis of such a device it is possible to see that official opinion is more concerned with Soviet policy than with general perspectives of Soviet society and in this respect tends to be remarkably consistent. In the opposite quadrant of the matrix, however, public opinion is more focused on images of Soviet society and as such is more variable in its concerns.

Even in this simple form, however, the matrix has to be seen in context. Taken overall, it is clear that British opinion in relation to the Soviet Union at all levels is generally very consistent. Britain has always been essentially hostile to Communist Russia and regarded it as an adversary. Exceptions to this, such as the Labour movement in the inter-war years, or the brief period of the Grand Alliance, are notable precisely because they are so exceptional. As a hostile superpower the Soviet Union cannot safely be ignored, but while it is a key factor in Britain's international environment it has not been a major focus of immediate or even mid–term policy. The range of political emotions through which relations are pursued is fairly narrow. Thus, when we examine variations in public or official attitudes towards the Soviet Union, preferences may be clear, or the centrality of the Soviet state in the international environment may be recognised, but there is a lack of intensity in British opinion. Debates about the Soviet Union tend to be part of debates about something else, whether the wisdom of disarmament, the level of defence spending, the politics of NATO, the supply of strategic resources or regional stability. This is in sharp contrast to opinion regarding the United States, for example, where a recognition of centrality, preferences, and an intensity of interest all go together. When it comes to British attitudes to the Soviet Union, variations occur within a collective mind set that is essentially consistent and which views the Soviet Union somewhat indirectly.

Secondly, the matrix is not timeless and some variations in emphasis can be discerned over a period. In particular, the last six years have marked something of a change which could turn out to be structural. It may well be that while official opinion maintains its consistency and its focus on Soviet policy, mass public opinion, and to some extent political opinion, have begun to change in their response to the Soviet Union. Typically, in the British case, however, this is as much a result of general environmental factors as of any clear reappraisal of Soviet society or its ideology.

In order to substantiate these points and to understand more clearly how far present changes may be a departure from the norm, I will review each of the major components that make up this view of a national perspective: the historical tradition, official opinion, political party debate, interest groups, the mass media and, finally, public opinion.

THE HISTORICAL TRADITION

Though the historical record of Anglo–Soviet relations is long and complex, the salient features of it, insofar as they have entered into our national perspective, can be stated fairly simply. The historical record, in other words, creates a series of expectations and stereotypes which are true enough in themselves, but which also serve to iron out the variations and ambiguities of a more complex reality.

Firstly, the historical record suggests that Britain's hostility to the Soviet Union is genuine and deep seated. The circumstances of the revolution, the immediate effect of it on the Allies fighting the Central Powers, the fate of the Romanovs, and the ideology for which they suffered, though not at all well-understood in British circles, created a distaste and a suspicion which set the pattern for the rest of the twentieth century. In a sense, successive British Governments handled this mutual animosity by ignoring the Soviet Union as far as possible. Conservative Governments during the 1920s were overtly hostile, and even the two Labour Governments of the decade, though they recognised the new state, were less than enthusiastic about it, and more concerned to recover the pre-revolutionary debts owed to Britain.[2] During the inter-war years, no serious official thought was given to the role that the Soviet Union might play in dealing with the fascist dictatorships. Insofar as there was a debate over whether Britain and France could afford to take the lead in world diplomacy during this period, it was about the role that the United States might or might not play. The Soviet Union was hardly recognised as a diplomatic player.[3] Even during the period of the Grand Alliance in the Second World War, British diplomatic efforts were centred around a powerful consensus to create an Anglo–American directorate to shape the diplomacy of the post-war world. Though this attempt did not seem to be successful at the time, the same result was effectively achieved by 1947 through a series of incremental actions. The special relationship with the United States was partly built upon this directorate.[4] It provided a platform for British diplomacy and a political strength that lasted for a long time and was far in excess of the country's tangible resources.

A second strand in the historical tradition has reinforced the first. When it was clear that the Soviet Union could no longer be excluded from a world that was destined to be essentially bipolar, British diplomacy favoured a *modus vivendi* with the Soviet Union. From the very beginning of the Grand Alliance, British policy-makers were always alert to the possibilities of a deal with the Soviet Union.[5] In 1943 the US would not hear of it because it smacked of dirty politics: in 1953 it was suspicious because it smacked of weak politics. British policy has traditionally been more consistent in this than has that of the USA. Thus, in the mid-1950s, Britain was keen to explore the possibilities of détente with the post-Stalin leadership in the Soviet Union, took the lead in trying to engineer some summit diplomacy in 1960 and in relation to the partial test-ban treaty of 1963, and right up to the present has shown a willingness to do deals with the Soviet Union that has often proved to be some way ahead of US assessments.[6] This has been partly facilitated by the fact that the Soviet Union has accorded Britain, on a number of occasions, a higher diplomatic status than many of its partners. This is derived from a Soviet respect for British diplomatic power within the Western Alliance; and is also partly due to a belief that Britain has some influence in Washington over and above that due to a European ally. The alertness of British officials to the possibilities of détente, however, should not be interpreted as a search for new beginnings in East–West relations. Successive British Governments have been more keen on the processes of détente than on its promises of political change. If good fences make good neighbours, then détente has been seen as a way of building better fences. British Governments have justified their policies as expressions of mature realism; cautious and pragmatic, playing for the longer term diplomatic benefits.

Thirdly, the historical tradition, at least from 1945, teaches British observers that Anglo–Soviet relations are a function of wider East–West relations. They have to be seen in their structural context. For this reason, Anglo–Soviet relations, except in those particular areas which have to be handled bilaterally, are in all major respects a matter of multilateral diplomacy.[7] Hence they are seldom direct. Britain does not have an arms control approach to the Soviet

Union, for instance, but rather an approach to arms control within the Atlantic Alliance which therefore becomes a multilateral arms control approach towards the Soviet Union. Of course, there have been differences of emphasis with the United States; over the conduct of the Korean War, for example, or the wisdom of involvement in Vietnam. But Prime Ministers and Foreign Secretaries, from Churchill and Eden almost without exception up to the present day, have predicated their East–West diplomacy on the need to establish Anglo–American agreement about all the essentials.[8]

Finally, the history of Anglo–Soviet relations leaves us with a clear perception that the vast majority of the general public has backed up this diplomatic continuity, though for somewhat different reasons. From the very beginning of the Soviet State, the overwhelming perception of the Soviet Union in the public's mind has been that it is a Communist power. Public attitudes have always been, and continue to be, a reflection of this fact. It is fair to say that the British public never knew very much about Russia, still less about communism; and there have never been any natural vehicles in British culture to convey such knowledge. Nevertheless the image in Britain of communism is extremely strong, if somewhat blurred, and the image of Soviet Russia has always been as that of a totalitarian extreme of the Left. For this reason, the history of public attitudes to the Soviet Union is really the history of an essentially internal debate. After the unsuccessful war of intervention and the onset of the depression, there was a good deal of sympathy for the Soviet Union on the Left of British politics. To defend the Soviet Union was a way of upholding the principle that there was an alternative to failed and decadent capitalism.[9] The Communist Party of Great Britain was never numerically strong, even in the 1930s, by the standards of other major European countries. Even in 1937 it recorded only 12,000 members. Nevertheless, it did, for a time, constitute the left wing of mainstream polical argument in Britain. But the Nazi–Soviet Non-Aggression Pact and the outcome of the war in Eastern Europe destroyed communism as a credible political force in mainstream British politics. By 1950 it was a fringe belief, serving as a home for displaced leftist activism. But the left wing of mainstream political argument in Britain. But the Nazi–Soviet Non-Aggression Pact and the outcome of the war in Eastern Europe destroyed by those who feared it during the 1960 and 70s. Its shadow far exceeded its stature.

This identification of the Soviet Union with a failed political ideology was mitigated only a little and for a limited period during the Grand Alliance, when the Soviet Union was perceived as a brave and suffering ally. Apart from that, and a certain grudging admiration for the Soviet industrial achievements since then, the British public have displayed towards the Soviet Union what Ivor Crewe has described as a 'wary attitude' of 'rocklike stability apparently unaffected by the ebb and flow of East–West relations'.[10]

THE PERSPECTIVES OF OFFICIALS

Official perspectives are mainly derived from what are regarded as the perennial realities of any relationships with Communist countries. Official opinion, insofar as it can be divorced from the personal opinions of the individuals who become officials, is conditioned by what the Whitehall memory knows about the specifics of relations between the two countries.

One of the most obvious lessons that the official memory learns is that the contacts between Britain and the Soviet Union are not in themselves very intense. Any number of cultural and economic interests could be cited as the real substance of bilateral relations, but they do not loom large in the general framework of British interests. Anglo–Soviet trade has never been worth more than a few hundred million pounds per annum and has normally constituted less than 2 per cent of Britain's world trade, even before the decline of recent years. Cultural and educational contacts are so few that they can be individually named and listed. The real essence of Anglo–Soviet relations, in other words, is the general 'political work' for which the Foreign and Commonwealth Office and foreign embassies are normally responsible, and the procedural work of facilitating visits, political contact and normal diplomatic relations.[11]

A second reality that the official memory understands is that virtually all of these rather meagre bilateral relations are constrained by formal agreements. There are three central sets of arrangements between London and Moscow: the 'Joint Commission' concerning science, technology, trade and economic relations; the Joint Maritime Commission; and the Cultural Agreement, first signed in 1959 and updated every two years. The 'protocol on consultations' of 1975 had fallen into disuse but has recently had new life breathed into it.[12] Officials know, therefore, that any change in the nature of bilateral relations is less a matter of natural political developments than a formal agreement to permit a natural development, or to manufacture one which, in time, may perhaps become natural.

It is not surprising, therefore, that the official memory also knows that the positive aspects of bilateral relations are easily overtaken by the antagonistic issues. Just as cultural and economic relations are used as symbols of a growing détente, so their curtailment is also used as an expression of displeasure when détente is in decline. As Curtis Keeble shows in chapter 2, the diplomacy of Anglo–Soviet relations tends to be a cyclical affair: a gradual expansion of relations where contacts are deepened and extended, followed by a diplomatic crisis, followed in turn by an attempt to rebuild the edifice.[13]

Finally, the official memory knows that bilateral relations do not have a genuinely independent existence outside the general structure of East–West relations. The 'crisis' which brings about a decline in bilateral relations may be

73

over a particular Anglo–Soviet issue, such as a series of multiple diplomatic expulsions as occurred in 1971, 1985 and again in 1989. It is more likely, however, that the crisis is occasioned by wider East–West problems, such as the issue of Czechoslovakia, Afghanistan, or the NATO dual-track decision of 1979.[14] Indeed, even events such as these have to be set in a broader political context. The Soviet intervention in Hungary in 1956, for example, caused much deeper and more lasting official hostility than did the intervention in Czechoslovakia in 1968, because of the different atmospheres in superpower relations prevailing at each time.[15] Equally, the crisis in superpower relations over the 1973 Middle East War did not have a significant impact on the procedures of détente that were being so hopefully pursued at the time, whereas the Angolan Civil War in 1975 and the intervention in Afghanistan in 1979 had a major impact on East–West perceptions because from 1975 the general climate was significantly more adversarial. When compared with these forces, the impact of Anglo–Soviet bilateral relations cannot be regarded as significant in themselves. Officials understand, therefore, that Anglo–Soviet relations are determined by the multilateral context.[16] Multilateral concerns set the level of political expectations; they are intrinsically important, and no British policies stand much chance of success unless they are part of Atlantic Alliance policy, or European Community policy, or, if not part of a multilateral policy, are at least derived from a process of allied consultation to ensure that national policies are compatible.

All of these factors have conditioned the professional governmental view over recent years. It is not that officials are cynical or unenthusiastic. But they are genuinely wary and interpret their task as one of reflecting the prevailing state of Anglo–Soviet relations, rather than initiating new approaches. In a sense, the official stands as more moderate than the politician and as less involved than the interest group. The official perspective tends to take major East–West crises in its stride. Whereas Czechoslovakia, Poland or Afghanistan dramatically tilt political and public perceptions, and certainly excite a degree of vitriol, officials are noted for their willingness to inject as much normality into relations as possible. After announcing a package of sanctions to be taken against the Soviet Union following the Afghanistan invasion, for instance, the Foreign Secretary, Lord Carrington, aptly expressed the official view when he stressed that Britain must nevertheless continue to seek 'commercially justified trade' with the East.[17] Or again, though the CSCE process spent its first decade after 1975 to the accompaniment of increasingly bitter Cold War rhetoric, the official perspective on the CSCE remained that it was a useful process, no great expectations were entertained for it, but it could be pursued as normal diplomacy that might turn out to have a productive outcome.[18]

THE PERSPECTIVES OF POLITICIANS

One would expect the opinions of politicians to be more volatile than those of officials and indeed this is observably so. There are some singular examples of political leaders being noticeably more keen than their officials to make summit approaches to the Soviet leadership. In the 1950s, both Winston Churchill and Anthony Eden felt (presumably on the basis of their experience of Grand Alliance diplomacy) that they could handle the Soviet leadership and found themselves up against the scepticism of their Foreign Office officials.[19] If Britain was alert to the prospects of détente during these years then it is fair to say that the impetus came from politicians more than officials. In the late 1950s and early 1960s there was great political interest in the post-Stalin leadership and Macmillan was personally keen to help promote East–West détente, or at least be part of it. Again, Harold Wilson in 1965 and 1967 undertook two fairly novel but quite unsuccessful attempts to end the Vietnam War through a process of Commonwealth and Anglo–Soviet diplomacy which flew in the face of official advice. On both occasions, official scepticism was seen to be entirely justified.[20]

In the same way, the opinions of politicians and political parties have often been far more damning to the Soviet Union, in reaction to specific events, than have those of officials. Calls for sanctions and reprisals against the Soviet Union have been heard loud and often after Soviet interventions in Eastern Europe or in Afghanistan. Human rights issues and the problems of Jewish emigration have loomed largest on the parliamentary agenda when the Soviet Union has been criticised. But officials have never been particularly preoccupied by these matters.[21] Indeed, when officials did take up human rights cases as a more major East–West issue in the 1980s, it was against the inclinations of the Foreign and Commonwealth Office and was the result of explicit political direction to do so.[22] Probably the greatest divergence between political and official opinions occurred during the first Thatcher Administration.

As soon as she became leader of the opposition in 1975, Mrs Thatcher offered the country a robust anti-Sovietism. In fact she made very few statements about East–West relations whilst in opposition, indicating both hostility and disinterest in diplomatic contact with the East. She earned the cachet of being the 'iron lady' for a single speech.[23] Like many of Mrs Thatcher's political stances, it was not particularly consistent or intellectualised: it was a strong mixture of political instinct and short-term tactical calculations. When she became Prime Minister in 1979, Mrs Thatcher's outspoken anti-Sovietism broke with the more moderate, cautious tradition of most official views. She defended policies that she had effectively inherited from the previous government – to increase defence expenditure, to support NATO's dual-track decision on cruise and Pershing missiles, and to tackle the Polaris replacement question – in highly anti–Soviet terms.[24] She argued that 'our way of life' would be put at risk without a nuclear deterrent;[25] that 'a bully always goes for the weakest'[26] and that the Soviet Union presented Britain with 'the greatest threat since Munich in 1938'.[27] In 1980 she was very clear that the British Olympic Committee should boycott the Moscow Olympics in response to the Soviet intervention in Afghanistan. She claimed to be 'astonished' at the stance the British Olympic Committee took when they disagreed.[28] The declaration of martial law in Poland in December 1981 provided an interesting contrast. For while Lord Carrington expressed the FCO view in the House of Lords that the government regretted the turn of events and declared strict non-intervention in the matter, Mrs Thatcher told the Commons that her government 'totally condemned' the 'oppression of the present regime' and 'bitterly and deeply regretted that action is being taken to extinguish the flame of freedom that started in Poland'.[29] Nor was the Prime Minister overly interested in taking any of the normal diplomatic opportunities that were offered to her. In 1982 she chose not to attend Brezhnev's funeral. In 1984 she attended Andropov's funeral, but did not speak to his successor or even shake hands with him.

The divergence between politicians and officials could hardly be more marked than in the case of the first Thatcher Government. Nevertheless, it is testimony to the power of consensus that operates in British foreign policy that this approach was thoroughly reappraised by the Government in 1983. Since then, Anglo–Soviet and Anglo–East European diplomacy has been very busy. There is some discussion over what caused this change of emphasis. One view has it that the FCO simply managed to persuade the Prime Minister over a number of months that a more active diplomacy towards the East would be advantageous. Some view it as a natural evolution of Mrs Thatcher's self-image as a stateswoman of the West; Geoffrey Howe has claimed that it was a natural, timely and independent reassessment of Britain's Eastern relations; others have seen in it a response to pressure from Britain's allies. All agree, however, that this reappraisal was highly dependent on the more general context of visibly improving East–West relations after 1984.[30]

This is, in fact, the key to an understanding of political perspectives on the Soviet Union. For while there certainly are cases of an independent difference of view between senior politicians and officials, and while the Thatcher examples of 1975 and 1984 are undoubtedly the most obvious, the reality is that the political perspectives of the Soviet Union are reflections of other arguments. Those party political debates in Britain that have discussed the Soviet Union have not been about Anglo–Soviet relations as such, or even about the Soviet Union itself; rather, they have been debates over arms control, NATO unity, or the attitude towards the United States. In all such debates, attitudes towards the Soviet Union are essentially unchanging. The Soviet threat is taken as a given.

Since defence became a matter of party political debate, many attitudes have been polarised. In order to defend their policies, Conservatives have constantly reiterated the nature of the threat that the Soviet Union is thought to pose to Britain. Parliamentary debates reveal how prevalent this threat is believed to be. The success of the Intermediate Nuclear Force negotiations in 1987, according to Foreign Office Minister Lynda Chalker, was due to the fact that the West 'have taken such a firm stand in recent years in our dealings with the Soviet Union'.[31] In this she was echoing a very clear assumption of the Prime Minister that an INF deal constituted 'a vindication of the policy of firmness'. And notwithstanding the deal itself, Trident should be purchased and the full panoply of weapons necessary for flexible response should be maintained, because the Soviet threat would remain undiminished.[32] The spectre of nuclear blackmail haunts Conservative views of the Soviet Union. Mrs Thatcher alludes to it frequently and for that reason told the Commons flatly that her government 'simply will not stand for the denuclearisation of Europe', which would 'leave us dangerously exposed to Soviet superiority'.[33]

The essence of all of these views lies in the fact that Conservative thinkers are fearful that the policies of the Labour Party during the 1980s would have left the country essentially defenceless. A Labour Britain, Mrs Thatcher told the Commons, 'would have no answer to nuclear blackmail'.[34] The concern, therefore, was to establish in the political arena the unquestionable need for existing defences rather than to reappraise the nature of the threat itself. There are, of course, shades of opinion on the Conservative benches. Members, such as Sir Anthony Kershaw or Peter Temple-Morris, who take an interest in foreign affairs, tend to reflect a 'foreign office' conservatism about Anglo–Soviet relations. But it is interesting that within Conservative ranks the only notable dissent as intellectual critique has come from Enoch Powell. He has criticised Government policies on the grounds that they ignore the possibility of a rational calculation of interests on the part of the Soviet leadership: it is simply irrational for the Soviet Union to threaten Western Europe, but such a threat continues to be assumed by Western governments, rather than analysed, and used as justification for existing policies.[35] In this respect, Conservative opinions are faithfully echoed in many Centre party statements and also find some sympathy on the Right of the Labour Party.[36]

None of this is particularly surprising in an era in which defence issues have been the focus of heated party debate. The Conservatives have stuck to their defence policies and argued them without close reference to the nature of the threat. More surprisingly, however, the Labour Party has done the same. For while Labour defence policies became far more radical and specific than ever before during the 1980s, there was nevertheless little alternative thinking about the Soviet Union beyond a general consensus that the threat was overestimated and a relief that the new leadership in Moscow made détente policies look less naive than hitherto. Rather, the real focus of Labour defence debates remained, as it had always been, the United States and the Atlantic Alliance.[37]

For the Labour Party, the premises behind its opposition to INF deployments, to a Polaris replacement, or to British support for the Strategic Defense Initiative, were all concerned essentially with the wisdom of American leadership. If anything, Labour spokesmen were wary of tackling the question of the Soviet Union, lest they seem like fellow-travellers and open themselves to Conservative criticism that they were either very naive or downright sinister. The assumption contained in Labour's message to the electorate in 1987 was not that we need to take a fresh look at the Soviet Union or at the threat, so much as that we need to take a fresh look at how we combat the threat.[38] Labour Party conference debates about Britain's membership of NATO are expressed almost exclusively in terms of the problems of being 'powerless to divorce ourselves from this American foreign policy'.[39] And debates about the possibilities of adopting a non-nuclear policy are overwhelmingly set in terms of whether this would be practical in the context of the Alliance. There is indeed a parochialism about the Labour Party in these matters. The number of backbenchers genuinely interested in East–West relations is extremely small. Denis Healey is the acknowledged expert in the party, and by far the most experienced politician on whom the leadership can call. Out of power for over a decade, the Labour Party has no younger generation of specialists who have been able to build up governmental experience of East–West issues. Lacking substance, Labour's attitudes have tended to be reactive and tuned to intra-party arguments. Thus, just as Labour Party defence debates in the late 1940s were not about Communism, but about the policies of the Western camp, and the debates of the late 1950s were for the ideological soul of the party, so those of the 1980s are also, in essence, internal debates. The Soviet Union is not ignored in these arguments but there is little detailed knowledge of the country and a somewhat detached interest in it.[40]

The same may be said of the Centre parties, indeed, with even greater force. For while the Liberal Party and the Social Democrats were intuitively nearer to Conservative emphases on the nature of the Soviet threat, defence issues emerged as a prime vehicle of the power struggles both within and between the two Alliance parties and their factions. The fact that defence became such a plague on the attempts to create some electoral unity out of the Centre parties reflected a lack of consensus about the policies of the United States and NATO, and about Britain's proper role in the defence of the West.[41] There was some attempt in the key Alliance document of 1986 to suggest a reappraisal of the context of Anglo–Soviet relations, but it is typical of the nature of the debate that a reappraisal of the Soviet Union was written, but not included in the official document, and that this aspect of the report was, in any case, ignored in the debates which attended it.[42]

Party political debate in Britain, therefore, insofar as it is about the Soviet Union, is about differences in emphasis rather than analysis. The onset of *glasnost'* has not altered this fact, though it has created some curious political juxtapositions since Mrs Thatcher displayed, in her second term, such willingness to engage in Anglo–Soviet diplomacy and to praise the leadership of Mr Gorbachev.

INTEREST GROUPS AND BRITISH PERSPECTIVES

One of the reasons why the official perspective of the Soviet Union is so influential is that there is so little outside the governmental process that can offer a detailed critique of it. There are few interests whose main concern is the Soviet Union, though there are many who have some peripheral interest or involvement with it. Since Anglo–Soviet trade only accounts for less than 2 per cent of Britain's world trade, at a value of less than £1 billion per year, it is not surprising that there are few British companies directly involved with the Soviet Union. Fewer than twelve British Embassy staff in Moscow are responsible for Anglo–Soviet commercial relations and only a handful of major banks and companies – fewer than 15 – have their own representation in Moscow.[43] Many businesses claim to have an interest in dealing with the Soviet Union. By one estimate there are more than 600,[44] but in truth the Soviet market is extraordinarily difficult to break into (see chapter 10). The inflexibilities of five-year planning, the conditions under which Western companies operate, and the initial outlays required, all tend to debar other than large, established companies from operating. Lead times on manufacturing projects seem to be 3–4 years longer than on projects undertaken in Western Europe:[45] the costs, even of establishing an office in Moscow to facilitate some breakthroughs in the Soviet market, are thought to rule out most companies with a turnover of less than $10 million.[46] These are long-standing realities of Anglo–Soviet trade. In the wake of all Mrs Thatcher's summit diplomacy during 1987, both she and Mr Gorbachev agreed that they would try to increase Anglo–Soviet trade by some 40 per cent by 1990.[47] Whether or not this proves to be possible, it is unlikely to increase greatly the number of commercial interest groups who figure in the picture. Such an increase would be against a declining trend in Anglo–Soviet trade in relation to trade between the Soviet Union and other West European states. More importantly, it is being handled through the existing machinery of the Joint Commission and the usual conditions will apply. Only those companies already experienced in dealing in the Soviet market are likely to gain from any new impetus.

The same is true of cultural and educational relations. As John Morison shows in chapter 8, the number of organisations that have an active interest to promote is small and the work of such groups is highly specialised. Anglo–Soviet cultural contacts all fall within the framework of the Cultural Agreement and their number is such that they can be listed separately: activities of the Anglo–Soviet Friendship Society, or the Great Britain–USSR Association; contacts between parliamentarians, and so forth.[48] And when Soviet and British leaders use the framework of cultural contacts to show an intention towards improved diplomatic relations, as they periodically do, then cultural contacts are enriched with a number of highly specific and prestigious events. Cultural relations between the two countries could not be described as ubiquitous. Personal travel back and forth is not great. The Soviet Union and Eastern Europe account for about 0.5 per cent of passenger transits to and from Britain in any one year.[49] The number of Soviet students in Britain learning English has been increasing but still barely runs to an annual three-figure total.[50] Meanwhile Soviet studies in Britain have been in steady decline for lack of resources. The East European Trade Council united with academic interests in 1987 to press the Government for expanded funding for Soviet and East European studies, but received little practical support.[51]

The British trade union movement has sometimes been thought of as an interest group that has wanted to promote Anglo–Soviet relations. But this has been more shadow than substance. The Soviet Union has used the fraternal links between some British and Soviet unions to make a political point, as during the miners' strike in 1985; but these links have never been anything more than a vehicle for symbolic fraternity. Indeed, they have had a negative effect both on public opinion and on intra-union debates in Britain. And there is absolutely no evidence that British trade unionism, unlike Polish trade unionism, has had any impact on Soviet society.

Interest groups do exist, therefore, and they are consulted by government on occasions. But they do not form a politically significant force either separately or together. Nor, despite the recent improvement in relations, is there any real indication that the scope or number of interest groups will grow. Though the Soviet leadership is well aware both of its need for modern technology and of the fact that it cannot isolate itself from the information explosion in the West, there is no immediate sign that Anglo–Soviet relations will be expanded to account for this. British firms that have won definite orders in the Soviet Union as a result of the attempts to boost bilateral trade have been in the engineering sector: British firms are not well placed to take advantage of the Soviet Union's need for computer technology and software, since Moscow has established a joint Soviet/French/Italian enterprise to manage its most pressing needs. The British Invisible Exports Council has, however, been active in promoting British financial services in Moscow for the first time and it is quite possible that as the Soviet Union moves into the world of Western finance, a new and powerful form of British economic interest will arise in this sector.[52] This, however, represents the only significant departure from past trends on the immediate horizon.

PUBLIC OPINION AND THE MEDIA

At the broadest level of national perceptions reliable information is extremely scarce. This, in itself, is testimony to the relative lack of intensity displayed in British views of the Soviet Union. Both the media and public opinion can be said to have a thin slice of 'interested' and 'well-informed' opinion contained within them, but they are otherwise characterised by largely unstructured views that are centred more on images than on specific opinions.

In 1976 Mikhail Ozerov, the London correspondent of Tass, lamented the ignorance of the British in relation to his country. He criticised the 'bourgeois' British press for its 'meagre and slanted coverage of the USSR'.[53] One may suspect his motives for putting it in this way and the overall picture of the media is not so one-dimensional, but it is difficult to argue with his analysis of the practical outcome. It is not one-dimensional because 'the media' consists of a quality as well as a tabloid press, and of television as well as newspapers and magazines. The quality press in Britain does display a genuine interest in the Soviet Union and accords it no less coverage than other major areas that are not in the immediate political vicinity of British policy makers' concerns. As one possible index of interest during 1987, some 7 per cent of the total number of editorials in *The Times* and 5 per cent of those in *The Independent*, as two representative examples, were concerned with the Soviet Union or Eastern Europe in some way. These figures represented around one sixth of the editorial interest in foreign affairs generally. Moreover, these proportions appear to be relatively consistent over time. Of course, many caveats should be entered here. Editorials are no clue as to the amount or style of news reporting, and though these figures might not seem unreasonable when viewed against the totality of Britain's foreign news interests, the year 1987 witnessed some of the most dramatic changes in the nature of Soviet politics and the greatest progress in arms control up to that time. In these circumstances, it may be surprising that there was not more coverage.

Television also provides a very potent source of serious news reportage on the Soviet Union. Some 20 million adults watch one of the two major channel evening news programmes every day and, according to one survey, over 80 per cent of older secondary school children claim to watch television news regularly.[54] Moreover, television is obliged by law to attempt to maintain standards of impartiality and certainly has tried to preserve the ethos of this, whereas the British press is, on the whole, openly partisan. Television, we may assume, has a major effect on the formation of public images, and has visibly affected the ways in which Britons perceive the United States and the Soviet Union via the presentation of the personality of their leaders. A reasonable proposition would be that the Soviet Union, as a society, continues to receive a bad press in a medium that is otherwise so dominated by American culture, whereas Gorbachev, as a statesman and leader, has had very favourable media coverage.

Despite these considerations, however, the gross facts of British media coverage of the Soviet Union are all too familiar. The quality press is not read by many outside an 'interested' audience and the power of television to create images is more potent in programmes other than news coverage. When the House of Commons Foreign Affairs Committee examined the role of the media in Anglo–Soviet relations, it had nothing to say beyond the comment that the media merely amplified 'the occasionally strident tone of ministerial comments on the Soviet Union . . . when relations are not at their best'.[55]

On the basis of these facts it may be surprising that public attitudes, insofar as they can be ascertained, are as perceptive as they are. Any analysis of public opinion must begin from the assumption that precise attitudes are not discernible. It is possible, however, to be reasonably certain about general attitudes over time where comparable opinion poll findings reveal some curious public attitudes towards the Soviet Union.

In the first place, there is no question that the British public prefers Western society and the American model of modernity to anything that the Soviet Union has to offer. There is no sense in which changes in public attitudes reflect changes in social preferences. The post-Brezhnev leadership in the Soviet Union excited a certain amount of public curiosity but the image of Russia, as a society, remains consistently negative in Britain.[56] However, the British public's attitude towards Soviet policy and the actions of Soviet leaders has changed a good deal over recent years. When it comes to a judgement about actions, there is some real differentiation in the public mind. The Gallup Organisation has consistently asked over a number of years whether respondents have approved or disapproved of the role 'Russia is now playing in world affairs'. A summary of these results is presented in table 4.1. For many years the 'disapproval' rating of the Soviet Union stood consistently at over 70 per cent. But from the end of 1983 the figure began to drop progressively, until by January 1988 it had fallen as low as 30 per cent. This general trend is supported by data on more specific issues such as arms control and the diplomacy of East–West relations.[57] While the public's fear of war fluctuates somewhat with events, its fear of the Soviet Union, as a specific threat, has steadily declined.[58]

This dramatic turnaround has to be seen in the context of a changing public view of the United States. In the 1960s British public perceptions of the US were consistently favourable, certainly on East–West relations, notwithstanding the damage done to the image of the US by its involvement in Vietnam. But from the late 1960s the public's faith in the wisdom of specific US policies and its qualities of leadership has slipped dramatically. In April 1986 the 'disapproval' rating of the United States was greater than that for the Soviet Union for the first time ever, and has continued to be higher ever since. Individual policies excite particular criticism, such as the invasion of Grenada, or the Strategic Defense Initiative; President Reagan's personal standing with the British public was low, especially in relation to Mr Gorbachev; and a clear majority of Britons – 50 per cent to 28 per cent – have claimed that they would favour the development of a 'Western European defence policy independent of America'.[59] Clearly, though there is no mirror image between the two superpowers in the public's mind, there seems to be some relationship between the loss of confidence in one and gradually increasing acceptance of the other.

Finally, all of these trends in opinion should be set in context. Though it is possible to discern some real differentiation in attitudes to Soviet and American policies, the more pressing fact is that most of the public display a marked cynicism about both superpowers and a fatalism about Britain's effect on them. In clear contrast to the good will that attended President Kennedy's summits with the Soviet Union, well over two-thirds of the public were cynical about the motives and the effects of President Reagan's summit diplomacy.[60] Mrs Thatcher's Moscow summit in April 1987 was not treated with the same scepticism: respondents generally felt that it was a worthwhile and sincere attempt at improving relations with a superpower that wanted to be friendly.[61] But in respect of the way the superpowers behave towards each other there is a clear sense of equivalence in the public mind.[62] In December 1985 a poll indicated that the public was neatly divided into equal thirds on the question of who was the greatest threat to European peace; one-third felt it was the Soviet Union, one-third felt the USA, one-third thought 'both equally' or could not decide at all.[63] This cynicism is reflected particularly in the attitudes of younger people. Surveys undertaken by the British Atlantic Committee and by the Richardson Institute of the attitudes of sixth formers towards East–West relations show a reasonable degree of factual knowledge on the part of pupils but a powerful cynicism and fatalism about superpowers: a *realpolitik* view of the world in which the superpowers are morally equivalent.[64]

The issue of salience is also important in any consideration of public opinion context. For the public will display clear preferences when asked for them but this is no indication of the intensity with which such views are held. The British public is not preoccupied with the Soviet Union as a society, in marked contrast, for example, to the West German public.[65] There is a far greater degree of preoccupation with the United States and all things American, which may account for some anomalies in public perceptions. For all that Russia is more acceptable to Britons in the 1980s, there is no sign that Soviet behaviour has had any discernible effect in creating an outcry against the policies of NATO.[66] Equally, there is an asymmetry in its view of the two superpowers since so much more is known about the United States. In the absence of a major crisis – a new Afghanistan or Czechoslovakia that would reinforce the image of the Soviet threat – the public which judges the USA so harshly tends to assess the Soviet leadership on its general image and the seriousness and sensibleness with which it talks about European politics. For the British public holds its opinion about the USA with a good deal more intensity than its opinions about the Soviet Union.

The public's cynical image of the nature of world politics, however, is a widespread perception that is held with some intensity and which appears to be a long-term trend. In this respect, the present anomalies cannot be regarded as temporary – as a reflection of particular superpower leaders who happened to coincide in the 1980s. It goes deeper than this. Any future consideration of the British public's perception of the Soviet Union must begin from the premise that the old consensus with the United States – the view of the Cold War as 'a brave and essential response of free men against aggression' – has gone forever.[67]

CONCLUSION

If we try to characterise current British perspectives on the Soviet Union then we have to recognise that they are a mixture of static and dynamic elements. The matrix that we outlined at the beginning exists within an essentially consistent and fairly narrow conceptual focus. Anglo–Soviet relations are not intense and are not a matter of great public interest in Britain. Nevertheless, there are some interesting changes within the matrix.

The official view, and that of the present government, remains essentially cautious in its attitude to the Soviet Union. Officials have seen détente and arms control before and there is, as yet, no reason to believe that this is anything more than a welcome upswing in a Cold War cycle. They have not, of course seen *glasnost'* before and officials are uncertain what to make of it. There is a recognition that *glasnost'* represents a genuine attempt at structural change within the Soviet Union, but rather less certainty as to what it might mean for Anglo–Soviet relations. Officials therefore fall back on a position that they can hold with more certainty: that we will respond to *glasnost'* as and when we see the results of it in those matters which are important to Britain. The approach is cautious and reactive.

This is backed up by the attitude of Mrs Thatcher and the present government. The Prime Minister undoubtedly likes Mr Gorbachev and has gained considerable prestige in her dealings with him. She believes that his attempts to achieve change are 'bold' and 'courageous' and she wishes him well with them. On the other hand, the Soviet Union has to be recognised for what it is; a 'big bureaucracy' where 'the individual counts for virtually nothing'. Mr Gorbachev, she believes, 'is constrained by the Communist system'.[68] Sir Geoffrey Howe has made much the same point. Reykjavik, he admits, constituted 'a great shaking of the kaleidoscope'. But at the end of it 'the key components remain in place'. The Soviet threat still has to be looked at 'from our end of the European land mass'.[69]

The official and governmental perspective, therefore, waits to see how change will be expressed in specific policy terms. When the conditions under which trade and human contacts are conducted have changed; when Soviet diplomatic stances have been seen to evolve; when Soviet tank armies in Eastern Europe begin to be demobilised or redeployed, then the British Government will have something positive to which to respond. Until then, the onus is on the Soviet Union to express its new approach in tangible ways.[70]

Public attitudes, on the other hand, are much more concerned with broad images of the Soviet Union and in this respect there has been some rapid and perhaps irrevocable change. The press and broadcasting organisations have become fascinated by the Soviet Union as they have gained unprecedented access to it. In part, this is due to the sheer novelty of being able to operate more deeply in a system that has been hitherto so full of inhibitions. It is also due in part to the skill with which Mr Gorbachev has handled the Western media. Nevertheless, it is clear that the Soviet leadership, if not the Soviet Union as such, has a far better public image in Britain than at any time since the period of the Grand Alliance.

It might be possible to dismiss this as faddish public interest – another surge of curiosity in another new leadership – were it not for the fact that there has been so much change in the context within which public attitudes now exist. It is impossible any longer to divorce consideration of the Soviet Union from a series of other issues: the public's view of the nature of superpowers, of the policy of the United States, of Britain's role in diplomacy, of the evolution of politics in Europe. Perhaps most significant of all, there is every indication that defence will remain an important party political issue in British politics well into the 1990s. Though defence debates have all but ignored the Soviet Union in the past, it is reasonable to suppose that a reassessment of our attitudes towards Russia is the next logical step in the argument.

Michael Clarke

Overt changes in public attitudes are not likely to occur quickly. The number of interest groups who may want to promote Anglo–Soviet relations shows no signs of significant growth, and the public's view of Soviet society will probably remain wary. But it may be that the salience of Anglo–Soviet relations will be heightened in the public mind as the Soviet Union comes to figure more largely in the politics of an interdependent Europe. In this situation, the official perspective may find itself expressing a reactive conservatism which is no longer wholeheartedly supported by an unspoken public consensus. In this respect, the Thatcher diplomacy toward the Soviet Union and Eastern Europe, ironically, may have given more respectability to communist societies than the government would regard as healthy. The media and public opinion do not make careful distinctions between atmosphere and policy. Yet in pursuing an initiative based on policy, the government has made, as it were, an involuntary contribution to a more general change of atmosphere in European and East–West relations.

86

Table 4.1 *Gallup Poll questions Approval/Disapproval of the role of the superpowers 1983–1988*

Question: Do you approve or disapprove of the role the United States is now playing in world affairs? (Approve/Disapprove/Don't Know.)
And what about the role of Russia? (Approve/Disapprove/Don't Know.)

Percentage of respondents answering 'Disapprove'.

	Disapprove of US %	Disapprove of Russia %
November 1983	55	75
February 1984	59	71
June 1984	53	74
August 1984	53	69
November 1984	49	73
January 1985	47	62
July 1985	51	58
September 1985	52	65
October 1985	48	59
March 1986	45	54
1 April 1986	56	53
16 April 1986	59	51
21 April 1986	58	46
28 April 1986	55	50
June 1986	57	52
October 1986	50	48
August 1987	56	41
September 1987	50	37
October 1987	46	35
November 1987	47	38
January 1988	41	30

Note: The US attack on Libya took place on 14–15 April 1986.
Extracted from *Gallup Political Index* 282, 285, 286, 288, 291, 294, 299, 302, 307, 308, 309, 310, 314, 324, 325, 326, 327, 329; February 1984–April 1988.

NOTES

1. Only in 1988 did the Soviet Union announce the establishment of a first national public opinion study centre. See *The Times*, 29 March 1988.
2. A. J. P. Taylor, *English History 1914–1945* (Oxford University Press, 1965), pp. 217–18.
3. See G. Ross, ed., *The Foreign Office and the Kremlin: British Documents on Anglo–Soviet Relations, 1941–45* (Cambridge University Press, 1984), pp. 3–25. Also, R. Ovendale, *Appeasement and the English Speaking World* (University of Wales Press, 1975), pp. 98–116, 266–7.
4. See also, R. Ovendale, *The English Speaking Alliance* (George Allen and Unwin, 1985), pp. 273–8.
5. One of the best expressions of this is to be found in William H. McNeill, *America, Britain and Russia: Their Cooperation and Conflict 1941–46*, Survey of International Affairs, 1939–46 (Oxford University Press, 1953), pp. 238, 532–5.
6. J. Frankel, *British Foreign Policy 1945–1973* (Oxford University Press, 1975), pp. 194–5, 200–1.
7. See M. Clarke, 'Anglo–Soviet relations' in G. Flynn, ed., *Domestic Roots of Foreign Policy Towards the Soviet Union* (Atlantic Institute, forthcoming).
8. Ovendale, *The English Speaking Alliance*, pp. 273–88.
9. B. Jones, *The Russia Complex: The British Labour Party and the Soviet Union* (Manchester University Press, 1977), pp. 11–14.
10. I. Crewe, 'Britain: two and a half cheers for the Atlantic Alliance', in G. Flynn and H. Rattinger, eds., *The Public and Atlantic Defense* (Croom Helm, 1985), p. 16.
11. The best account of the substance of bilateral relations is to be found in Second Report from the Foreign Affairs Committee, 1985–86, *UK–Soviet Relations*, Vol. 1, HC 28-1 (HMSO, 1986).
12. *Ibid.*, pp. xxvii–xxviii.
13. An excellent account of this phenomenon can be found in a memorandum to the Foreign Affairs Committee submitted by Sir Curtis Keeble in *ibid.*, Appendix A. See also *ibid.*, p. xxvi.
14. B. White, 'Britain and East–West relations', in M. Smith, S. Smith and B. White, eds., *British Foreign Policy: Tradition, Change and Transformation* (Unwin Hyman, 1988), pp. 149–67.
15. See a statement in evidence by Lord Carrington to the Foreign Affairs Committee, 1979–80, *Foreign and Commonwealth Office Organisation*, HC 511, 362 i–iv (HMSO, 1980), p. 114.
16. This is officially stated in *UK–Soviet Relations: Observations by the Government* to the Second Report from the Foreign Affairs Committee, 1985–86, Cmnd 9842, July 1986, pp. 2–3.
17. P. Hanson, *Trade and Technology in Soviet Western Relations* (Macmillan, 1981), p. 248.
18. See M. Clarke, 'The implementation of Britain's CSCE policy 1975–84', in S. Smith and M. Clarke, eds., *Foreign Policy Implementation* (George Allen and Unwin, 1985).
19. See John Colville, *The Fringes of Power: Downing Street Diaries, 1939–55* (Hodder and Stoughton, 1985), pp. 673, 697–8, 701–3: R.R. James, *Anthony Eden* (Weidenfeld and Nicolson, 1986), pp. 400–2, 417–18: Richard Lamb, *The Failure of*

the Eden Government (Sidgwick and Jackson, 1987), pp. 10–11.

20. See H. Wilson, *The Labour Government 1964–70* (Weidenfeld and Nicolson, 1971), pp. 117–23, 344–67; A. Roth, *Sir Harold Wilson* (Macdonald and Jane's, 1977), pp. 51–3; G. Brown, *In My Way* (Victor Gollancz, 1971), pp. 142–6.

21. D. Wilson, 'Anglo–Soviet relations: the effect of ideas on reality', *International Affairs*, 50: 3 (July 1974), pp. 390–1.

22. M. Clarke, 'The implementation of Britain's CSCE policy, 1975–84', p. 158.

23. *Sunday Times*, 25 Jan. 1976; *Daily Telegraph*, 29 Jan. 1976; *Sunday Telegraph*, 1 Feb. 1976. Other Soviet publications showed her as a cartoon witch and penned verses such as 'Mrs Thatcher, trouble hatcher' and 'Tory leader, Cold War pleader'. See *The Times*, 26 Feb. 1976; *The Economist*, 18 June 1983, p. 34.

24. See N. Bowles, 'The defence policy of the Conservative Government', in D. S. Bell, ed., *The Conservative Government 1979–84: An Interim Report* (Croom Helm, 1985), pp. 184–6; L. Freedman, *Britain and Nuclear Weapons* (Macmillan, 1980), pp. 54–5.

25. *Parliamentary Debates 1980–81, Commons*, 23 July 1981, col. 498.

26. *The Times*, 10 Sept. 1981.

27. In a speech to the Bournemouth Young Conservatives, 12 Feb. 1983, *Keesings Contemporary Archives 1985* (Longman, 1985), p. 33351.

28. *Parliamentary Debates 1979–80, Commons*, 6 Mar. 1980, col. 652.

29. *Parliamentary Debates 1981–2, Lords*, 14 Dec. 1981, col. 9; *Parliamentary Debates 1981–82, Commons*, 22 Dec. 1981, cols. 866–7.

30. See accounts in H. Young and A. Sloman, *The Thatcher Phenomenon* (BBC, 1986), pp. 106–7; W. Wallace, 'Foreign Policy: The Management of Distinctive Interests', in R. Morgan and C. Bray, eds., *Partners and Rivals in Western Europe: Britain, France and Germany* (Gower, 1986), p. 222; White, 'Britain and East–West Relations', pp. 150–3.

31. *Parliamentary Debates 1986–87, Commons*, 26 June 1987, col. 217.

32. *Ibid.*, 12 Nov. 1987, cols. 23–5.

33. *Ibid.*, 2 Apr. 1987, cols. 1227–9, 1223–4.

34. *Ibid.*, 12 Nov. 1987, col. 23.

35. *Ibid.*, 7 Apr. 1987, cols. 199–200. See also H. Thomas, *Our Place in the World* (Conservative Political Centre, 1983).

36. Evidence of the essential agreement on the unchanging nature of the Soviet threat is offered by the Report of the Joint SDP–Liberal Alliance Commission, *Defence and Disarmament* (SDP and Liberal Parties, 1986), especially in the 'Note of dissent' by Brian May, p. 51. Since the 1987 General Election and the foundation of the SLDP, the attitude of the centre parties on this issue shows no signs of significant change.

37. A good example of these attitudes is provided by a Labour researcher. See M. Gapes, 'The evolution of Labour's defence and security policy', in G. Burt, ed., *Alternative Defence Policies* (Croom Helm, 1988), pp. 82–105.

38. See Labour Party, *Defence and Security for Britain* (Labour Party, 1984), pp. 10–12; M. Gapes, *No Cruise, No Trident, No Nuclear Weapons* (Labour Party, 1981), pp. 7–8; *Britain Will Win: Labour Manifesto* (Labour Party, 1987), pp. 15–16.

39. 'Defence and arms control at the 1986 party conferences', *ADIU Report*, 8: 6 (Nov.–Dec. 1986), p. 14.

40. To appreciate the historical continuity of the Labour Party in this respect, compare the history provided by Jones, *The Russian Complex*, especially pp. 200–12, with the more recent concerns of the Left as expressed in M. Kaldor, D. Smith and V. Vines,

eds., *Democratic Socialism and the Cost of Defence* (Croom Helm, 1979); P. Tatchell, *A Non–Nuclear Alternative Democratic Defence* (GMP Publishers, 1985).

41. *Britain United: The Time Has Come. The SDP/Liberal Alliance Programme for Government* (SDP/Liberal Alliance, 1987), p. 21.

42. See B. May, *Is Russia Really A Threat?*, Liberal Challenge Booklet, 7 (Liberal Party, 1986); B. May, 'Why the red card is never a trump', *The Guardian*, 22 Sept. 1986. For a general analysis of the terms of the argument see *The Financial Times*, 26 Sept. 1986; *The Times*, 25 Sept. 1986; and an interview with David Owen in *The Times*, 13 Sept. 1986.

43. Second Report from the Foreign Affairs Committee 1985–86, Vol. 1, pp. xxxiii–xxxviii; also Appendix B, pp. ciii–cxiv; Foreign Affairs Committee 1985–86, *UK–Soviet Relations*, Vol. 2, Minutes of Evidence and Appendices, HC 28–II (HMSO, 1986), pp. 271–2, 277–89. See also Department of Trade and Industry, *Overseas Trade Statistics of the United Kingdom*, Quarterly (HMSO). A general review is to be found in P. Hanson, *Western Economic Statecraft in East–West Relations* (RIIA/RKP, 1988).

44. Second Report from the Foreign Affairs Committee 1985–86, Vol. 2, pp. 32, 66–7.

45. Long–term survey quoted in P. Hanson, *Trade and Technology in Soviet Western Relations*, pp. 190–201.

46. Second Report from the Foreign Affairs Committee 1985–86, Vol. 2, p. 358.

47. *The Times*, 11 Dec. 1987.

48. They are set out in Second Report from the Foreign Affairs Committee 1985–86, Vol. 1, pp. 1–ixl.

49. Central Statistical Office, *Annual Abstract of Statistics 1985*, tables 10.36, 10.37, pp. 215–6.

50. According to a British Council Memorandum in Second Report from the Foreign Affairs Committee 1985–86, Vol. 2, pp. 70–4.

51. *The Independent*, 7 Dec. 1987. On the Government's keen support, but lack of any extra funding, see *UK–Soviet Relations: Observations by the Government*, pp. 9, 12.

52. On the engineering sector see *The Financial Times*, 9 Dec. and 19 Dec. 1987. On computer technology see *The Times*, 2 Feb. 1988. On financial management see *The Financial Times*, 14 Dec. 1987.

53. *The Times*, 29 Jan. 1976.

54. B. Munske, *Attitudes and Knowledge of Schoolchildren Towards the Soviet Union* (Richardson Institute for Conflict and Peace Research, Occasional Paper, 1986), p. 25.

55. Second Report from the Foreign Affairs Committee, *UK–Soviet Relations*, Vol. 1, p. xviii. Discussion, in fact, is almost exclusively on the nature of the Soviet media, pp. lxxv–lxxix.

56. Crewe, 'Britain', p. 16: Clarke, 'Anglo–Soviet relations'.

57. The Soviet Union is perceived as being more likely than the USA to honour arms control agreements, more likely to make concessions to get them, less likely than the USA to 'worsen' the situation in the Gulf, and less likely to be the first to use nuclear weapons. See *Gallup Political Index*, 321 (May 1987), p. 22: 326 (Oct. 1987), p. 41: 327 (Nov. 1987), pp. 21–2.

58. On the variable fear of war, see *British Public Opinion*, 7: 1 (1985), p. 4. See also D. Capitanchik and R. C. Eichenberg, *Defence and Public Opinion* (RIIA/RKP, 1983), pp. 21–2. By June 1987 86 per cent of respondents felt that the Soviet Union posed

'little or no' or 'not great' danger to Britain according to *Gallup Political Index*, 322 (June 1987), p. 28.

59. On reactions to arms control, the invasion of Grenada, or the Strategic Defence Initiative, see *British Public Opinion*, 5: 9 (Oct. 1983), p. 6; *Gallup Political Index*, 294 (Feb. 1985), p. 18; 297 (May 1985), p. 23; 300 (Aug. 1985), p. 21. On President Reagan's standing see a MORI survey reported in *The Times*, 8 Dec. 1987. On a West European defence policy see *British Public Opinion*, 6: 3 (1984), p. 7.

60. *Gallup Political Index*, 290 (Oct. 1984), p. 34.

61. *Gallup Political Index*, 319 (Mar. 1987), p. 17; 320 (Apr. 1987), p. 25.

62. *British Public Opinion*, 5: 9 (Oct. 1983), p. 6; *Gallup Political Index*, 300 (Aug. 1985), p. 22; 313 (Sept. 1986), p. 24.

63. *Gallup Political Index*, 304 (Dec. 1985), p. 21.

64. Munske, *Attitudes and Knowledge*; British Atlantic Committee, internal study for Ministry of Defence, 1985.

65. T.G. Ash, 'Quiet flows the Rhine', *The Spectator*, 12 Mar. 1988, pp. 9–11.

66. P. Sabin, 'Assessing a "peace offensive": the impact of Gorbachev on British public opinion about defence', *RUSI/Brassey's Defence Yearbook 1987/88*.

67. J. Wheeler-Bennett and A. Nicholls, *The Semblance of Peace* (Macmillan, 1972), p. 556.

68. *International Herald Tribune*, 3 Dec. 1987; *The Guardian*, 11 May 1988.

69. Interview in *The Independent*, 23 May 1988.

70. See Peter Hennessy, *ibid.*

5   The security dimension

CHRISTOPH BLUTH

INTRODUCTION

Great Britain and the Soviet Union emerged from the Second World War as victors, as two of the Big Three powers. The central factors of the balance of power in the post-war world, namely the strategic role of nuclear weapons and the resultant bipolarity of world power relations, and the new alignment of world economic relations did not emerge for some time after the war. For these reasons, there was at first a marked continuity in British foreign policy in the first years of the post-war era, in which Britain continued to pursue its Great Power role in terms of global commitments and as the major power in Western Europe.

Despite impressive elements of continuity, however, profound changes were already beginning to make themselves felt. The United States had without any doubt emerged as the dominant partner of the Allies. Britain, while still clearly the third most powerful nation in the world, could not come near to matching American or Soviet power. As a result of the war and the consolidation of Soviet power in Eastern Europe, Moscow soon began to assume a central position in British defence and foreign policy. The conciliatory attitude to the wartime ally did not last as long in London as it did in Washington, and thus for Britain the Soviet Union assumed at a much earlier time the central position as the main threat to Western security.

In the early post-war period, Britain was clearly the most important European power from the Soviet perspective. Militarily, it represented the only potential opponent of significance apart from the United States. However, United States ground forces in Europe had already been substantially reduced and an American commitment to a permanent presence in Europe did not emerge for some time. Although the significance of Britain in Soviet perceptions declined somewhat in later years, relations with Britain continued to occupy an important place, partly because Britain was a nuclear power and because of a substantial British commitment to the defence of Central Europe. Furthermore, Britain could bring some influence to bear on both the United States and the European NATO members (in particular West Germany); the latter connection gained considerably in significance when Britain became a member of the European Community.

As a result of the confrontational character of East–West relations and the perceived military threat from the Soviet Union facing Western Europe, security policy has been central to British–Soviet relations. It is not surprising that issues of defence policy, arms control or wider aspects of international security generally dominate the diplomatic agenda. British–Soviet relations in this sphere are obviously characterised by asymmetry. While the Soviet Union is the central security concern of the United Kingdom, for the Soviet Union the United States is of much greater importance and therefore Soviet security policy is determined more by relations with the United States. The approach adopted here is to examine the general environment in which security policy has to be formulated, and then look more specifically at how British and Soviet interests interact on contemporary issues. One principal focus will be the British 'independent nuclear deterrent', the debate in Britain about the justification for the role of the independent nuclear deterrent in the defence of the country and as a contribution to NATO. Soviet perceptions of these issues will be assessed. Another focus will be Britain's role in the arms control process, in particular the INF controversy, the implications of the Strategic Defense Initiative and the place of British strategic nuclear forces in arms control. Particular attention will be devoted to British views on arms control after the Reykjavik summit and the implication of Gorbachev's 'new thinking'.

SOVIET AND BRITISH SECURITY POLICIES: THE INTERNATIONAL ENVIRONMENT

The evolution of Soviet military policy

In the early post-Stalin period during the 1950s the Soviet military still conceived of a nuclear war as basically a more destructive version of World War II.[1] The establishment of the Strategic Rocket Forces in December 1959 was accompanied by a revision in Soviet military doctrine announced by Khrushchev.[2] In a speech before the Supreme Soviet in January 1960, Khrushchev declared the primary importance of nuclear weapons and missiles.[3]

Military opposition to Khrushchev's 'one–sided' emphasis on nuclear weapons, the emerging strategic nuclear parity between the Soviet Union and the United States and the adoption of 'flexible response' led to a shift in Soviet military thought; the avoidance of escalation to a strategic nuclear level became a positive objective of Soviet military doctrine. This shift occurred rather gradually in the period from the mid-1960s to the mid-1970s, when the Soviet armed forces were restructured to enable them to engage in warfare in the European theatre which could remain at the conventional level for a prolonged period.[4]

Despite the SALT agreements, both the United States and the Soviet Union substantially increased and modernised their strategic arsenals. The public position of the Soviet leadership in the 1970s emphasised the reality of nuclear strategic parity and mutual assured destruction. The 1970s saw the development and strengthening of theatre conventional and nuclear capabilities. The primary objective in a war in the European theatre would now be to deny NATO the option of mobilising its resources and exercising its options for escalation. This could only be done by the rapid occupation of Western Europe and eliminating American bases (the presence of which would make Great Britain a particular target), thus presenting the United States with the fait accompli of having been excluded from Europe. This strategy is of course greatly complicated by the presence of LRTNFs and British and French nuclear forces.

The acceptance of nuclear parity and the abandonment of the pursuit of superiority were clearly set out in Brezhnev's well–known speech in Tula in January 1977. He went as far as providing the rationale for a policy of no first use of nuclear weapons, and the same year the Warsaw Treaty Organisation proposed a multilateral treaty on 'no first use'. A unilateral 'no first use' pledge was made in 1982.[5] However, the strategic and operational implications were not readily accepted by the military, and it is evident that the development of nuclear and conventional war-fighting capabilities continued, along with naval deployments which resulted in capabilities for global power projection.[6]

Thus Nikolai Ogarkov, who was promoted to Chief of the General Staff in 1977 (almost one year after Dmitri Ustinov became Defence Minister), while paying lip service to official positions, clearly advocated a nuclear war-fighting strategy and defended the 'objective possibility to achieve victory' in such a war, although he denied the possibility of a successful strategic first strike. In 1981 Brezhnev renewed his re-assertion of the principle of mutual assured destruction (MAD) and went as far as denying the possibility of victory in nuclear war.[7] This statement came after the 26th Party Congress in March 1981 had decided a significant shift of resources away from defence and towards the civilian sector. Ogarkov, however, continued covertly to attack the Brezhnev–Ustinov line.[8] Ustinov's very strong support for MAD and his harsh critique of Ogarkov's views failed to whip the military into line, partly perhaps because of the state of political paralysis the Soviet Union had fallen into as Brezhnev's health deteriorated.

Andropov appeared to be determined to end the debates and impose Party authority. He succeeded at least in dampening the controversy and eliciting formal agreement from Ogarkov, while the Party leadership itself was moving towards a far more pessimistic assessment of the international situation, resulting in increased military allocations (including the 'counter-deployments' after NATO's LRTNF deployment began).[9] Ogarkov was removed from his key position in the aftermath of the Korean Airliner incident in 1984, but remained a significant figure in the Soviet military until 1988. His successor, Marshal Akhromeyev, held views similar to Ogarkov's (except for a somewhat more positive assessment of possible improvements in East-West relations).

The pessimistic assessment of the world situation in 1983, the perception of an increased risk of war and the resentment against the Reagan Administration resulted in a debate in the Party leadership about the future of relations with the West in which those favouring a more conciliatory line and a return to negotiations eventually won out, as became evident by September 1984.[10] Soviet–British relations improved as evidenced by Mikhail Gorbachev's visit in December 1984.

The removal of Ogarkov and the accession of Gorbachev to the leadership seem to have resulted in a relative strengthening of Party control. Akhromeyev and Ustinov's successor Sergei Sokolov both generally supported Gorbachev on East–West relations and arms control. The replacement of the Commander of the Strategic Rocket Forces, Marshal Tolubko, in 1985 by General Maksimov may have served to facilitate a more flexible approach to strategic arms control; there were also other notable personnel changes at the highest level of the Soviet military hierarchy. The 27th Party Congress provided indications of a decrease in military influence. None the less, it is undeniable that fundamental differences of view between the professional military and the Party leadership exist, as evidenced by military opposition to the unilateral nuclear test moratorium. Gorbachev's domestic priorities are clearly deeply inimical to the institutional interests of the military, but his *perestroika* cannot succeed without a fundamental shift in resources away from the military-industrial complex. His position may have been strengthened as a result of the penetration of Soviet defences and landing in Red Square by a West German pilot in 1987. This led to the dismissal of the Commander of the air defence forces A. Koldunov and Defence Minister Sokolov. The new Minister of Defence, Dmitri Yazov, was promoted by Gorbachev to the position of Chief of Personnel before assuming his present post. Yazov's former deputy in the Far East command, General Moiseyev, replaced Akhromeyev who resigned in December 1988 in the wake of the announcement of unilateral Soviet cuts in conventional forces. Whether military opposition will become a significant obstacle for Gorbachev in the implementation of his ambitious policies remains to be seen.

The British military force posture and strategy

With the decline of its empire and status as a world power at the end of World War II, Britain was faced with the vital issue of its role in the post-war world. For an economically weak Britain unable to maintain its overseas presence, the possession of nuclear weapons appeared to be one way for it to preserve its status as a major power.

The political implications of the pursuit of this objective were highly paradoxical. On the one hand the whole purpose of the independent nuclear deterrent, as it came to be called, was to preserve a degree of independence from the United States, even though it was clearly recognised that the defence of Europe depended on American strategic nuclear forces. In time, however, it became clear that Britain could not develop even a small strategic capability itself. Increasing reliance on technological assistance from the United States significantly diminished the independence of the British nuclear deterrent. Britain therefore continually emphasised the 'special relationship' with the United States; its preservation also became a principal objective in British foreign policy.

A central issue of British security policy is the fact that Britain is a nuclear power. Since 1969 the backbone of the British independent nuclear deterrent has consisted of four nuclear–powered submarines, until recently armed with 16 Polaris A-3 missiles (which replaced the nuclear-armed V Bombers). According to the IISS the Polaris missiles were armed with three nuclear warheads. From 1982 to 1985 a partial modernisation of the system was completed by the replacement of the A-3 warhead with the Chevaline. The Chevaline system is also a MRV (multiple re-entry vehicle) system with the same number of warheads as the Polaris A-3, but with improved manoeuvrability and a number of decoys to confuse Soviet ballistic missile defence. In the view of Soviet military experts the Chevaline represents a significant improvement of British strategic nuclear forces. The 'Moscow criterion', according to which it is essential for British nuclear forces to be capable of penetrating strategic defences in the Moscow area, is well understood by Soviet military experts. V.G. Trukhanovsky describes the need to be able to penetrate the Soviet ABM system as the primary rationale for Chevaline.[11] Like other Soviet commentators he assumes the maximum possible capabilities and cites a hypothetical estimate of six warheads (plus dummies) as the likely configuration.[12]

The official British description of its strategic nuclear forces is that of a minimum deterrent and a weapon of last resort. The objective to maintain a capability to inflict 'unacceptable damage' on the Soviet Union has direct implications for targeting (given that the British SLBM system is not well suited for counterforce strikes). Soviet military experts believe that the primary targets are political, followed by military and industrial targets.[13] Trukhanovsky expresses the view (citing Ian Smart) that the primary target of Polaris is the civilian population of the Soviet Union, then the destruction of industry and finally military targets.

Naturally Soviet commentators display great interest in the plans to replace the Polaris systems by the Trident D-5. Soviet analysts estimate that by the completion of Trident deployment Britain will have 512 strategic warheads with high accuracy and counterforce capability (a 'first strike potential'). However, Soviet analysts do not expect Soviet missile silos to be the prime targets and thus consider British strategy as quite different from American strategy. None the less, the question as to whether Britain will follow a national target plan or a warfighting strategy co-ordinated with the United States is one which Soviet analysts feel unable to resolve.[14]

The current official rationale for maintaining an independent nuclear deterrent was enunciated in a 1974 Memorandum from the Ministry of Defence in terms of giving NATO a second centre of decision making. A more recent full exposition of this view was given in a statement to Parliament in 1980 by the then Defence Secretary Francis Pym. Given the increased emphasis in current NATO strategy of flexible response on delaying the decision to 'go nuclear' in a European conflict, some uncertainty exists as to whether the United States would in a crisis be willing to provide extended nuclear deterrence to Europe and thus risk Soviet strategic nuclear retaliation. Pym was anxious to point out that such uncertainty might exist in Soviet and not British minds. The existence of an independent decision-making centre in London would mean that the Soviet risk calculus would be affected in two ways. For one, Britain would threaten to launch a nuclear attack on Soviet territory as a last resort to deter a Soviet attack on Britain itself. (An important element in British thinking, rarely acknowledged publicly, is the need to have some 'insurance' against a fundamental change in American policy towards Europe – even if British strategic nuclear forces are a somewhat inadequate form of such insurance given their dependence on American technical assistance.) But Pym was also careful to say that as a European power Britain was more closely threatened by Soviet aggression in Europe, the implication being that the Soviets should take into account British nuclear capabilities in contemplating military aggression in Europe which did not necessarily affect Britain directly.

Soviet military and political authors do not pay any great attention to these rationales for the British independent nuclear deterrent.[15] However, if we look at the issue from the perspective of Soviet military thought and planning, it is clear that the devastation of the Soviet homeland is no longer perceived as an inevitable consequence of war. It is thus a central priority in Soviet military thought that in the event of war Soviet territory should remain a sanctuary and thus the escalation to a strategic exchange between the superpowers be avoided. It is clear, therefore, that the British independent nuclear deterrent threatens the central objective of Soviet military doctrine. As a weapon of last resort, to be used when British territory itself is under attack, it could well assure the sanctuarisation of Britain in the same way as it does that of the superpowers.

The situation is less clear-cut if one looks at British strategic nuclear weapons in terms of a contribution to NATO. The commitment of the British strategic deterrent force to the defence of Europe was explicit in the Nassau Agreements under which the Polaris force was made available by the United States. It also continues to be part of Britain's declaratory policy. Furthermore, Britain is represented on the Joint Target Planning Staff in Omaha where targeting of the British SLBM force is undertaken. However, there is a distinct nationalist emphasis to this force which remains under exclusively British control, and separate target lists have been created. Thus Lawrence Freedman has pointed out:

Despite the assignation of Britain's nuclear forces to NATO, the assumptions and dominant plan surrounding their targeting do not, as far as can be gathered from the public record, naturally fit in with any NATO plans. The trend in British public pronouncements suggests that the 'standing alone' hypothesis is the underlying rationale for the nuclear force.[16]

As a result, a number of Western experts have raised doubts about the strength of the commitment of British strategic forces to the defence of Europe. It has been pointed out that the same arguments which cast doubt on American extended deterrence may apply, albeit with reduced forcefulness, to British nuclear guarantees to other European Alliance members. While Soviet military experts are well aware of the close co–ordination of targeting with the United States, some see the possibility that in the event of crisis British national priorities may predominate.[17]

The situation may be different with regard to Britain's other nuclear capabilities. The nine RAF strike-attack Tornado and two Buccaneer squadrons based in Britain and West Germany are capable of delivering nuclear as well as conventional bombs. Soviet analysts recognise that Britain's nuclear capabilities extend to all services but believe that the Royal Air Force or the Royal Navy would have a far more significant role in nuclear strike missions, given the small number of warheads available to BAOR and the fact that these are under American control. While Soviet military experts are thus in no doubt that Britain might engage in tactical nuclear strikes in Europe,[18] it is not clear that the notion of 'multiple decision centres' enhances the credibility of such use. It is difficult to conceive of a scenario in which Britain would start using tactical nuclear weapons in a Central European battlefield without a corresponding decision having been taken by SACEUR and the President of the United States. On the other hand, the Soviets believe that Britain may resist American attempts to unleash a limited nuclear war in Europe.[19]

The centrality of the 'special relationship' between Britain and the United States is stressed, particularly with regard to Britain's nuclear defence policy. While Britain is seen to benefit considerably from access to technical information, targeting plans, nuclear hardware and political influence, it is thus dependent on American technology and help. Britain is seen as the most pro-nuclear ally of the United States in Europe, as furthering militarism in Europe, giving further impetus to the arms race and supporting the widening of NATO's zone of action outside Europe.[20]

Soviet military experts interpret the British force posture in terms of seeking to maintain capability for out-of-area operations, with the Royal Navy being the main instrument of power projection.[21] (The best example of such an operation is, of course, the Falklands conflict.) However, they see the British force posture as being constructed mainly around the European theatre. Of fundamental importance from the Soviet point of view is the presence of British forces in Germany and their role in NATO's forward defence strategy. Unlike other European NATO members (with the exception of West Germany) Britain has a substantial fraction of its total manpower contribution to NATO's defence (about 56,000 men) stationed at the front line in peacetime.

Another important role played by Britain in the view of Soviet military experts is that of providing key bases for NATO's coalition warfare strategy. The United Kingdom is seen as the principal base for supplies, support and re-enforcement in the event of a conflict in the European Theatre of Military Operations (TVD).[22] Thus from the point of view of Soviet authors, Britain clearly plays a pre-eminent role in Europe, in some ways even more important than that of West Germany by dint of possessing of nuclear weapons and holding a prominent position in NATO. Soviet authors note that the British have a much greater representation in the NATO command structure than any other of the Allies and play a central role on NATO committees – a position which is used to preserve Britain's role and influence.

NUCLEAR ARMS CONTROL

Soviet and British objectives in arms control and disarmament

The Soviet Union has always tried to portray itself as being in the forefront of the 'struggle for disarmament'. Soviet disarmament policy in the early 1960s was pursued partly for purposes of propaganda, and given the large American superiority in nuclear strategic forces until the late 1960s the Soviet Union was not interested in agreements that would prevent it from catching up. None the less there was also some real interest in arms control. From the Soviet point of view, the military advantage of certain forms of arms control lay in their potential to restrain the growth of Western military power and prevent the spread of nuclear weapons to non-nuclear powers (particularly China and West Germany). The political value lay in the pursuit of détente with the United States and a more favourable international climate. The Partial Test Ban Treaty (1963) was an important success in this respect: it signified an improvement in East–West relations in the aftermath of the Cuban missile crisis and symbolised an apparent willingness of restraint, while not in fact restraining the build-up of Soviet strategic nuclear forces.[23]

The Partial Test Ban (PTB) Treaty provided a focus of Soviet–British interaction in security policy as Britain was involved with the United States in negotiating the PTB Treaty. British interest in the PTB was primarily political: it was a way for Britain to retain some of the trappings of Great Power status. Since then, British defence policy has been based on two fundamental principles: possession of the independent nuclear deterrent and participation in arms control. Indeed, those two strands became causally linked by the policy that Britain should have an independent deterrent with the objective of therefore having a seat at the arms control negotiations table. The net result was strong British support for the PTB and an official emphasis on Britain's role in bringing it about.[24]

Nuclear non-proliferation is another area in which Soviet and British interests have overlapped. The main target of Soviet policy in the negotiations for a Nuclear Non-Proliferation Treaty (NPT) in the 1960s – apart from China – was the American policy to disseminate nuclear technology within the Alliance and plans for a Multilateral Force (MLF) which would allow the European Allies, in particular West Germany, a degree of participation in nuclear control. The NPT became possible eventually because the MLF project was abandoned, and the Soviet Union compromised on nuclear consultation arrangements envisaged by the NATO Nuclear Planning Group.

British interests did not appear to be endangered by the NPT. The 'special relationship' with the United States appeared to be on solid ground; it was threatened more by the MLF or other nuclear sharing proposals.[25] The NPT is therefore an interesting case where British and Soviet objectives in arms control coincided to some extent at points where there were divergences with West Germany and the United States. As Britain's role as a nuclear power would remain unchanged by the treaty, the political benefits flowing from the possession of nuclear weapons could only be enhanced by the NPT. The same is true for the political effects of being involved in the negotiations.[26] In 1976, the Soviet Union and the United Kingdom joined with 15 other countries in the

London Club which, as a contribution to the non-proliferation of nuclear weapons, agreed on certain principles regarding the export of nuclear technology. As the Soviet Union clearly accords high priority to nuclear non-proliferation,[27] the NPT review conference, planned for 1995 to decide whether the treaty should continue to be in force indefinitely, may well see the USSR and the United Kingdom actively demonstrating a common interest in preserving and enhancing measures to prevent the further spread of nuclear weapons. One area for possible British initiatives lies in proposals for strengthening the procedures if proliferation is believed to have occurred, an area currently recognised as a central weakness of the non-proliferation network.[28]

Limitations on strategic arms, by contrast, stand out as an area of conflicting Soviet and British interests. The talks on strategic arms limitations were the first major set of arms control negotiations in which Britain did not participate, nor was it ever envisaged that it should. While the British position was one of support in principle, there were a number of ways in which the central goal of British defence policy, the maintenance of an independent strategic nuclear capability, could come under threat. The first lay in Soviet demands for the inclusion of British and French systems in the assessment of the nuclear balance on which a treaty would be based. The Soviet case is argued along the following lines. Third country systems were targeted against the Soviet Union and their control therefore constituted a legitimate Soviet security interest. As Britain and France were members of NATO, their systems should be counted on the Western side. Otherwise the principle of 'equal security' which forms the basis of arms control in the Soviet view would not be safeguarded.[29]

The British rejected the Soviet view entirely. It is ironic that one major British justification for maintaining an independent nuclear deterrent has been that it constitutes a 'ticket of admission' to arms control negotiations, while in the SALT era the primary objective of British arms control policy has been to exclude its own arsenal from any limitations and oppose measures that might restrict British access to new nuclear weapons technologies.

The US position has been that it cannot negotiate about the weapons systems of third countries. Furthermore in the American view the principle of 'equal security' cannot mean that the Soviet Union be allowed a strategic arms potential equivalent to that of the United States plus that of all third countries.

The problem of third country arsenals was not a major issue in the SALT I negotiations. Moreover, the Soviet Union has not, at any time, demanded that Britain should scrap or even reduce its arsenal, but merely that it should be taken into account in strategic arms limitation agreements. In a unilateral protocol to the SALT I interim agreement the Soviet side asserted the right to match any deployment of submarines by NATO (i.e. even if not American) beyond the agreed limits.[30] The United States delegation did not accept this protocol; in the event it was never put to the test since the United States never reached the limits for SLBMs laid down in the interim agreement.

While from a legal standpoint there is no question that the SALT accords do not include any compensation for third country systems, there has been some argument as to whether the Soviet Union was allowed some *de facto* compensation. Henry Kissinger's apparent unwillingness to sell Britain Poseidon missiles as a modernisation of Polaris and the higher number of heavy bombers granted the Soviet Union under the SALT II accords, for example, could be seen in that light. The declaratory position on this issue, however, never changed.

The most positive aspect of the SALT I accords from the British point of view was the ABM Treaty. Ballistic missile defences, while unlikely to give complete protection from nuclear attack, could seriously degrade the effectiveness of small nuclear forces. For this reason Soviet BMD capabilities have, since the late 1960s, had a significant effect on British strategic arms policy. The limitation of ABMs (to 200 and then to 100 launchers) was therefore a very welcome development from the British point of view.

With regard to SALT II, Britain also took a generally supportive position towards the negotiations and their significance in the overall context of East–West relations, again insisting that British forces should not be included. One important issue from the British perspective arose out of a Soviet proposal for a non-transfer clause which would ban the transfer of strategic missiles, their components, technical descriptions and blueprints to third parties (analogous to the non-transfer clauses contained in the ABM Treaty). While the Americans firmly and successfully resisted any Soviet attempt to introduce non-transfer clauses in SALT II, some degree of ambiguity resulted from the agreement not to circumvent the Treaty through third parties. American unilateral statements have expressed the interpretation that while the United States would not seek to circumvent the treaty, it would continue with its normal patterns of co-operation with its Allies. This interpretation has not been challenged, and has not affected negotiations between Britain and the United States about the future replacement of the Polaris force.

One set of arms control negotiations in which Britain was directly involved in the late 1970s were the talks about a Comprehensive Test Ban Treaty (CTBT). In March 1977 the United States and the Soviet Union set up a joint working party on this issue; in July 1977 the United Kingdom asked to join the discussions. The British and American position was to ban all nuclear explosions for five years with a view to negotiating a permanent ban after that. The negotiations did not get very far as a result of internal opposition in the United States to both SALT II and the CTBT. The problems raised by the Joint Chiefs of Staff were verification (only explosions above 5 kilotons could be reliably detected), the possible degradation of the existing weapons stockpile and the foreclosure of improvements in weapons technology. Evidently some of these concerns were shared by British nuclear scientists, without making much impression on the British Chiefs of Staff or the political leadership at the time. The Soviets contributed to the difficulties by insisting that seismic detectors used on Soviet territory to verify that no explosions were carried out had to be of Soviet manufacture, and both the United States and Britain were to install detectors on their soil (even though Britain conducts tests only on an American site in Nevada). The Callaghan Government would not consider footing the bill for such installations. The talks ended in 1980 and were not resumed after the Reagan Administration came to power. It objected to a CTBT first on grounds of verification, but when the Soviet Union compromised on verification, the US stated that the continued need for nuclear deterrence implied the need for testing. Gorbachev's pursuit of a comprehensive test ban has also been interpreted as aimed at crippling the Strategic Defense Initiative.

The British Government's position on this issue has been rather ambivalent. On 27 March 1982 Prime Minister Thatcher called for a speeding up of the CTBT negotiations. On 19 July 1982 President Reagan announced that the trilateral talks about a CTBT would definitely not be resumed. The official British position shifted in support of United States policy; Sir Geoffrey Howe followed the American line in justifying this position on the grounds of verification problems. A public debate on this issue ensued, in the course of which it became evident that as a result of Soviet concessions (such as accepting IAEA safeguards with regard to on-site inspections and peaceful nuclear explosions) and substantial breakthroughs in the technology of detecting and monitoring nuclear explosions, the argument against a test ban based on problems of verification was no longer sustainable. Once again the British Government aligned its position with that of the United States and emphasised the need to preserve nuclear deterrence. During the period of the unilateral Soviet test moratorium, Britain co-operated in two tests with the United States, and by April 1986 it had become clear that the tests required for the British Trident programme were virtually complete. There were repeated calls throughout 1985 and 1986 by Labour and Alliance MPs (notably former Prime Minister James Callaghan and former Foreign Secretary David Owen) for the British Prime Minister to invite President Reagan and General Secretary Gorbachev to begin trilateral talks on a test ban. This was rejected by the Government since the US Administration appeared to have made up its mind and London would merely waste political capital. At that time it was considered more important that Britain should encourage the administration to stay within the SALT II limits than promote a CTBT.[31] When Mikhail Gorbachev announced an extension of the unilateral moratorium during a television speech in August 1986, the FCO expressed the view that it regretted the Soviet preoccupation with unilateral approaches and suggested that more effort be directed at the negotiations in Geneva. This provoked a satirical response in *Pravda* which accused the FCO of rejecting an initiative simply because it came from the Soviet Union.[32] Other Soviet comments singled out Britain as an opponent of the moratorium and as a power whose interests lay in continued testing. It must be said, however, that were an American administration actively to seek a test ban agreement, the British government would be most likely to support such a policy.

The INF controversy

In the early 1970s at the initiative of British Defence Minister Denis Healey the NATO Nuclear Planning Group undertook detailed studies on the possible employment of theatre nuclear weapons. The studies pointed inescapably to the conclusion that even a large-scale use of theatre weapons would not necessarily result in regaining the military advantage. The conclusion arrived at by the Group was that the use of tactical weapons should have an essentially political purpose in convincing the adversary of the risk of continued military action – their use should be designed to restore a state of deterrence. Together with the report to Congress in March 1974 by US Defense Secretary James R. Schlesinger which proposed an even greater flexibility in the planning and targeting of nuclear weapons, on both the strategic and the theatre level, a momentum towards the modernisation of conventional and theatre nuclear weapons was established which resulted in the decision to deploy new longer range theatre nuclear forces (LRTNF) in Europe.[33]

An important stimulus to the gathering momentum for Theatre Force Modernisation was of course the considerable Soviet modernisation programme. One particular aspect, which came to play a pivotal role, was the replacement of SS-4/SS-5 INFs by the SS-20.[34] In October 1977, Helmut Schmidt gave the Alastair Buchan Memorial Lecture at the IISS in which he voiced some of his concerns.[35] While he welcomed the SALT process, Schmidt cautioned that the neutralisation of the strategic nuclear capabilities of the superpowers could be dangerous for Europe unless the disparities of military power in Europe were also removed.

The concern about the Soviet LRTNF modernisation programme was in stark contrast to previous attitudes to asymmetries in the European theatre. Despite the large number of Soviet medium-range missiles, for example, the United States withdrew all its equivalent systems during the 1960s such as the Thor and Jupiter ballistic missiles and the Mace and Matador cruise missiles.

Why did the SS-20 thus become the focus of such concern? In the age of American strategic superiority, Soviet medium-range systems were interpreted as serving the function of deterring the United States by holding Europe hostage. In the view of some European experts including Helmut Schmidt, the age of parity, as codified in SALT, implied the effective neutralisation of the strategic forces of the superpowers. With extended deterrence in doubt, the 'Eurostrategic balance' acquired a new significance. Furthermore, American forward-based systems capable of reaching Soviet territory (such as the F-111 and F-4 bombers) were losing their assured capability of penetrating Soviet air defences. In this light, the SS-20 appeared as the development of a new capability to undermine NATO's strategy of flexible response, engage in a limited nuclear war in Europe and thus exert considerable political pressure on Western Europe towards neutralism and concessions to Soviet political objectives.

It must be added that many British experts did not take the threat of the SS-20 as seriously as did Helmut Schmidt. Michael Howard, for example, warned of the exaggerated fears of the 'decoupling' of the defence of Europe from the strategic capabilities of the United States.[36] David Owen, then Foreign Secretary, told this author that he totally rejected the concept or the need for a 'Eurostrategic balance', nor did he accept the need to deploy new land-based missiles in Europe to counter 'decoupling'. The British perceived the need for theatre force modernisation as arising less out of Soviet deployments and more from the requirements of flexible response *per se*.[37] In the wake of the 'neutron bomb controversy', NATO decided on an approach combining a decision for deployment with an offer for arms control negotiations since it was believed that the modernisation decision might otherwise be politically unsustainable. In December 1979 the NATO 'dual-track' decision was announced to deploy 572 LRTNF warheads (on 108 Pershing-II and 464 land-based cruise missiles) subject to the outcome of arms control negotiations with the Soviet Union.

The Conservative Government which came to power in 1979 fully supported the 'dual-track' decision, and British officials frequently stressed the dangers for Alliance cohesion of not carrying it out. Differences between the German and British position emerged, however, during discussions in Bonn in 1981 when German officials supported the view that LRTNF deployment would not be necessary if the Soviet removed theirs. This view was opposed by British officials who argued for modernisation regardless of Soviet capabilities.

As a result of the 'dual-track' decision, a separate set of negotiations on INF was initiated. The opening negotiating position of the Reagan Administration, on the basis of a suggestion by Helmut Schmidt, was based on the so-called 'zero option' which offered to forgo the deployment of GLCMs and Pershing-II missiles in return for the withdrawal and destruction of all SS-4, SS-5 and SS-20 missiles. Proceeding from an intellectual framework opposed to détente and arms control in principle, the 'zero option' was adopted by the Reagan Administration primarily for reasons of public relations; it was taken for granted that the Soviet Union would not accept it.[38]

The position taken by the Conservative Government in Britain was also largely driven by the need to preserve the consensus for a nuclear defence policy. The 'dual-track' decision became the focus of a protest movement which found a great echo in the Labour Party and which was also directed against Britain's independent nuclear deterrent and the plans for its modernisation (the decision to modernise the Polaris by acquiring the Trident C4 system was announced in June 1980). At the Labour Party Conference in Brighton, the party endorsed an 'unambiguous commitment to unilateral disarmament', expressed its opposition to the deployment of American missiles in Britain and voted to eliminate Britain's own nuclear forces. Strong opposition to LRTNF modernisation also existed within the Liberal Party, while the Trident decision was rejected by the Liberal Party and the SDP. Anti-nuclear feeling in Britain gained further impetus when the Government announced in March 1982 that it was now going to purchase the Trident D-5 system instead of C-4, at higher cost and with greater military potential – both aspects came under attack.

The Soviet analysis of the security implications of LRTNF modernisation focused on perceived American endeavours to escape the realities of nuclear parity and recover military superiority and the capability to engage in military conflict either directly against the Soviet Union, or, if deterred by Soviet military might, against other Soviet foreign policy interests (such as national liberation movements). The NATO doctrine of 'flexible response' was described as a way of keeping nuclear war limited to Europe. The announcement of the Strategic Defense Initiative in March 1983 contributed to the view that the United States was seeking a first strike capability. In this context the deployment of cruise and Pershing-II missiles took on a quite different significance. It was not just an addition to NATO's theatre forces, or even a counter to the SS-20. It was seen as providing the United States with a completely new capability. It appears that despite exaggerations for propaganda purposes, these arguments reflected some genuine security concerns.

Soviet negotiating strategy was rather unimaginative. Initially it insisted that 'rough parity' in Eurostrategic systems already existed; after continuing the build-up of SS-20s to a level of 270 (in Europe) there was notable movement in the Soviet position. While the 'walk in the woods' formula was rejected (after having been rejected first by Washington), Andropov made an offer in December 1982 to the effect that the number of SS-20 missiles in Europe would be reduced to the number of missiles deployed by Britain and France (later specified to be

162) provided no cruise and Pershing-II deployment took place. A significant improvement on this offer occurred in 1983 when it was declared that the 81 missiles which were to be withdrawn would actually be destroyed rather than redeployed in Asia. This and other variants of Soviet proposals were based on the principle that the Soviet Union was willing to reduce the number of SS-20 as long as there was no NATO LRTNF deployment at all. The idea was not that the French or British should reduce their systems; they were simply used as a basis to argue for a retention of SS-20. The final Soviet offer ran along similar lines, though not involving French and British systems: both NATO and the Soviet Union would reduce their LRTNF warheads by 572. This would mean zero deployment for NATO, and leave 120 SS-20 in place. The failure of the negotiations and the arrival of the first missiles in Europe resulted in the Soviet walk-out of both the INF and the START negotiations in November 1983.

NON-NUCLEAR ARMS CONTROL

Conventional arms control

Britain has played a central role in the efforts to reduce conventional forces in the Mutual and Balanced Force Reduction negotiations which lasted from 1973 to 1988. Among the European NATO Allies, it was mainly the British and the West Germans who kept pressing for the initiation of such negotiations.

The main reason for the failure of MBFR lay in the divergence of the central objectives of the two sides. The WTO objective was to maintain the existing balance at somewhat reduced levels, whereas NATO sought an asymmetrical reduction to correct a perceived WTO superiority. An associated difficulty was the 'data issue', i.e. an unresolved disagreement about the actual level of existing forces. Verification also proved to be a stumbling block. Paradoxically, part of the problem was that the political objectives pursued in East and West were achieved (at least in part) without too much progress in the negotiations themselves. The WTO managed to get the CSCE process established, while the West Germans successfully pursued their *Ostpolitik*. The MBFR process contributed to averting the threat of unilateral force withdrawals by NATO members; domestic pressures in this direction had been central to American and British interest in MBFR.

None the less, there have been some successes in recent years. As a result of a proposal worked out by Britain and West Germany, Eastern and Western positions on MBFR converged considerably. The proposal tabled officially on 5 December 1985 proposed certain initial reductions in Soviet and American forces followed by a collective commitment not to increase the level of forces without having to resolve the data issue. Soviet commentators reacted positively to the Anglo-German proposal.[39] Soviet willingness to move closer towards Western views on verification was signalled in a speech by Gorbachev on 15 January 1986.[40]

Another milestone was the successful conclusion of the initial phase of the Conference on Confidence and Security Building Measures and Disarmament in Europe (CDE) which met in Stockholm from January 1984 to September 1986 with an agreement on a package of confidence building measures which indicate a willingness on the part of the Eastern side to greater openness and acceptance of more far-reaching verification measures than ever before.

The momentum towards nuclear arms control under Gorbachev has given renewed impetus towards conventional arms control. The need for progress in conventional arms control has been given particular emphasis by the British Prime Minister on the grounds that far-reaching nuclear arms reduction could allow the fear of conventional aggression to emerge, a problem also acknowledged by Soviet experts. On 18 April 1986, during a visit to East Germany, Gorbachev proposed the reduction of conventional forces in Europe 'from the Atlantic to the Urals'.[41] This was elaborated in the 'Budapest Appeal' of the Political Consultative Committee of the WTO on 11 July 1986. This involved a wide-ranging set of proposals, including troop reductions on both sides by 100,000 to 150,000 men and their armaments within a few years and extensive verification procedures, including on-site inspections.[42] The principle of negotiations about force reductions in the area 'from the Atlantic to the Urals' has been accepted by the Western Alliance, and talks on a mandate for such negotiations had by the end of 1988 reached agreement on all major issues.

There is certainly evidence of Soviet 'new thinking' in conventional arms control. Analysts in Moscow describe the goal of conventional disarmament as force reductions to a level of 'minimum sufficiency' (or 'reasonable sufficiency') and defensive force postures. In the view of some Soviet analysts:

. . . the level of reasonable sufficiency as applied to conventional armed forces must be determined not by the ability to win a major local conflict but by ensuring an adequate defence potential so that the aggressor should not be able to count either on a 'local blitzkrieg' or on escalating such a conflict with impunity.[43]

The central issue of conventional force reductions in Europe continues to be perceived imbalances. In July 1986 Gorbachev mooted the idea of asymmetrical reductions depending on areas of 'surplus' possessed by NATO or the WTO. This was reaffirmed by the Political Consultative Committee of the WTO in May 1987.[44] This does not mean that the Soviet Union has accepted the Western notion of a WTO superiority; it still insisted that:

an approximate parity in conventional weapons and troops strength of the two sides has long existed on the continent.[45]

The door is left open to compromise with the NATO position by the recognition of 'certain asymmetries' due to the deployments of 'certain types of weapons' and 'differences in the structures of the armed forces' which, as Soviet statements clearly imply, may also lead to asymmetric reductions.[46]

Given Britain's contribution to the defence of Europe and participation at MBFR, there is a great deal of scope for the United Kingdom to contribute to and influence the movement towards conventional arms control. For example, the British have resisted attempts by the WTO to include tactical nuclear weapons in the negotiations, at least in the initial phase, despite West German interest in the removal of battlefield nuclear weapons. The decision announced by Gorbachev at the UN in December 1988 unilaterally to reduce Soviet forces by 500,000 men over a two-year period underscored his anxiety both to influence the West European debate and to get the negotiations on conventional forces in Europe, scheduled to begin in early 1989, off to a good start. The most important task for the Western Alliance is to formulate and pursue a coherent set of objectives in these talks and for conventional arms control in general at the beginning of the 1990s.

Chemical weapons

Since the Second World War, both NATO and the WTO have built up very sizeable stocks of chemical warfare agents, although the United States has not produced any chemical weapons (CW) since 1969 and Britain abandoned the production and storage of its own chemical weapons in the late 1950s. Thus British efforts in this field have been concentrated exclusively on passive defensive measures, such as protective clothing and gas masks. In the United States a new generation of chemical warfare agents known as 'binary weapons' (consisting of two chemical agents which, only when combined, produce a highly lethal substance) have been developed. The issue of CW modernisation is very important from the British point of view, because American F-111 bombers based in Britain will be one of the main delivery vehicles of chemical warheads. The British Army on the Rhine has the equipment to fire the two other binary weapons which have been developed by the US Army (a 155 mm shell and a rocket artillery warhead). The British position has been that CW will not be stored on British soil in peace time, but this policy is subject to review depending on circumstances.[47]

In the eighteen-nation Disarmament Conference in the 1960s discussions were initiated aiming at a comprehensive ban of chemical weapons. These talks did not make a great deal of progress. In 1976, Britain injected new life into them by tabling a draft Chemical Weapons Convention, some aspects of which are still relevant for the discussions on CW today. However, the United States and

USSR had since 1974 been moving towards bilateral discussions, and multilateral talks thus were put into abeyance from 1976 until 1980.

In 1982 multilateral discussions received a new lease of life in the context of the 40-nation Conference on Disarmament (CD) at Geneva. The United Kingdom again played an active role. In March 1983 Douglas Hurd, then Minister of State at the FCO, made a proposal on verification measures (involving the monitoring of key chemicals known as 'precursors' of nerve gases in chemical industries). Another major proposal on verification (relating to on-site inspections) was tabled by Hurd's successor Richard Luce in 1984.

Verification is of course the key issue and is much more intractable when it comes to CW than in nuclear arms control, given that it will require rather intrusive inspection procedures and monitoring of civil chemical industries. This must be seen in the light of a widespread view in the West that the Soviet Union has been engaged in the development and production of biological warfare agents despite its claim to have adhered to the ban on such weapons. However, there are hopeful signs that the objective of the official policy positions of NATO and the WTO, namely an agreement to ban chemical weapons completely (including the destruction of all existing stockpiles) may be achieved together with appropriate verification measures. A CW ban has derived considerable impetus from the actual use of chemical warfare agents by Iraq since 1984, as well as from the current momentum in arms control in other areas. Of particular significance is a greater willingness on the Soviet side to accept verification, as demonstrated in the visit by CD delegates in October 1987 to Shikhany, one of the main Soviet chemical weapons establishment, where chemical weapons were shown and demonstrations of their destruction given.

In July 1987 Britain submitted a paper to the CD on practical steps to ensure effective implementation of a CW ban. Soviet–British interaction is therefore likely to make an important contribution as negotiations proceed towards a total ban on chemical weapons.

SHIFTING PATTERNS OF INTERACTION

European defence co-operation

One of the important shifts in the general environment of security policy has been the increased emphasis on European defence co-operation. The revival in the early 1980s of the problems of European Defence Co-operation as a pressing concern resulted in the decision (following a French proposal) to reactivate the WEU at a meeting of Foreign and Defence Ministers. One important source of pressure lies in the divergent views on strategic and arms control issues and the conduct of East–West relations between Europe and the United States. These divergences were brought into sharp focus as a result of the enhanced radiation warhead issue, by the INF controversy, and later by the policy of the Reagan Administration on East–West relations in general and arms control in particular. The existence of perceived differences of view and political interests is an incentive for a stronger and more united assertion of Europe's responsibilities for its own defence. Furthermore, as the European Community is striving towards greater co-ordination in foreign policy, the tendency to include security issues in the European Political Co-operation increases.

These factors have been complemented by the emergence of doubts about the wisdom of American commitments to the defence of Europe among important sections of opinion in the United States, accompanied by the attempt of the 1984 Nunn amendment to push Europe to assume a greater share of the burden for its own defence. The obvious advantages of joint arms production, given widespread cynicism about a 'two-way street' with the United States in this area, also provide a powerful push in the direction of greater West European security collaboration.[48]

Soviet authors see developments in European defence co-operation mainly as a way of strengthening the Western Alliance. Thus S. Madzoevsky, (Maclean) and G.V. Kolosov focus on the military significance of Eurogroup and the IEPG.[49] Soviet authors definitely see a shift in the correlation of forces between the United States and Western Europe in favour of the latter. Greater European co-operation (in which Britain is seen to play a leading role) is interpreted as an attempt to prolong the life of the North Atlantic Alliance, the main emphasis being on military-industrial co-operation. Kolosov sees as one of the fundamental aims of the IEPG the strengthening of the position of the European defence industries *vis-à-vis* the US, but observes that this has so far not happened.[50] Although Soviet authors like to emphasise the diverging interests of Western European members of the Alliance and the United States, some claim that European Defence Co-operation is supported by 'American ruling circles' as a means to strengthen their grip on Western Europe.

The greater co-ordination of European efforts is seen as a process of centralisation which will enable the United States to exercise greater control. The United States is seen (in part contrary to fact) as encouraging the formation of groupings such as WEU with the purpose of restricting the national sovereignty of Western European countries. The leadership role taken by Britain and West Germany, as the most important members of the Alliance, is viewed as being designed to force a closer adherence to American plans on smaller European states.[51] Divergences of interests and viewpoint between European NATO members and the United States are a frequent theme of Soviet writings.[52]

Soviet commentators generally do not seem to see European Defence Co-operation as a likely road to Europe becoming an independent military superpower, but interpret it rather as a way to preserve American influence, even if some authors discern a growing West European identity.[53] Soviet writings do emphasise differences of interest between the United States and Europe and would certainly encourage divisions in the Western Alliance. While the Soviet leadership would see a Europe de-coupled from the United States and independently militarily strong as the least desirable option (in particular if this involved an independent nuclear arsenal), some loosening of military ties with the United States would clearly be seen as a positive development.[54]

A new departure in arms control?

Margaret Thatcher distinguished herself even while Leader of the Opposition as a stern critic of the Soviet Union. Her natural instincts to take a strong line against the Soviet Union bear some resemblance to those of President Reagan. But despite British insistence on the reality of the Soviet threat, the need to maintain an adequate defence posture (which for Britain included nuclear weapons), despite joining in the condemnation of the invasion of Afghanistan and Soviet pressure on Poland over Solidarity, perceptions in London of the security environment were markedly different from those in Washington. Thus British officials and defence experts generally discounted the notion of ICBM vulnerability ('the window of vulnerability') as being of strategic significance in view of the invulnerable second-strike force of SLBMs. There was no sense in London of the imminent threat to deterrence stability projected by the Administration and its supporters in Washington. The British Government was also unwilling to have its trade interests damaged by the deterioration in East–West relations.

These fundamental differences in perception and implied policy preferences were usually obscured by Britain's public position in order to maintain the spirit of the 'special relationship' with the United States and avoid adding to the negative sentiment about US foreign policy developing in sections of the British population. But such differences were starkly revealed by the announcement of the Strategic Defense Initiative in March 1983. The rationale for SDI was couched in language which strongly questioned the morality of continued nuclear deterrence and thus the entire basis of NATO defence policy. Having withstood formidable political pressures with regard to INF, European governments, including the British, were not keen to have another great defence controversy. Furthermore, as was pointed out earlier, Britain had always been sensitive to the potential of Soviet BMD to degrade the effectiveness of Britain's independent nuclear deterrent, a spectre that might raise its head again if the limitations of the ABM Treaty were discarded.

The final position adopted by the Prime Minister on SDI, while giving qualified political support to it, saw a role for the programme substantially different from that envisaged by President Reagan. In Thatcher's view, the goal of the SDI should be to enhance deterrence, not do away with it. SDI-related research should be conducted within the confines of the narrow interpretation of the ABM Treaty; if it came to development and deployment of any systems this should be subject to negotiations with the Soviet Union. Similarly qualified support for SDI was expressed in a speech by the Foreign Secretary, Sir Geoffrey Howe, in March 1985; because of its tone it was interpreted as more hostile to SDI.[55]

In the aftermath of the breakdown of the INF talks the need for a new departure was increasingly recognised by Soviet arms control experts. One of the important developments discernible in the thought of some prominent Soviet specialists is the recognition that the arms race has an inherent dynamic of its own and that the Soviet Union has also contributed (or at least must be careful not to contribute) to it.[56] Soviet arms control policy under Gorbachev has shown a far greater degree of flexibility than before, involving initiatives and unilateral gestures which have often surprised the West, as well as far greater openness to verification. The direction of the policies appears to be firmly towards a substantial demilitarisation. The pursuit of a comprehensive test ban is clearly directed against SDI, but its realisation would also inhibit the modernisation of existing nuclear arsenals.

The 'new thinking' became dramatically apparent at the Reykjavik summit in October 1986; both leaders agreed in principle to the desirability of a zero option with regard to INF and deep cuts in strategic ballistic missiles, with the objective of their eventual total elimination. The British Government, like other European Governments, responded to the Reykjavik proposals with considerable (if publicly restrained) alarm. From the British perspective, the purpose of arms control is to legitimise nuclear deterrence and provide it with a degree of stability, not to eliminate nuclear weapons. The Reykjavik proposals threatened to undermine both extended deterrence and the legitimacy of the British independent deterrent. Not surprisingly, Gorbachev has characterised the reaction by Thatcher and other European leaders to the Reykjavik summit as 'the fruit of obsolete thinking'.[57] With regard to INF, Britain urged the inclusion of shorter range missiles which eventually became the 'double zero solution' of the INF agreement signed in Washington.

On the positive side, Gorbachev did not insist that British and French nuclear systems should be included in a Soviet/American INF agreement. But it is also clear that if the obstacle which SDI currently poses to deep cuts in strategic arsenals is overcome, the British nuclear force will become an issue, particular after its modernisation. Before Reykjavik, in May 1986, Gorbachev had offered talks for a bilateral agreement with Britain on the basis that the Soviet Union would match any reductions in British nuclear weapons by cuts in its own arsenal, and revived a proposal made by his predecessor Chernenko to guarantee not to target nuclear weapons on Britain were British nuclear weapons completely eliminated. The British accept in principle that at some stage their arsenal will have to be put on the table, but all that is said so far is that this can only happen after substantial reductions (i.e. more than 50 per cent according to a statement by Margaret Thatcher in December 1987) in strategic weapons have been achieved.

During Thatcher's visit to Moscow in 1987 she forthrightly took issue with Gorbachev's vision of a nuclear-free world and stressed the need to maintain nuclear weapons for deterrence. British Government statements voiced their concern about European denuclearisation while a large imbalance of conventional forces remained, and Thatcher's response to an impending INF deal in 1987 was that denuclearisation in Europe had now gone far enough. Both the Thatcher visit to Moscow and Mikhail Gorbachev's stop-over in Britain on his way to the Washington summit are indicative of a Soviet perception that Britain has an important role to play in East–West relations. It is also clear British influence facilitated the compromise over SDI which was a prerequisite for the signing of the INF Treaty.

Mikhail Gorbachev has presented the West with a general set of objectives in East–West security. This involves deep cuts in nuclear weapons, leading eventually to their total elimination. He has also accepted the need to correct imbalances in conventional forces and taken the first steps to reduce Soviet levels. The Western Alliance, and Britain in particular, is faced with a stark challenge. The Western Alliance lacks a common concept of what it would see as the ultimate goal in relations with the Soviet Union: is the West going to encourage Gorbachev in proceeding with the denuclearisation and even the demilitarisation of East–West relations? If not, other objectives will have to be defined. There is much to be said for Europeans coming to an agreed position on the broad objectives and seeking agreement with the United States before strategic and conventional arms control gathers even more momentum. Britain will have to play a vital role in any such process, a part that will underscore the continued centrality of the security dimension to its relations with the Soviet Union.

NOTES

1. See Raymond L. Garthoff, *The Soviet Image of Future War* (Public Affairs Press 1959); H.S. Dinerstein, *War and the Soviet Union* (Frederick A. Praeger, 1962).
2. For more detailed analysis of Soviet strategic arms policy and foreign policy under Khrushchev see Christoph Bluth, 'Defence and security', in Martin McCauley, ed., *Khrushchev and Khrushchevism* (Macmillan, 1987), pp. 194–214; J.M. Mackintosh, *Strategy and Tactics of Soviet Foreign Policy* (Oxford University Press, 1962); Thomas W. Wolfe, *Soviet Power and Europe 1945–1970* (Johns Hopkins University Press, 1970), pp. 73–236.
3. *Pravda*, 15 January 1960.
4. For more detail, see Christoph Bluth, 'The evolution of Soviet military doctrine', *Survival* (March–April 1988), pp. 149–62.
5. *Pravda*, 19 January 1977; see also L.I. Brezhnev, *Na strazhe mira i sotsializma* (Politizdat, 1979), pp. 491–2; for discussion see Tsuyoshi Hasegawa, 'Soviets on nuclear-war fighting', *Problems of Communism*, 35: 4 (July–August 1986), pp. 68–79; Robbin F. Laird and Dale R. Herspring, *The Soviet Union and Strategic Arms* (Westview Press, 1984), pp. 20–2; David Holloway, *The Soviet Union and the Arms Race* (Yale University Press, 1984), pp. 48–64; Michael MccGwire, *Military Objectives in Soviet Foreign Policy* (Brookings Institution, 1987), chapters 2 and 3; David R. Jones, 'Soviet military doctrine and space in the 1980s', in Carl G. Jacobsen, ed., *The Uncertain Course* (Oxford University Press/SIPRI, 1987), pp. 93–135.
6. Holloway, *The Soviet Union and the Arms Race*, p. 50.
7. *Pravda*, 21 October 1981.
8. Marshal N.V. Ogarkov, *Vsegda v gotovnosti k zashchite otechevstva* (Voenizdat, 1982).
9. For a detailed analysis of the Ustinov–Ogarkov debates, see Hasegawa, 'Soviets on nuclear-war fighting'. See also MccGwire, *Military Objectives*, chapters 13 and 14. A recent authoritative account of contemporary Soviet military doctrine, critical of the Sokolovskii volume, is given in M.A. Gareev, *Frunze – voennyi teoretik* (Voenizdat, 1985).
10. Statements about military allocations at the time indicate a decision that while some additional resources would be made available, the general structure of the social programmes of 1981 (with all the implications for resource allocations) would not be changed. Cf. MccGwire, *Military Objectives*, p. 312 where the documentary evidence is cited.
11. V.G. Trukhanovsky, *Angliiskoe iadernoe oruzhie* (Mezhdunarodnoe otnosheniia, 1985), p. 179; for a general article on British and French nuclear weapons see V. Poshcupkin, 'Schet po raschetu', *Kommunist vooruzhennykh sil*, 5 (March 1985), 82–6.
12. Trukhanovsky, *Angliiskoe iadernoe oruzhie*, p. 180. On the other hand, Trukhanovsky accepts the official British version that the Chevaline system is not MIRVed. The claim that Chevaline is MIRVed is made in (for example): I. Vladimirov, 'Voennaia politika Velikobritanii', *Zarubezhnoe voennoe obozrenie*, 7 (1981), 7–12, p. 8; A. Karemov and G. Semin, 'Nekotorye polozheniia voennykh doktrin osnovnykh evropeiskikh stran NATO', *Zarubezhnoe voennoe obozrenie*, 6 (1983), 7–14, p. 10.

13. This is argued in a report by Robbin F. Laird and Susan Clark, *Soviet Perspectives on British Security Policy* (IDA, 1986), p. 20.

14. See *ibid.*, p. 21.

15. Trukhanovsky's discussion of Pym's speech, for example, merely discusses the technical features of the Chevaline system and says nothing about Pym's justification for a British deterrent. See Trukhanovsky, *Angliiskoe iadernoe oruzhie*, chapter 8, in particular p. 179 f.

16. Lawrence Freedman, 'British nuclear targeting', *Defence Analysis*, 1:2 (1985), 81–99, p. 96. See also Edward A. Koldziej, 'Modernization of British and French nuclear forces: arms control and security dimensions', in Jacobson, ed., *The Uncertain Course*, pp. 239–54.

17. G.V. Kolosov, *Voenno-politicheskii kurs Anglii v Evrope* (Nauka, 1984), p. 64; see also Kolosov in N.S. Kishilov, ed., *Zapadno-evropeiskaia integratsiia: politicheskie aspekty*, p. 243; Kolosov is in my opinion one of the more perceptive Soviet observers of Western European security policies. Colonel Poshchupkin on the other hand seems to be convinced that Margaret Thatcher would 'press the button' in the event of war in Europe even if it meant the destruction of Britain; see V. Poshchupkin, 'Schet po raschetu', p. 84.

18. See A. Karemov and G. Semin, 'Nekotorye polozheniia', for a detailed discussion of Britain's military options, including the distinction between 'general nuclear war' involving strategic weapons and limited warfare, involving only conventional weapons or theatre nuclear strikes.

19. See Lawrence Freedman's chapter in J. Roper and K. Kaiser, eds., *British-German Defence Cooperation: Partners within the Alliance* (Jane's for the Royal Institute of International Affairs and Forschungsinstitut der Deutschen Gesellschaft für Auswärtige Politik, 1988).

20. Trukhanovsky, *Angliiskoe iadernoe oruzhie*, chapter 8; Vladimirov, *Zarubezhnoe voennoe obozrenie*, according to whom the Tory Government adapts its policies to the interests of US imperialism (p. 9). See also Karemov and Semin, 'Nekotorye polozheniia', p. 8.

21. With regard to the Royal Navy, see Iu. Galkin and S. Grechin, 'Voenno-morskie sily Velikobritanii', *Zarubezhnoe voennoe obozrenie*, 2 (1983), pp. 69–75; for a survey of British military capabilities, see S. Azherskii, 'Vooruzhenye sily Veilikobritanii', *Zarubezhnoe voennoe obozrenie*, 9 (1984). See also Laird and Clark, *Soviet Perspectives*. For an interesting contribution about the recent defence debate in Britain, see G. Kolosov, 'Bor'ba po voprosam voennoi politiki v Anglii', *MEMO*, 1 (1988).

22. Trukhanovsky gives a fairly good account of the debate in Britain as to whether the United Kingdom will have adequate control over the use of American nuclear weapons from British territory. Trukhanovsky, *Angliiskoe iadernoe oruzhie*, p. 196 f.

23. For more detailed analysis, see Robin Ranger, *Arms and Politics 1958–1978* (Macmillan, 1979). For a Soviet study on nuclear disarmament from the post-war period to SALT, see A.E. Efremov, *Iadernoe razoruzhenie* (Mezhdunarodnye otnosheniia, 1976).

24. Christoph Bluth, 'British–German defence relations 1950–80: a survey', in Roper and Kaiser, eds., *British–German Defence Cooperation*, pp. 1–40.

25. The Polaris force was given to Britain on the understanding that it would form part of a multilateral force.

26. Ranger, *Arms and Politics*, part IV; Freedman, *Britain and Nuclear Weapons*, pp.

88–91. The author also benefited from a discussion with Lord Chalfont on these questions.

27. Konstantin Borisov, 'The problem of nuclear non-proliferation', *International Affairs* (Moscow), 6 (1987), pp. 28–34, 61.

28. For more detailed discussion, see John Simpson, *Ploughshares into Swords? The International Nuclear Non-Proliferation Network and the 1985 NPT Review Conference*, Faraday Discussion Paper No. 4 (Brassey's Defence Publishers for The Council for Arms Control, 1985).

29. Karin Eifert, *Die britische Nuklearstreitmacht* (Quorum Verlag, 1986), p. 58.

30. Freedman, *Britain and Nuclear Weapons*, p. 97.

31. *Ibid.*, pp. 91–6.

32. *Pravda*, 20 August 1986, p. 4.

33. Helga Haftendorn, 'Das doppelte Missverständnis – zur Vorgeschichte des NATO–Doppelbeschlusses von 1979', *Vierteljahreshefte fur Zeitgeschichte*, 33:2 (April 1965), 244–87, p. 249; J. Michael Legge, *Theater Nuclear Weapons and the NATO Strategy of Flexible Response* (Rand Corporation, 1983), pp. 26–8; this section also benefited from personal conversation with former Defence Secretary Lord Mulley, former Foreign Secretary Dr David Owen, former Inspector General of the Bundeswehr Jurgen Brandt and officials in the German Ministry of Defence; for more detailed analysis see Christoph Bluth, 'British–German defence relations'.

34. See David Holloway, 'The INF policy of the Soviet Union', in Hans Henrik Holm and Nikolaj Petersen, eds., *The European Missile Crisis* (Frances Pinter, 1983), pp. 92–114; MccGwire, *Military Objectives*, Appendix D. American success in having Soviet medium-range systems such as the SS-11 and the Backfire counted as strategic compared with the Soviet failure to have American INF counted as such is remarkable (particularly in the Backfire case).

35. Schmidt later claimed to have some of the concerns expressed in his speech known at the NATO summit meeting in May 1977.

36. Michael Howard, Letter to the Editor, *The Times*, 3 November 1981; for discussion see Jane M.O. Sharp, 'Understanding the INF debacle: arms control and Alliance cohesion', *Arms Control*, 5:2 (September 1985), 95–127, p. 116 f.

37. For more details, see John Cartwright and Julian Critchley, *Cruise, Pershing and SS-20, A North Atlantic Assembly Report* (Brassey's Defence Publishers, 1985); and Freedman, *Britain and Nuclear Weapons*, chapter 11.

38. This emerges clearly from the analysis of Strobe Talbott, *Deadly Gambits* (Picador, 1985); see also Alexander Haig, *Caveat* (Weidenfeld and Nicolson, 1984), p. 229. It should be noted that there was of course a diversity of views in the US Administration; some who were seriously seeking an INF agreement opposed the 'zero option' for this reason.

39. Konstantin Borisov, 'For progress at the Vienna talks', *International Affairs* (Moscow), 6 (1986), pp. 110–15.

40. Wilfrid Aichinger, 'Die Wiener Truppenabbauverhandlungen – eine Bestandsaufnahme', *Osterreichische Militärische Zeitschrift*, 22:3 (Mai–Juni 1984), pp. 189–95; see also Canadian Centre for Arms Control and Disarmament, *Arms Control Chronicle*, 9 (August 1985), pp. 18–29; 11–12 (Nov. 1985–Jan. 1986), pp. 23–4; 13 (Jan.–Feb. 1986), pp. 16–18; *Survival*, 28:3 (May–June 1986), pp. 261–8, p. 53 f.; Michael Sheehan, 'A more inane Congress: twelve years of MBFR', *Arms Control*, 6:2 (September 1985) pp. 150–69.

41. *The Guardian*, 19 April 1986.

42. *Pravda*, 12 June 1986; see also BBC Monitoring Service, *Summary of World Broadcasts*, EE/8582/C/3, 1 June 1987; for discussion see 'Conventional shrinkmanship', *The Economist*, 28 November 1987, pp. 21–4; Karl-Heinz Kamp, 'Perspectives of conventional arms control in Europe', *Aussenpolitik*, 38:4 (1987), pp. 331–43; David S. Yost, 'Beyond MBFR: the Atlantic to the Urals gambit', *Orbis*, 31:1 (Spring 1987), pp. 99–134. What is remarkable about David Yost's article is that apart from a perfunctory footnote there is no reference to Gorbachev's speech or the Budapest Appeal and the main text of his article reads as if this was a 'NATO initiative for a new conventional arms forum' (p. 99) and not a WTO initiative in any sense.

43. Vitaly Zhurkin, Sergei Karaganov, Andrei Kortunov, 'Reasonable sufficiency – or how to break the vicious circle', *New Times*, 12 October 1987, pp. 13–15, p. 15; see also V.V. Zhurkin, S.A. Karaganov and A.V. Kortunov, 'O razumnoi dostatochnosti', *SShA*, 12 (1987), pp. 11–21; A. Kokoshin, 'Razvitie voennogo dela i sokrashchenie vooruzhennykh sil i obychnykh vooruzhenii', *MEMO*, 1 (1988), pp. 20–32.

44. Quoted from BBC SWB (see note 42).

45. Gennadi Stakh, 'European disarmament programme', *International Affairs* (Moscow), 11 (1987), pp. 106–14, p. 107.

46. *Ibid.*, p. 108.

47. Ministry of Defence, 'Chemical weapons: a background note', *The Council for Arms Control Bulletin*, 34 (December 1987), pp. 4–5; see also Nicholas A. Sims, *Chemical Weapons – Control or Chaos?*, Faraday Discussion Paper No. 1 (Council for Arms Control, 1984); J.P. Perry Robinson, 'Disarmament and other options for Western policy-making on chemical warfare', *International Affairs*, 63:1 (Winter 1986/87), pp. 65–80.

48. For more detailed analysis, see Bluth, 'British–German relations'; the inclusion of security issues in the EPC has long been opposed by Ireland, Denmark and Greece.

49. S. Madzoevsky and Efim S. Khesin, 'Velikobritaniia v sovremennom mire', *MEMO*, 8 (1980), pp. 50–63, p. 56; G. Kolosov, *Voenno-politicheskii kurs Anglii v Europe* (Nauka, 1984), p. 184; see also G. Kolosov, 'Voenno-politicheskie aspekty zapadnoevropeiskogo integratsionnogo protsessa', *MEMO*, 4 (1987), pp. 34–42, p. 38. For a less differentiated analysis, see A. Migalot'ev, 'Voenno-promyshlennye kompleksy stran NATO na sluzhbe voiny', *Kommunist vooruzhennykh sil*, 1 (1985), pp. 77–81.

50. See Kolosov, *Voenno-politicheskii*.

51. E. Kirichenko 'On certain specific features of inter-imperialist rivalry', *International Affairs* (Moscow), 6 (1985), pp. 78–86, p. 86.

52. For instance see A. Bovin, 'Western Europe: "strategic concerns"', *International Affairs* (Moscow), 12 (1985), pp. 94–101.

53. See for example Sergei Vybornov, Andrei Gusenko and Vladimir Leontiev, 'Nothing is simple in Europe', *International Affairs* (Moscow), 3 (1988), pp. 34–41; V. Beletsky, 'What lies behind the "European Defence Initiative" project', *International Affairs* (Moscow), 6 (1986), pp. 49–55.

54. As V.F. Davydov has explained:

> It appears that supplementing political détente with military détente would allow the United States the possibility of reducing the expenses of its involvement in the so–called 'defence' of Western Europe; in turn, for the West European countries the processes of gradually abolishing the NATO structures formed

during the 'cold war' years would open up the way of decreased dependence on the US without needing a sharp increase in military expenditures, including on nuclear forces, which presupposes the redistribution of the 'burden of responsibility' within NATO.

V.F. Davydov, 'Diskussiia o evropeiskikh iadernykh silakh', *S Sh A*, 3 (1976), pp. 71–2. English translation quoted from Robbin F. Laird, *The Soviet Union, the West and the Nuclear Arms Race* (Wheatsheaf Books, 1986), p. 223. See also Vsevolod Kniazhinsky, *West European Integration: Its Policies and International Relations*, (Progress Publishers, 1984); Vitaly Gusenkov, 'Another pillar of NATO', *New Times*, December 1984, pp. 10–11.

55. For a Soviet view, see Bovin, 'Western Europe', *International Affairs*; see also G. Vorontsov, 'Zapadnaia Evropa i SOI', *MEMO*, 3 (1987), pp. 41–8.
56. The arguments outlined in this section have been developed in considerable detail in Pat Litherland, *Gorbachev and Arms Control: Civilian Experts and Soviet Policy*, Peace Research Report Number 12 (Bradford University School of Peace Studies, 1986); Stephen Shenfield, *The Nuclear Predicament* (Routledge and Kegan Paul/RIIA, 1987). A. Bovin, *Izvestiia*, 20 October 1979.
57. M.S. Gorbachev, *Perestroika i novoe myshlenie* (Politizdat, 1987), p. 211.

6 Anglo-Soviet relations: political and diplomatic

MARGOT LIGHT

INTRODUCTION

Mr Gorbachev's stopover in Britain on the way to his summit meeting in Washington with President Reagan served to symbolise the good working relationship which has developed between the British Government and the Soviet leadership since Mr Gorbachev became General Secretary of the Communist Party of the Soviet Union (CPSU) in March 1985. It was also evidence of the fact that there has been 'new political thinking' in both the Soviet Union and Britain.

In the Soviet Union, Gorbachev's attempt to revitalise Soviet foreign policy included the adoption of a set of principles which have become called the 'new political thinking'. Although they primarily concern relations between the superpowers, they include a new emphasis on interdependence and on the need for flexibility in foreign policy. The Soviet leadership has also declared that the Soviet Union should diversify its foreign relations, in particular so that they are not all seen through the prism of Soviet–American relations. An important aspect of the Soviet view of interdependence is the recognition, first, that Europe has a common history and common problems and second, that the Soviet Union is part of Europe.[1] In Britain, although the term 'new political thinking' is not used, there has been a change in policy towards the USSR. During the first Thatcher Government from 1979 to 1983, there was little contact with the Soviet Union. During 1983, however, a decision seems to have been made to raise the profile of bilateral Anglo-Soviet relations.

The invitation to use Britain as a transit point and its acceptance attested to the success of the change in British policy, just as Mrs Thatcher's warm reception in Moscow in March 1987 demonstrated that Mr Gorbachev accords importance to negotiation and dialogue with leaders of other countries irrespective of their political beliefs.

As we have seen in chapter 2, before World War II Anglo-Soviet relations had fluctuated according to fluctuations in political power in Britain. Underlying mutual mistrust and hostility remained but relations improved from time to time. But even when they were good there was limited contact between the two governments. From 1941 to 1945, the two countries co-operated in achieving their common interest, the defeat of Germany, but the underlying suspicion remained. Once Germany had been defeated their shared superordinate goal disappeared. Mutual suspicion once again became manifest. But by then Britain no longer had the military or economic power to play the dominant role in Western policy towards the Soviet Union. Asymmetries developed in Anglo-Soviet relations. While Britain remained preoccupied with Soviet power and potential for further expansion, the major part of Soviet attention and hostility shifted to the United States which had taken over the dominant role in Western policy. Britain concentrated on co-ordinating a collective Western response to the Soviet threat. Bilateral relations become less salient to both sides.

During and after the Cold War Anglo-Soviet bilateral relations continued to fluctuate but even when they were relatively good, contacts remained limited. Unlike the French Government in the early 1960s, the German Government at the end of that decade and the American Government in the early 1970s, the British Government concentrated on multilateral relations with the Soviet Union and did not attempt to forge independent political and diplomatic relations. On the Soviet side Britain's relative coolness towards détente caused some resentment. The change in British policy in the 1980s was, therefore, all the more welcome.

Does this indicate that the problem noted in chapter 2 of achieving a stable and satisfactory bilateral relationship has been solved? Or was it significant that Gorbachev was on his way to a summit meeting with President Reagan in Washington? In other words, how important are bilateral relations to the British Government? And are Anglo-Soviet relations *per se* important to the Soviet leadership? Or are they cultivated less for their own sake than in the hope that Mrs Thatcher will use her influence on President Reagan? Does the Soviet leadership look to Britain to intercede with its European partners in the European Community (EC) or the North Atlantic Treaty Organisation (NATO) when necessary to adopt more conciliatory policies towards the Soviet Union? Have there been alterations in the respective foreign policy institutions that suggest changes in bilateral Anglo-Soviet relations?

This chapter will begin with an examination of the institutions which are responsible for the bilateral relationship in each country. An assessment of the Soviet Union's place in the overall foreign policy strategy of Britain and the importance of Britain in Soviet foreign policy will follow. The historical record of Anglo-Soviet political and diplomatic relations since the early 1970s will then be considered to see what conclusions can be drawn about the future course of Anglo-Soviet relations.

In establishing the importance of each country in the other's foreign policy it is clearly essential to take mutual perceptions into account. Perceptions are to a large extent dependent upon history. The subject matter of this chapter, therefore, complements chapters 2, 3 and 4, in which history and perceptions are dealt with in greater detail. In the same way that it is difficult to separate perception and policy, political and diplomatic relations cannot easily be considered in isolation from other kinds of relations. The political and diplomatic relationship between two countries provides the context within which other kinds of relations flourish or diminish. In the absence of reasonably amicable diplomatic relations there are unlikely to be active economic and cultural relations. Diplomatic, economic and cultural relations and defence policies are instruments of foreign policy. When political relations deteriorate, diplomatic, economic and cultural sanctions frequently follow and defence policy may become more belligerent. This is not to suggest that economic, cultural and defence policies are entirely determined by political relations. They also reflect domestic conditions (particularly in the case of defence policy). But the relationship between these various aspects of foreign policy is even more complex. Changes in economic, cultural and defence policy will also (sometimes inadvertently) affect political and diplomatic relations.[2] Anglo-Soviet political and diplomatic relations cannot, therefore, be considered without paying some attention to other aspects of the bilateral relationship. The subject matter of this chapter will, therefore, also complement that of chapters 5, 8, 9 and 10.

MAKING AND IMPLEMENTING ANGLO-SOVIET RELATIONS

Although British foreign policy is rather more preoccupied with the Soviet Union than vice versa, the asymmetry is not reflected in major differences in the respective sections of their foreign policy establishments that deal with bilateral relations. In fact, in so far as there is an imbalance, it is that on the Soviet side foreign policy is not the sole preserve of the Government. The CPSU is concerned in formulating Soviet policy in a far more direct way than is the political party in power in Britain at any given time.

The conduct of British policy

Foreign policy is regularly debated in the House of Commons. There is also an all-party Select Committee on Foreign Affairs which studies various aspects of British foreign policy, taking evidence from interested outsiders as well as government officials. From time to time it reports on Anglo–Soviet relations. But political responsibility for foreign policy rests with the Cabinet. The Secretary of

State for Foreign and Commonwealth Affairs steers policy as a member of the Cabinet. He reports major developments and recommends policy changes to the Cabinet and to the Cabinet Committee, chaired by the Prime Minister, that deals with questions of foreign policy.[3] He is aided by a Minister of State with particular responsibility for relations with the Soviet Union and Eastern Europe. The Foreign Secretary also reports to the Prime Minister, of course. Prime Ministers vary both in the extent to which they play an active role in foreign policy and in the issues to which they accord the kind of priority that requires their active participation.[4] Since the Soviet Union is perceived to be Britain's major adversary, Anglo-Soviet relations may be assumed to be accorded high priority. As a result, Foreign Secretaries and Prime Ministers are reputedly less prone to direction by the relevant officials in the Foreign and Commonwealth Office than they might be with regard to other aspects of British foreign policy. They participate consistently and actively at all stages of policy planning and implementation. Nevertheless, since the Secretary of State is responsible for all of British foreign policy and is constantly heavily committed, he is clearly very dependent in a number of ways on the department which he heads, the Foreign and Commonwealth Office (FCO).

Within the FCO Anglo-Soviet relations are the prime concern of the Soviet Department which initiates policy and is responsible for the conduct of day-to-day policy. The Soviet Department submits advice both to the Foreign Secretary and to the Minister of State responsible for relations with the Soviet Union and Eastern Europe. It also liaises with the many other departments within the FCO and in other ministries that deal with Soviet affairs and it gives instructions to the Embassy in Moscow.[5] At present, there are about nine people working in the Soviet Department (excluding support staff). A small unit concerned with matters relating to the Conference on Security and Co-operation in Europe (CSCE) is attached to it. Neither arms control nor defence policy are dealt with by the Soviet Department and nor are questions concerning NATO or Germany. Within the FCO there are two departments that deal with arms control: the Security Policy Department deals with conventional and nuclear arms negotiations (MBFR and CBM as well as START, INF and SDI) while the Arms Control Department deals with chemical weapons and UN disarmament fora. Defence policy, on the other hand, is the preserve of the Ministry of Defence.

All cultural relations, including those with the USSR are dealt with by the FCO Cultural Relations Department. It works through the British Council for cultural and educational relations with the Soviet Union (the Department of Education and Science plays no part in Anglo-Soviet educational exchanges). Since Anglo-Soviet cultural exchanges are regarded as having broad, if rather nebulous, political relevance and importance, the Soviet Department keeps a watchful eye on them.[6] The salience of cultural relations and of ensuring that there is a bilateral flow of information has increased since the CSCE process began.

Two other establishments play a role in planning and executing British foreign policy. The FCO Planning Department has little to do with day-to-day policy, but it is responsible for formulating a broad view of British foreign policy. It also keeps contact with unofficial (including academic) opinion, co-ordinates seminars, writes speeches and briefs. The Cabinet Office services the various Cabinet Committees, including the Committee on foreign policy.[7]

Within the FCO there is a Research Department. Unlike other departments in the FCO which are staffed by rotating diplomats, it has a permanent staff (although Soviet research specialists may be posted in the British Embassy in Moscow). It is thus well equipped to develop expertise, offer advice on particular issues, and write research memoranda and papers.

There are about sixty British diplomats in Moscow (compared to thirty-eight French and eighty-seven West German diplomats).[8] The task of Embassy staff is to implement British policy and to assist in the formulation of that policy. British diplomats in Moscow analyse developments in the Soviet Union, complementing the work of the Soviet Department with the insights obtained from being on the spot and being able to travel around the country. In most respects the British Embassy in Moscow is not unlike other British Embassies elsewhere. The major differences are first, a concentration on political developments (elsewhere economic considerations often predominate) and, second, the fact that the political section reports both on domestic and foreign policy (in most other British Embassies, the political section concentrates on domestic politics).

Listing the British ministers and departments involved with the Soviet Union and their functions does not, of course, describe how their policy is formulated. One political analyst points out that foreign policy is rarely 'made' or changed in a clear cut and final manner. Changes evolve 'out of an accumulation of small decisions, of adjustments to circumstances and reactions to situations'.[9] Another shows that important and controversial issues (usually referred to as 'high politics') are dealt with by high policy holders in the Cabinet with the help of civil servants and diplomats. Parliament and the media play a critical role in exposing the issues to public debate. Important policy changes in Anglo-Soviet relations are dealt with in this way.

But within the broad framework provided by 'high politics', most foreign policy most of the time concerns less controversial and more routine 'low politics'. It is dealt with by a sectoral process 'based on a set of agreed assumptions about policy within a limited area'.[10] In other words, the FCO and other relevant government departments, with or without the participation of outsiders (interested members of parliament and/or pressure groups) deal with the issues without recourse to high policy holders, by negotiation and consultation within and between 'sectors' (which are separate departments which specialise in particular spheres of government activity).[11] Little media or public attention is paid to these issues; Parliament plays a minor role, although the Cabinet may act as a senior co-ordinating body. The Anglo-Soviet Cultural Agreement is usually negotiated in this way (see chapter 8) and this is how most day-to-day Anglo-Soviet relations are conducted. However, 'low politics' can (sometimes quite suddenly) become controversial and turn into 'high politics'. This can happen in the bilateral relations between any two countries (for example, when one of two trading partners suddenly imposes quotas or tariffs that affect the trading relationship) but it is particularly prevalent in the case of Anglo-Soviet relations, where the bilateral relationship is fundamentally antagonistic.

The conduct of Soviet policy

Until 1989 the Ministry of Foreign Affairs (MFA) was constitutionally responsible for executing Soviet foreign policy which was said to be formulated in the Supreme Soviet (each chamber of which had a Standing Commission on Foreign Affairs which could co-opt specialists) or in its Presidium between Supreme Soviet sessions.[12] Although in practice the Supreme Soviet as a whole rarely debated foreign policy, senior MFA officials reported to the Standing Commissions on Foreign Affairs which did discuss policy. When parliamentary exchanges took place between the Soviet Union and other countries, the Soviet delegates were usually members of one of the Standing Commissions. Gorbachev, for example, paid his first visit to Britain in 1984 as chairman of the Commission on Foreign Affairs of the Supreme Soviet Council of the Union. The new Supreme Soviet which came into being in 1989 as a far stronger parliament will probably have livelier debates on foreign as on domestic policy. The Standing Commissions are likely to monitor MFA performance more searchingly and make some substantive changes to Soviet foreign policy.

The current upgrading of the role of Supreme Soviet notwithstanding, the leading role in Soviet society will probably continue to be played by the CPSU. There is general agreement amongst specialists that foreign policy is formulated by the Politburo of the Party. But since the Politburo deals with all aspects of Soviet policy and is heavily burdened, it must depend upon a number of Party and state institutions for information, recommendations and policy implementation.[13] For the first two of those functions it relied both on the MFA and on the International Department of the Central Committee (for relations with capitalist states) and the Department for Liaison with Socialist States (for relations with socialist states). These two departments acted as Party foreign policy organs parallel to the MFA. In late 1988 they were merged and subordinated to a new umbrella body for the co-ordination of the Party's external policy, the Central Committee Commission on International Affairs headed by Aleksandr Yakovlev.

Implementation of the foreign policy formulated by the Politburo remains the preserve of the MFA. This is the institution that has most to do with day-to-day Anglo-Soviet relations. Its structure is not unlike that of Western foreign ministries. It is divided into geographic and functional departments. The Second European Department has responsibility for Anglo-Soviet relations.[14] The British section within this department consists of three or four people. But contact with Britain is not confined to it. On functional matters – for example, negotiations about chemical weapons, consular matters, or regional conflicts – the British Embassy deals with the relevant department in the MFA. Similarly, in matters of trade the Department of Trade and Industry deals with the foreign trade bodies. Since the reform introduced in January 1987, other Soviet ministries and departments have the right to trade directly with foreign partners and foreign trade will be co-ordinated by the new Foreign Economic Relations Commission (see chapter 10). In the same way that the Soviet Department in the FCO co-ordinates other departments and ministries that have dealings with the Soviet Union, the British section of the MFA liaises with other departments within the MFA or other ministries and state committees that are in contact with Britain, and it also instructs the Soviet Embassy in London which reports to it.

Extensive changes in the MFA under Shevardnadze, not only in personnel but also, and perhaps more importantly, in style, certainly convey the impression that both its professionalism and its prestige have increased. None the less, the role that it plays in policy *formulation* (as opposed to implementation) remains ambiguous. It has a Planning Department which probably formulates the broad outlines of Soviet foreign policy and considers how various aspects of policy are to be co-ordinated. But detailed planning is more likely to have been the preserve of the International Department of the Central Committee (ID).[15]

After Gorbachev became General Secretary of the CPSU, Anatoly Dobrynin was appointed head of the ID. In late 1988 he was replaced by Valentin Falin. Certain structural changes were made within the ID, but it remained divided, like the MFA, into geographic and functional departments, each headed by a deputy head and subdivided into sub-sectors, organised along geo-linguistic or functional lines. Its highly competent and well-educated permanent staff are aided by consultants co-opted from the Academy of Sciences research institutes.[16]

The ID does more, however, than provide information to the Politburo and Secretariat. In effect, its implements the *Party's* foreign policy. It 'has responsibilities for the entire non-Communist world, including state-to-state relations'.[17] While for a time in the late 1980s it appeared that the ID would be playing an important role in state-to-state relations, by 1989 it seemed clear that its main focus was at the party-to-party level. It maintains relations with non-ruling Communist parties and with other political parties, revolutionary groups and national liberation movements. In relation to Western Europe, therefore, it maintains links with Communist, socialist and social democratic parties, encourages socialist–Communist co-operation and attempts to strengthen Soviet–West European relations and to expand Soviet influence. It must, therefore, have similar functions *vis-à-vis* Britain. It contains a British sector which has links with the Labour Party (and therefore indirectly with Ministers when the Labour Party is in power).

As in the British case, listing departments or individuals and their functions does not really explain how policy is made. And it is unlikely that the process is any less complex than in Britain. The Politburo is probably primarily concerned with 'high policy' when substantial doctrinal, personnel and policy changes are considered. In the Soviet case, the ID and MFA both provide the support and information that is provided in Britain by the FCO. The major difference between Soviet and British decision making on matters of 'high politics' is in the function of the media and the public. In Britain, the media may draw public attention to an issue which only then becomes salient to high policy holders and FCO personnel. In the Soviet Union, even with *glasnost'*, it is unlikely that the media and the public could introduce an issue into the foreign policy agenda in an analogous way. It is far more likely that foreign policy issues only reach the public domain when high policy holders give explicit instructions that they should be publicised.

But in the Soviet Union, as in other countries, most foreign policy most of the time concerns 'low politics'. And 'low politics' are probably dealt with by a similar 'sectoral' approach to the one described for Britain. In other words, the MFA and the ID probably negotiate, consult and co-ordinate policy within and between sectors specialising in particular spheres of activity without recourse to high policy holders. But in the Soviet Union, too, 'low politics' may become controversial quite suddenly and turn into 'high politics'.

The higher profile that Anglo-Soviet bilateral relations have taken since 1985 has not been reflected in institutional changes. Although there have been major changes in foreign policy personnel and also alterations to the institutional structures in the Soviet Union since Gorbachev became General Secretary of the CPSU, they are the product of rationalisation and a more general attempt to put the 'new political thinking' into practice. They do not seem to be the result of a particular change in policy towards Britain.

BRITAIN AND THE USSR IN EACH OTHER'S OVERALL FOREIGN POLICY STRATEGY

There are asymmetries between the importance that the Soviet Union has assumed in British foreign policy and the British role in Soviet foreign policy, particularly since World War II. They are a reflection of the relative power each country possesses and the role each plays in its respective alliance structure. But both before and after the war their mutual perceptions of hostility have been more or less symmetrical. Britain loomed large in Soviet demonology as the chief imperialist power and the most likely initiator of the inevitable attack by capitalism upon socialism. British hostility to the Bolshevik regime and its possible pernicious influence on the British Empire was equally strong. These early perceptions continue to affect the role each occupies in the other's foreign policy strategy.

The USSR in Britain's foreign policy strategy

Since the October 1917 Revolution fear of the spread of socialism has often made Western, including British, policy makers attribute to the Soviet leadership 'a unique share of wickedness'. There has been a tendency to discount the idea that Soviet foreign policy might, like any other foreign policy, be based on *raison d'état* and that its primary consideration might be the enhancement of national security.[18] As a result Britain's relations with Soviet Russia since 1917 have always been uneasy. Even when the two countries have been allies in a common cause, each has suspected the other of having other, more nefarious aims.[19]

British policy towards the Soviet Union after 1945 has been characterised as armed vigilance coupled with a search for agreements. In fact, it was perceived by hardliners in the United States and Western Europe as a tendency towards the same kind of appeasement that had produced disastrous consequences in the 1930s. Thus 'by the time President Nixon and Secretary of State Kissinger were making *détente* with Russia the centrepiece of their foreign policy, British ministers had tired the world with talking about it'.[20]

The willingness to negotiate with Soviet leaders has not diminished the perception held by both Labour and Conservative Governments since World War II that Britain's chief adversary is the Soviet Union. While British leaders have traditionally followed a dual policy, on the one hand trying to ensure that their allies remain alert to the danger of Soviet expansion while, on the other hand, attempting to keep bilateral and multilateral channels of negotiation open, occasionally warnings about the Soviet threat have taken precedence over dialogue. This appeared to be the position during the first term in office of the present Conservative Government. Mrs Thatcher's initial attitudes towards the Soviet Union were implacable (they earned her the epithet 'iron lady' in the Soviet Union). Anglo-Soviet political and diplomatic relations fell to a low ebb. In 1983, however, Mrs Thatcher modified her approach and the British Government reverted to its traditional policy. The Soviet Union was still perceived to be hostile, but it was acknowledged that it was a flawed superpower, 'a military giant with political and social feet of clay'.[21] And the fact that after 1985 the Gorbachev leadership itself appeared to recognise that the Soviet economy was ailing and seemed intent on scaling down the size of the military giant while improving the quality of its political and social feet served to make diplomatic and political relations more fruitful without reducing the perceived Soviet threat. But as with détente in the 1970s, there was some scepticism about the 'new political thinking'. Mr Gorbachev might be sincere in wishing to reconstruct the domestic economy but only time would tell whether this had positive implications for Soviet civil rights or Soviet foreign policy. Meanwhile the correct precepts for British policy were 'realism, vigilance, and an open mind',[22] together with the recognition that nuclear deterrence remained the only reliable insurance against a revival of the Soviet threat. In other words, after the brief interlude from 1979 to 1983/84, there has been a return to a policy of a search for agreements combined with armed vigilance.

While mutual perceptions of hostility have mirrored one another since 1945, the importance each country has in the other's foreign policy strategy has become less equal. The fact that the Soviet Union is perceived as Britain's main and most dangerously armed adversary whereas Britain is only one (albeit nuclear) armed adversary of a large number of perceived enemies facing the Soviet Union is the most obvious source of the asymmetry. A great deal of British foreign policy is directly or indirectly concerned with the Soviet Union. But, in contrast to the increasing importance accorded to bilateral relations in French foreign policy when Franco-Soviet détente was launched in the 1960s and in West German foreign policy at the end of that decade when *Ostpolitik* was adopted, Anglo-Soviet bilateral relations seem to have become less salient to British foreign policy than forging co-ordinated policies towards the Soviet Union at other levels.[23] On the one hand, this may be a function of Britian's declining power (and, perhaps more importantly, of the recognition that declining power imposes limitations on British foreign policy). On the other hand, it also reflects a tradition of international co-operation. Britain therefore has 'conceived its function as that of alliance management and multilateral co-operation in East–West relations.'[24] Until recently, therefore, Britain has not attempted to adopt an autonomous policy towards the Soviet Union. As a result, Britain's problem has remained the one to which Curtis Keeble draws attention, namely, how to use bilateral Anglo-Soviet relations to improve general

East–West relations when the latter tend to be dominated by the superpower security relationship.

The aim of all foreign policy is the preservation of security and the enhancement of prosperity. Since the Soviet Union is perceived to be the main threat to British security, the main aim of British foreign and defence policy has been to deal with the threat. British policy within NATO is, of course, directly and almost predominantly concerned with the Soviet threat. The fostering of a 'special relationship' with the United States after World War II was also primarily concerned with achieving a co-ordinated policy *vis-à-vis* the Soviet Union. Once Britain joined the EC and attempts were launched to co-ordinate the foreign policies of the member states, some of that effort also concerned relations with the Soviet Union and the states of Eastern Europe. In other words, even when traditional bilateral relations had become less salient, much of British foreign policy was directed towards the Soviet Union.

In the last few years bilateral relations have become more important. British policy has aimed not only at dealing with the military threat, but also at working through high and low level contacts in the hope of improving the flow of information and reducing the chance of misunderstanding between the two countries. British policy towards the Soviet Union once again includes both defence and dialogue. But the increasing importance accorded to dialogue has generated a new problem: how publicly and privately to exhort the Western Alliance not to lower its guard in the face of an only marginally reduced Soviet threat without losing the momentum of an improved constructive and businesslike bilateral relationship with the Soviet Union.

Britain in the Soviet Union's foreign policy strategy
As we have seen in chapter 3, the predominant Soviet perception of Britain since 1917 has been that Britain, whether led by a Conservative or Labour Government, is hostile to socialism and to the Soviet Union.

At best, British hostility towards the Soviet Union is thought to be punctuated from time to time by sensible leaders who understand that the inevitable competition between the two social systems need not detract from good interstate relations.[25] Those sensible leaders are not necessarily members of the Labour Party. Soviet commentators believe that within the British bourgeoisie as a whole there have always been 'moderate sections' which oppose the 'short-sighted adventurist tendency which has frequently dominated British policy'.[26] Occasionally the moderate sections prevail temporarily over negative tendencies and there is some improvement in Anglo-Soviet relations. But the temporary nature of the improvement lends an inherent instability to the relationship. As a result, Anglo-Soviet relations are 'characterised by extreme changeability, alternating between periods of movement and periods of stagnation.'[27]

It should be stressed that Soviet leaders and political commentators consistently perceive Britain to be the source of the instability in Anglo-Soviet relations. The Soviet Union is always described as constant in its desire for normal and stable relations.[28] Moreover, although Labour Governments are not generally thought to be markedly less anti-Soviet than Conservative Governments, a more positive evaluation is made of the policy of the Labour Government of 1974 which is thought to have put an end to the preceding 'anomaly which had occurred . . . under the Conservative Government, and which was expressed in the way that Britain remained on the sidelines of the process of détente'.[29] By the end of the 1970s, however, the Callaghan Government had, in the Soviet view, changed course, adopting a more hostile attitude towards the Soviet Union. This led to a new deterioration in Anglo-Soviet relations.[30]

Although the policies of Labour Governments are not always interpreted as favourable to good Anglo-Soviet relations, Labour policies in opposition are frequently contrasted positively to those of the Conservative Government of the day. Conservative policies in opposition, on the other hand, rarely receive a favourable Soviet press. But the line taken by Mrs Thatcher when she became leader of the Conservative opposition in 1975 was believed to be more than usually hostile. It seemed to some Soviet analysts to epitomise a move to the right in the Conservative Party which had begun to be noticeable under Mr Heath's leadership. Once in power Mrs Thatcher geared British policy to American strategy. Bilateral Anglo-Soviet relations almost came to a complete halt.[31]

The change in British policy which took place after the 1983 election must have seemed another example of its perennial mutability. By 1985, however, it could be interpreted as a realistically minded response to the 'new political thinking' in the Soviet Union. The British Government's negative attitude to various Soviet nuclear arms proposals has remained a disappointment to the Gorbachev leadership, which claimed to have shown enormous trust in not taking British and French nuclear arms into account during the negotiations to reach the INF treaty signed in December 1987.[32] Mrs Thatcher's insistence that the independent British nuclear deterrent will not be brought into any arms deal until the superpower strategic cuts have gone much further than the 50 per cent presently on the negotiating table indicates that she does not share Mr Gorbachev's conviction that British and French missiles should be included in present negotiations.[33] Moreover, she has played an active role in trying to ensure that NATO nuclear weapons are modernised in the wake of the INF agreement. Despite disagreements about the possible 'denuclearisation of Europe', however, both sides have expressed the determination to build on the present goodwill and understanding between the two leaders.[34] The positive role that Britain has played in breaking the deadlock between the United States and the Soviet Union has been considered particularly valuable by the Soviet leadership.[35]

The British and French nuclear forces present particular difficulties to the
Soviet leadership. Although British nuclear arms are officially part of the NATO
nuclear deterrent, and although they are aimed at the Soviet Union, the British
Government has not agreed to include them in negotiations to reduce either
strategic or intermediate-range missiles. Moreover, the decision to replace
Polaris with Trident was interpreted as an attempt to launch a new round in the
arms race (see chapter 5). It was also said to have been accompanied by an
increase in hostility towards the Soviet Union and by the arrival of Pershing 2
and cruise missiles in Britain. These measures were believed to be aimed at
destabilising the nuclear balance in Europe and achieving NATO military
superiority.[36] They could not fail to have a negative effect on Anglo-Soviet
relations. But by the time Gorbachev visited Britain in December 1984, the
Soviet leadership seemed to have had a change of heart. Political relations could,
it seems, improve despite Britain's nuclear policy. But the problem of where and
when the British independent deterrent will be counted in the nuclear balance
remains to be resolved.

Soviet foreign policy, like British, is aimed at preserving Soviet security and
enhancing prosperity. Since Britain is perceived to threaten Soviet security,
Soviet foreign and defence policy is concerned with dealing with that threat. But
Britain presents less of an independent threat, despite its possession of nuclear
weapons, than it forms part of the combined threat of NATO and, potentially, of
a future militarily integrated EC. And that is why the 'special relationship' and
Britain's role in the EC are important aspects of the role that Britain plays in the
overall foreign policy strategy of the USSR. It can be argued that bilateral
relations have always been important to the Soviet leadership in part because of
the potential effect they might have on the policy of the Western Alliance
towards the Soviet Union and the WTO. But they are also important for their
own sake, irrespective of Britain's influence on either the United States or the
EC. In part this is because of British military power. But good bilateral relations
imply recognition of Soviet status in the international political system and at
least partial acceptance of the avowed aims of Soviet domestic and foreign policy.
In other words, they contribute to the legitimation of the Soviet leadership and
of what it considers the rightful place of the Soviet Union in the international
community of states. Achieving that recognition has been an important aspect of
Soviet foreign policy ever since the October Revolution in 1917. And Britain has
always held a key role in the granting or withholding of that recognition.

ANGLO–SOVIET POLITICAL AND DIPLOMATIC RELATIONS, 1971–1987

In the relatively short time since the early 1970s Anglo-Soviet political and
diplomatic relations have undergone similar vicissitudes to those that have

always characterised the relationship. But the amplitude of change has not been very great. Relations have never become so strained that there has been a danger of rupture. On the other hand, even at the best of times, the level of interaction has not been very intense.

British policy makers tend to explain the vacillations in Anglo-Soviet relations in terms of Soviet policy: British policy is constant and relations deteriorate when the Soviet leadership pursues an aggressive foreign policy (not necessarily towards Britain), when it expands its military power or when it adopts a more repressive domestic policy. Soviet policy makers offer a mirror image explanation. In their view Soviet policy towards Britain is constant. They dismiss the idea that shifts in British policy are responses to Soviet political and military behaviour. They explain the frequent deterioration in Anglo-Soviet relations by reference to a struggle between positive and negative tendencies within the British ruling establishment, both Labour and Conservative. Relations improve when positive tendencies are dominant. But they rarely remain dominant, so Anglo-Soviet relations are characterised by inconstancy.

These two sets of explanations are not necessarily mutually exclusive. Both could contain some truth. But neither explanation is sufficient to explain the instability of the bilateral relationship. Although Soviet foreign, domestic or military policy can cause relations to deteriorate, it is also the case that relations sometimes improve before any change can be noticed in Soviet policy. And although there may be an underlying hostility towards the Soviet Union in British governments irrespective of which party is in power, it is sometimes difficult to detect a shift between tendencies at the time that relations deteriorate or improve. In other words, even if there are times when one or the other explanation for the instability of Anglo-Soviet relations is true, there are other, additional reasons for the changes that occur.

There have been two relatively high points in Anglo-Soviet relations since 1971. The first occurred in 1975 and it lasted until late 1977, when relations began to deteriorate once again. The second began slowly after Mr Gorbachev's visit to Britain in 1984. It has lasted until the present (although the rhetoric that has recently been employed by the British Government with regard to Soviet military policy casts doubt on whether the present amicable relations can be sustained). In both cases there were real improvements in relations. But the improvements seemed more dramatic than they actually were because they followed periods of minimum bilateral contact and publicly expressed hostile attitudes.

After the decision by the British Government to reduce the number of Soviet diplomatic and trade officials in London in 1971 and the expulsion of 105 Soviet representatives for spying, bilateral political and diplomatic links became extremely limited. The Soviet Government responded by expelling British diplomats, journalists and academics (some of whom have only recently been allowed back to the Soviet Union for the first time). Cultural contacts were affected and bilateral trade declined (see chapters 8 and 9).³⁷ Franco-Soviet relations continued to be good during these years and contacts between the two superpowers were particularly active. Moreover, Soviet relations with the FRG expanded after the successful negotiation of the Moscow Treaty (between the USSR and the FRG) and the quadripartite agreement on Berlin. In contrast to this burst of diplomatic and political activity, Anglo-Soviet relations seemed particularly thin. Contacts were gradually resumed in 1972 at the level of the MFA and FCO. The Foreign Ministers of the two countries began meeting soon afterwards from time to time at international conferences. But a public signal that official relations had improved was given when the Duke of Edinburgh and Princess Anne went to the Equestrian Games in Kiev in 1973. In December 1973 Sir Alec Douglas-Home, British Foreign Minister, went to Moscow for talks with Gromyko. Both sides expressed the intention of improving bilateral relations at all levels with the aim of establishing regular consultations. Relations continued to improve in 1974 but France and West Germany were far more active in European détente than was Britain. Soviet policy makers responded by paying far more attention to bilateral relations with those countries than to Anglo-Soviet relations.³⁸

The Labour Government which came to power in 1974 thus inherited an improvement in Anglo-Soviet relations which it developed further. The climax in the improvement of Anglo-Soviet relations in the 1970s was the visit paid to Moscow by Prime Minister Harold Wilson and Foreign Minister James Callaghan in February 1975. A Protocol was signed on regular political consultations, as well as a ten-year agreement on industrial and economic co-operation in science and technology, a long-term agreement on industrial and economic co-operation, an agreement on co-operation in medical and health care and a joint declaration on the non-proliferation of nuclear weapons. During the visit a long-term credit agreement was signed but only a small part of the credit was used and it did little to improve bilateral trade.³⁹ Soviet analysts particularly emphasise the importance of the Protocol since it envisaged regular annual meetings at the level of Foreign Minister or his representative to discuss matters of mutual concern in bilateral relations and international affairs.⁴⁰

It is ironic that 1975 was the climax in this period of improved Anglo-Soviet relations (because of Prime Minister Wilson's visit to Moscow) and in European détente generally (the Final Act of the CSCE was signed in August of that year in Helsinki). There are two reasons for this. First, the two events were barely connected. The British Government remained unimpressed by détente and its rhetoric. British policy remained pragmatic and the Final Act did little to contribute to the improvement in Anglo-Soviet relations. The second reason why it is ironic that 1975 was the climax of détente is that it was also the year in which East–West relations began to deteriorate. Soviet interest in Mozambique and Angola in Southern Africa made Western policy makers suspicious of the real aims of détente.

As far as superpower relations were concerned, the linkage in 1975 by the US Congress of Most Favoured Nation status with freedom of emigration from the USSR marked the beginning of strained relations. Human rights issues acquired a new salience in US foreign policy during the presidential election campaign and it became the dominant theme in Carter's foreign policy. The human rights provisions in the Helsinki Final Act gave Western policy makers ammunition to attack Soviet performance in this field. Disappointment began to be expressed with the results of the CSCE.

Paradoxically, since the British leadership had limited expectations of both détente and the CSCE process, it was rather less disappointed than were the American administration and the other West European governments.[41] The 1975 summit meeting between Brezhnev and Wilson had given a certain momentum to bilateral relations and it took some time for it to wind down.

For the first two years after the meeting there was a considerable amount of activity in Anglo-Soviet relations. A number of different delegations exchanged visits. The International Department of the Central Committee made contact with the Labour Party. A CPSU delegation visited Britain in 1976 headed by Boris Ponomarev.[42] Regular round-table discussions were set up between the Institute of World Economy and International Relations in Moscow and the Royal Institute of International Affairs in London. Bilateral military contacts were initiated. Gromyko visited London in 1976 and when David Owen, the new British Foreign Secretary, paid a return visit in 1977, an agreement was signed on the prevention of accidental nuclear war.[43] But by then both public opinion and government policy had become less enthusiastic about relations with the Soviet Union. The first follow-up meeting of the CSCE had assembled in Belgrade. Soon mutual recriminations by Eastern and Western representatives about non-fulfilment of the Helsinki Final Act lent a negative tone to East–West relations in general, including the bilateral Anglo-Soviet relationship.

Apart from human rights issues and Soviet activity in Southern Africa three sets of events in 1977 and 1978 contributed to the new coolness in Anglo-Soviet relations. The first was the enthusiasm shown by the Labour Government for developing relations with China. The Soviet Government was particularly perturbed by the proposal to sell Harrier jets to the Chinese government. The second was the Cuban/Soviet intervention in Ethiopia in 1977. The third set of events concerned the positive reaction of the Labour Government to the proposal to develop a neutron bomb. The Soviet leadership launched an impassioned campaign against the neutron bomb. British approval of the bomb was interpreted to mean that anti-Soviet tendencies had again come to the fore in

the Labour Party.[44] Thus when the Conservative Party won the general election
in 1979 the new government inherited an already strained relationship with the
Soviet Union. The Conservative Party had itself been growing increasingly
hostile to the Soviet Union since 1975. Soon after the Conservatives came to
power the Soviet Union intervened in Afghanistan in December 1979, bringing
superpower détente to an end and disrupting European détente.

The British response to Soviet actions in Afghanistan was no less disapprov-
ing than that of the American administration. There was, however, some
disagreement between the two governments about the best means of responding
to Soviet action. President Carter was determined to impose economic sanctions
and encouraged his European allies to follow suit. The British Government was
wary of economic sanctions, believing that they were unlikely to alter Soviet
behaviour and that they might even have a negative effect on Soviet policy.
Together with its fellow members of the EC, the British government agreed to
tighten up COCOM policies. They were unwilling, however, to curtail
machinery exports.[45] Nonetheless, the British response to the intervention was
very firm. Anglo-Soviet military exchanges ceased, there was some curtailment
in economic and 'high visibility' cultural relations, although low level exchanges
were unaffected. British athletes were discouraged, but not prohibited, from
attending the 1980 Olympic Games in Moscow (see chapter 8). For a time
communication was reduced to the bare minimum. Visits were cancelled and
Soviet functions boycotted. But there was no intention on the British side of
closing the channels of communication completely between London and
Moscow.[46] In sum, the British response to the intervention in Afghanistan was
more severe than that of France and the FRG. But it was less severe than the
American response.

Despite the cool relations which followed the intervention, some political
contacts were retained by the two governments. Meetings took place between
their respective Foreign Ministers (for example, in May and September 1980
and in July 1981). In 1981 Lord Carrington, in his capacity of Chairman of the
EC Council of Ministers, proposed a plan for settling the Afghan conflict. It
involved a two-stage set of negotiations. The participants in the first stage would
be the permanent members of the UN Security Council, regional powers and the
UN Secretary General. The Afghan Government would not take part until the
second stage, when the rebels would also be invited to construct a new neutral
government. The plan was rejected by the Soviet Union in no uncertain terms.[47]

Although Soviet intervention in Afghanistan continued, bilateral relations
might have improved in due course (as they did, for example, after the 1968
intervention in Czechoslovakia). But Soviet attitudes to developments in Poland
impeded recovery. In December 1981 martial law was declared in Poland in an
attempt to deal with Solidarity. This affected Anglo-Soviet relations and it also

provoked ill-feeling within the Western Alliance. Once again the American administration imposed economic sanctions on both the Polish and the Soviet Governments and pressed its European allies to follow suit. And once again West European Governments were reluctant. When the United States attempted to impose secondary sanctions against European firms that continued supplying equipment for the Urengoi gas pipeline, Atlantic unity was threatened as the disagreement spilled over into other issues.[48] Economic sanctions did not affect Soviet behaviour and the disagreement within NATO did not improve Anglo-Soviet relations. By then the build up of conventional forces in the Warsaw Treaty Organisation (WTO) and the Soviet deployment of SS-20s on the one side, and British support for the decision to modernise NATO intermediate range nuclear forces by deploying Pershing-II and cruise missiles in Europe on the other had given new grounds for mutual suspicion and hostility.

There was a great deal of criticism of the British Government published in the Soviet press as a result of the Falklands War and some diplomatic exchanges on the matter. But it did not really affect Anglo-Soviet relations. In fact, there is reason to believe that the Soviet leadership was secretly impressed by Mrs Thatcher's firm response. The issues which continued to affect bilateral relations were Poland, Afghanistan and disagreements about arms deployments. None the less meetings continued to take place between the MFA and the FCO and between the respective Foreign Ministers. Although they did not produce any concrete results, they demonstrated that relations had not deteriorated to the same extent as they had after the expulsion of the Soviet diplomats ten years previously, although the issues dividing the two countries were far more contentious.

Brezhnev died in November 1982. The initial hopes that Andropov would modify Soviet policy and improve East–West relations were never realised. Whatever he might have intended in the long run, there was little change in Soviet foreign policy and no modification in the Western response. In fact, relations deteriorated sharply when a Soviet fighter plane shot down a South Korean passenger airliner in September 1983. When the deployment of cruise and Pershing-II missiles began, the Soviet team walked out of the arms control negotiations in Geneva. East–West relations had reached their lowest point for years.

After Brezhnev's death there was a growing realisation within the British Government that the hostility that had followed the intervention in Afghanistan and the events in Poland was unproductive and could not be sustained. The American administration's attitude to the Soviet Union had become increasingly intransigent. East–West relations had reached an impasse. A more constructive relationship was required and Britain could perhaps initiate it. In 1983 Mrs Thatcher and Sir Geoffrey Howe decided that the most important foreign policy task facing the government in its second term of office would be to improve Anglo-Soviet relations. But it was not until 1984 that there were signs that the Soviet side, too, wanted to retreat from intransigence. In December 1984 Mr Gorbachev visited Britain at the head of a Supreme Soviet delegation. He made a favourable impression on Mrs Thatcher who declared that he was a man with whom she could do business. Within a very few months he had become General Secretary of the CPSU and she had the opportunity to do just that.

In fact, the issues which divided the two countries remained intractable. The factors which had led, on the British side, to the deterioration were no more acceptable. Soviet troops were still fighting in Afghanistan and Cuban troops were in Angola and Ethiopia. Although martial law had been abandoned in Poland, the position of Solidarity had not improved. SS-20s had continued to be deployed and shorter range SS-12 missiles had been moved forward to the German Democratic Republic and Czechoslovakia. There had been no reduction in WTO conventional troops. The Soviet record on human rights continued to make progress in the CSCE process impossible. On the Soviet side, objections to Western policy had not produced any modification to that policy. Pershing-II and cruise missiles had continued to be deployed in Europe and the decision to replace British Polaris missiles with multi-warhead Trident IIs meant that British nuclear strength would increase dramatically (see chapter 5). The Soviet leadership reacted sharply against the Strategic Defense Initiative (SDI) for which President Reagan was seeking the support of America's allies.[49] What *had* changed on both sides was the political will to embark on constructive dialogue.

Gorbachev soon announced a programme of domestic reforms. He also presided over extensive personnel changes within the MFA and the ID. A new ambassador, Mr L.M. Zamyatin, a full member of the Central Committee (previously head of the now disbanded International Information Department of the Central Committee), arrived in Britain. A new set of principles governing Soviet foreign policy, called the 'new political thinking', was announced. It was accompanied by a new diplomatic style. Soviet diplomacy became more flexible, pleasant and polite. There was less recourse to rigid positions and discussion became more open. On both sides there was more readiness to take the other side's perceptions into account.

The climax of the new period in Anglo-Soviet relations so far has been Mrs Thatcher's visit to Moscow in March 1987. Three agreements (on space co-operation, on improving and upgrading the hotline between the Kremlin and Downing Street and on the mutual provision of new embassy sites) and a memorandum of understanding relating to co-operation in the sphere of information, culture and education were concluded. But perhaps more important than the agreements was the rapport that clearly developed between the two leaders and the warm reception which Mrs Thatcher received in the Soviet Union.

The rapport has not, however, been sufficient to resolve the differences between the two countries. British attempts to persuade the Soviet leadership to agree to a UN Security Council sponsored arms embargo against Iran (for failure to comply with a ceasefire in the Iran–Iraq war), for example, failed. And the Soviet leadership has got no closer to persuading the British Government that short-range nuclear weapons in Europe should be abolished rather than modernised. By the time Sir Geoffrey Howe visited Moscow in February 1988 the tone of both the British Government and the Soviet leadership had become more combative. The visit did not produce any signs of further improvements in bilateral relations. Nor did Mr Gorbachev's visit to London in April 1989, which consolidated the political dialogue yet pointed up continuing differences on arms control issues.

It is clear from this examination of Anglo-Soviet diplomatic and political relations from 1971 to the present that deterioration and improvement are not solely caused either by Soviet conduct (as the British frequently argue) or by a shift in the dominant tendency within the British ruling elite (as Soviet analysts maintain). These factors certainly affect bilateral relations, but there are others which influence them at the same time. One of these factors has already been noted in section 3 above. It concerns Britain's role in the Western Alliance.

British policy towards the Soviet Union has not, in fact, changed very much since 1945. Then the British Government was concerned to ensure a continuing American commitment to Western Europe while trying to maintain multilateral and bilateral dialogue with the Soviet leadership. A British nuclear deterrent was considered essential in case American commitment could not be retained. The insurance of an independent deterrent is still regarded as essential. But since it is a minimum, last-resort deterrent, it is still vital to keep the United States committed to the defence of Europe. It is no less important to maintain East–West dialogue.

The difficulty for British policy makers remains what it was then: how to persuade Britain's European allies to contribute to Western defence and the USA to continue its European commitment while at the same time sustaining a constructive relationship with the Soviet Union. The former task requires raising the level of the perceived Soviet threat, while the latter calls for a softer, more flexible approach. The problem is that when the former approach is too successful, East–West relations tend to become stuck in an impasse. And when the latter is too successful, the Western Alliance seems to be in danger of losing its commitment to the armed defence of Europe. A balance is required, but it is almost impossible to achieve.

The changes in British policy have been caused as much by shifts between these two approaches as by responses to Soviet conduct. Moreover, these are systemic aims which concern the role British policy makers believe that Britain should play in the Western Alliance and in the bipolar balance of power. They are not always compatible with promoting constructive bilateral relations and they are never consonant with stability in the bilateral relationship. Invariably Britain's role in the Western Alliance has taken precedence over bilateral relations.

The Soviet perception that British policy is inconstant is not, therefore, entirely wrong. But this does not mean that Britain is always to blame for a deterioration in Anglo-Soviet relations. Successive Soviet leaders have traditionally found it difficult to accept that Soviet conduct outside of Europe affects its bilateral and multilateral relations in Europe as well as East–West relations in general. They have also shown scant concern for Western security perceptions and little facility for discriminating between messages designed to strengthen or demonstrate Western resolve and those intended more directly to affect the bilateral relationship. They have usually refused, therefore, to modify their conduct elsewhere for the sake of better East–West or Anglo-Soviet relations. And they have been quick to reply to belligerent messages with belligerent responses. Gorbachev, however, seems intent on changing the habits of Soviet foreign policy. He has demonstrated a determination to keep talking even when the initial response is negative and to search for compromise solutions to problems. And the 'new political thinking' defines security as indivisible and stresses the importance of understanding the security concerns of others.

This has not yet had dramatic effects on Anglo-Soviet bilateral relations in the sense of new treaties and agreements, but it is clear that a better working relationship has developed. There appears to be some optimism on the British side that domestic change will occur in the Soviet Union, and some on the Soviet side that more positive changes are possible in Anglo-Soviet relations.

CONCLUSION

Gorbachev maintains that his 1984 visit to Britain and his 1985 visit to France set him thinking about the role and place of Europe in the world. He gained a new awareness that Russia is part of Europe and that Europe requires a 'pan-European policy'.[50] His immediate reaction was to stress the concept of 'Europe as the common home of Europeans'. He also offered to deal with the EC as a political entity.[51]

If Britain is regarded as one of the major members of the EC and if Gorbachev is intent on developing a new European policy, then Anglo-Soviet bilateral relations clearly must be considered an integral part of this initiative. But bilateral relations with France and the FRG would obviously be considered equally or more important by the Soviet leadership. And yet a comparison of Mrs Thatcher's reception when she visited the Soviet Union in March 1987 and that of the French Prime Minister a short while later suggests that Anglo-Soviet relations are more salient to the Soviet leadership at present than Franco-Soviet relations. Similarly, Soviet relations with the FRG have not been as warm or as active as relations with Britain (although they have improved markedly since 1987). Does this mean that Britain has come to be regarded as more important than either of the two other large countries in the EC? Or is it that Mrs Thatcher has been in power for longer than her French and German colleagues and is, therefore, perceived to be the more senior and the more important statesperson? Is it merely a question of personalities and the fact that Mrs Thatcher has developed a better personal relationship with Mr Gorbachev than either President Mitterand or Chancellor Kohl? On the other hand, has the Soviet leadership adopted a divisive strategy?

The answer to these questions probably lies less in the relative importance of those countries than in the response of their leaders to Gorbachev's domestic and foreign initiatives. The Soviet leadership tends to respond positively to approval and Mrs Thatcher's positive assessment of Soviet *perestroika* has been appreciated. The more it is confirmed by increased contacts and concrete agreements, the Soviet leadership probably calculates, the harder it will be for her to backtrack on her present policy. And the fact that she previously took hardline positions towards the Soviet Union is valuable in this regard. For one thing, it highlights the change in *Soviet* policy, for what else could have prompted Mrs Thatcher's conversion? For another, it makes it more likely that other world leaders and politicians will be won over to the 'new political thinking' by her example. Her support of the INF agreement, for example, was considered important in reassuring the US Senate that it was safe to ratify the treaty.

Anglo-Soviet relations have an intrinsic value for the Soviet leadership. Good relations help to legitimise the changes which are taking place in the Soviet Union. And the aim of the Soviet leadership is probably to unite the Western Alliance in policies favourable to the Soviet Union. In other words, Anglo-Soviet relations are also useful because of the positive effects they may have on Soviet relations with other countries, including both the United States and the countries of Western Europe.

From the Soviet point of view, there are two serious impediments to further improvements under the present Government. First, the British Government remains firmly committed to the continuation of nuclear deterrence while the Gorbachev leadership is in favour not only of a nuclear-free Europe, but of a nuclear-free world. Second, it is almost inconceivable that the present British Government would agree to negotiate reductions in Britain's nuclear forces. If the Soviet leadership entertained any doubts on either of these issues, they must have been dispelled by the decision to invest in a new air-launched missile for the RAF and Mrs Thatcher's stance in favour of the modernisation of NATO tactical weapons at the NATO summit meeting in Brussels at the beginning of March 1988.[52] The removal of these impediments requires a Labour Government. But this presents a dilemma to the Soviet leadership. For one thing, it is not unknown for Labour Governments to renege on their manifesto promises and, in any case, the Labour Party has now abandoned its belief in a non-nuclear policy. For another, many of the advantages of good relations with a previously implacably hostile Western leader who is, at the same time, a senior international statesperson would be lost if the Conservative Party lost power. And finally, there is the danger that a non-nuclear Britain would provoke a more hardline policy towards the Soviet Union in the United States or encourage Franco-German nuclear co-operation.

From the British point of view the same impediments exist. In other words, if Gorbachev insists that British nuclear weapons must be reduced if Anglo-Soviet relations are to improve further, the British Government is unlikely to make concessions. The present policy is based on vigilance and an open mind. No matter how far the domestic changes go in the Soviet Union, it is unlikely that British vigilance will be lowered to the extent of abandoning nuclear defence. On the contrary, there have been signs recently that British nuclear vigilance is to increase and a resolute NATO defence policy is to be encouraged. Both sides face a challenge if bilateral political and diplomatic ralations are to fulfill the hope and optimism expressed by their leaders in their first few encounters.

NOTES

1. See M. S. Gorbachev, Political Report to the 27th Congress of the CPSU, *Pravda*, 26 February 1986; M. S. Gorbachev, Speech at the meeting in honour of the 70th anniversary of the October Revolution, *Literaturnaia gazeta*, 4 November 1987, p. 4 for the 'new political thinking'. For Gorbachev's views on Europe, see M. S. Gorbachev, *Perestroika: New Thinking for Our Country and The World* (Collins, 1987), pp. 190–5.
2. See P. A. Reynolds, *An Introduction to International Relations* (2nd ed. Longmans, 1980), chapter 6 for the instruments of foreign policy.
3. James Barber (*Who Makes British Foreign Policy?* (Open University Press, 1976,) p. 22) points out that usually 'while the Cabinet is kept informed, it seldom debates foreign policy'.
4. *Ibid.*, pp. 14–17.
5. There are a number of functional departments within the FCO that deal directly with the Soviet Union over which the Soviet Department keeps a watching brief. The new Narcotics and Aids department has been a beneficiary of the 'new political thinking' in the Soviet Union and there has been increasing co-operation in those fields.

Among the government ministries that are currently actively involved in bilateral contacts with the Soviet Union are the Department of Energy (particularly after the Chernobyl accident and as a result of the initiatives undertaken by Peter Walker); the Department of Agriculture; the Department of Health; and the Department of Trade and Industry, which has responsibility for the Joint Consultative Commission, established in 1968 to monitor the progress of Anglo-Soviet economic, scientific and technological co-operation agreements. See Malcolm R. Hill, *East–West Trade, Industrial Co-operation and Technology Transfer: The British Experience* (Gower, 1983), pp. 179–80.

6. There is a difference between the goals that the British and Soviet governments hope to achieve through cultural relations. In Britain the hope is that they will help to break down barriers and get more information across about Britain. John Morison argues (see chapter 8) that the British Government tends to use the Cultural Agreement as a means of developing bilateral political relations. The Soviet Government tends to channel and control its cultural relations rather more purposively. Apart from wanting to impart information about the Soviet Union, it is often thought to use cultural relations to acquire technology. Thus in scholarly and scientific exchanges, the British side favours the humanities and social sciences, while the Soviet side prefers sending natural and technical scientists to Britain.

7. Barber, *Who Makes British Foreign Policy?* p. 50.

8. *Information Moscow* (Jupiter Press, Spring–Summer 1986). The number of British diplomates fluctuates as a result both of the normal traffic as diplomats change their postings and of the tit-for-tat expulsions that have become a feature of Western–Soviet diplomatic relations. The British Embassy, like the Embassies of other European countries, employs a number of locals. (The American Embassy used to employ Russians but after the expulsion of Soviet diplomats from the UN mission in New York, the Soviet government retaliated by withdrawing local employees from the American Embassy.)

9. William Wallace, *The Foreign Policy Process in Britain* (Royal Institute for International Affairs, 1975), p. 6. Charles Lindblom, *The Policy Making Process* (Prentice Hall, 1980) calls this process 'disjointed incrementalism'.

10. Barber, *Who Makes British Foreign Policy?* quote on pp. 43–4.

11. Wallace, *The Foreign Policy Process*, pp. 4–11.

12. *Constitution (Fundamental Law) of the Union of Soviet Socialist Republics* (Novosti Press Agency Publishing House, 1985).

13. Although Soviet foreign policy specialists rarely comment on Soviet decision making, Valentin Falin, then a senior member of the Central Committee apparatus, has been quoted as saying that 'all foreign policy and national security questions must be discussed and decided in the Politburo' (Gottemoeller, quoting Henry Brandon, in Robbin F. Laird and Erik P. Hoffmann, *Soviet Foreign Policy in a Changing World* (Aldine, 1986), p. 160). A prominent Soviet *émigré* maintains that the MFA is directly responsible to the Politburo and not to the Council of Ministers or the Central Committee departments. The MFA initiates policy and only in rare cases does the Politburo fail to adopt a ministry proposal. (Arkady N. Shevchenko, *Breaking with Moscow* (Knopf, 1985), p. 187). The Politburo has a foreign policy committee, but its composition is unclear. Shevchenko, for example, maintains that the circulation of some information is restricted to the General Secretary and a few others.

14. A Soviet textbook on the diplomatic service listed 17 territorial and 16 functional departments in 1977. It also maintained that the Foreign Minister supervises the foreign dealings of other ministries and authorities. See V. Zorin, *Osnovy diplomaticheskoi sluzhby* 2nd ed. (Mezhdunarodnye otnosheniia, 1977), p. 126. The MFA underwent a *perestroika* in the middle of 1986. The Second European Department used to deal with Britain, Ireland, Canada, Australia and New Zealand. Canada has been transferred to the US department, Australia and New Zealand have joined the newly formed Pacific department and Scandinavia has been added to the Second European department.

15. Elizabeth Teague ('The foreign departments of the Central Committee of the Communist Party of the Soviet Union', *RFE-RL Research Bulletin Supplement*, 27 October 1980) points to the frequent interchange of personnel between the Central Committee foreign departments and the MFA. A prominent recent example was the appointment of Dobrynin as head of the International Department after twenty-four years as Soviet Ambassador to Washington. Teague believes that the Central Committee foreign departments play the leading role in formulating policy and are superior in the hierarchy to the MFA (p. 27). Shevchenko, as we have seen (fn. 13), takes the opposing view, but maintains that 'Despite tensions that sometimes arise from overlapping each other's turf, diplomats and ideologues in the Central Committee more often than not try to compromise their differences' (p. 189). For another view that the MFA is more important than the ID, see A. Brown, 'The foreign policy-making process', in C. Keeble, ed., *The Soviet State. The Domestic Roots of Soviet Foreign Policy* (Gower for RIIA, 1985), p. 215, n.37.

16. The academic consultants co-opted to the ID conduct in–depth research and long-range studies. They also draft doctrinal statements. The Institute of World Economy and International Relations and the Institute of the USA and Canada are the major providers of this expertise. See Kitrinos, in Laird and Hoffman, *Soviet Foreign Policy*, pp. 194–7.

17. Brown, 'The foreign policy-making process', p. 203.

18. F.S. Northedge and Audrey Wells, *Britain and Soviet Communism: The Impact of a Revolution* (Macmillan, 1982), p. 134.

19. F.S. Northedge, 'Russia and the lessons of history', *Millennium: Journal of International Studies*, 11:1 (Spring 1982), p. 52.

20. Northedge and Wells, *Britain and Soviet Communism*, pp. 6, 133–4, quote on p. 6. The belief in Britain that diplomatic relations with Soviet Russia were necessary despite the nature of the regime can be traced back to the early years after the revolution. See, for example, Lloyd George's explanation after the failure of the Genoa conference in Stephen White, *The Origins of Détente: The Genoa Conference and Soviet-Western Relations, 1921–1922* (Cambridge University Press, 1985), pp. 192–4.

21. Sir Geoffrey Howe, 'East–West relations: the British role', *International Affairs*, 63:4 (Autumn 1987), p. 556.

22. *Ibid.*, p. 558.

23. Elizabeth Young, 'Britain: lowered guard', in G. Ginsburg and A.Z. Rubinstein, eds., *Soviet Foreign Policy Toward Western Europe* (Praeger, 1979), p. 148.

24. Angela Stent, 'The USSR and Western Europe', in Laird and Hoffman, *Soviet Foreign Policy*, p. 451. Frankel maintains that the outstanding characteristic of British foreign policy is a tradition of international co-operation. See J. Frankel,

British Foreign Policy 1945–1973 (Oxford University Press, 1975) pp. 119–24.

25. See, for example, V. I. Gantman, ed. *Razriadka i konfrontatsiia: dve tendentsii v sovremmenykh mezhdunarodnykh otnosheniiakh* (Nauka, 1987), p. 254.

26. V. Matveev, 'Krupny shag na puti pretvoreniia v zhizn' Programmy mira: K itogam sovetsko–angliiskoi vstrechi na vysshem urovne', *Kommunist*, 4 (1975), p. 46.

27. Gantman, *Razriadka*, p. 252.

28. See, for example, *ibid.*, pp. 252–3 and the statement made by Gromyko on arrival in Britain in 1970, *Pravda*, 27 October 1970.

29. Matveev, 'Krupny', p. 49.

30. A. A. Gromyko and B. N. Ponomarev, eds., *Soviet Foreign Policy 1945–80* (Progress, 1981), p. 617.

31. *Ibid.*, p. 618.

32. Mikhail Gorbachev, *Perestroika*, pp. 202–9.

33. Mrs Thatcher's answer to questions at the press conference following her meeting with Mr Gorbachev at Brize Norton, reported in *The Guardian*, 8 December 1987.

34. House of Commons Debates (HCD), 2 April, 1987 and see Gorbachev, *Perestroika*, p. 202.

35. See, for example, the interview with Zagladin, reported in *The Guardian*, 28 May 1987; Mr Gorbachev's statement at Brize Norton, reported in *The Guardian*, 8 December 1987.

36. On the decision to deploy cruise and Pershing missiles in Europe, see Brezhnev's report to the 26th Congress of the CPSU in L. I. Brezhnev, *Izbrannye proizvedeniia*, Vol. 3 (Izd-vo politicheskoi literatury, 1981), p. 503; on counting British nuclear weapons, see Y. V. Andropov, *Speeches and writings* (Pergamon, 1983), p. 312; and on Trident, see Gantman, *Razriadka*, p. 260.

37. For the year-to-year changes in Anglo-Soviet trade, see chapter 9. It should be noted that some analysts believe that factors other than the expulsion of Soviet diplomats affected bilateral trade. For example, bilateral trade was affected when Britain joined the EC in 1973. The enlarged Community assumed powers to conduct commercial policy with the Eastern bloc on behalf of its members. See Elizabeth Young, 'Britain: lowered guard', p. 141.

38. Compare, for example, Brezhnev's treatment of Franco-Soviet and Soviet–West German relations in his foreign policy speeches in these years to his neglect of Anglo-Soviet relations. See L. I. Brezhnev, *O vneshnei politike KPSS i Sovetskogo gosudarstva: Rechi i stat'i* (Politicheskoi literatury, 1973).

39. Gantman, *Razriadka*, pp. 254–6. See chapter 9 for fluctuations in trade. Soviet export earnings had been boosted by the OPEC price rises and commercial suppliers offered better terms for credits. On the credit agreement, see *ibid.*, p. 250 and Hill, *East–West Trade*, pp. 179–80.

40. See, for example, Gantman, *Razriadka*, p. 255. Note, however, that despite the improvement in Anglo-Soviet relations, Brezhnev concentrated on Franco-Soviet and Soviet–West German relations in his report to the 25th Congress of the CPSU. See L. I. Brezhnev, *Izbrannye proizvadeniia*, pp. 18–77.

41. Phil Williams, in Kenneth Dyson, ed., *European Détente: Case studies of the Politics of East–West Relations* (Frances Pinter, 1986), pp. 221–4.

42. Party contact would, in the Soviet view, have a beneficial influence on bilateral state relations. See Gromyko and Ponomarev, *Soviet Foreign Policy*, p. 616.

43. An account of these activities is given in *ibid.*, pp. 616–17.

44. For typical official Soviet views of the neutron bomb, see Brezhnev's replies to questions by a *Pravda* correspondent, 24 December 1977, in Leonid Brezhnev, *Peace, Détente and Soviet–American Relations* (Harcourt Brace Jovanovich, 1979), pp. 196–7 and A. A. Gromyko, 'Practical ways of ending the arms race: speech at a Special Session of the UN General Assembly devoted to disarmament, 26 May 1978' in A. A. Gromyko, *Peace Now, Peace for the Future: Selected Speeches and Writings* (2nd ed.; Pergamon Press, 1984), p. 27. The downturn in Anglo-Soviet relations and in Labour Party attitudes to the Soviet Union is described in Gantman, *Razriadka*, pp. 256–7.

45. Angela Stent, 'Economic Strategy', in Edwina Moreton and Gerald Segal eds., *Soviet Strategy Toward Western Europe* (Allen and Unwin, 1984), pp. 228–9. For a discussion of the use of sanctions in East–West relations, see Philip Hanson, *Western Economic Statecraft in East–West Relations: Embargoes, Sanctions, Linkage, Economic Warfare and Détente*, Chatham House Papers 40 (Routledge and Kegan Paul for the Royal Institute of International Affairs, 1988), chapter 6.

46. House of Commons, Fifth Report from the Foreign Affairs Committee, Session 1979–80. *Afghanistan: The Soviet Invasion and the Consequences for British Policy.* HC 745 (HMSO, 1980).

47. *Pravda*, 5 August 1981.

48. Stent, 'Economic Strategy', pp. 229–30.

49. A few months later Sir Geoffrey Howe made a public speech (published in *Journal of the Royal United Services Institute for Defence Studies*, June, 1985, pp. 3–8) which cast doubt on both the feasibility and the wisdom of SDI. Nonetheless, the British government soon decided to join the scheme of co-operation between Europe and the USA which offered research contracts and the technological spin-offs they might produce in return for support for SDI research.

50. Gorbachev, *Perestroika*, pp. 190–5, quote on p. 195.

51. Report on Gorbachev's visit to France in *The Guardian*, 4 October 1985. See also *Warsaw Treaty: New Initiatives*, Documents of the Meeting of the Political Consultative Committee of the Member States of the Warsaw Treaty Organization, Budapest, June 10–11 1986 (Novosti Press Agency Publishing House, 1986), p. 25.

52. For reports on the air-launched missile to be carried by Tornado fighter-bombers and the NATO summit, see *The Observer*, 6 March 1988.

7 The Soviet Union and the Left in Britain

MIKE BOWKER AND PETER SHEARMAN

In this chapter we first examine Soviet perceptions of the 'Left' in Britain, for an assessment of Soviet views will provide us with a clearer understanding of what motivates Soviet policy in relation to such important groups as the Labour Party, the trade unions or the peace movement. The second part of the chapter assesses, in the light of Soviet perceptions, interactions between the Soviet Union and these major components of the British Left during the 1980s.

The sources that are available are ultimately all under the control of the CPSU and are heavily censored, which severely limits the freedom of individuals to express their views openly and candidly. Yet these limitations are also in a way advantageous, for until very recently what is permitted to be published is likely to reflect the dominant views of the political elite at any particular time. Furthermore, if there does exist any polarisation of views among the political elite this too may be identified in the opposing positions among the academic community. Published views though, given the nature of the Soviet political system, often contradict what proponents of these views say in private conversation. In order to compensate for this problem, and to complement our analysis, we interviewed a number of representatives of the Left who have direct dealings with Soviet officials.

Under the broad term 'the Left' we have decided to focus on four groups: the Labour Party, trade unions, the Communist Party of Great Britain (CPGB), and the peace movement. Some readers will take issue with us for leaving out other groups. But our choice was made on the basis of the importance these groups have in *Soviet* perceptions of the Left in Britain, which is our subject. The Labour Party is the leading representative of the Left in the country; it has been in government and is the most likely alternative to the Conservatives to form the next government. Trade unions are seen as the leading representatives of the working class; they play an important role in industrial relations, and they are influential in the Labour Party. The CPGB is still seen as the leftist organisation most sympathetic to the Soviet Union which plays an important role in the workers' movement. Placing the peace movement in the broad category of the Left is more debatable, but the Soviets have looked upon it as representing the interests of the 'masses', and one interesting question here is the extent to which they attempted to influence the peace movement for Soviet foreign policy objectives.

THE LABOUR PARTY

The Labour Party's attitude towards the Soviet Union has been mixed, and has shifted over time. In 1920 the Labour Party annual conference passed a resolution calling for a general strike if the British Government provided military support for the Poles following their intervention against Russia in April of that year. In 1939 the Labour Party condemned the Russian invasion of Poland. Allied with the Soviet Union against fascist Germany, the Labour Party sang the praises of the glorious Red Army. In 1956 and 1968 the Labour Party condemned Soviet military interventions in Eastern Europe. In the middle of the 1970s the Labour Government was forging ahead in developing economic and political ties with the Soviet Union. In the late 1970s the Labour Party was condemning Soviet violations of human rights. In the middle of the 1980s the Labour Party was calling for unilateral nuclear disarmament and for a more co-operative relationship with Moscow. Whilst these attitudes to the USSR are not necessarily contradictory, based as they are on changing circumstances and changes in Soviet behaviour, they do indicate an ambiguity in the Labour Party's attitude towards the world's first socialist state, an ambiguity which can be traced back to the Russian Revolution of 1917.[1]

I. E. Gorodetskaia produced an interesting study in the middle 1970s which was unusual in attaching an important role to the electoral process and to parliamentary politics in the struggle for 'left, democratic forces'. Using Western sources on voting behaviour and political culture in Britain, she portrays a complex society not simply based on two opposing classes, but rather comprising a diverse range of stratification based upon political, economic, social and demographic factors.[2] She seems to accept that the government in Britain, of whatever hue, is at least in part accountable to the wider British population, and not just the capitalist class. She further notes that Britain has 'long democratic traditions', and cites Lenin when referring to the English as 'cherishing their political freedoms' to a greater extent than they do in the continental European countries.[3] Whereas earlier Soviet specialists condemned the Labour Party for its 'reformism', especially in the Stalinist period, Gorodetskaia seeks to explain it in the context of British political history and political culture.

During the 1970s and early 1980s positive or negative Soviet assessments of the Labour Party depended to a very great extent on the party's position on international issues, particularly détente. The Wilson and Callaghan Governments were largely perceived to have had a positive effect on the easing of international tensions. Likewise, Ryzhikov noted that relations between the USSR and Britain improved substantially during this period, although there still existed sharp contradictions between words and deeds in the realm of disarmament and independence from the United States. (Ryzhikov, for example, refers to Denis Healey at this time as a 'rabid anti-communist', a perception that would change in the 1980s.)[4]

A continued emphasis on the 'special relationship' between the USA and Britain led the Labour Government of the 1970s to support US policies in Vietnam and the Middle East.[5] Many Soviet studies of this period note that a significant number of leading Labour Party officials saw détente as a one-way process benefiting only the Soviet Union. Strong criticism was made of Callaghan's decision to accept the deployment of US cruise and Pershing II missiles in Britain.[6] Nevertheless, in general the Labour Party was seen to be taking a more realistic view of Britain's limited role in global politics epitomised by its retreat from East of Suez. Towards the end of the 1970s Moscow saw Labour as the more predictable, 'realistic' and 'constructive' party with which to conduct bilateral UK–Soviet relations. This perception increased during the first years of the Thatcher Government and into the 1980s. The splits in the Labour Party in the 1980s, with the resultant constitutional changes and formation of the Social Democratic Party, were perceived to be of critical importance in Moscow, marking a major advance for the left wing. The constitutional changes calling for reselection of MPs and the establishment of an electoral college for electing the party leader and deputy leader were seen in a very positive light in the Soviet Union. According to S. P. Peregudov of IMEMO these changes in the Labour Party caused 'deep alarm' among the 'British establishment' out of fear that now unilateral nuclear disarmament and other left-wing policy prescriptions would be supported by a leadership accountable to the mass membership.[7] Soviet commentaries were generally optimistic about the political prospects of the Left, noting that the split in Labour ranks had driven out of the party many of the reformist right-wing leaders who had always distanced themselves from the 'masses' and tended to uphold the position of the bourgeoisie.[8] But even here, however, they recognised that the formation of the SDP, supported by the British establishment, restricted the electoral chances of Labour in forming another government.[9]

Throughout the 1980s, then, Soviet perceptions of the Labour Party have been for the most part very positive, seeing the party now as firmly committed to 'realistic' and 'constructive' policies. These relate more to foreign than they do to domestic politics, marking a continuation of the linkage between Soviet perceptions and the Labour Party's stance on issues directly affecting the USSR.

This refers in particular to Labour's position on issues of nuclear disarmament and détente. The Labour leadership under Kinnock is seen as being consistently committed to nuclear disarmament and for a more co-operative economic relationship with the socialist bloc. Furthermore, with the constitutional changes in the party, the leadership is now seen as less likely to renege on conference decisions and to be therefore more likely to carry out in government what it says it intends to do when in opposition. One Soviet report of Kinnock and Healey's Washington visit just before the 1987 British General Election noted that even in the face of strong US pressure the Labour leaders maintained their unilateral stance. This, it was said, is evidence of 'new thinking'. It has been pointed out by many commentators in Britain that Healey's position did indeed reflect 'new thinking', given his previous stance on nuclear disarmament. But whereas many British editorials interpreted Healey's new thinking as opportunism, the Soviets saw it as reflecting genuine new thinking related to new concepts of international security.[10] Previous Labour leaderships have been condemned by the Soviets for 'opportunism', and perhaps the most significant change in perceptions during the past decade concerns Labour's foreign and defence policy orientations.

A number of recent Soviet evaluations of social democratic and labour parties in Western Europe have stressed that, despite ideological differences, they are coming to share with the Communist parties a common position on important issues of peace, disarmament, and détente.[11] Gorbachev expressed a similar view at the 27th congress of the CPSU, and then again in his report to the Kremlin meeting celebrating the seventieth anniversary of the Russian Revolution, where he noted that social democratic and labour parties are playing an increasingly important and influential political role in international relations.[12]

We will see now how this is reflected in Soviet interactions with the Labour Party during the 1980s. The Labour Party in power during the 1960s and 1970s had not been a major force in the European détente process – the principal actors were the West Germans and the French. It is clear that the Soviets have correspondingly accorded the British Labour Party less attention and taken it less seriously than they have the French Socialist Party and the German Social Democratic Party (SPD). Between 1975 and 1985 the NEC only once, in 1981, invited an 'observer' from the CPSU to the annual party conference. Although erratic, the NEC has extended invitations far more often to the other ruling parties in Eastern Europe, with the exception of Czechoslovakia. In 1981 a Labour Party parliamentary delegation led by Michael Foot and Denis Healey paid a visit to Moscow. That same year the Soviet Union sent an observer to the party conference at Brighton, and official correspondence was exchanged between the two parties on defence and disarmament issues. However the following year, due to Labour condemnation of the Polish Government's actions against the Solidarity trade union movement, relations and interactions reached a low ebb. Relations again began to improve following Neil Kinnock's election to the leadership and the Labour Party's expressed commitment to unilateral nuclear disarmament.

Kinnock and Healey visited Moscow in November 1984, and were given a very warm welcome by senior party officials and an audience with General Secretary Chernenko. Although the Soviet media gave far more prominence to the announced resumption in superpower negotiations set for the New Year in Geneva, the Labour Party delegation was taken very seriously.[13] Kinnock and Healey had six separate meetings with Boris Ponomarev, head of the International Department and candidate Politburo member, and four meetings with his deputy, Vadim Zagladin. Healey, well experienced with many previous meetings with Soviet officials, was very impressed with Zagladin whom he found to be friendly, open and intelligent. For the first time in his dealings with the Soviets Healey felt that 'he was having a real conversation with a Soviet leader and not just having a prepared position or propaganda speech'.[14] With Kinnock, seen as a committed unilateralist, being elected leader of the party, the Kremlin was clearly taking Labour's defence policy seriously. In his talks with Kinnock and Healey, Chernenko stated that if a future Labour Government did give up Britain's nuclear forces and closed down American nuclear bases then the Soviet Union would reduce and dismantle a corresponding number of its nuclear forces. Although the Soviet leadership encouraged the Labour Party to adopt a unilateralist stance, and made what was clearly a serious response, the Soviets were nevertheless somewhat dubious about Labour's commitment to implement such a policy should it gain power. But at least now the Soviet Union was seeking to establish a closer, more constructive relationship with the British Labour Party. Whilst still not given the same level of attention as the major parties of the left in France and West Germany, Labour was being courted to a much greater degree than hitherto.

With Gorbachev's rise to power this process of improving the Soviet ties with socialist and social democratic parties in the West has gained momentum. Healey and George Robertson, Labour frontbench spokesman on Foreign Affairs, attended the VE Day celebrations in Moscow in 1985, where they were accorded a great deal of attention from Soviet officials and the media. Healey was treated with considerable respect. The two Labour MPs were accommodated in the special CPSU Central Committee hotel in Moscow. The visit took place just before the sweeping personnel and policy changes that followed the succession of Gorbachev to the head of the Soviet Communist Party. Robertson commented on the fact that Foreign Minister Gromyko then still appeared to be very much in control of Soviet foreign policy, noting that he 'was already negotiating at Potsdam well before I was born'.[15]

Just one year later Robertson headed a Labour Party delegation to the 27th Congress of the CPSU, where he was struck by a 'dramatic sea change which will have its repercussions far beyond Russia'.[16] The remarkable thing here, of course, is that the Labour Party and other socialist parties were invited to participate in a congress of the Soviet Communist Party which in previous years had been restricted to fraternal Communist parties and a number of national liberation movements. Clearly the Soviet leadership was changing its attitude to non-Communist parties of the Left, in part as a recognition of their much greater influence and prospects for power in their respective countries.

Whilst it is perhaps interesting to draw some comparisons between Thatcherism and Gorbachevism, there is actually a remarkably close correspondence between Labour Party foreign policy proposals and 'new thinking' in Soviet foreign policy. For example, if one compares the Labour Party programme for the 1987 election, *Modern Britain in a Modern World*, with many of Gorbachev's speeches on foreign affairs, the two parties share a number of complementary policy goals.[17] Both talk of the need for a 'new détente', of 'collective security', a 'nuclear test ban', 'no first use' of nuclear weapons, 'mutual problem solving', 'disarmament', increased trade between East and West, a review of COCOM restrictions, multilateral links between the EEC and the CMEA, and a greater role for international organisations such as the UN. Gorbachev has stressed that these objectives are for the mutual advantage of all nation states, irrespective of different ideologies – a sentiment echoed by Robertson in the interview he gave to an *Izvestiia* correspondent during his attendance at the 27th Congress.

That the Soviet leadership under Gorbachev seem intent on broadening contacts with a wider spectrum of the European Left than the traditional Moscow-oriented communist parties was underlined by the invitations issued to socialist parties to attend the Kremlin meeting in November 1987 celebrating the seventieth anniversary of the Russian Revolution. Again Robertson headed the British Labour Party delegation, and once more the Soviet hosts were far more attentive to the British socialists, compared to other European socialists present, than hitherto. Labour Party contacts with the Soviet Communist Party have increased sharply since Gorbachev came to power, which is indicative of what appears to be a genuine attempt to forge some common ideological ground in rethinking the broad Left's attitudes on fundamental issues of international relations. In addition the Soviet leader wishes to gain support among leading political parties and opinion makers in Western Europe for his disarmament and arms control policies. During Mrs Thatcher's visit to the Soviet Union in 1987 Gorbachev made it clear that disarmament was one of his chief concerns, and that: 'At this critical moment for Europe, it is its nuclear powers – Britain and France – that we are addressing in the first place.'[18]

THE COMMUNIST PARTY OF GREAT BRITAIN

Communist parties in developed capitalist societies are regarded, in Soviet ideological formulations, as the vanguard of the working class, a central component of the 'world revolutionary process'. Therefore, unlike the Labour Party, the CPGB's strategy and tactics are supposedly based upon a scientific mode of analysis and are part of an integral political alliance of Communist parties actively pursuing a socialist path of development.[19]

Whatever one's ideology, the weak position of the CPGB in British politics has to be acknowledged. Established in 1920, its electoral fortunes have never come close to matching those of Communist parties in a number of other West European countries. In the same year that the CPGB was formed the Independent Labour Party made an application to join the newly created Comintern (Third International), but the response from Moscow 'was such a fierce and abrasive condemnation of the ILP and its leaders that much support was alienated'.[20] The British Communist Party was to become the officially accredited representative of the working class in the Moscow-controlled Comintern, and has retained close (although not always tension-free) relations with the CPSU ever since. However the CPGB has never posed a real challenge to Labour in a competition for working-class support, either in terms of membership or in elections. So how does the Soviet Union view the Communist Party and its marginalised role in British society?

Many of the books and articles on British politics already cited devote very few pages to the CPGB, reflecting its lack of influence in the conduct of UK–Soviet bilateral state-to-state relations. For example, recalling his visit to Britain in the spring of 1956 Khrushchev does not even mention meeting members of the CPGB, but provides much detail of his meetings with Eden and other government ministers, opposition Labour leaders, military figures and the Queen.[21] Most Soviet scholars do give a little space to the party, usually contrasting its solid class position with the Labour leadership's reformism, opportunism, and anti-Sovietism. Many also point to a split in the Labour Party, between its right-wing leadership and more peace-loving and radical left-wing mass membership. Yet, of course, if the leadership is out of tune with the working class, then the latter do have an alternative in the form of the Communist Party, which is said to represent its interests. Why then has membership in and voting for the CPGB remained so weak?

Part of the answer for some Soviet British specialists seems to lie in what one may term national distinctions. For example, Gorodetskaia contrasts the weak position of the British Communist Party with its counterparts in France and Italy, noting the proverbial British tendency to compromise rather than take extreme opposing positions. In the context of British political history and culture she notes also the lasting and powerful role of certain traditions which has led to a rather conservative society (here she refers to opinion polls showing that even the working class is very strongly in favour of retaining the monarchy as an institution). Gorodetskaia uses this to explain the 'false class consciousness' among British workers, and hence the weak position of the Communist Party compared to France and Italy.[22]

Other writers tend to stress the structure of capitalism which controls the entire system from the ideological apparatus through to the political and judicial institutions. Zagladin notes that the CPGB is much weaker politically than the Communist parties in France, Italy, Finland, Portugal and Greece, having no parliamentary representation or mass support among the electorate, but that it does have considerable influence in the trade union movement.[23]

Recognising that the Communist Party has no chance of gaining power through the ballot box, Soviet writers do not then go on to advocate violent revolution. Apart from fostering political awareness and class consciousness in the unions, the CPGB's other important function in Soviet perceptions is to strengthen the left wing of the Labour Party. Gorodetskaia sees this as the most important role of the British Communist Party. The objective should be to wage an 'ideological struggle' within the working-class movement for the victory of revolutionary socialism over the ideas of right-wing Labourites.[24] What all Soviet writings on the CPGB have in common is the perception that it is: (1) a genuine vanguard Marxist-Leninist party, (2) it represents the interests of the working class, (3) working within the particular objective conditions of the British political system its chief function should be to gain influence in the trade unions and to support a left-wing orientation in the Labour Party.

The Communist Party in Britain is also viewed as a consistent supporter of Soviet proposals for peaceful coexistence, détente and arms control and disarmament. However, there have been frictions between the CPSU and the CPGB over the latter's stance on certain aspects of Soviet domestic policies and relations with Eastern Europe and other fraternal Communist parties. The CPGB supported the 1956 intervention in Hungary, but was critical of repression of the Prague Spring in 1968; with only one dissenting vote the Executive Committee of the party condemned the Soviet invasion. Soviet pressure to prevent the issue from appearing on the agenda of the CPGB Congress in 1969 failed, and Congress, following heated debate, approved the condemning resolution. Although the Soviet Union did not directly denounce the CPGB, criticisms of the party appeared in the Czechoslovak press.[25]

The British Communist Party under the leadership of John Gollan became more critical of the CPSU into the 1970s. Gollan wrote an article criticising certain aspects of Soviet society in *Marxism Today* (the organ of the Eurocommunist element within the CPGB) in January 1976, which reportedly produced a private message of protest from Moscow (the pages of the journal containing Gollan's article were torn out before distribution in the USSR).[26] The new party programme published the following year, containing a guarantee for political pluralism, marked a further move towards an independent position from Moscow, but reports in the Soviet media played this down.[27] Along with the larger West European Communist parties the CPGB denounced the Soviet invasion of Afghanistan in 1979 – with General Secretary MacLennan doing this openly at the 26th CPSU Congress. The CPGB also opposed the establishment of martial law in Poland in 1981. Soviet sources now began to criticise Eurocommunist tendencies, arguing that they undermined the interests of the 'international communist movement'.[28]

It should be noted that the CPGB itself has been split, with no unanimity of views supporting a Eurocommunist trend. The traditionalists in the party, for example, controlled the *Morning Star* daily newspaper and maintained this control after their expulsion from the party. Although relatively restrained in its reporting and interpretation of this split, the Soviets seemed to side with the traditionalists. For example, shortly before the 39th CPGB Congress Alexei Kozlov wrote to *Marxism Today* complaining that the journal had a 'generally unfriendly attitude to our party and to Soviet society', referring to 'malicious fabrications' in its pages.[29] When the CPGB Congress met in May 1985 it was divisive and *Pravda* reported the 'fierce struggle in the party' centred around a number of members who were also on the editorial board of the *Morning Star*. These members were accused, *Pravda* noted, of 'overestimating the role of the working class in the struggle against Thatcherism', and taking too uncritical an attitude towards the socialist countries. Although not taking sides itself directly, the fact that *Pravda* (before the rise of *glasnost'*) went on to report the successful resolution to expel those so accused perhaps indicated a change in Soviet attitudes to fraternal parties. Indeed, Gorbachev had only just taken over as General Secretary of the CPSU in March 1985, and since that time the Soviet Communist Party has been re-evaluating its perceptions of and relations with other Communist parties.

In his report at the meeting to celebrate the seventieth anniversary of the Russian Revolution, Gorbachev stated that the Soviets 'have become convinced of there being no "model" of socialism to be emulated by everyone' and that all Communist parties are 'completely and irreversibly independent'.[30] These statements indicate a radical revision of the Brezhnev doctrine.[31] These developments, linked to Gorbachev's domestic economic and political reforms and changes in style, personnel and policies in the USSR, have substantially improved mutual perceptions between the CPSU and CPGB.

With Gorbachev in power in Moscow a convergence of views has developed between the two Communist parties. Both party leaderships now articulate similar views on most aspects of Soviet domestic and foreign policies and on the role of the 'international communist movement'. Gorbachev has noted that there does not exist an organisational centre directing the policies and strategies of individual Communist parties, and that 'the time of binding international conferences is over'. The world Communist movement, he said, 'is at a turning point'.[32] The CPGB monthly, *Marxism Today*, has featured many articles on the USSR since 1985 which demonstrate strong approval of the Soviet Union. If Gorbachev's 'new thinking' proves to be long lasting, a turning point could well have been reached and relations between the CPGB and the CPSU will continue to improve.

THE TRADE UNIONS

Lenin had continuously emphasised that trade unions should not limit their activities to improving the economic interests of the workers, but should mould class consciousness among the proletariat 'and become a very important channel of political agitation and revolutionary organisation'.[33] The trade unions in Britain, however, have rarely, in Soviet perceptions, operated outside the narrow bounds of serving the economic interests of their members. The trade unions have no institutionalised ties with the Communist Party, which, as the vanguard of the working class, should be their most natural ally. Rather, the trade unions are tightly integrated into the Labour Party, a result of the particular historical circumstances in which the party was established (by trade union and socialist groups at the turn of the century). Soviet writings on the trade unions during the Stalinist period took a similar line to assessments of the Labour Party: a right-wing, opportunist leadership serving the interests of corporate capitalism, and a more radical rank-and-file membership whose interests were not being served. Although similar assessments are made today, many Soviet writers on the British trade unions recognise the 'political passivity of wide sections of the working class', and the diverse nature of the trade union movement.[34] For Peregudov the trade unions have been a particularly 'reformist' element within the working class movement.[35] Gorodetskaia traces the growth in white-collar workers and the decline in membership of trade unions representing workers engaged in physical labour.[36] And recent Soviet evaluations have had to account for an increasing tendency of blue collar workers to vote Conservative and a lack of 'class solidarity' in the face of the Thatcher Government's 'anti-union' legislation and the defeat of the miners' strike in 1985.

The miners' strike was seen in the Soviet Union as a major struggle between labour and capital, an example of the unions acting out the role assigned for them by Lenin. Thus, in assessing Soviet perceptions of the British trade unions in the 1980s we will focus upon Soviet interpretations of the miners' strike, for these should provide us with a clear picture of how the Soviets perceive the role, functions, strengths and weaknesses of the unions in contemporary Britain.

On the eve of the miners' strike, Soviet perceptions of British trade unions seemed to portray an increasingly politically conscious, militant trade union movement strongly influenced by the CPGB whilst at the same time having itself a strong, radical influence on the Labour Party.[37] The National Union of Mineworkers (NUM) has always been viewed by the USSR as being the most militant of British trade unions. Most Soviet scholars saw the strike as an event of major significance.[38] Gorodetskaia, for instance, viewed the strike in terms of a 'class conflict' and, comparing it to the General Strike of 1926, she described as a 'major event in the history of the British workers' movement'.[39] Why then did the strike fail and the miners return to work in March 1985 without having achieved their objectives?

Zak and Khesin note the difficult position in which the Labour Party leadership under Kinnock found itself during the strike. Support for the miners would have led to an increase in influence for the Left within the party and hence undermined the unity achieved following the split which had helped to vitiate Labour's electoral prospects during the 1983 election. Yet to refuse support 'could have sparked a conflict with the trade unions' whose support, financial and political, was necessary to win the next election.[40] In the event Kinnock gave the miners only token support, trying to steer a middle course which did little to help the NUM's cause. Gorodetskaia is openly critical of Kinnock and Hattersley (and indeed Norman Willis, General Secretary of the TUC) for not giving unequivocal backing to the miners[41] and she, with most other Soviet analysts, pays tribute to the CPGB for its steadfast and class-conscious solidarity with the NUM.

The picture which emerges from an examination of Soviet specialist analyses of the miners' strike is one of recognition of the relative weakness of the British trade union movement in the 1980s. This view contrasts with Soviet writings of the 1970s which were optimistic about increased class consciousness and radicalism among the working class. A number of factors are said to explain this weakness, but principal among them are the Thatcherite restructuring of the economy and anti-union legislation.

All the works cited here relating to the miners' strike are clear in their bias towards the miners – indeed, interpreted as a class struggle they would have to support the strike movement to be in line with Soviet Marxist-Leninist ideology. The Soviet media certainly supported the miners in rhetoric, Soviet trade unionists provided some economic assistance and funded holidays for some strikers' families on the Black Sea coast, but the Soviet official state apparatus did very little for the miners.[42] On the contrary, Soviet ships were used to transport Polish coal to British ports. According to a report in 1986, Kim Howells, a

Research Officer for the South Wales Area NUM maintains that coal imports from Poland and fuel deliveries in Soviet tankers played a 'crucial role . . . in defeating the NUM in 1984/5'.[43] A secretary of the Soviet mineworkers union did make an announcement on Soviet television in October 1984 that trade unions had decided not to export coal and fuel to Britain. However, a Soviet foreign trade ministry official denied that such a decision had been taken – and indeed, no such embargo was ever imposed.[44] The NUM called off its strike the same month that Gorbachev became General Secretary of the CPSU. Thus it would be appropriate finally to assess briefly if there have been any noticeable changes in Soviet views of British trade unions since March 1985.

The Armenian economist Abel Aganbegyan, one of Gorbachev's advisers, stated in a recent interview with *Izvestiia* that: 'In the Donbas there are almost 30 mines consuming a huge amount of resources and producing a scanty amount of coal. If these 30 mines are closed down, the money released would be enough to produce three times as much coal'.[45] Such a rationale is very close to that of the National Coal Board (NCB) and the Thatcher Government in 1984 concerning the profitability of some British coal mines – the very cause of the miners' strike. Gorbachev is seeking to reform the Soviet economy on the basis of economic viability and cost-accounting in which profit will be the operative word. Following on from this logic it is debatable whether Gorbachev would have sided with the NUM in its struggle against the Coal Board. References to trade unions in the West since Gorbachev came to power are related increasingly not to the class struggle within their own countries, but to an internationalist stance in favour of disarmament and other 'globalist' issues. For example, Gorbachev's own message to the meeting of the World Federation of Trade Unions in 1985 focused for the most part on disarmament.[46] The General Secretary of the WFTU writing in the pages of *International Affairs* noted the trade unions' important role in 'mobilising the masses' to oppose the arms race, pointing out that in Britain unions supported the Greenham Common women and consider 'peace' as legitimate to 'trade unions' business'.[47]

Although neither the unions, the TUC nor Labour Party showed complete solidarity with the miners' strike, the fact that the labour movement and its vanguard the CPGB are now united on the most 'fundamental' and 'universal' issues of peace and disarmament, is seen in Moscow as of great significance. For if one accepts the reformist view promoted by Gorbachev that imperialism is no longer inherently militaristic then it is the trade unions and the Left generally which in a mutually supportive alliance can temper the militarism still prevalent in capitalist circles, and thus assist in the 'peace process'. In October 1987 a working party of the International Confederation of Free Trade Unions (ICFTU) on Peace, Security and Disarmament held a meeting in Moscow with Gorbachev. (Norman Willis was the head of the British contingent.) At the meeting Gorbachev noted that relations between the ICFTU and the Soviet

Union had been improving following years of mutual suspicion and tension. The Soviet leader said that he had read the ICFTU statements on security-related issues covering the past three years and subscribed to 99.99 per cent of the policies proposed. It was in 1983 at its congress in Oslo that the ICFTU first proposed the policy of 'disarmament for development', a concept that Gorbachev has since taken up himself. Gorbachev's arms control and disarmament initiatives have won the Soviet Union wide support among trade unions in Britain.

There has generally been a marked improvement in relations between British and Soviet trade unions since 1985, and contacts have gone beyond formal bureaucratic meetings to real working collaboration on industrial problems. In the same year as the Chernobyl disaster the TUC set up a Nuclear Energy Review Body to examine all aspects of the nuclear industry, particularly that relating to safety. The TUC made a request to their Soviet counterpart for members of the Review Body to visit the Soviet Union to discuss the implications of Chernobyl. In the event the request was granted and, in April 1987, the highest level British TUC delegation to the Soviet Union in many years had meetings with government, trade union, and health and safety officials in Moscow, Kiev and Chernobyl itself.[48] Generally the TUC delegation left Moscow very impressed with the openness and frankness of the responses they received to the very direct questions they put to the Soviet officials.

Earlier in 1987 Norman Willis had attended and addressed the 18th Soviet Trade Union Congress. He made clear the TUC's continuing support for Solidarity in Poland and for the right of trade unions to maintain their independence of the state.

THE PEACE MOVEMENT

We use the term 'peace movement' as a generic label for those groups, principally the Campaign for Nuclear Disarmament (CND) and the European Nuclear Disarmament (END), whose main objective is to act as pressure groups to further the cause of nuclear disarmament. We use the term because it is widely employed to refer to those groups, like CND and END, actively engaged in anti-nuclear campaigns.

The Soviets have had an uneasy and ambiguous relationship with the British peace movement, generally considering it a useful vehicle for furthering the foreign policy and defence interests of the Kremlin, whilst simultaneously, certainly in the case of END, viewing it as a troublesome and intrusive critic of Soviet nuclear arms policies. However, under the leadership of Gorbachev there has been a marked improvement in relations between the official, state-run Soviet Peace Committee (SPC) and the peace movement in Britain, along with a reappraisal of Soviet thinking on issues of national security and defence policy. In this section of the chapter we assess Soviet attitudes towards CND and END since the early 1980s, and trace the links between these groupings and party and state organisations in the USSR.

CND grew dramatically in the early 1980s and, in contrast to the 1960s, a broader European 'peace movement' developed throughout Western Europe. At the end of 1979 total CND membership amounted to less than 3,000. By 1984 this figure had reached some 110,000 individual members, excluding affiliated local groups.[49] CND organised a number of large public rallies and demonstrations throughout Britain during this period.[50] This clearly impressed Soviet officials.

Soviet media coverage of CND activities gave the impression that the British public generally supported its objectives. Soviet officials who have dealings with Western peace groups had always acknowledged that the British peace movement was not a unified, monolithic bloc, but contained different currents.[51] However, the rise of CND in the early 1980s was seen as marking a 'qualitatively new stage' in CND's development.[52] Soviet commentators seemed to place great hope in CND's potential to influence government thinking on INF deployment, noting its large, broad-based membership and capacity to organise mass demonstrations against cruise and Pershing. Many references were made to the composition of the membership, representing a broad array of radical and left-wing groupings of Communists, labourites, trade unionists, and progressive elements from the churches and professional bodies, supported by large sections of the masses. It was noted also that even former senior military personnel, such as Field Marshal Lord Carver, had attacked certain aspects of Mrs Thatcher's defence policy.[53]

The actions of the women holding vigil at Greenham Common were portrayed in heroic terms in the Soviet media. The greater awareness of women and young people, and their willingness to actively campaign against the Government's nuclear arms policy, were explained by the fact that these groups have suffered most from the economic recession in the West.[54] The activism of Western youth was a particularly hopeful sign for the Soviets for it demonstrated evidence of a new, peace-loving generation unburdened by the ideological baggage of the Cold War and blind anti-communism. All in all the Soviet commentators were generally optimistic that the Western peace movements would be able to put sufficient pressure on their governments to reverse the decision to deploy new INF missiles.

Furthermore, the British peace movement of the 1980s was initially seen as one area where the Left had successfully united on an issue conducive to achieving Soviet objectives (i.e., no deployment of cruise or Pershings), incorporating the CPGB, the Labour Party and the trade union movement.

Soviet writings evidenced great faith in the influence of public opinion and pressure groups in Western societies on state policy, representing a significant shift in the Soviet perception on the workings of bourgeois democracy. In these assessments there was little or no acknowledgement that Soviet actions and rhetoric often effectively undermined the chances of the peace movement decisively influencing the decisions of Western Governments.

Although much has been made about the links between the Western peace movements and Soviet, or Soviet-sponsored bodies, with claims of CND being little more than a Soviet Communist Party Front organisation, relations have been at times fairly strained.[55] CND has always been an organisation designed to influence *British* policy on nuclear weapons and as such, given its unilateral stance, the Soviets have understandably supported its aims. Following NATO's dual-track decision, CND put its energies into pressurising the government not to proceed with the deployment of cruise missiles – which was of course in line with Soviet demands. Although CND did not accept that cruise was a response to Soviet SS-20s deployed in Eastern Europe, and although its sole purpose was to lobby the British Government, there is no logical connection between this and support for Soviet defence policy. For example, at the height of the CND campaign, at the moment when it had its largest membership and had just held its largest rally, it had organised in December 1984 'Operation Christmas Card' in which cards and letters were sent to Soviet, Czech and East German officials expressing CND's opposition to INF deployments in Czechoslovakia and the GDR.[56] As Meg Beresford, vice-Chair of CND has written: 'CND's opposition to nuclear weapons is fundamental and comprehensive: it does not differentiate between US and Soviet weapons of mass destruction.'[57] Following the Reykjavik summit between the superpowers CND issued a 'Defence Briefing' in which it was stated that the zero-zero proposal should not be held hostage or linked to either SDI or conventional forces, a stance not then shared by Soviet officials.[58]

Between January 1984 and May 1987 there were four CND delegations to Moscow, and on each successive occasion there was a marked improvement in the level of relations between CND and their Soviet hosts. This was not a result of CND coming closer to Soviet positions, for example on INF, but rather as a consequence of 'new political thinking' in Soviet foreign and defence policy, which actually brought Soviet views closer to those already held by CND. At the invitation of the SPC a five-member CND delegation, headed by Joan Ruddock, visited the Soviet Union in September 1985. Members of the delegation were at first refused access by the KGB to the home of a member of the Moscow Trust Group (an unofficial independent peace group). Yuri Zhukov, then head of the SPC, spent much time at one meeting attacking individual members of the Trust Group, going as far as quoting directly from private correspondence and medical reports. CND's request to meet with members of the International Department was not granted, and the SPC generally reacted with contempt to many of the proposals for disarmament made by the British visitors.[59] The most fruitful meetings the delegation had were with members of IMEMO and the Scientific Council of Problems of Peace and Disarmament, who discussed CND's proposals seriously and, unlike SPC officials, were willing to engage in rational, fairly candid debate.

Ruddock led another CND working delegation to Moscow, just before the Reykjavik summit in December 1986. Zhukov, still head of the SPC (he was replaced shortly after the visit), was a little more ready to admit that both sides in the arms race had made mistakes. The visitors found a far greater degree of openness even among SPC officials, and this time they did get to meet with a leading figure of the International Department (Zagladin, its First Deputy Head) at Central Committee Headquarters. At this time Gorbachev's reform programme inside the Soviet Union was gaining momentum, and the CND delegation was struck by the lack of consensus and unity of views among the institutes, the SPC, the foreign and defence ministries.[60]

In March 1987, at the invitation of the CND, an SPC delegation visited Britain. It was headed by the new SPC First Vice President Vladimir Oryel who had previously worked in the International Department. The leadership of the SPC had recently been revamped, with new blood from the party apparatus, the diplomatic service, and the media. Many of these new officials were representatives of new thinking: one of the SPC delegates on the visit to London, Aleksandr Lebedev, an associate editor of the *New Times*, gave an interview to Stephen Brown, international worker for CND, for CND's journal, *Sanity*. Lebedev stated that the new political thinking involved a shift away from 'parity' as a central concept of defence policy, and in one statement acknowledged that the decision to deploy SS-20s in Eastern Europe was unnecessary and contributed to an escalation in the arms race.[61] On their return to Moscow Lebedev and Oryel co-authored an article for *New Times* in which they admitted that: 'About two-thirds of Britain's population . . . still advocate maintaining its nuclear status.'[62] These admissions of some Soviet responsibility for the arms race, and that the bulk of the British population supported Britain's independent nuclear deterrent marked a radical revision of previously held views by former leading figures in the SPC. CND paid its third visit to Moscow within eighteen months in May 1987 to participate in an Information Seminar hosted by the SPC. CND members joined with other Western peace groups in successfully lobbying the SPC to permit representatives of the Trust Group to attend the seminar. One Trust Group member, Irina Krivova, was allowed to take the floor and outline her organisation's aims and difficulties.[63] She received a mixed response from the official East European delegates, with many of the Soviet participants referring to the Trust Group as an agent of imperialism. But the fact that the

Trust Group was allowed to attend some of the seminar proceedings was a clear sign of the changes underway in the SPC.

However, there was evidence that 'old thinking' still lived on among some individuals, including Grigori Lokshin who headed the Soviet delegation to END's 6th Convention in Coventry in July 1987, and much of his report for the Soviet media consisted of an attack on the Trust Group.[64]

Compared to CND, END's relationship with the SPC has been fractious and tense. In 1980 E.P. Thompson published his pamphlet *Protest and Survive*, in which he proposed a nuclear-free zone in Europe from Portugal to Poland, for which *all* governments in Europe, East and West, should be lobbied and pressurised. It was in this context that END was born, and the organisation has constantly criticised the USSR and other East European states for not allowing independent peace and human rights groups to operate freely. END has also argued that responsibility for the arms race is shared by both East and West. Soviet officials were quick to denounce such claims and END has been subjected to the most severe attacks for making them.[65] Many individual leaders of END have been criticised directly in Soviet writings, but, as with CND, as Gorbachev's reforms and new thinking have progressed, relations between END and the SPC have improved. An END delegation visited Moscow in May 1987 and discovered among Soviet officials a much greater degree of openness than in previous years and serious debate underway concerning defence issues. At an international seminar organised by the *World Marxist Review* in 1987 Oryel, representing the SPC, stated 'we are prepared to hear out even those who make anti-Soviet statements . . . not everything the opponent says always appears to be absolutely wrong. Experience shows that many ideas from the midst of the anti-war movement, which at first looked suspicious and were simply brushed off, turned out to be highly valuable and useful.'[66] Professor Tair Tairov, the International Department's main representative on the World Peace Council wrote in 1987 that 'many elements of the new thinking (in Soviet defence policy) originated in the ranks of the peace movement'.[67] CND, despite early optimism in Moscow, failed to force a change in government policy on cruise, yet ultimately, with the INF deal agreed by Reagan and Gorbachev at the Washington summit, Soviet policy and thinking on disarmament came to resemble that long advocated by the British peace movement. Oryel and other members of the SPC have, following the earlier optimism regarding the power of the peace movement to influence government policy, suggested that they placed too much faith in the anti-nuclear movement in the early 1980s.[68]

CONCLUSIONS

First, Soviet perceptions of and policies towards the Left in Britain depend to a great extent on the views and objectives of the current Kremlin leadership at any particular time – and of course these change over time. Under Stalin, for example, the Left was seen, through a simplistic ideological curtain, as representatives (with the exception of the CPGB) of bourgeois interests. Gorbachev, however, appears to be making an effort to forge a closer working relationship with radical and leftist forces in order to further globalist and humanist values, downplaying the opposing ideologies of capitalism and Communism. We have examined the level of success the new Soviet leader has achieved in increasing and improving ties with all segments of the British Left.

The second conclusion is that Soviet attitudes towards the Left in Britain depend upon the stance each takes on issues of concern to the USSR. It is Soviet *state* interests which are paramount, and not any question of seeking to establish an ideological consensus on the meaning of socialism. This is the key to understanding Soviet relations with leftist parties and groupings, and is perhaps best summed up by Lebedev and Oryel: 'As for which of Britian's leading parties the Soviet public sympathises with, these sympathies, regardless of the ideological aspect, derive above all from the actual policy pursued, be it by the Conservatives, Labour, the Liberals or the Social Democrats.'[69]

NOTES

1. See Bill Jones, *The Russia Complex: The British Labour Party and the Soviet Union* (Manchester University Press, 1977).
2. I. E. Gorodetskaia, *Velikobritaniia: Izbirateli, vybory, partii, 1945–1970* (Nauka, 1974), p. 219. Gorodetskaia draws heavily on the works of Butler and Stokes as well as Almond and Verba.
3. *Ibid.*, p. 219.
4. V. A. Ryzhikov, *Zigzagi diplomatii Londona* (Mezhdunarodnye otnosheniia, 1973), pp. 161–3.
5. V. G. Trukhanovsky and N. K. Kapitonova, *Sovetsko-angliiskie otnosheniia, 1945–1978* (Mezhdunarodnye otnosheniia, 1979), p. 218.
6. A. A. Gromyko and B. N. Ponomarev, eds., *Soviet Foreign Policy 1945–1980* (Progress, 1981), p. 585.
7. S. P. Peregudov, 'Leiboristskaia partiia Velikobritanii i strategiia tsentrizma', *Rabochii klassi sovremennyi mir*, 6 (1981), pp. 139–44, p. 140.
8. Peregudov, 'Leiboristskaia partiia', p. 140. See, also V. A. Ryzhikov, *Sovetsko-angliiskie otnosheniia: osonovye etapy istorii* (Mezhdunarodnye otnosheniia, 1987), pp. 237–238; G. Kh. Shakhnazarov, ed., *Contemporary Political Science in the USA and Western Europe* (Progress, 1985), p. 216; G. V. Kolosov, *Voenno-politicheskii kurs Anglii v Evrope* (Nauka, 1984), p. 204.
9. Shakhnazarov, *Contemporary Political Science*, p. 213; and L. Zak and E. Khesin, 'Velikobritaniia: konservatory ostalis' u vlasti', in O. N. Bykov *et al.* eds., *Mezhdunarodnyi ezhegodnik: politika i ekonomika, 1984* (Politizdat, 1984), pp. 145–51.
10. See *New Times*, April 1987.

11. See, for example V. Pan´kov, 'Sotsial-demokraty ob ekonomicheskom sotrudnichest-ve v Evrope', *Mirovaia ekonomika i mezhdunarodnye otnosheniia*, 10 (1987), pp. 121–127; and S. P. Peregudov, 'Sotsial-demokratiia pered litsom novykh problem', *Mirovaia ekonomika i mezhdunarodnye otnosheniia*, 6 (1986), pp. 16–30.
12. See Gorbachev's Congress Report and his Report celebrating the 70th anniversary of the Russian Revolution. Both can be found in translation in *Soviet News*, 26 February 1986 and 4 November 1987, respectively.
13. See *Pravda*, 27 November 1984.
14. As reported in *The Observer*, 2 December 1984.
15. George Robertson, 'Peace and an opportunity lost', *Glasgow Herald*, 13 May 1985.
16. George Robertson, 'Gorbachev: changing rules of Communism', *Glasgow Herald*, 4 March 1986.
17. See *Modern Britain in a Modern World* (The Labour Party, 1987), *Europe: A New Détente* (The Labour Party, 1987), and M. Gorbachev, *Speeches and Writings*, Vol. 2 (Pergamon, 1987).
18. *Soviet News*, 1 April 1987.
19. V. V. Zagladin, 'The International Communist Movement as a vanguard political force of the world revolutionary process', in V. P. Jerusalimski, V. A. Trofimov, V. V. Zagladin *et al.*, *Theory and Tactics of the International Communist Movement* (Progress, 1985), pp. 41–68, p. 43.
20. Jones, *The Russia complex*, p. 6.
21. Talbott, ed., *Khrushchev Remembers*, pp. 401–14.
22. Gorodetskaia, *Velikobritaniia*, p. 12. Vsevolod Ovchinnikov notes the conservative and conformist attitude the English display to 'money, to words, and to emotions'; see his *Korni duba: vpechatleniia i razmyshleniia ob Anglii i anglichanakh* (Mysl´, 1980), p. 286.
23. Zagladin, 'The international communist movement', pp. 44–5.
24. Gorodetskaia, *Velikobritaniia*, pp. 71–3.
25. Interview with Monty Johnstone of the CPGB.
26. *Marxism Today*, January 1976, pp. 4–30; *The Guardian*, 13 February 1976; interview with Monty Johnstone.
27. See, for example, *Pravda*, 15 November 1977.
28. Iu. Krasin, *The Contemporary Revolutionary Process* (Progress, 1981), pp. 115–16.
29. *Marxism Today*, May 1985, p. 6.
30. See 'October and *perestroika*: the Revolution continues', *Soviet News*, 4 November 1987.
31. For an analysis of a possible revision in the Brezhnev doctrine, see Karen Dawisha and Jonathan Valdez, 'Socialist internationalism in Eastern Europe', *Problems of Communism*, March–April 1987, pp. 1–14.
32. Gorbachev, 'October and *perestroika*'.
33. A. M. Rumiantsev, *A Dictionary of Scientific Communism* (Progress, 1984), p. 266; Zagladin, 'The international communist movement', p. 157.
34. S. P. Peregudov, *Antivoennoe dvizhenie v Anglii i leiboristskaia partiia* (Nauka, 1969), p. 237.
35. Peregudov, 'Leiboristskaia partiia', p. 141.
36. Gorodetskaia, *Velikobritaniia*, p. 78.
37. E. K. Silin, 'Rol´ obshchestvennykh sil Evropy v borbe protiv voennoi ugrozy', in S. L. Tikhvinsky, ed., *Diplomaticheskii Vestnik, 1984* (Mezhdunarodnye otnosheniia,

1985), pp. 151–61; Peregudov, 'Leiboristskaia partiia', p. 141; Trukhanovsky and Kapitonova, *Sovetsko-angliiskie otnosheniia*, p. 257; Gorodetskaia, *Velikobritaniia*, p. 78; Ryzhikov, *'Sotsializm' po-leiboristski – mify i real' nost'* (Politicheskaia literatura, 1971), p. 51.

38. L. Zak and E. Khesin, 'Velikobritaniia: rezkoe obostrenie klassovoi borb'y' in O. N. Bykov *et al.*, eds., *Mezhdunarodnyi ezhegodnik*, p. 156; S. A. Ershov, 'Obshchenatsional'naia zabastovka shakhterov v Velikobritanii: prichiny, kharakter, znachenie', *Rabochii klass i sovremnnyi mir*, 1 (1985), pp. 83–95.

39. I. Gorodetskaia, 'Stachka dlinoi v god', *Novaia i Noveishaia istoriia*, 1 (1987), pp. 39–54, p. 39.

40. Zak and Khesin, 'Velikobritaniia', p. 157.

41. See Gorodetskaia, 'Stachka'.

42. On aid to the miners, see Michael Crick, *Scargill and the Miners* (Penguin, 1985), p. 132.

43. *International Labour Reports*, January–February 1986.

44. See *News Line*, 9 April 1985.

45. Reported in *Soviet Weekly*, 24 October 1987.

46. See *Pravda*, 1 October 1985.

47. Ibrahim Zakaria, 'Trade Unions in the Struggle for Peace and Social Progress', *International Affairs* (Moscow), 6 (1986), pp. 65–8.

48. See TUC Nuclear Energy Review Body, *Report of a Delegation Visit to the USSR, 2–5 April 1987*.

49. Paul Mercer, *Peace of the Dead* (Policy Research Publications, 1986), p. 160.

50. For example, in 1981 a demonstration organised by CND drew a crowd of between 15,000 (claimed by *The Times*) and 250,000 (claimed by its sponsors) – see Mercer, *Peace of the Dead*, p. 162. The massive rally in October 1983 was said by CND to have attracted 400,000 people.

51. For example, see I. N. Shchelokova, *Problemy evropeiskoi bezopasnosti i politika Anglii* (Mezhdunarodnye otnosheniia, 1982), p. 115; and V. I. Shveitsev, 'Sotsial-demokratiia i antivoennoe dvizhenie v zapadnoi Evrope', *Voprosy Istorii*, 7 (1986), translated in *Soviet Law and Government*, Winter 1986–87.

52. V. Shaposhnikov, 'The current anti-war movement', in N. N. Inozemtsev, ed., *Peace and Disarmament* (Academic Studies, 1982), p. 120.

53. P. V. Kolosov, *Voenno-politicheskii kurs Anglii v Evrope*, (Nauka, 1984).

54. N. Berezhnaya and Ye. Blinova, *Women Fight for Peace* (Nauka, 1987), pp. 6–7.

55. For a detailed examination of CND's links with the SPC see Mercer, *Peace of the Dead*.

56. CND, 'Press Information', 3 December 1984.

57. Meg Beresford, 'New Perspectives', in Gerard Holden, *The Second Superpower: The Arms Race and the Soviet Union*, (CND Publications, 1985), pp. 76–97, p. 85.

58. 'After Reykjavik', *CND Defence Briefing*, November 1986.

59. See, 'Back from the USSR', *Report of CND Delegation to the Soviet Union, 18–28 September 1985* (CND, 1986), and Jane Mayes, 'And the twain shall meet', *Peace News*, 13 December 1985. (Mayes was a member of the CND delegation.) The delegation gave an interview on their experiences and perceptions of the visit in *Sanity*, December 1985. Also see Jane Mayes, *New Statesman*, 11 November 1985; and Joan Ruddock, *Sunday Times*, 29 September 1985.

60. Joan Ruddock reported on this visit in *Sanity*, February 1987.

61. See *Sanity*, June 1987.
62. Alexandr Lebedev and Vladimir Oryel, 'The other Britain', *New Times*, 20 April 1987.
63. A report on the Moscow visit can be found in *Sanity*, July 1987.
64. See, for example, Grigori Lokshin, *The Anti-War Movement: East–West Dialogue* (Novosti, 1986); Lokshin, 'Moscow dialogue – new people and new atmosphere', *XX Century and Peace*, Information Seminar, see *Index on Censorship*, 9 (1987).
65. Grigori Lokshin, 'Coventry appeal', *XX Century and Peace*, 10 (1987), pp. 8–15.
66. *END Journal*, December–January 1987/88.
67. See, Tair Tairov, 'Moments of truth', *New Times*, 18 May 1987.
68. See, for example, *New Times*, 20 July 1987; *World Marxist Review*, July 1987, pp. 49–63.
69. Lebedev and Oryel, 'The other Britain'.

8　Anglo-Soviet cultural contacts since 1975

JOHN MORISON

THE HISTORICAL BACKGROUND

Cultural relations serve as a barometer of Anglo-Soviet political relations. They are seen by both sides as an important element in developing and consolidating a burgeoning political relationship, but are adversely affected when the political climate deteriorates.

Cultural and scientific contacts between the Soviet Union and Britain were minimal during the Stalin period. Military co-operation during the Second World War led the British Foreign Office to hope for a friendly political atmosphere and proper cultural relations, including student exchanges, with the USSR after the war. However, the advent of the Cold War made the establishment of meaningful contacts unrealisable. Stalin's death opened the way for scientific and cultural exchanges with the West. These were to be a by-product of Khrushchev's reformation of Soviet foreign policy and of his quest for peaceful coexistence. One major advantage of détente would be the possibility of ending Soviet separation from world science. Unlike Stalin, Khrushchev saw that isolation from Western scientists and lack of contact with recent developments contributed to technological backwardness.[1] Khrushchev's and Bulganin's visit to Britain in April 1956, during which specific references were made to increased cultural, scientific and technological exchanges, seemed to herald a breakthrough. The Suez, Hungarian and Berlin crises delayed the signing of the Agreement on Relations in the Scientific, Technological, Educational and Cultural Field, 1960–61, until 1 December 1959.[2]

This Cultural Agreement has subsequently been renegotiated every two years and spells out in considerable detail the scientific, educational and cultural exchanges which it is intended should take place. However, this is essentially an enabling document, and the extent to which its provisions have been implemented has been significantly influenced by the political climate, in addition to other factors such as financial stringencies and Soviet bureaucratic inefficiency. Although the British expulsion of 105 Soviet spies in 1971 led to a short period of Soviet retaliatory cussedness, the initiative in using the Cultural Agreement as a weapon to express political disapproval of actions by the other side has usually been taken by the British Government. Moral outrage at the Soviet invasion of Czechoslovakia in 1968 was expressed by the cancellation of a visit by the Red Army choir. Politicians can, when it suits them, have very short memories. Improving political relations and a specific pledge in the 1975 Helsinki Agreement to increase cultural links encouraged the Labour Government to seek an expansion in contacts and trade. The series of agreements which were signed in Moscow in 1975 by Wilson and Brezhnev included detailed programmes for co-operation in science, technology, medicine and public health. The importance of cultural links was stressed and it was proclaimed that the visit 'marked the opening of a new phase in Anglo-Soviet relations'.[3] This supposed new phase did not last long. Human rights issues and Soviet involvement in Africa, Afghanistan and Poland undermined détente. The British Government's response to the Afghanistan crisis was to make various gestures of disapproval, to add a little substance to its words. Amongst these, and in addition to the not very effective attempt to organise a boycott of the Moscow Olympics, was the decision to reduce cultural exchanges with the USSR and its Eastern European allies. 'High visibility' activity was suspended, including visits by officials of Deputy Minister status or above, and tours by major theatre, ballet and opera groups. Medical and cultural exchanges ceased to operate. Nevertheless, most of the programme of cultural interchange continued unabated. A British Council report for 1981–82 aptly described the situation: 'Our present work has been described as a fairly large jug of milk with the cream taken off.' Mrs Thatcher's Government thus tacitly agreed with the Soviet view that it was useful to keep low-level and uncontroversial contact going even in times of tension. This contrasted sharply with the suspension of official cultural exchanges implemented by the United States and some other Western countries. In 1983, the British Government decided to embark on independent moves towards rapprochement with the USSR, a process hastened by Gorbachev's own striking initiatives since 1985. The resulting increase in cultural contacts served as a signal on the political barometer of a serious commitment to an improved relationship in other areas. The November 1985 Geneva summit emphasised scholarly and cultural contacts. To quote an authoritative American observer, there began 'a major Soviet cultural offensive designed to demonstrate to the world the reasonableness of the system, the benign intentions of the leadership, and its willingness to engage in international contacts at a variety of societal levels'.[4]

British plans for exchanges of visits by major theatrical and ballet companies and for an exhibition of twentieth-century art which had been abandoned after the occupation of Afghanistan were now revived. Steps were taken to reactivate areas of the Cultural Agreement which had lain dormant. Thus the Royal Ballet completed a season at Moscow's Operetta Theatre and in Leningrad in 1987, and in the opposite direction the Kirov Opera from Leningrad and dancers from Moscow's Bolshoi Theatre have toured England. Many other visits have taken place, and the level of cultural interchange in the performing arts had been set by 1987 on a sharply upward curve. By 1987, medical exchanges had restarted and, although the section on agricultural exchanges was deleted from the 1987 Cultural Agreement, it was intended, at Soviet request, to replace it by a memorandum of understanding between the relevant ministries in both countries. During Mrs Thatcher's pre-election visit to Moscow in March 1987, a seal of official approval was laid on the increase in scientific and cultural contacts by the signature of an agreement on space collaboration and a memorandum of understanding 'concerning new directions in co-operation in the fields of information, culture and education'. These documents did not mark the cultural conversion of Mrs Thatcher, but rather her use of cultural relations to underpin an improving political relationship and to help her emergence as an honest broker between the two superpowers. On the Soviet side, they demonstrated a willingness to make significant concessions to Western opinion, such as ending the jamming of the BBC, allowing direct television discussion programmes and home visits by schoolchildren, in order to achieve better relations with the West and to give substance to the policy of greater openness in Soviet society. These concessions were of general application, coincidental to but not dependent on Mrs Thatcher's visit.

CULTURAL POLICY AND ITS FORMATION

Sharp contrasts in their cultural policies have strewn difficulties in the way of the smooth development of cultural relations between the two countries. Although not clearly stated in black and white terms, Soviet cultural policy seems to be relatively clearly etched and to be mostly hard headed in its objectives.

The Soviet Union wishes to promote the Russian language as a world-wide means of communication and Russian culture as rich and universal in its achievements. There are deep historical roots for this aspiration, going back to the mid-nineteenth century Slavophiles. Since World War II, the Soviet Union has indisputably become a superpower, the only equal in military terms of the USA on the world stage. It is therefore galling to see the adoption of English as the pre-eminent world language, whether it be in science, air traffic control or popular youth culture. In terms of mass culture, the world's youth takes the USA rather than the USSR as its model. Hence, the Soviet Government lays great stress on the development of Russian language studies abroad. Foreign tours by celebrated Soviet performers and the promotion abroad of works by

Soviet writers, composers and artists mark an attempt to claim superpower status in cultural as well as military matters. The USSR successfully used its influence to persuade UNESCO to establish MAIRSK, the International Association for the Study and Dissemination of Slavic Cultures, a body which seems to be inappropriately nationalistic in its objectives for sponsorship by an international body. The Russian language and Soviet culture are also agents for the promotion of an ideology of supposedly universal significance. In training Russian language teachers from all over the world at the Pushkin Institute in Moscow the Soviet Union hopes to make them into cultural agents who will promote, through the study of the Russian language, a sympathetic attitude towards the USSR and its ideological message. Soviet language materials are written so as to contain a political message. Large numbers of students from socialist and Third World countries are enlisted on five-year courses and are subjected to intensive political education before being returned to their countries of origin.

Britain is a singularly unpromising cultural partner for the Soviet Union in this respect. Russian language studies have never operated on more than a small scale in Britain, and have been in decline in British schools since 1968. The British Government has done little in practice to check this decline. Moreover, popular attitudes in Britain, supported and stimulated by the British press, have in general been extremely unsympathetic to the Soviet ideological message.

Britain does, however, offer more fertile soil for the achievement of another Soviet objective. In promoting cultural exchanges, Khrushchev set as a deliberate Soviet aim the systematic acquisition by this means of advanced scientific and technological information and the stimulation of Soviet science and technology through direct contact between Soviet scientists and their Western counterparts. The restricted range of Western periodicals available in the USSR, and the censorship maintained over them even in scientific fields, makes even access to British academic libraries a valuable experience. The extensive nature of Soviet industrial espionage, co-ordinated by the KGB, is relatively well known, although espionage, used in the context of the cultural exchange, is perhaps a dramatic turn of phrase to describe the acquisition and analysis of information which is in the public domain.[5]

On a more mundane level, the Soviet side has laid great stress in the 1980s on obtaining courses to improve the level of their teachers of English, which it is hoped will in turn improve general competence in English in the USSR. This will, *inter alia*, facilitate wide-scale access to American and British scientific and technical information.

British cultural policy is a singularly elusive concept. Summoned to appear before the Foreign Affairs Committee of the House of Commons, the Foreign and Commonwealth Office produced, apparently for the first time, its definition of British cultural policy. This was so general that the Committee acidly commented: 'this list of objectives is a list of objectives for diplomacy in general rather than cultural diplomacy specifically'.[6] Nevertheless, it is clear that the Foreign and Commonwealth Office in general views cultural policy in terms of the promotion of an image of Britain which will yield political, scientific and commercial benefits for the United Kingdom.[7] In its evidence to the same committee, the British Council laid its stress on cultural relations, the aim of which should be 'to develop over time a greater understanding and appreciation between peoples and institutions for their mutual benefit', in contrast to cultural diplomacy which made specific use of cultural relations for national benefit. To quote John Mitchell, 'the purpose of cultural relations is not necessarily, and in advanced thinking hardly at all, to seek one-sided advantage. At their most effective, their purpose is to achieve understanding and co-operation between national societies for their mutual benefit.'[8] If its emphasis on the fostering of good will and the countering of prejudice seemed to make the British Council more altruistic in its objectives than its main paymaster, it did also posit as aims the countering of 'the adverse image of Britain as a static, class-ridden society in economic decline' and the promotion of British achievements with the intention of enhancing Britain's international status and facilitating its trade.[9] To complicate matters further, Malcolm Rifkind, Minister of State at the Foreign Office, seemed to side with the British Council in his evidence to the Foreign Affairs Committee on 27 November 1985 when he said: 'what we wish to do is to maximise the opportunity for British and Soviet citizens to meet, to have contact, to see each other's way of life, to travel, to have access to the literature and culture of each society, to maximise the prospect of trade and economic links and in that way not only to achieve objectives that are valuable in their own right, but also indirectly to reduce tension between our two societies, two states, which will be helpful in terms of the wider political issues'.[10]

Cultural relations, as defined by John Mitchell, have hitherto not been possible with the Soviet Union. On the one hand, the Soviet Union has sought to present a highly propagandistic image of itself. On the other hand, any British desire to foster genuine collaborative ventures and mutual understanding between Soviet and British citizens has been seriously impeded by a plethora of Soviet restrictions, for instance on travel within the Soviet Union. Any British wish to transmit an honest and balanced picture of contemporary Britain to Soviet citizens has been obstructed by severe restrictions on the access of Soviet citizens to such information. The one Russian-language journal, *Angliia*, which Britain is permitted to distribute inside the Soviet Union, has a very limited circulation. Nevertheless, it has remained an aspiration of British policy to foster genuine mutual understanding, in particular by inter-personal exchanges. The transition of the Soviet Union under Gorbachev from being a closed society to becoming a more open one has made this objective appear in 1987 to be far less unrealistic than in the past.

If British policy has at times been presented as being altruistic in purpose, it does have its political aspects. The achievement of genuinely two-sided cultural relations would inevitably hasten liberalisation and political change in the Soviet Union. Additionally, the Cultural Agreement seems to be regarded by official circles as a document of value to Britain primarily as a means to the real objective, that of sustaining and, when appropriate, developing a political relationship with the Soviet Union. In other words, the content of the Agreement is secondary to its main purpose as a document *per se*, which, merely by its existence, has a political significance.

The precise contents of the Agreement are, in general terms, negotiated in response to pressures from below, as articulated by interested parties, rather than on specific lines dictated from above by ministerial diktat. This reflects a common-sense approach. Higher political and foreign policy needs compel the British Foreign Office to negotiate a Cultural Agreement with the Soviet Union, thus granting cultural relations a higher status than they are normally accorded in British diplomacy. Financial constraints imposed by the Treasury on the general Foreign Office budget impose limits on the scale of operations possible under this agreement. Within these limits it is thought to be sensible to adjust the contents of the agreement to reflect to a considerable degree the level of demand for the various opportunities offered. Consultative committees of interested parties enable those concerned to make their case at regular intervals.

British cultural policy towards the Soviet Union is thus formed by a complex interaction between the Soviet and Cultural departments of the Foreign Office (not always in complete harmony), the British Council, and a wide range of outside advisers or pressure groups, including academics, arts administrators and practitioners, librarians and archivists. The net result tends to be an accommodation of interests rather than a clear-cut policy. Analysis of the process by which Soviet policy is formed in any area is necessarily speculative, such is the cloud of secrecy that descends over it. The decision to resume meaningful cultural contacts in 1959 was clearly taken at the highest level. Since then, the renegotiation of the Cultural Agreement every two years has been a relatively routine matter, the Soviet Union adopting a pose of injured innocence in response to Western use of cultural relations as a twig with which to beat the USSR as a painless indication of disapproval of various of its acts. Negotiated by the Soviet Ministry of Foreign Affairs, the agreement concerns a wide range of other ministries and official bodies, including notably the Ministries of Education, of Higher and Specialised Secondary Education (now merged into the State Committee for Public Education), of Culture and of Health, and the Academy of Sciences. They can provide an input on detailed points, and can indicate new needs in their areas. Interest groups can perhaps exert occasional influence.

THE CULTURAL AGREEMENT

Britain is not used to conducting its cultural relations by means of an inter-governmental treaty, preferring to operate through the British Council, as an independent agent, and through initiatives by autonomous bodies and individuals. The Soviet Government, and most of its allies in Eastern Europe, demand that such contacts must take place under the umbrella and within the confines of a formal agreement. Although the British side may wish, and hope ultimately to operate otherwise, it has had to accept the Cultural Agreement as the essential keystone of its cultural relations with the Soviet Union. This Soviet insistence is in large part a reflection of the historical reality of the highly centralised nature of the Soviet system of government. It also denotes a determination to supervise and control in detail the activities of its citizens, and in particular their contacts with foreigners. If the Soviet side is concerned to use cultural diplomacy and relations as a means of mounting a world-wide ideological offensive, it is also very conscious that such a cultural offensive, whether by accident or design, may operate in reverse.[11] A policy of cultural relations may bring material advantages to the Soviet Union, but it also brings the risk of encouraging unwelcome social or pluralistic tendencies. The recently adopted policy of greater openness in Soviet society may have widened the range of debate and discussion inside the USSR, but it has not lessened the need, as perceived by the leadership and the KGB, to guard against subversion from outside. The practical consequence of these suspicions is that the British Council is severely impeded in its work to develop genuine cultural relations with the Soviet Union. It has only recently been promised a separate office in Moscow. Its three representatives in Moscow (planned in 1989 to be increased to four) have had to work as diplomats, confined within the Embassy, entrance to which is strictly controlled and effectively barred to ordinary Soviet citizens. No open lending library or the wide range of cultural activities normally associated with a British Council office abroad have been possible. Even the harmless film shows put on in their tiny office can be viewed only by the select handful of Soviet citizens able to accept personal invitations. The very few British lectors teaching English in Soviet universities are strictly controlled in what they teach, and how they teach it. They, together with British students and all other non-Soviet citizens, are subject to severe travel restrictions, which make it extremely difficult to leave the bounds of the city to which they have been granted a visa. In this respect, the USSR is far more restrictive than its East European allies or China. This state of affairs is very one-sided, since retaliatory measures have been applied in Britain only to Soviet diplomats, journalists and trade officials; others can wander freely.[12]

The Cultural Agreement, which has the status of a treaty, is renegotiated every two years. At Soviet insistence, inter-personal exchanges are strictly reciprocal, and are calculated on a person–month basis. As differing needs have developed, so various of the categories have gone into imbalance, but nevertheless the sum total of person–months exchanged has remained in balance. Thus, for instance, the increased number of places for British students of Russian has in large measure been offset by a rise in the number of places for Soviet teachers of English. Much of the agreement is devoted to laying out the exchanges that should take place over a two-year period. Not all quotas are in fact fulfilled; the Soviet side in particular is insistent that it should receive no more British participants than the number of Soviets despatched to Britain. Additionally, the agreement contains facilitating clauses, which authorise links outside those specified in detail in the treaty. Without such authorisation, direct contacts have tended to founder at an early stage in the seas of Soviet bureaucratic obstruction. An extremely detailed administrative annex on protocol emphasises that this is not an agreement between gentlemen but between two wary and mutually suspicious partners.

As a result of the strait-jacket imposed on Anglo–Soviet cultural relations by the Cultural Agreement, their success depends in large measure on the efficiency of the ministries and other bureaucratic bodies entrusted with its administration. Serious problems have arisen over the years. In the USSR, much of the agreement is implemented by the Ministry of Higher and Specialised Secondary Education, which had been described by the British Council as being 'by any standards . . . monumentally inefficient'.[13] Further problems have been created by the rigidity of the Soviet bureaucratic structure, leading to singular lack of co-operation between different ministries. Since an academic visitor might, for example, be hosted by a university under the command of the State Committee for Public Education but wish to work in archives controlled by three other bodies, the delays and difficulties encountered are easy to envisage. The administrative motes in the British Council's eye have resulted from lack of continuity resulting from an excessive movement of personnel at all levels, in part by accident but also by policy. The Soviet side often waxes indignant at the long delays frequently encountered by its citizens in obtaining visas. It is sometimes itself to blame for submitting applications late, but this criticism has some foundation. The performance of the visa department of the Home Office is widely considered to be a national scandal. However, having once reached Britain, the average Soviet visitor will find far fewer impediments in his way than will his British counterpart in the Soviet Union.

SCHOLARLY AND SCIENTIFIC EXCHANGES AND CONTACTS

The Cultural Agreement is the main vehicle for scholarly and scientific exchanges.[14] It is generally used by the Soviet side to send natural scientists and technologists to Britain, whereas Britain responds predominantly with scholars and postgraduates in the humanities and social sciences.[15] There is a clear tendency for the Soviet visitors to concentrate on specific topics in computer science, electrical, electronic and fuel engineering and physics, although there has been a wide range of other subjects from methods of harvesting fruit and cattle breeding to textiles and molecular biology. Most British postgraduates have been specialists in Russian history or literature, although in most years three musicians have been included – one of the more rewarding sections of the exchange since their practical training at Soviet conservatoires has usually been excellent. British scholars in the USSR have tended to concentrate at Moscow and Leningrad universities, whereas Soviet scientists in Britain have been distributed among a wide range of universities and institutes. The small exchanges in medicine and agriculture were largely inoperative between 1979 and 1984, casualties of the political climate. Since 1984 there have been two or three visits a year of agricultural specialists in each direction.[16] In 1987, agriculture was removed from the Cultural Agreement at Soviet insistence, a gap prospectively to be filled by a separate arrangement between the respective Ministries of Agriculture. There has also been a revival of medical exchanges and signs of increased co-operation between the two Ministries of Health. In most years there has been an exchange of two or three town planners and architects. The agreement also allows small groups of British and Soviet educationists to observe each other's systems at close quarters for short periods and to produce reports varying from the useful to the naive.

A separate agreement between the British Academy and the Soviet Academy of Sciences provides Soviet scholars in the humanities and social sciences with a rare opportunity to undertake research in Britain, with political scientists and economists predominating, many of them coming from the Institute of the World Economy and International Relations in Moscow. Some historians have been included, notably historians of Africa. This exchange is particularly popular with British social scientists and historians who need contact with scholars located in Institutes controlled by the Academy of Sciences, access to whom is difficult on exchanges administered by the Soviet State Committee for Public Education, such is the rigid compartmentalisation of Soviet bureaucracy.[17]

The main avenue for Anglo-Soviet scientific contacts is provided by the agreement between the Royal Society and the Soviet Academy of Sciences.[18]

The cream of Soviet scientists work for the Academy, and most important research projects are located in its institutes. Hence, British scientists find this agreement of far more value to them than the Cultural Agreement, which provides entry to the universities. In reverse, Academy scientists desperately need the Royal Society agreement if they are to maintain contact with British science. For many years after the first agreement in 1956 the level of British interest was low. Few British scientists knew Russian. The general standard of equipment in Soviet laboratories was perceived to be low. Lack of information about Soviet science was widespread. Bureaucratic obstacles abounded, and Soviet scientists were frequently denied exit visas. Many British scientists were concerned about human rights issues in the USSR, and about the defence connections of some of Soviet science, which in turn excluded British visitors from some areas in which the USSR excelled. Security considerations and technology transfer regulations also excluded Soviets from some British laboratories. Fears exist that British patents will not be sufficiently respected in the USSR.

This situation has recently changed. Gorbachev's reforming activity has aroused general interest in Soviet affairs and given the impression that fruitful collaboration is possible. Improvements in human rights, the return of Sakharov from exile, the granting of more exit permits to Jews, and steps taken to curtail the abuse of psychiatry in the suppression of dissent have improved the Soviet Union's image. The publicity attendant on Mrs Thatcher's visit to the Soviet Institute of Crystallography in March 1987, and her reception of President Marchuk of the Soviet Academy in November 1987, demonstrated high-level support for increased links. Above all else, more British scientists have realised that there are positive advantages to be gained from co-operation with their Soviet counterparts. The Soviet scientific establishment is the largest in the world, has traditionally attracted most of the best Soviet brains to it, and is especially strong in theory and in fundamental research. Huge Soviet investment in science means that long-term projects are possible in the Soviet Union which financial considerations prevent in Britain. Physics and maths are areas of especial strength. The Soviet side is impressed by British applied science, and the speed with which its results can be introduced into industrial production. The prospects for increased collaboration seem bright. Marchuk has stated his intention to send young Soviet high-fliers to Britain on extended visits. The Royal Society has received the right to nominate up to a quarter of the Soviet scientists to visit Britain, thus increasing the possibility of developing meaningful collaboration with individuals of interest to British scientists. The establishment of an information service by the Royal Society will help British scientists to locate Soviet counterparts in their particular specialisms. Problems may nevertheless remain. The hitherto obstructive bureaucracy of the Soviet

Academy may be imperfectly reformed and British finances are likely to remain inadequate to meet demand. Moreover, the British desire to co-operate in areas where Soviet science is strong and the Soviet desire to improve fields in which it is weak may lead to some incompatibility of purpose.

The possibility exists for direct scholarly contacts outside the formal framework of the agreements. The Helsinki accord of 1975 gave a big impetus to the development of such links, not least because it persuaded the British Government to allocate earmarked funds to promote such contacts with the USSR and Eastern Europe.[19] Official British policy is to respond to demand rather than to create one artificially. Hence, if Polish schemes receive far more than Soviet ones, this is in large measure because Polish scholars are far freer to travel outside their own country if funds are forthcoming to support them than are Soviet scholars. Long delays in replying to invitations, or complete failure to reply, have been the Soviet norm rather than the exception. Even when invitations have been accepted, official approval has often been withheld at the last minute. The innumerable problems and frustrations involved have been sufficient to deter all but the most determined of prospective British partners in direct academic links with the Soviet Union. Nevertheless, some progress has been made. The Royal Society had records of twenty-six collaborative scientific research projects in operation in 1987, although many of these were operating in a low key.[20] In the arts and social sciences, any collaboration has tended to be personal and informal. However, round-tables organised by the Royal Institute of International Affairs and Moscow's Institute of the World Economy and International Relations, and the 'Edinburgh conversations', now organised by Edinburgh University, have become regular and well established. These meetings involve high-ranking defence experts, political figures and academics on both sides, take place in private, and explore in depth political, economic and defence topics. Both sides have seen such seminars as means of bringing influence to bear on policy making in the other country.[21] The number of other, more academic seminars has also increased. There has been a significant movement in both directions of individual specialists attending general conferences on all manner of subjects, even if relatively few Soviets have surmounted the bureaucratic obstacles and actually arrived and many British scholars have been deterred by the high costs involved.

The achievements in the field of scholarly and scientific contacts have been real but patchy, with failures outnumbering successes in many years, particularly when political relations have been at low ebb. Frustrations on the British side have been numerous, ranging from visa delays to difficulty of access to Soviet archives and other materials, restrictions on travel for scholarly purposes and frequently poor working conditions. Ironically, the Soviet side has gained less than it might have done from these exchanges over the years as a result of the self-defeating inefficiency of its own bureaucracy which has frustrated many potentially useful contacts. Nevertheless, Soviet scientists have gained access to a wide range of laboratories and expertise, even if some of their scholars have been criticised for gathering information rather than engaging in fundamental research. The British side has been enabled to do fundamental research in Russian culture and history and Soviet society. This is valuable in its own right, and has also heightened British critical awareness and understanding of the Soviet Union. Some valuable scientific contacts have also been made. Given recent improvements in contacts, prospects for improved and more beneficial collaboration seem good.

RUSSIAN AND ENGLISH LANGUAGE STUDIES

The scale of exchanges of language teachers and students has increased sharply over the past decade. British students of Russian had no opportunity to study in the Soviet Union until the 1965–67 agreement which provided a one-month summer school for twenty-eight British students. In the late 1960s, a shortfall in the number of qualified British postgraduates and the refusal of the Soviet side to reduce this quota, which was important to it, opened the way for handfuls of British undergraduates to spend a year in the USSR on language studies, in the guise of postgraduates. Rapid progress has been made since 1973; in 1988, over 250 were scheduled to spend between three and ten months in the Soviet Union.[22] At all institutions except the Pushkin Institute, the British students live in hostels with Soviet students. Thus, although they are taught separately, they have the opportunity to mix with their Soviet counterparts even if various obstacles are placed in the way of such personal contacts. The inefficiency of such obstacles has been demonstrated by the significant number of Anglo-Soviet marriages that have resulted from these exchanges.

Soviet students of English receive a raw deal under these exchange agreements. Apart from the few direct links, their opportunity to visit Britain is to qualify for one of the forty-five places available annually on courses lasting 30 days for students from teacher training colleges and departments of education. By deliberate act of Soviet policy, students have been replaced by teachers of English on all the other exchanges, with the result that the Soviet Union is now the largest customer of courses for teachers of English organised directly by the British Council.[23] Any restrictions on their movement and contacts with British citizens are only those imposed internally by their group leaders. The decline in the teaching of Russian in Britain helps to explain the limited provision for school teachers in the Cultural Agreement. It has proved difficult to fill even the twenty-five places available on a summer holiday course organised for them in Leningrad. The agreement also makes possible the exchange of three teachers a year to teach in schools for up to three months each, and the engagement of three Soviet teachers in British schools and of three British teachers in Soviet pedagogical institutes for the year. These clauses are generally implemented and are invaluable in the development of direct contacts. Expansion on any scale seems unlikely, given the problems that the few English teachers of Russian have in obtaining leave of absence and the traditional reluctance of the Soviet authorities to allow the prolonged presence in their schools of alien, and so by definition potentially disruptive, influences. One British teacher had to be specifically instructed not to display any British newspapers, except the *Morning Star*.[24]

British language students go in large numbers to schools in many countries to serve as language assistants. This is not yet possible in the Soviet Union. Recent graduates are sent as lectors on a wide scale to foreign universities. The opportunities in Soviet universities are very limited for them. The Cultural Agreement provides for the exchange of up to twenty lectors a year. In 1985–86 and 1986–87 only thirteen were exchanged. This section of the Cultural Agreement is mutually beneficial. Although British students of Russian as a group still have significantly less chance of practising their Russian than their counterparts in other languages, the expansion in opportunities for residence in the Soviet Union has raised the general standard achieved in the spoken language and has provided invaluable insights into the Soviet system and society. The maintenance of a large pool of Russian speakers is necessary if British commercial, pedagogical, academic, defence and other needs are to be met. Likewise, Soviet teachers have been given greater opportunities to raise their standards, to the benefit of their students. Notwithstanding a frequent lack of a spirit of adventure, they do achieve some contact with British life, particularly in those centres where they are boarded out with British families, and therefore obtain a more realistic and balanced view of the country they are studying. On both sides, genuine personal contacts are possible, thereby satisfying the more altruistic objectives of cultural relations.

YOUTH EXCHANGES

Youth exchanges are encouraged by the Cultural Agreement. However, developments in this area have hitherto been generally unsatisfactory. British groups going to the Soviet Union have found themselves in the hands of Sputnik, the Soviet Union's Youth Travel Bureau, which is closely linked with the Young Communist League. They have been offered tourist programmes, with some items of a tendentiously political nature. Contact with young Russians and joint activities have been severely restricted. Political activists posing as 'official friends' have found it difficult to provide genuine human contact with their British visitors, and have deterred 'unofficial' contacts. Soviet groups visiting

Britain are as a rule significantly older in their membership than is usual in youth exchanges, creating problems for their hosts. Moreover, they have been led to believe that they have paid for a normal tourist visit rather than a genuine exchange. International Youth Camps in the Soviet Union, such as that held at Noorus in Estonia in the summer of 1987, tend to devote much of their programmes to political indoctrination. The Bradford Youth Players, the Huddersfield Youth Jazz Orchestra and Dundee Junior Showtime are among youth arts groups that have visited the Soviet Union.

In terms of genuine personal contacts, exchanges made under the aegis of town twinning arrangements have tended to be far more successful. Indeed, youth exchanges are unlikely to be successful unless they bring together partners with interests in common, preferably on a long-term basis. Hitherto, Soviet policy has been to obstruct such arrangements, but there are indications that recent political developments are leading to a change in attitude. An exchange of youth drama groups between University College, London, and the Latvian State University in Riga may presage regular interchanges of the sort that have proved so fruitful with some other Eastern European countries. Children from schools in Canterbury and Vladimir went on an exchange visit in early 1988. They visited lessons and stayed in each other's homes, a notable breakthrough.

TOWN TWINNING ARRANGEMENTS

There were nineteen town twinnings in existence in 1987, not all of which were active. Where they work well, they provide opportunities for genuine personal contacts. The Cardiff-Voroshilovgrad link has led to groups of young Russians in Welsh homes, and to a continuity in relationships. Sheffield's link with Donetsk stands out for its longevity and scale of operations. Started in 1956, it is financially supported at both ends by the city councils. Sheffield and Donetsk weeks have been held in the respective cities, youth and tourist exchanges taken place, alongside visits by brass bands, civic dignitaries, football teams and the like. Three London boroughs are twinned with Moscow districts. Lambeth's link has led not only to the presence of Soviet schoolchildren in London but also that of a London artist in Moscow on an extended visit to record scenes of ordinary life.[25] Although, in the context of Anglo-Soviet relations, town twinning may have produced some notable examples of co-operation, it cannot be denied that twinning arrangements with other countries have been much more productive and widespread.

RELIGIOUS AND PEACE GROUPS

The status of religious bodies is such in the Soviet Union that the prospects for contacts between Soviet and British Christians would seem at first sight to be scanty. However, the Soviet Government has found the Foreign Relations Department of the Orthodox Church to be a useful tool in promoting its foreign policy objectives, with the result that there has been a significant interchange of church delegations. The British Council of Churches has also enabled Baptists to meet their opposite numbers. British Quakers have been especially active in seeking to promote contacts with Soviet citizens and, in their genuine commitment to peace, have been able to co-operate with the Soviet Peace Committee, a far from independent body which defines peace in terms of official policy. Seminars have been held, many British Quakers have visited the Soviet Union and made personal contacts, and young British volunteers participated in Soviet work camps. Bodies like Pensioners for Peace, Mothers for Peace, Teachers for Peace, Scientists against Nuclear Arms, Schools against the Bomb, and the UK–USSR Medical Exchange Programme and CND have developed links with Soviet counterparts.[26] Soviet objectives are well served by such contacts since they enable official policy, embellished with suitable terminology, to be explained to representatives of British public opinion considered to be 'progressive' as a result of their idealism. The Soviet Union greatly relishes being able to claim support for its policies in all countries.

FRIENDSHIP SOCIETIES

The Union of Soviet Societies for Friendship, based in Moscow, maintains contacts with 9,000 organisations and many activists in 140 countries.[27] One of its 78 constituent societies is the USSR–GB Society, now headed by the publicity-conscious eye surgeon, Professor S.N. Fedorov. From the Soviet point of view, friendship societies are a valuable means of maintaining unofficial contacts with sympathisers throughout the world, of extending Soviet influence and promoting the USSR's image, of counteracting anti-Soviet propaganda and of controlling Soviet citizens' contacts with foreigners. A Soviet commentator has noted with approval how friendship societies in Europe have actively opposed the neutron bomb and American 'Eurorockets' and have supported Soviet disarmament initiatives.[28] The three British societies which might usefully serve these objectives are negligible in size and influence.[29] Their membership is minute, their publications have a small circulation and their activities generally low-key. Nevertheless, they are highly praised by Soviet commentators. Their main value in Soviet eyes must be in maintaining a network of sympathisers and in entertaining Soviet visitors. Nothing is potentially more effective than anti-British propaganda from British mouths.

The Great Britain–USSR Association is different in character. It was founded in 1959 with government support and funding to provide an alternative channel for unofficial and personal contacts with the USSR, the existing friendship societies being considered to be subject to Soviet influence or control. It does not aim to be a mass organisation, but rather to maximise contacts between Soviet and British people of similar interests. It has organised colloquia for writers, lawyers, journalists and television directors, and has helped British theatre directors to make visits to the USSR to do research for new productions of Soviet plays in Britain. It organised a British week in Novosibirsk in 1978, helped to set up a Soviet Festival in Birmingham in 1988 and will co-ordinate a reciprocal British event in Kiev in 1990. It has helped Soviet visitors in many fields to make contact with British counterparts. Categorised in Soviet eyes as an appendage of the British Foreign Office, it has frequently been criticised by Soviet writers.[30]

SPORT

In February 1979, the British Government signed a memorandum of under-standing with the Soviet Committee for Physical Culture and Sport which envisaged the exchanges of coaches and of information, joint seminars and conferences, as well as participation in competitions in both countries. This memorandum has been largely worthless. A year later, Prime Minister Thatcher was writing to Sir Denis Follows of the British Olympics Association, 'for British athletes to take part in Games in Moscow would be for them to seem to condone an international crime' (the military occupation of Afghanistan).[31] Mr Jeeps of the Sports Council affirmed that the loss of this memorandum would not be of any great loss to sport 'since no money had been provided to implement the terms of the agreement: it was simply evidence, in the Sports bodies' eyes, of a government agreement entered into without consultation and forgotten in the present situation'.[32] Notwithstanding this generally discouraging atmosphere, some regular contacts have been made, particularly in gymnastics and chess. Co-operation between coaches takes place at routine matches.[33] The Soviet side is used to dealing with one appropriate co-ordinating body, and finds the proliferation of autonomous governing bodies for individual sports in Britain to be totally bewildering. British bodies find the financial demands made by visiting Soviet teams, particularly for pocket money in addition to living expenses, to be generally beyond their means. Despite the encouraging atmosphere of 1987 significant progress is unlikely to be made. Even if extra funds were to be made available, the prospect of the amateurs running individual British sports sinking their differences and forming a co-ordinating committee to liaise with the Soviet Committee for Physical Culture and Sport is an unlikely one, although such an arrangement would be very likely to be to Britain's advantage, given Soviet sporting pre-eminence.

THE ARTS

The Cultural Agreement signed in 1960 made reference to visits in each direction to be made by named major ballet, theatrical and other companies and orchestras. These specific references have been dropped in recent years to be replaced by facilitating clauses and phrases of encouragement. The Soviet side would like to restore specificity, but the British Government cannot exert sufficient control over autonomous bodies in the arts world to be able to guarantee to fulfil any precise pledges made. The terms on which the exchange of visits by major companies and orchestras takes place are financially disadvantageous to the British side. Soviet companies deal with British impresarios, who are able to charge high ticket prices and to pay Goskontsert, the responsible Soviet agent, a sum in convertible currency sufficient to cover all touring expenses and to leave a significant surplus. Wages are anyway covered by the large state subsidies and paid in roubles; the pocket money allowance paid in pounds to Soviet visitors is at a miserly level that would not be tolerated by Equity or the Musicians' Union. Where the books do not balance, large subsidies have to be raised in Britain, as in the case of the visit of the Maiakovskii Theatre to the National Theatre in October 1987. British companies and performers touring the USSR are paid by Goskontsert largely in non-convertible roubles, leaving a large deficit in the wages, often at double rate on foreign tours, which have to be paid in sterling but cannot be recovered from income for the tour. The net result is that the British side has to subsidise visits by British groups to the Soviet Union, and also to underwrite many Soviet tours of Britain, a very one-sided arrangement. Soviet companies and orchestras can perform where they like in Britain; Goskontsert severely limits the itineraries of British artists and so the extent to which British culture can be directly appreciated by Soviet citizens. Even in Moscow and Leningrad, major British companies are seen only by a limited sector of the populace, since influential contacts are usually needed for ordinary citizens to obtain tickets. The British embargo on tours by major companies following the occupation of Afghanistan in 1979 was effective, although it did not prevent visits by privately funded individual musicians or lesser-known theatrical groups. The change in policy in the mid-1980s has been followed by an increased number of visits by prestigious companies in both directions, with the Russian theme in the 1987 Edinburgh Festival marking a high point. The Soviet side sees this interchange in terms of traditional cultural diplomacy, preferring to concentrate on excellence in high culture, even if some Soviet rock and jazz musicians have recently been allowed to perform in Britain. The British side, not least on financial grounds, would like to demonstrate the liveliness and variety of British culture by sending more fringe groups, jazz and folk groups and pop musicians. Hitherto, this policy has met with only limited success.

The 1987 Cultural Agreement contains a new clause for the exchange of composers. The fruitful results of Benjamin Britten's friendship with Shostakovich and other Soviet musicians are well known. More recently, representatives of the new generation of Soviet composers like Schnittke, Gubaidulina and Denisov have visited Britain and a reasonable number of performances of their works have taken place. British composers like Nigel Osborne have responded vividly to inspiration from Russian literature. The new clause in the agreement may help to remedy the situation whereby Britten and the communist Alan Bush are virtually the only twentieth-century British composers whose works are performed in the Soviet Union.

LITERATURE AND THE MEDIA

A frequently heard Soviet complaint is that the British reading public is denied access to Soviet literature. British publishers are commercial organisations and not controlled by the British Government. Nevertheless, the range of Soviet literature which has been translated and published has been quite wide in the 1970s and 1980s. Perhaps the unacknowledged thrust of the Soviet complaint is that many of the authors published, such as Solzhenitsyn, are living in exile, but that is the responsibility of the Soviet rather than the British Government. Soviet publishers do bring out many translations into English of Soviet works. Much of this material is propagandistic and designed mainly for Third World countries. Lack of commercial acumen, and in some cases the quality of the translations, limits the circulation in Britain of the more worthwhile of these publishing ventures. Soviet publishers may sell freely to the British public. British publishers, even when promoting British book exhibitions to the USSR, are denied similar facilities and are dependent for sales on orders from the central purchasing authorities. The result is that only a very limited range of British publications, in small quantities, are made available for purchase in foreign language bookshops in a few of the larger Soviet cities. A limited number of British novels have been translated into Russian. Writers like Graham Greene, Alan Sillitoe and Stan Barstow are very popular. Soviet public demand for British books is great and largely unsatisfied; British public demand for Soviet books is limited and generally satisfied.

Many British authors have visited the Soviet Union. Some have addressed large audiences of admirers; others have gone in order to spend rubles which they have accumulated in royalties. A steady stream of Soviet novelists, poets and playwrights of varying reputation have been to Britain, often with the co-operation of the friendship societies and sometimes in connection with performances or publication of their works.

In 1987 and 1988 the quality British newspapers were regularly publishing serious and detailed reports from correspondents resident in Moscow. However, the large majority of the British public reads mass-circulation newspapers in which reporting about the Soviet Union is intermittent, often frivolous and seldom objective. Soviet complaints on this score have much justification. In these circumstances, British radio and television bear a great burden of responsibility to develop an informed British public opinion about the Soviet Union. The BBC in particular has responded admirably to this challenge especially since it is able to maintain television as well as radio correspondents in Moscow.[34] The memorandum of understanding signed during Mrs Thatcher's visit to Moscow in March 1987 laid stress on improvements in co-operation between the national television and radio companies. Before the advent of Gorbachev to power, the BBC had already managed to produce a Russian language series in co-operation with Soviet TV, but many other projects had been frustrated. The changed atmosphere since 1985 has led to a flood of programmes on the USSR produced with Soviet co-operation. Soviet spokes-men are regularly interviewed and discussion programmes shot in Moscow. Much stress has been laid on Russian and Soviet culture, and BBC Radio 3's Russian Festival has been only the most conspicuous of an extensive and continuing series of events. These developments have been made possible by a general change in Soviet policy, and have enabled a wider section of British and other Western public opinion to be better informed about the Soviet Union than previously.

In 1985 the Soviet Union had eighteen journalists resident in London.[35] As a result of their efforts, Soviet newspapers, radio and television have maintained a coverage of British news which has been highly selective, slanted and sometimes inaccurate. The deliberate intention has been to present a view of Britain which is ideologically acceptable in Soviet terms by portraying Britain as a class-divided society in decline, with 'progressive' forces in society subjected to brutal police repression. Recent developments in the policy of *glasnost'* have enabled this picture to be punctured at moments by live discussions on 'telebridges' with politicians and others in the USA, Britain and other countries. Even the live interview of Mrs Thatcher in forthright form on Soviet television in March 1987 doubtless had a salutary impact.

Despite *glasnost'*, Soviet citizens receive a biased and extremely selective view of the outside world from Soviet sources. Unlike some of their neighbours in the Warsaw Pact countries, nearly all Soviet citizens are geographically too distant to be able to pick up Western television broadcasts to give them an alternative view of the world.[36] They are, however, able to pick up Western short-wave radio transmissions when these are not jammed. The BBC World Service programmes in English have always been accessible in theory to Soviet listeners, but the weakness of the British transmitters has made reception difficult. The commissioning of new transmitters at Rampisham and Orfordness should improve the situation and increase the BBC's (admittedly low) audience figures for its English-language programmes.[37] The BBC has concentrated its attention on its Russian language broadcasts, for which it claimed a monthly Soviet audience of about 18 million in 1985, despite comprehensive Soviet jamming. The number of hours broadcast has been increased over ten years from 32 to 46 a week.[38] An opinion research centre based in Paris judged the BBC to be considered by its listeners to be more objective and effective than any of its Western rivals.[39] It probably owes this favourable evaluation to its policy of providing a centrally controlled news bulletin common to all its foreign language broadcasts,[40] and to a stricter control over the voicing of the political prejudices of its *émigré* employees. The BBC has been presented with new opportunities by the Soviet decision in January 1987 to stop jamming its broadcasts, whilst for a time continuing effective disruption of stations like Radio Liberty. It has responded with a new half-hour daily magazine, 'Argument', with reports in Russian from BBC journalists around the world and items on trends and developments in Britain. New English lessons and a discussion programme aimed at Soviet youth have also been introduced.[41]

The Soviet Union has a very large film industry, with particularly active studios in republics like Georgia and Latvia, as well as in Moscow and Leningrad. It often complains that its films are not distributed in Britain, a complaint that has been echoed by many independent British film producers unable to find favour with the commercial distributors. Special seasons at the National Film Theatre and other minority venues in London and to a lesser extent elsewhere have shown some of these films to a limited audience. More important in this respect has been the BBC which has shown many recent and classic Soviet films to large late-night audiences. The British film industry is minuscule by comparison, and some of its products objectionable to the Soviet censors on moral or political grounds. A very few British films have achieved wide distribution, but the British entry to the 1983 Moscow Film Festival was banned. On the other hand, a few British television films like 'The Forsyte Saga' have been very popular with Soviet television audiences.

TOURISM

In the aftermath of the Chernobyl disaster, the number of British tourists visiting the USSR in 1986 fell to 55,000, but reached 73,000 in 1987.[42] The vast majority of these go on standard package tours with Intourist, Thomsons or other mass operators, are whisked from city to city, given the officially desired view of the country by Soviet guides and shielded from real contact with the local population by their ignorance of the Russian language. Special interest study tours arranged, for instance, through the Soviet Council of Trade Unions, show small numbers different aspects of the Soviet system, again from an official point of view. Soviet tourists visit Britain in very much smaller numbers. They tend to be based on Soviet cruise ships docked at ports like Tilbury, which saves hotel bills and minimises contact with British society. Shepherded around in tour buses, their meetings with local inhabitants are usually limited to social events organised by pro-Soviet friendship societies. Individual tourism is possible in the Soviet Union, but is expensive, difficult to organise and limited to those roads and cities open to foreigners. Individual Soviet tourism in Britain is inconceivable save for those who, like Soviet diplomats, are based here. Theoretically it has been possible for individual visits to be made in both directions by personal invitation, but in practice these have nearly always been nipped in the bud by the Soviet visa authorities. In 1987, this obstructive policy was changed but the flow of such visitors in each direction is still likely to be very limited.

Thus those who believe that the foundations of a successful cultural relations policy can be laid by mass tourism can find little comfort in the Soviet experience, such has been the usual success of the Soviet authorities in conducting such interchange on its own terms. Whether the general proposition is valid is open to doubt, as a visit to the Costa Brava would indicate.

FUTURE PROSPECTS

In 1987 it became apparent that Gorbachev's policy of *glasnost'* was not only leading to internal changes but also to a reassessment of the Soviet Union's cultural relations with the outside world. Former bureaucratic obstacles are shrinking as obstructive administrators are denounced in the press. Soviet officials emphasise that policies have changed and that initiatives which in the recent past were theoretically possible but in practice unrealisable may now go ahead. Whilst Soviet officialdom is still likely to be cautious in making proposals off its own bat, it is now much less likely to resist the pressure from below for a great increase in scientific and cultural contacts with the West. A change in the law whereby foreign guests are now able to stay in Soviet homes should lead to an expansion in personal contacts between citizens. More direct link and school exchanges of various sorts were concluded in 1988. The exchange of scientists through the Royal Society and the Academy of Sciences will double, if words are translated into deeds. Barring political changes in the Soviet Union, the main obstacle is likely to be a financial one. The Soviet Union continues to be extremely reluctant to spend any convertible currency on such contacts. Consequently, any increase in activity will entail additional expenditure by the British side at a time when financial stringencies are curtailing much general activity in education, the arts and science. A modest increase in the British Council's annual spending on its operations in and with the Soviet Union has already led to a significant increase in activity under the Cultural Agreement.[43] The main thrust of any further expansion is likely to be in contacts outside the Cultural Agreement, provided that a large and positive response be made to the the initiatives from and aspirations of Soviet society. Large-scale expenditure on visits by prestigious British theatrical companies is not needed, unless cultural consolidation of an improving political relationship is perceived to be necessary. Further visits by the Royal Ballet are likely only to strengthen Soviet convictions of their own superiority in that art form, and there is no hard evidence to support the view that such visits influence Soviet officials to buy British goods.

When China opened itself to the West, the British Government responded with a large injection of money to foster cultural and scientific contacts. Now that the Soviet Union is opening up, there has been a modest increase in funding; in early 1989 an additional £800,000 was allocated for establishing 'closer contacts' with the Soviet Union.[44] Since Britain seems now to enjoy better political relations with the Soviet Union than at any time since the Second World War, London has an unprecedented opportunity to take the lead in responding to the pressure from Soviet society for greater contact, thereby furthering the cause of democratisation and opening up of Soviet society which has long been an aim of British policy. Whether or not this opportunity will be seized to the full still remains to be seen, despite all the hopeful signs. What is needed is moderate continuing funding for scientific and cultural relations, as opposed to ostentatious gestures of cultural diplomacy. Otherwise the lead will again be ceded to countries like France.[45]

NOTES

1. M.J. Berry, 'Science, technology and innovation', in Martin McCauley, ed., *Khrushchev and Khrushchevism* (Macmillan, 1987), p. 73.
2. Agreement had already been concluded with France in 1956 and with the USA in 1958. *Keesing's Contemporary Archives*, 16–23 June 1956, pp. 14934–5; Yale Richmond, *US–Soviet Cultural Exchanges, 1958–1986* (Westview Press, 1987), p. 2.
3. *Soviet Union No. 1*, Cmnd 5924, 1975, p. 23.
4. Allen K. Kassof, 'Report of the Executive Director', International Research and Exchanges Board, *Annual Report 1985–1986*, Princeton, New Jersey, 1987, p. 7.
5. See, for instance, Philip Hanson, *Soviet Industrial Espionage: Some New Information* (RIIA, 1987).
6. House of Commons, Fourth Report from the Foreign Affairs Committee, 1986–87, *Cultural Diplomacy*, HC24 (HMSO, 1987), pp. v–vi, 55.

7. *Ibid.*, p. 230.
8. J.M. Mitchell, *International Cultural Relations* (Allen and Unwin, 1986), p. 5.
9. House of Commons, *Cultural Diplomacy*, pp. 1–2.
10. House of Commons, Foreign Affairs Committee, session 1985–86, *UK–Soviet Relations*, vol. II (HMSO, 1986), p. 302.
11. John Morison, 'The political content of education in the USSR', in J.J. Tomiak, ed., *Soviet Education in the 1980s* (Croom Helm, 1983), pp. 147–8; John Morison, 'Recent developments in political education in the Soviet Union', in George Avis, ed., *The Making of the Soviet Citizen* (Croom Helm, 1987), p. 28.
12. *UK–Soviet Relations*, vol. II, pp. 272–3.
13. *Ibid.*
14. The Cultural Agreement for 1987–89 provides for up to ten senior academics from each side to make short visits of up to a fortnight to give lectures or make contacts, for up to 25 academics to make research visits of at least a month in duration, and for 45 Soviet postgraduates and young scholars under the age of 35 to visit Britain for up to a year with 30 British equivalents going to the Soviet Union for a similar period. The aggregate of all these categories entitles the British side to a total of 322 person-months each year, as opposed to the Soviet quota of up to 470 person-months. This imbalance is rectified elsewhere in the agreement by the provision of undergraduate places for British students of Russian.
15. At postgraduate and junior scientist level, the Soviet side sent 30 technologists and natural scientists in 1981–82, and only three in arts and sciences (one lawyer, one economist and one musicologist). In 1982–83, 24 scientists and technologists were balanced by six others (one student of British folk tales, two linguists, one international lawyer, one lexicologist and one historian studying British attitudes to resistance movements in World War II). In 1983–84, the respective figures were 28:5, in 1984–85, 27:3, in 1985–86, 26:6 and in 1987–88, 28:8. In the reverse direction, Britain sent 26 arts and social science postgraduates in 1981–82 with one physicist and one pharmacologist. In 1982–83, 1983–84 and 1984–85 Britain could muster only 16 postgraduates per year (with some Soviet visa refusals contributing to this), with a solitary scientist among them, studying the foraging habits of birds. In the following two years, the figures reached a total of 17 and 19, but included no scientists.

    At a more senior level, similar tendencies are observed. The available records show that between 1982 and 1987 the Soviet side sent in the exchange of lecturers for research purposes 36 specialists in science and technology, 10 social scientists and two linguists. In the same period the British despatched 23 historians, 14 literary scholars, 4 linguists, 13 social scientists and one specialist in forestry. In the short visits for up to a fortnight by senior scholars, the Soviet participants have again been almost exclusively natural scientists and technologists, but British involvement has been much more mixed, with the inclusion of a significant number of scientists.
16. Soviet visitors have studied sugar beet, viral diseases of animals, molecular biology and the like in exchange for British investigation of the breeding of textile fibre producing goats, plant health controls, collective farming, irrigation and soil science.
17. The present agreement between the British Academy and the Soviet Academy of Sciences was signed in 1977 and provides for the annual exchange of ten scholars in the humanities and social sciences for periods of between two weeks and three months, to a total of 15 person-months a year.

18. A new agreement in 1986 allowed for exchanges of postdoctoral scientists in the natural sciences or technology on short visits or fellowships between one and nine months, to an annual total of not more than 15 and 50 person-months respectively. A protocol signed during the visit of the head of the Soviet Academy of Sciences to Britain in November 1987 provided for an immediate increase of 50 per cent in these quotas, with a further 50 per cent increase envisaged in 1988. The tendency is for British scientists to prefer short visits, usually of two weeks. In contrast, the Soviet Academy prefers to send its participants on longer fellowships.

19. In 1986–87, a total of £98,790 was made available. A large percentage of this, £45,000, was diverted to support of the flourishing scheme for academic links with Poland. £35,000 was made available to support such links with the rest of Eastern Europe and the USSR. (In 1985–86, 23 per cent of this portion went to the USSR.) The remaining £18,790 was distributed to a variety of individuals and institutions active in this area.

20. In 1980, radio astronomy was singled out as an area in which collaboration had been of benefit to both sides, and the agreement between the British Geological Survey and the Institute for the Physics of the Earth in Moscow has worked well. Other viable contacts include those between Birkbeck College and the Institute of Crystallography in Moscow, between Leeds and Novosibirsk in gas flame structure, between Oxford and Moscow in mathematics, and between Sheffield, Birmingham and Moscow in space research. See Sir Michael Stoker, 'Some foreign affairs', *Royal Society News*, 5 (October 1980), p. 2; House of Commons, Fifth Report from the Foreign Affairs Committee, 1984–85, *UK Membership of NATO* (HMSO, 1985), HC 461, p. 78; *The Guardian*, 20 and 21 October 1987.

21. *Times Higher Education Supplement*, 2 October 1987, p. 6; *Scotland–USSR News*, 1 (1981), and 3 (1983); *The Scotsman*, 25 September 1984, p. 6; V. Kobysh, 'Vzgliad s britanskikh ostrovov', *Literaturnaia gazeta*, 14 October 1981, p. 9. Similar Soviet–French and Soviet–German meetings are held.

22. Under the Cultural Agreement for 1987–89, 38 students will spend an academic year at Soviet universities on language courses, and a further 114 will attend three-month courses. Fifty more will study for five months at the Pushkin Institute in Moscow, a special establishment designed to train future and actual teachers of Russian from all countries save the Soviet Union. Direct links between five British universities and Soviet pedagogical or language institutes provide further opportunities, and more direct link agreements are expected to be signed in 1988.

23. In the 1987–88 academic year, 114 young Soviet teachers of English will come to Britain on three-month courses, 48 more mature teachers will come for four months, and 40 senior teachers will arrive for one month.

24. Michael N. Brannan, 'Teaching English in the Soviet Union', *Modern Languages in Scotland*, 21–22 (May 1981), p. 73.

25. *Britain–USSR*, 75 (December 1986), pp. 9–11.

26. Claire Ryle and Jim Garrison, *Citizen's Diplomacy* (Merlin Press, 1986), pp. 54–5.

27. Z.M. Kruglova, 'Soiuz Sovetskikh obshchestv druzhby i kulturnoi sviazi s zarubezhnymi stranami', *Voprosy istorii*, 12 (1981), p. 37.

28. Kruglova, 'Soiuz sovetskikh obshchestv', p. 39.

29. The British–Soviet Friendship Society now has a membership of about 3,000, works in close collaboration with the Soviet Embassy, and is very pro-Soviet. It is especially active in providing hospitality to Soviet visitors. The Society for Cultural Relations

with the USSR had only 1,076 members in 1986–87 and was facing a financial crisis, despite unidentified donations. It is generally sympathetic to the USSR, and is especially active in organising language courses, and small exhibitions. The Scotland–USSR Society is based in Glasgow, and has over 2,000 members. Its activities have included the 'Edinburgh Conversations' and a 'Scottish–Soviet Peace Forum' in 1983. It is closely linked with Sovscot Tours, a travel agency which takes many youth and tourist groups to the USSR (Progressive Tours, with its strong links with the Communist Party, performs a similar function for the English friendship societies). See Society for Cultural Relations with the USSR, *Annual Report*, 1986–87, pp. 11, 15.

30. A.V. Golubev, 'Sovetsko-angliiskie sviazi po linii obshchestvennykh organizatsii v 1979–1982 gg', *Vestnik Moskovskogo Universiteta, Seriia Istoriia*, 14 (1984), pp. 31-8; V. Korotych, 'O chem zvoniat kolokola', *Pravda*, 11 February 1985, p. 6.

31. House of Commons, First Report from the Foreign Affairs Committee, Series 1979–80, *Olympic Games 1980* (HMSO, 1980), HC 490, p. vi.

32. House of Commons, *Olympic Games 1980*, p. 17.

33. Ryle and Garrison, *Citizens' Diplomacy*, 29-32.

34. ITN established a base in Moscow in 1988.

35. *UK–Soviet Relations*, vol. II, p. 271.

36. Estonians can, and do, watch and understand Finnish television.

37. *UK–Soviet Relations*, vol. II, pp. 89-93, and Memorandum Submitted by the BBC World Services, House of Commons Foreign Affairs Committee, Sessions 1988–89, *Eastern Europe and the Soviet Union* (HMSO, 1989), p. 275.

38. *UK–Soviet Relations*, vol. I, p. lxxviii.

39. *UK–Soviet Relations*, vol. II, pp. 387-388.

40. Peter Frankel, 'The BBC External Services: broadcasting to the USSR and Eastern Europe', in K.R.M. Short, ed., *Western Broadcasting over the Iron Curtain* (Croom Helm, 1986), p. 142.

41. *The Daily Telegraph*, 14 September 1987.

42. *The Guardian*, 7 November 1987, p. 8; *The Sunday Times*, 28 February 1988, p. F3.

43. The British Council's annual spending on its operations in and with the Soviet Union, after suffering an earlier cut, rose from £704,000 in 1984–85 to £1,097,000 in 1985–86, underwriting a doubling of inward and outward visits under the Cultural Agreement between 1983 and 1985 to 500 in each direction per annum. See *UK–Soviet Relations*, HC 376, pp. 70, 78.

44. See *Eastern Europe and the Soviet Union*, p. xxxviii.

45. For example, if France has many more lectors working in the Soviet Union than has Britain, this is not because the Soviet Union has adopted a cultural policy deliberately discriminating in favour of France nor because it wishes to promote the study of French rather than of English. The reason lies in the fact that in 1986 France was spending nearly three and half times as much as Britain on cultural diplomacy, and was therefore able to pay its recruits at a rate to make even service in a Soviet provincial town attractive. At the same time, it was able to place Soviet lectors in France.

9   Trade relations: patterns and prospects

MICHAEL KASER

The United Kingdom was the first country to sign a trade agreement with the USSR, three-and-a-half years after the Bolshevik Revolution, and for many years up to and soon after the Second World War it was the biggest Western partner. Today each side represents only one per cent of the other's foreign-trade turnover. Despite fluctuations induced less by commercial than by political considerations, the bilateral relationship has been more stable than the corresponding trade of other Western partners. On statistical grounds it is even possible to speak of some priority among such partners for the UK when the USSR allocates its funds for convertible-currency imports; for significant periods the UK has done better in selling equipment to the USSR than British competitiveness on world markets would have justified. Nevertheless in the 1980s British equipment has done worse in the USSR than it has done elsewhere.

Over the full seven decades of Soviet trade with the United Kingdom, exchanges, as with other market economies, have been sensitive historically to the degree of international tension, from the end of the Civil War in Russia (1920) through the German invasion of the USSR (1941) to the Soviet invasion of Afghanistan (1979). The bilateral relationship has, however, not escaped the impact of political issues in the United Kingdom. Trade agreements with the USSR have usually been made soon after changes in administration – four by a Labour Government (1924, 1930, 1947 and 1975), two by a Conservative ministry (1934 and 1959) and two by a coalition (1921 and 1942). Constrained as they have been within such a political fluctuation, economic relations have also been activated or depressed by the domestic requirements of the USSR (though not of the UK) and by British multilateral commitments – to wartime allies in 1920 and 1942, to the Commonwealth in 1932 and to NATO, under policies of selective embargo, since 1949.

TRADE WITH BRITISH PRIMACY

The Red Army's victory in the Civil War allowed both Soviet Russia and the Western powers to move towards normalising economic relations. Within a month of the evacuation of mainland Russia by counter-revolutionary forces, a Soviet trade delegation met an emissary of the Supreme Economic Council of Allied Governments and, within days, the latter (at the San Remo Conference, 25 April 1920) directed its permanent Executive Committee to 'take all steps necessary to secure the development of trade relations between Russia and the Allied Countries'. The United Kingdom took its decision within that inter-Allied accord and was the first to sign a trade agreement: negotiations began on 31 May 1920 and signature took place in London on 16 March 1921. Similar treaties were made within the year by the principal European nations, but that with Germany at Rapallo was outside the Allies' understanding and profoundly surprised them by establishing close political and economic links (and, later, military) between the two 'outsiders' of Europe.

George Kennan perceived that two Soviet objectives had emerged as early as 1918. One was to 'produce a second, and genuinely Soviet, revolution in Germany' on the way to a European revolution. But the second, pending achievement of the first, was to persuade the Western Allies to withdraw interventionist troops and 'to establish with the Soviet regime such official relations as would assure against a renewal of intervention and would make possible a modicum of renewed trade and perhaps of economic assistance from Western countries'.[1]

The readiness of the Allied powers to engage in trade with a country that had nationalised all foreign property without compensation and renounced all pre-revolutionary bonds was grudging and was followed by diplomatic recognition only after considerable delay. The keenness of Soviet Russia to open up relations lay in its urgent need of imports for famine relief. The first public warning of the impending harvest disaster coincided with the start of negotiations and its magnitude became clear with the creation in June of an All-Russian Committee for Aid to the Hungry and agreement with the American Relief Administration in July for supplies. The Anglo-Soviet trade treaty signalled the end of Russian economic isolation: a month after its signature Lenin observed 'it is important for us to open one window after another . . . Thanks to this treaty we opened a certain window.' Lenin's accolade was long beneficial, as it proved, to British business.

More fundamentally, a reorganisation of the Soviet economic mechanism underlay the abandonment of self-sufficiency practised under 'War Commun-ism' (1918-21) and in almost every way the 'New Economic Policy' (1921-28) re-introduced an open economy. The state monopoly of foreign trade (decreed in

1918) was re-interpreted as state control: private as well as state enterprises could engage in foreign trade under licence, foreign firms could establish subsidiaries as 'concessions', most of which laid down certain obligations on the import of technology or in 'mixed companies'; expatriate professionals could be employed; the rouble, quickly stabilised after the hyper-inflation, was made internationally convertible and a tariff was applied to imports. Between 1922 and 1930 (when the concessions scheme was withdrawn to leave the way clear for complete socialisation of the means of production) UK firms had 9 wholly owned concessions and participated in 19 mixed companies (out of 127 and 95 respectively).[2]

Bilateral trade (as table 9.1 shows) rapidly expanded after the 1921 agreement to a peak in 1925, the year following the resumption of diplomatic relations and the signature of a Treaty of Commerce and Navigation. The rupture of those relations and the non-ratification of the commercial treaty in 1925, followed by the abrogation of the 1921 trade agreement in 1927, reversed the trend. Anglo-Soviet turnover (the sum of imports and exports) fell to a nadir in 1928. The United Kingdom returns show 1928 as 59 per cent of 1925 (a turnover of £26.4m against £44.6m) and the Soviet returns, adopting a year from 1 October to 30 September, put 1927/28 at 58 per cent of 1925/26 (71m rubles against 122m). The impact of the political deterioration can be measured by the 38 per cent increase, over those same years, of Soviet trade with all other countries.

By 1929, the first full year of the Five Year Plan, orders for capital equipment were pushing Soviet demand upward and the UK shared in the boom. But the bilateral upswing to 1931 can also be partly attributed to the return of a Labour Government in 1929 and the restoration of diplomatic links and a commercial agreement (1930). Given the low overall trade dependence of the USSR, then as now, it is significant that British supplies in 1929 constituted 0.5 per cent of the Soviet national income and UK purchases absorbed 0.7 per cent of that national income.

Towards the end of the First Five Year Plan (1928–32), the USSR began rapidly to phase out even that modest trade dependence; self-sufficiency was induced not only by the nature of the 'command economy', which is inherently averse to foreign trade,[3] but also by a disastrous deterioration of the Soviet terms of trade. As an exporter of primary commodities with which to buy manufactures (capital equipment comprised 55 per cent of total Soviet imports in 1932), the USSR was so badly hit by the differential impact of the Depression that in 1932 its export price index as a ratio of its import prices was a mere 72 per cent of 1929. During that Five Year Plan UK supplies peaked at 13.1 per cent of USSR imports in 1932, but dropped at the start of the Second Plan in 1933 to 8.8 per cent. The value of bilateral trade reflected also the price decline of the Depression: British exports fell from £10.6m in 1932 to £4.3m in 1933 and – on the Soviet returns – from 32.0m rubles to 10.7m. On the British side the Conservative landslide in the 1932 election and public protest at the sentencing of British nationals in the Metropolitan-Vickers trial of 1933 brought termination of the commercial agreement in early 1933, but economic commitments to the Commonwealth under the Ottawa Agreements (1932) played their part. Political opposition also contributed: the Soviet policy of selecting an import requirement and selling just enough exports to meet that bill had no place for comparative costs on which market economies traded and could be interpreted as dumping to disrupt capitalist trade. An American book of the time stridently asked:

What chance is there of the formation of a European economic bloc to boycott the Soviet Union and what chance is there of . . . a counterpart to the Soviet Foreign Trade Monopoly? . . . in a period when foreign trade of all non-Soviet countries is falling rapidly, Soviet foreign trade is increasing by leaps and bounds.[4]

The economic aversion to trade by the Soviet planners and the political antipathy on the part of many in the West reduced Soviet exports by the end of the Second Plan (1937) to only half a per cent of Soviet national income, compared with 3.5 per cent in 1930. Within this overall shrinkage, Anglo-Soviet trade responded positively to the conclusion of a long-run trade agreement in 1934, and in 1935, when imports from the UK were 18 per cent of the Soviet total, Britain became the USSR's biggest partner, overtaking both Germany and the United States.

THE SECOND WORLD WAR

Only weeks after the Nazi invasion of the Soviet Union the British and Soviet Governments signed an agreement (16 August 1941) on mutual deliveries on credit. The initial loan for UK supplies of £10m was increased under subsequent protocols.[5] The USSR has never published its valuation of UK wartime deliveries, confining the record to statements of physical quantities of *matériel* and civilian goods and to the calculation that during 1941-45 they were the equivalent of 4 per cent of Soviet industrial production.[6]

Of the $13.0 billion Allied deliveries to the USSR during the war, the biggest contribution ($11.2 billion) was from the United States, the settlement of which was agreed in 1972 but of which only a very small part was remitted. In addition to Lend-Lease and the equivalent British and Canadian supplies, the USSR imported goods to the value of 813m roubles, chiefly from the Allies, between 1942 and 1945. Deliveries from the UK and its major pre-war share of the market (17 per cent of Soviet imports in 1938, though by then second again to the United States) encouraged expectations of a high level of commerce after the war. Such expectations were realistic in the light of Soviet needs for reconstruction, the temporary nature of UNRRA assistance, the 1947 Anglo-Soviet Trade and Payments Agreement and Soviet participation in the multilateral conference to reform the world economic system. A Soviet delegation was at Bretton Woods, which created the IMF and the World Bank, but did not in the event appear at Havana, which would have established an International Trade Organisation.

TRADE UNDER EAST–WEST TENSION

A school of Soviet economists, benefiting from Stalin's authorisation in 1941 of Marxian value theory as applicable under socialism, contended that state intervention and the growth of the public sector in capitalist countries, promoted by the war and pursued as Keynesian policies in peace, had materially postponed the 'general crisis of capitalism'. The leading spokesman of that school, Eugene Varga, Director of the Institute for World Economy, concluded that there was only one 'world market', but he was dismissed in 1948 and Stalin explicitly formulated a theory of 'two world markets' – socialist and capitalist – in 1952. Although the punitive sanctions against holding the 'one market' view were lifted on Stalin's death, some traces of the conceptual divergence persist: the Institute for World Economy and International Relations (the successor to Varga's Institute and headed until 1989 by a close advisor to Mikhail Gorbachev, Evgeny Primakov) propounds the unity of a world economic system, while some economists from the planning and financial agencies (such as Gennady Sorokin and Meriam Atlas) have stressed the differentiation of socialism from capitalism.

The prospect of East–West co-operation was destroyed from many sides: first, the Cold War which from 1949 brought specific embargoes on sales to the USSR and its allies through the Coordinating Committee for Multilateral Export Controls (COCOM); second, Soviet non-participation in, or withdrawal from international economic agencies (and even briefly from its seat at the United Nations); and, third, a purge which included economic officials who might have modified the 'command economy'. Soviet domination of Eastern Europe and, between 1949 and 1961, alliance with a Communist China, forced the Soviet Union out of autarky, but the expansion of its international trade was channelled towards its allies; the Council for Mutual Economic Assistance (COMECON) was set up in January 1949, and trade with the West withered.

The year 1950 was the low point in Soviet trade with the market economies. Only 15 per cent of turnover was with the industrial West, but within that small share the UK had the leading position at 23.9 per cent, making 4.4 per cent of total turnover. The high British ranking could be attributed not only to the efficiency of UK traders, but also to the virtual disappearance from trade partnership of Germany and the United States which had rivalled the UK in

Soviet trade before the war. Germany was divided, the GDR joining COMECON and the FRG lacking standing in Moscow until 1955. The United States rigorously limited its Soviet trade – a mere 1.7 per cent of Soviet turnover in 1950, compared with 23.7 per cent in 1946.

But although Britain was the USSR's biggest Western partner, the Soviet Union took only 0.6 per cent of UK exports and sold to the UK 1.3 per cent of imports in 1950; in that year the UK closed its Commercial Secretariat at the Moscow Embassy, not to reopen it until the trade treaty of 1959. The 1959 agreement, negotiated with panache by Harold Macmillan (whose immense hat of white fur made front pages), came at an opportune moment. Khrushchev had formulated the concept of 'peaceful, competitive coexistence' and was opening doors to the West in trade as in other ways. He had the previous year formulated a policy of urgent and widespread *khimizatsiya*, the accelerated application of chemicals in industry and agriculture, the quickest achievement of which was by the import of complete chemical plants, a branch of engineering in which the UK was as advanced as the USSR was backward. Hanson rightly sees the 1964 contract with the Polyspinners consortium of UK companies to build a polyester fibre plant at Mogilev as a turning-point in Soviet policy on turnkey projects, contesting the view of Hardt and Holliday that the fulcrum was the Italian Fiat deal for a motor works at Tolyatti.[7] The author of a Soviet book on post-war Anglo-Soviet relations[8] observes that 'from the conclusion in May 1959 of the long-term trade agreement between the two countries their mutual turnover increased by 1970 to 3.3 times the 1958 level. In the 1960s Great Britain regularly occupied one of the first places in USSR trade with developed capitalist countries.'[9]

A renewed impetus came with the bilateral Navigation Treaty of 1968. Although the better relations were associated with enlarged imports and exports then and in the two following years, the expulsion of 105 Soviet personnel from the UK in 1971 brought a new downturn in exchanges. The same Soviet author notes the downturn without the slightest reference to the diplomatic friction: 'In 1970-74 trade developed more slowly: mutual turnover by value rose by 39 per cent within a decrease of the import of British goods by the USSR. In 1973 imports by value were 22 per cent and in 1974 10 per cent lower than in 1970. Exports of Soviet goods to Great Britain fell by volume but increased somewhat in value because of the world price rise for energy and raw materials.'[10] He goes on to place considerable weight on the agreement signed in Moscow in February 1975 between Harold Wilson and Aleksei Kosygin: he points to the establishment of representative offices of large British firms and of British commercial delegations to the USSR and banks in Moscow (16 by the time he wrote in early 1979) and the conclusion of framework agreements between those firms and others.[11] Another writer takes 'the first bilateral agreement in history' on economic, technical and industrial co-operation of May 1974 as the turning-point.[12] Certainly commerce picked up after that agreement although little use was made of the government-backed credit of £950 million simultaneously offered.[13] Soviet trade remained above one per cent of UK exports and imports until 1980. Again, a political event, the Soviet invasion of Afghanistan, adversely affected trade, not only for the UK but for other NATO members.

The early 1980s saw a further instance of a trade reduction in response to alignment with allied policy – a tightening of COCOM restrictions – and also a case of alliance policy divided on trade with the USSR. In 1981 the United States Government dispatched a mission to several NATO Governments, led by its Under Secretary of State for Economic Affairs, Myer Rashish, to press its view that the USSR should neither be supplied with equipment to build a natural gas pipeline from its Urengoi desposits in North-West Siberia to its western frontier nor sell its gas to Western utilities. The 'Rashish Raid' failed but the US Government suspended licences for the sale to the USSR of pipelaying vehicles and turbine rotor sets (for the compressor stations along the pipeline) and in June 1982 purported to ban the West European licences which had contracted to supply rotor sets. Such 'extraterritorial' claims were rejected by the United Kingdom. The Prime Minister's stand earned praise from Moscow:

When Washington attempted to launch another campaign of pressure on the Soviet Union in order to frustrate the construction of the Siberia–Western Europe gas pipeline, Margaret Thatcher was among the first to speak up in defence of the British companies delivering the necessary equipment to the USSR . . . she doubtlessly defended the broader interests of British business which could not tolerate the extension of American legislation outside the USA.[14]

In the words of Stern's contemporary account:

The focus of the [US] administration's argument has shifted away from the dangers of dependence on Soviet gas supplies and toward a policy of waging economic war against the USSR. Reagan believes that the Soviet Union is now on the point of economic collapse and that withholding Western technology and equipment from the pipeline project could hasten this collapse or at least force Moscow to take a more moderate stand on Poland and other international issues.[15]

A factor which exacerbated US relations with its allies and with Japan was the extremely favourable financial terms on which the pipeline contracts were negotiated[16] and the settlement which the NATO members concerned and Japan concluded tacitly with the United States administration seem to have involved an extension of the COCOM lists. Tighter export controls may have helped to depress Soviet trade with the developed West, but a more proximate cause was the decline in the price of the principal Soviet exports to those partners in line with the OPEC fall beginning in March 1983.

It was hence with a downward trend to record that Mr Gorbachev, during his visit to London in December 1984, publicly spoke of potential for a 40 to 50 per cent increment in Anglo-Soviet trade. Due to the unfavourable Soviet terms of trade in 1985 UK exports in current price were only 73 per cent of those of the previous year and imports from the USSR were 85 per cent of the 1984 level. Unwillingness to cut trade further may have influenced the Soviet Government – unlike its counter measures to the similar events of 1971, there was no Soviet economic riposte when in two waves 33 Soviet personnel were expelled from the UK in September 1985 nor when a further three were sent away in 1989.

A Soviet author writing in 1986 laid particular stress on inter-governmental and commercial agreements outside standard trade treaties, notably the establishment in 1970 of the Inter-Governmental Commission and the broad 1974 agreement already mentioned (which in 1985 was prolonged for a further five years).[17] He and others then found opportune the development of compensation arrangements and other forms of counter-trade; in 1986 the Exports Credits Guarantee Department announced that in future counter-trade deals could qualify for its insurance cover. Nevertheless, as Woolcock has pointed out, 'British companies have resisted the counter-trading practices of the CMEA state traders more than their Western European competitors.'[18]

These and other forms of barter were not part of any long-run Soviet policy. Gorbachev surprised the 1989 economic summit of the seven leading Western powers by a letter which declared that full Soviet participation in international economic organisations was an integral element of his *perestroika*. Participation in GATT requires a relationship between domestic and export prices which can be defended in terms of reciprocity and non-discrimination among its contracting parties; IMF membership complements this by progress towards an effective exchange rate and domestic adjustment mechanism.[19] Both the United Kingdom and the Soviet Union should perceive advantage in widening Soviet access to the gains of international trade and multilateral payments.

THE POST-WAR PATTERN OF BRITISH-SOVIET TRADE

At no time since the war has either side been significantly dependent on mutual bilateral trade. On 1984 returns (the last year of the Soviet oil windfall), the Soviet Union purchased 1.3 per cent of its imports from the UK and sold 1.9 per cent of its exports (4.2 and 6.5 per cent respectively if Soviet trade only with the industrial West is taken); the UK sold 1.0 per cent of its exports and bought 1.1 per cent of its imports from the USSR. Such similar shares on either side are historically standard. In the 35 years since 1950 the USSR has reached only a maximum of 1.7 per cent of UK exports (in 1961) and 3.6 per cent of UK imports (in 1959 and 1963). Current levels are somewhat low in terms of Soviet shares: the USSR took 3.6 per cent of its imports from the UK and sold 5.7 per cent of its exports in 1950, and 2.1 and 3.7 per cent respectively in 1966.

Since 1948 the UK has had a visible deficit with the USSR – usually substantial, although UK returns show imports exceeding exports by only a narrow margin in 1968, 1970, 1975 and 1981. Soviet returns generally show a surplus for the USSR, save in 1963 when there was a deficit. The trade statistics of any pair of partners hardly ever tally exactly but in British–Soviet exchanges UK reporting practices diverge in that exports are fob and imports are cif on the standard conventions, whereas both Soviet flows are franco frontier. Furthermore, UK imports include all re-exports, for some of which the Soviet authorities will have recorded not the UK, but the country of ultimate destination. Statistical procedures do not of course explain away all the consistent British deficit (Soviet surplus) and both Conservative and Labour administrations have urged for more balanced trade to the Soviet Government, whose counter-argument has been set out by Likhotal'. He claims that up to half of UK imports from the USSR are re-exported 'usually after additional fabrication which means that their selling price is very much increased' and that in recent years the UK bilateral deficit has worsened 'because of its decline in the competitiveness of its exports from the standpoints of price, quality and delivery delay'.[20] The reality was that until the expulsions the USSR was buying more British machinery than its competitive position on rest of the world's market justified (as the statistical appendix shows); after the expulsions the USSR bought less than the competitiveness of British equipment exports would indicate.

It is likely that the UK deficit on visible trade, however defined, has been at least partly offset by a favourable balance in invisible earnings. No bilateral estimates seem to have been published.[21] On the UK side there are the City of London's very large earnings on financial and insurance services, to be set against the substantial Soviet net balance on transport. The latter is a recent phenomenon due to Soviet determination to carry maritime traffic to and from the USSR in its own shipping,[22] to the rapid expansion of container transport by rail between the Pacific and Europe (the 'Trans-Siberian Land-bridge') and the carriage of goods between Iran and Europe during the Gulf War. Tourism is a net hard-currency earner for the USSR.[23] Portes estimates the USSR to have shifted from a net debtor to a net creditor in its convertible-currency current balance in 1979.[24] In the first half of the 1980s the USSR consistently ran a surplus on hard-currency invisibles (rising from $0.9 bn in 1980 to $1.1 bn in 1985[25]) and enlarged its deposits in Western commercial banks (from $3.6 bn in 1981 to $13 bn in 1985[26]). Its sales of gold (earning an estimated $1.6 bn in 1980 and $4.0 bn in 1985[27]) have also brought considerable income to the City of

London, where revenue from sales of diamonds through the Diamond Trading Corporation and at auctions of Soviet furs is also substantial.

The net British balance with the USSR – other than on merchandise trade, excluding re-exports – is likely to diminish. City financial earnings could fall due to a combination of greater caution on the part of Soviet borrowers (already evident in 1987[28]) and concern among Western bankers at over-exposure to a country which now seems set to be regularly in deficit in its visible balance in convertible currencies. Supplementary imports of consumers' goods – 10 billion roubles (£10 billion) in 1989, only a little less than total imports from the industrial West in 1987 (13.9 billion roubles) – will, however, almost certainly have to be covered by borrowing. British tourism to the USSR should increase (as public opinion gains a wider and favourable impression of *glasnost'* – unless ethnic disturbance mars the scene) by more than the likely rise in Soviet travel abroad (for enterprises can now use some of the foreign currency they earn for staff travel for business or leisure). The USSR is already selling more diamonds in Antwerp and Amsterdam, gold in Zurich and furs in Leningrad to the proportionate disadvantage of London. Soviet net transport earnings should rise even now that the Iran–Iraq war has ended because the Baikal–Amur Mainline will eventually offer more capacity for Europe–Pacific through traffic.[29] The prospects for visible trade depend on the overall purchasing policy of the USSR and within it any preference for maintaining trade with the UK. This in turn is influenced by relative UK competitiveness, particularly in engineering and chemicals exports, and in British purchases of Soviet products. Returns for 1987 promised a bleak prospect because the USSR cut its imports from the UK severely, but those for 1988 mitigated the fall; in both years the UK visible deficit widened.

THE STABILITY OF BRITISH–SOVIET TRADE

Over the very long run, as is shown by country shares of turnover (imports plus exports) with Russia in 1913 and with the USSR in 1930 and 1984 (table 9.2), UK trade with the Soviet Union has greatly declined, while the proportion of Soviet trade with other West European countries has been much steadier. The United States, which supplied between one-fifth and a quarter of Soviet imports from 1926 to 1931, has not since the 1940s reached its high inter-war share.

Since the Second World War, however, the United Kingdom has experienced greater stability in sales to the USSR than have the principal Western competitors. The statistical appendix examines exports to the USSR of France, the Federal Republic of Germany, Italy, Japan and the United States over the 31 years 1954–1985, for comparison with UK exports to the USSR. It is a fair conclusion from the statistics that the USSR pursues broadly similar policies towards the six Western partners in setting itself a target in convertible-currency spending, but because relative prices and commodity composition alter over time, there is less similarity in the value than in the volume figures. The UK showed much greater stability in its exports to the USSR than the other five countries, particularly in the earlier period 1954–68. Over the whole 31 years the three European countries examined – the FRG, France and Italy – were the next steadiest, while Japanese exports were more variable and the United States were the most fluctuating. The fluctuation of the United States exports can probably be explained over the long term by the variability of Soviet grain purchases (first made in 1963, not resumed until 1972 and variable with the Soviet harvest subsequently) and by changes in US strategic embargoes. By extension the constancy of the UK relationship with the USSR suggests that changes of COCOM coverage have not particularly affected the flow of UK goods. Some of that stability is also attributable to the complementarity of the British and Soviet economies as revealed by trade, for the UK sells very few products in the commodity groups from which it purchases. Such intra-industry trade is discussed in the statistical appendix, but the trade in equipment is particularly noteworthy (table 9.3). Whereas in 1965 Soviet imports of British engineering goods amounted to thirty times the value of those which the UK took from the USSR, by 1985 the gap had narrowed to 3:1 (this was due particularly to the sale of Soviet cars – notably the Lada – in the UK). Correspondingly the share of engineering goods in UK exports to the USSR fell while that of the Soviet return flow rose. The combined effect of changes in commodity composition and of relative prices was also least for the UK.

In real terms, that is in constant prices, UK exports to the USSR peaked in 1980, as did those of the FRG and France; Italy and the United States had peaked earlier and Japan peaked later (in 1982). From these various peaks the UK was neither the most nor the least cut. The Soviet reduction of imports was severest for Italy (to 37 per cent of its peak); France was affected the same as the UK (both to 46 per cent) and the United States much less (53 per cent), but the FRG and Japan were the least touched (53 and 68 per cent respectively). The two last countries were spared deep cuts because they export large-diameter steel pipe to the USSR which the UK does not. All are likely to be affected by Mr Gorbachev's concern that too much Western equipment has been bought:

We underestimated our scientific potential and placed too great a reliance on external ties . . . We have drawn the necessary conclusions, started the necessary research and development and the production of what we once proposed to purchase, so Western firms will ultimately be the losers . . . we decided to put a firm end to the 'import scourge'.[30]

Only Japan has recently been spared from a Soviet reduction in the equipment share of its imports among the six Western countries, but in earlier years it was the UK which had some preferential, or more competitive, entrée to the Soviet market for equipment. Intermittently between 1955 and 1961 and consistently between 1966 and 1970 the UK had a higher share of equipment going to the USSR than it had to the rest of the world.

The analysis of fluctuation and composition of Western sales to the USSR is of course for proportions of trade which are small for all Western partners. In 1984 Soviet turnover with the UK was 1.6 per cent of the total, with France 3 per cent, with the FRG 5.4 per cent, with Italy 3.2 per cent, with Japan 2.1 per cent and with the United States 2.2 per cent. On the other hand, the turnover of the USSR as a whole has been rising. In 1973 it ranked tenth among world exporters (3.7 per cent) and importers (3.6 per cent), but 1984 it was sixth among exporters (4.8 per cent) and seventh among importers (4.0 per cent). Although the current Five Year Plan (1986-90) established no specific target for the expansion of trade, it envisaged a reduction of Soviet reliance on the export of energy and of raw materials in favour of manufacturers. In introducing the Plan to the Party Congress on 3 March 1986, the Chairman of the Council of Ministers, Mr Ryzhkov, foreshadowed a reform of foreign trade organisation which would encourage Soviet domestic enterprise to 'unite their interests with the demands of the foreign market'. The implementing measures began in 1987 when 20 ministries and 70 domestic enterprises were endowed with foreign trading rights and decrees were promulgated to allow Western firms to have minority holdings in joint ventures on Soviet territory. The first UK–USSR joint venture (in computer software) was registered just before that year ended. In 1987 also a framework agreement for trade and finance was negotiated between the UK and the USSR. The extension of foreign trade rights to all Soviet state or co-operative enterprises in 1989 and the authorisation at the same time for majority holdings in joint ventures enhanced the penetration of market forces in the Soviet economy.

STATISTICAL APPENDIX

The computation for these measures of trade with the USSR was undertaken by Georg Lisiecki, graduate student of St Antony's College, Oxford, on programmes advised by Giuseppe Mazzarino, a staff member of the Institute of Economics and Statistics, Oxford University. The measure of competitiveness was suggested by Professor Philip Hanson, of Birmingham University, in his comments on the Study Group draft.

The coefficient of variation was computed for the exports to the USSR during 1954 to 1985 of the UK and five other major Western partners, the FRG, France, Italy, Japan and the United States (a) in current values in national currencies from national trade returns; (b) in current values in US dollars from OECD abstracts; and (c) in valuta roubles from Soviet trade returns. For the five partners, (b) is (a) at national currency exchange rates, but for the UK (a) includes, while (b) excludes, re-exports; (a) differs from (c) for the reasons most trade partners returns differ but Soviet statistics seem to show more variation because they and a partner's widely differ even where it involves only cross-border trade (e.g. with Mongolia and Poland) in which the divergences between fob/cif and franco frontier valuation is insignificant and goods move from the one country to the other in the same reporting period.

The coefficient of variation for the UK in (a) is 0.890 for the whole period of 31 years, but because the trend is markedly different in current prices (slow growth in 1954–68, inflation and real growth in 1969–85), the sub-periods show a better fit (on the least-squares method) – 0.471 and 0.531 respectively. The preferential stability of UK exports in relation to the other five partners is most marked in the first sub-period. Thus the coefficient for the United States was 1.666, because it was successively imposing and relaxing a series of restrictions and controls on trade with the USSR over this time. The West European states clustered around a coefficient of 0.6 (FRG 0.567, Italy 0.592 and France. 0.660) but Japan was less stable (0.877). By contrast, the later sub-period showed more similar stabilities, and the ranking only changed within Western Europe (Italy 0.538, FRG 0.559 and France 0.594); Japan's trade was more variable (a coefficient of 0.617) and the United States the least steady of the six countries (0.648). Remarkably, in view of the differences in values when individual years are compared, the coefficients of variation in (c) were very close to (a). For example, for France the coefficient for the whole period was 1.082 (1.127 for (a)) and for 1969–85 0.528 (0.594 for (a)).

A correlation matrix of series (a) for the full time span showed them all to be very highly correlated with each other. The best (and almost perfect) fit was between French exports to the USSR and FRG exports to the USSR ($R = 0.986$) and the most divergent between US exports to the USSR and UK exports to the USSR ($R = 0.899$). This closeness suggests that the Soviet authorities pursue a similar policy towards their main partners and operate (at least with respect to the six countries investigated) a valuta-rouble limit for their purchases year by year (the valuta rouble being merely a statistical reflection of the cross rates of the main Western currencies). This interpretation is strengthened by the correlation matrix of series (b) where the relationships are much weaker, but UK exports to the USSR nevertheless exhibit more stability than the exports to the USSR of any other of the five Western partners. Italy in the sub-period 1969–85 showed the same stability as the UK, which suggests that for those two countries the combined effect was least (among the six chosen partners of the USSR) of changes in commodity composition and in relative prices.

Series (b) was also inspected for peaks in real volume of exports to the USSR: Italy peaked earlier (1975), followed by the United States (1979), but the UK peaked in 1980 with two others, the FRG and France; Japan was the last of the six to peak (1982). From those peaks the decline to 1985 was most acute for Italy (to 37 per cent of its 1975 peak) and for France and the UK (to 46 per cent in 1980). The United States was cut to 53 per cent but the FRG (to 68 per cent) and Japan (to 76 per cent) were the least affected.

The conclusion that, before the 1987 reforms, the USSR Ministry of Foreign Trade decided its import bill on a basis of reasonably stable valuta-rouble allocations by main Western partners is strengthened by analysis of those partners' exports of machinery and equipment (SITC 7). Western country returns show considerable variations in the share of SITC 7 in total deliveries, due to the bunching of large consignments typified in complete plant sales. Over the period when Soviet purchases have been substantial and normal – taken as 1969–83 – the share of machinery in total exports was fairly stable from the FRG, Italy and the UK, but declined from France and the United States (in both cases displaced by agricultural produce) and rose in the case of Japan (consistent with the increase in Japanese sales of high-technology items worldwide).

The equipment import cuts which the Soviet Union undertook from 1984 as its terms of trade declined are shown to have been particularly severe for France, the UK and the United States; the share of equipment in Japanese sales to the USSR continued on the other hand to increase. The high share of equipment in exports to the USSR, except for the United States, for the period as a whole justified the second broad topic for statistical analysis, relative competitiveness in equipment.

The procedure was used by Hanson for the period 1960–75. He concluded that 'how well a Western country performs in selling to the Soviet Union, at least in machinery exports, is evidently very strongly influenced by its size and general competitiveness as an exporting nation'.[31] The present analysis takes the measure he uses for earlier and later periods to coincide with series (a), (b) and (c) above.

The first stage was to calculate from Western trade returns (as reported in dollars by the OECD) the share of each country in the SITC 7 exports of 14 countries (13 for 1954–59 when UK data were used and comparable Swiss data were unavailable) to the USSR and to the rest of the world. A similarity of the two shares indicates that the country's competitiveness in the Soviet market reflected its competitiveness in all markets. During 1954–59 this was shown for the UK, the FRG, Italy and Japan; Austria and France outperformed their world showing on Soviet markets; but United States and Canadian shares were far below their general competitiveness.

For the period since 1975, the calculation adopts Hanson's adjustment for 1960–75 which excludes Canadian exports of SITC 7 to and from the United States because of the particular economic relationship between the two countries. The number of years in which the share to the USSR exceeded the share to the rest of the world indicates relatively greater access to the Soviet market than its general competitiveness would indicate. The United Kingdom had two such periods, intermittently between 1955 and 1961 and consistently between 1966 and 1970; its worst year was 1974 which was also its second least competitive situation in any of these post-war years. The impact of the 1975 Anglo-Soviet trade agreement was evident in its recovery: by 1980 the share of exports to the USSR (7.5 per cent) had nearly reached its share to the rest of the world (9.7 per cent), but after 1980 the share to the USSR fell off rapidly (reaching in 1985 its worst-ever situation) whereas the share to the rest of the world declined only slightly, largely due to the crowding out by the rapid rise of Japanese sales of equipment to the rest of the world. Japan's expanding share of equipment trade to the USSR paralleled its expansion to all markets save for a remarkable boom in exports to the USSR between 1960 and 1967, when it greatly outstripped shares on all markets. Exporters which showed a regularly higher share of equipment sales with the USSR than elsewhere have been FRG, France, Italy, Switzerland and Austria. Countries in the contrary position, with Soviet-directed shares much under the average for their other markets, have been the United States, Belgium-Luxembourg, the Netherlands, Canada and Norway.

The final measure of Anglo-Soviet trade used in this study is of specialisation within single industries. Such intra-industry trade has grown at the expense of inter-industry trade among industrially developed countries and its standard measure shows its share in total bilateral trade within a given commodity group. The coarser the commodity grouping, such as denominated by one or two digits of SITC, the greater is intra-trade. The measure, as defined by Grubel and Lloyd[32] is for each commodity group:

$$\frac{(\text{Exports} + \text{imports}) - (\text{exports} - \text{imports})}{(\text{exports} - \text{imports})}$$

As UK trade shows a permanent import deficit with the USSR, an adjustment is made to bilateral trade in each commodity group to allow for this, again following Grubel and Lloyd. Even so, the average of all commodity groups quoted in the UK returns to 3 SITC digits is trivial – only 3 per cent during 1964–68 (when 88 per cent of exports to the USSR and 96 per cent of imports from the USSR were published to 3 digits of SITC in 1964 and 95 and 97 per cent respectively in 1968). After 1975 UK trade returns were revised so that commodities by country were distinguished only to two SITC digits. The coarser measure exhibits of course higher averages, but they are still much lower than those between industrially developed market economies: although it was 26 per cent in 1964 and 25 per cent in 1976, later years have shown a marked decline – up to 19 per cent in 1977 and an average of 16 per cent during 1978–85. For comparison, UK intra-industry trade with France and the United States is shown with the UK trade with the USSR in table 9.4.

The virtual absence of Soviet–West intra-industry trade is due to the concentration of each partner's exports on a few commodity groups. On the British side machinery and equipment has dominated throughout the period but in a diminishing share as UK exports have diversified. Thus power-generating equipment was 35 per cent of all UK sales to the USSR in 1964 and almost reached half (49.7 per cent) in 1968. It was still the biggest single group in 1981 and 1982 (10 per cent in each year) and in 1983 it was the second highest.

Table 9.1 *Anglo–Soviet Trade*

	UK returns: millions of pounds			Soviet returns: millions of valuta roubles	
	From USSR	*To USSR*		*From USSR*	*To USSR*
1921	3	3	1921	3	22
1922	8	5	1921/22	6	19
1923	9	4	1922/23	10	13
1924	20	11	1923/24	29	17
1925	25	19	1924/25	67	39
1926	24	24	1925/26	77	45
1927	21	11	1926/27	77	35
1928	22	5	1927/28	54	17
1929	26	7	1929	71	19
1930	34	9		98	28
1931	32	9		93	26
1932	20	11		48	32
1933	17	4		30	11
1934	17	8		24	11
1935	22	10		30	8
1936	19	23		29	8
1937	29	20		42	5
1938	20	17		28	13
1939	8	8		10	9
1940	1	1		—	1
1941	1	29		..	..
1942	3	75		..	..
1943	2	59		..	..
1944	2	56		..	..
1945	3	30		..	..
1946	5	11		28	8
1947	8	14		39	32
1948	27	7		123	24
1949	16	21		61	33
1950	34	14		92	36
1951	60	24		142	70
1952	58	37		117	112
1953	56	12		81	48
1954	57	15		100	47
1955	82	32		152	64
1956	75	56		133	67
1957	141	52		159	101
1958	93	52		131	66
1959	154	35		149	82
1960	113	53		173	97
1961	165	69		204	115
1962	122	57		192	106

Table 9.1 *(cont.)*

1963	192	64	104	117
1964	186	40	215	93
1965	150	47	262	137
1966	119	50	297	152
1967	105	64	273	178
1968	125	105	330	246
1969	133	95	384	216
1970	114	102	418	223
1971	119	89	405	200
1972	117	90	371	187
1973	164	97	541	175
1974	225	110	691	200
1975	236	211	591	368
1976	460	242	825	408
1977	545	347	958	378
1978	489	423	857	669
1979	492	416	1093	811
1980	422	450	859	953
1981	427	408	645	858
1982	645	356	813	752
1983	730	445	1185	632
1984	854	735	1393	819
1985	725	537	1218	685
1986	695	539	1274	515
1987	875	492	1586	524
1988	732	512	1794	623

Note: — signifies negligible . . signifies not available

Note: Returns by both partners are for the USSR within contemporary frontiers. Soviet returns for 1921–40 (provided by Professor R. W. Davies, University of Birmingham) are in valuta roubles of the gold content defined on 1 March 1950, but – for comparison with the series 1946–85 – are in the 1961 denomination (when 10 'old' roubles were exchanged for one 'new' rouble). All returns are at current prices except for Soviet data for 1921–1923/4 which are at the average price of 1913. When returns reverted to the calendar year in 1928 the exports for October–December that year were 16m roubles, but imports were negligible. The equivalent of the valuta rouble for Soviet foreign-trade valuation as the chervonets between 1922 and 1947.

Source: UK returns from *Overseas Trade Statistics of the United Kingdom* (HMSO annual); Soviet returns from *Vneshniaia torgovlia SSSR* (annual) and *Vneshniaia torgovlia SSSR za 1918–1940 gg* (Vneshtorgizdat, 1960).

Table 9.2 *Country shares of turnover with Russia/USSR*

| | Percentages | | | |
	1913	*1939*	*1984*	*1988*
Belgium and Luxembourg	2.6	1.6	1.2	0.9
France	5.1	3.5	3.0	2.1
Germany	38.3	7.4	5.4[9]	10.7[9]
Italy	3.1	3.0	3.2	2.3
Japan	0.2	0.2	2.1	2.4
Sweden	1.0	1.2	0.6	0.5
United Kingdom	15.3	17.2	1.8	1.8
United States	3.2	14.6	2.2	1.6

Note [9] Federal Republic
Source: as for tabe 9.1.

Table 9.3 *Trade in machinery and transport equipment (SITC 7) between the UK and USSR*
Percentages and thousands of pounds sterling

| | Shares | | Value | |
	UK exports	UK imports	UK exports	UK imports
1965	41.4	0.6	19,403	622
1970	44.9	0.4	40,224	947
1975	47.3	5.9	91,593	13,264
1980	33.7	5.2	151,940	21,954
1985	16.2	4.3	89,589	30,959
1986	16.7	5.8	90,715	40,819
1987	16.1	6.7	79,195	58,235

Source: Overseas Trade Statistics of the United Kingdom (HMSO, annual).

Table 9.4 *Intra-industry trade of the United Kingdom*

| | Percentages | |
	One SITC digit	Two SITC digits
With the USSR		
1965	37.99	26.36
Peak (1974)	59.81	28.69
Trough (1984)	23.07	11.75
1985	33.66	16.80
With France		
1985	74.84	64.19
With the United States		
1985	83.55	62.07

Note: The measure is that of Grubel and Lloyd 1975 with their adjustment for the aggregate UK deficit in the visible balance.
Source: as for table 9.3.

Michael Kaser

NOTES

1. George F. Kennan, *Soviet Foreign Policy 1917–1941* (Van Nostrand, 1960), p. 24.
2. Anthony C. Sutton, *Western Technology and Soviet Economic Development 1917 to 1930* (Hoover Institution, 1968), Appendix B, pp. 353–63.
3. The command economy, by according a passive role to money and prices, only very imperfectly identifies the comparative advantage of its own products in terms of those which it could exchange or for which it could bring in investment. The central planning authorities, in an environment of widespread and persistent shortage (variously seen as 'repressed inflation' or 'supply-side allocation'), normally resort to rationing imports and imposing quotas for exports.
4. H.R. Knickerbocker, *Soviet Trade and World Depression* (Bodley Head, 1931), p. 3. A more balanced analysis of inter-war trade is Alexander Baykov, *Soviet Foreign Trade* (Princeton University Press and Oxford University Press, 1946). See especially p. 65 on the trade consequences of the 1927 Arcos raid and Soviet reaction to restrictions imposed by other states on the grounds of dumping or the use of forced labour.
5. Ministerstvo inostrannykh del SSSR, *Sovetsko-angliiskie otnotsheniia vo vremia velikoi otechestvennoi voiny 1941–1945* (Politizdat, 1983), Vol. 1, pp. 13, 20.
6. *Ibid.*, p. 28.
7. Philip Hanson, *Trade and Technology in Soviet–Western Relations* (Macmillan, 1981), p. 108, referring to J.P. Hardt and G. Holliday, 'Technology transfer and change in the Soviet economic system', in F.J. Fleron, ed., *Technology and Communist Culture* (Praeger, 1977).
8. *Leninskii vneshno-politicheskii kurs v deistvii. Ukazatel' literatury 1976–1980* (Institut nauchnoi informatsii po obshchestvennym naukam, 1980) p. 85 (item 703) list Cheklin and A.A. Likhotal', *Sovetsko-angliiskie otnosheniia na sovremennom etape* (Moscow, 1978).
9. Vladimir N. Cheklin, *SSSR–Velikobritaniia: razvitie delovykh sviazei* (Mezhdunarodnye otnosheniia, 1979), pp. 61–2.
10. *Ibid.*, p. 63. It is significant that Cheklin writes of the downturn starting in 1970, the year of the expulsions, not 1971 when the decline could have been a policy action. Contracts take time to adjust to policy, even within a monopolistic Ministry of Foreign Trade, and it is the case that Soviet exports to the UK declined in 1970 on UK (though not on Soviet) returns. Mr Alan Brooke Turner, HM Minister in Moscow at the time, told the Study Group that the British Government took the downward trend into account in assessing the consequences of the expulsions. Peter Wright in *Spycatcher* (Heinemann, 1987, pp. 344–5) claims that the expulsions were made because by numbers and technique Soviet agents in the UK had outstripped the Security Service's surveillance resources.
11. *Ibid.*
12. Ye. V. Gumenyuk, ed., *Ekonomicheskie i nauchno-teknicheskie sviazi SSSR s Velikobritaniei 1971–1981* (VGBIL, 1984), p. 5.
13. The partial utilisation by 1979, when the UK terminated the credit offer, was due primarily to the windfall earnings in convertible currency which the USSR gained when oil earnings were on a sharply rising trend (1973–79) and to commercial supplier credits being available on better terms than those under the agreement.

14. S. Volodin, 'USSR–Britain: 60 years of diplomatic relations', *International Affairs* (Moscow), April 1984, p. 63.

15. Jonathan P. Stern, 'Specters and pipe dreams', *Foreign Policy*, 48 (1982), p. 32.

16. Axel Lebahn, 'Die "Jamal-Erdgasleitung" UdSSR–Westeuropa im Ost–West Konflikt', *Aussenpolitik*, 34 (1983), pp. 256-80.

17. Ye V. Korzun, 'Khoziaistvennoe sotrudnichestvo SSSR s Velikobritaniei' in Yu. V. Andreev *et al.*, eds., *SSSR–Zapadnaia Evropa: Problemy torgovo-ekonomicheskikh otnoshenii* (Moscow, Mezhdunarodnoe otnosheniia, 1986), p. 223.

18. Stephen Woolcock, *Western Policies on East–West Trade*, Chatham House Papers 15 (RIIA and Routledge and Kegan Paul, 1982), p. 57.

19. See two *Public Policy Papers* published by the Institute for East–West Security Studies, New York, 1989: Harald B. Malmgren, 'The Soviet Union and the GATT: Benefits and Obligations of Joining the World Trade Club', and Richard E. Feinberg 'The Soviet Union and the Bretton Woods Institutions: Risks and Rewards of Membership.'

20. Likhotal', 'Sovetsko-angliiskie otnosheniia', p. 32.

21. UK–Soviet balances of payments are not separately calculated in the two studies found: Oleg Betcher, *La balance des paiements de l'Europe occidentale avec l'Europe orientale de 1960 à 1970* (Institut universitaire des hautes études internationales, 1976) and OECD, *Financial Market Trends*, 24 (March 1983), which analyses Soviet payments balances for 1977–81 with Austria, FRG, France, Japan, Sweden and the United States. The estimates annually published by the Secretariat of the UN Economic Commission for Europe (*Economic Bulletin for Europe*, December issue) are aggregated by country-group.

22. In a comment to the Study Group, Professor Hanson, who has Soviet shipping among his many fields of expertise, termed the policy 'Soviet-style flag discrimination'.

23. Joan F. MacIntyre, 'The USSR's hard currency trade and payments position', Joint Economic Committee of the US Congress, *Gorbachev's Economic Plans* (US Government Printing Office, 1987), Vol. 2, p. 481.

24. Richard Portes in *Deficits and Détente: Report on an International Conference on the Balance of Trade in the Comecon Countries* (Twentieth Century Fund, 1983), p. 68.

25. MacIntyre, 'The USSR's hard currency trade', p. 480.

26. Banks reporting to the Bank for International Settlements which issues quarterly reports on *International Banking and Financial Market Developments*; data here taken from Iliana Zloch-Christy, *Debt Problems of Eastern Europe* (Cambridge University Press, 1987), p. 53.

27. MacIntyre, 'The USSR's hard currency trade', p. 480.

28. Soviet gross debt to BIS reporting banks and officially guaranteed non-bank trade credits was constant between December 1986 and September 1987 compared with a rise of $12 bn over the two previous years (BIS, *International Banking Developments*, Third Quarter, 1987, February 1988).

29. The current Five Year Plan (1986–90) requires by 1990 full operations on the Baikal-Amur Mainline (BAM), which would have carried 75m tonne-km by 1990, but only one-third of its length was fully operational in 1985. Abel Aganbegyan told Victor Mote in 1983 that BAM would not haul more than 30 m tonne-km before the end of the century (Victor L. Mote, 'Regional Planning: the BAM and the Pyramids of

Power', in Joint Economic Committee, *Gorbachev's Economic Plans*, Vol. 2, p. 379).

30. M.S. Gorbachev, *Perestroika: New Thinking for Our Country and the World* (Collins, 1987), pp. 93–4. This quotation was drawn to the Study Group's attention by Dennis Ogden (Polytechnic of Central London) in comments on the draft of this chapter.

31. P. Hanson, 'The trade-partner composition of Soviet trade with the West', in Z. Fallenbuchl and C.H. McMillan, eds., *Partners in East–West Economic Relations* (Oxford University Press, 1980), p. 213.

32. H. Grubel and P. Lloyd, *The Theory of Intra-Industry Trade* (Macmillan, 1975), p. 22.

10 Doing business with the USSR

ANNA DYER

The intention in this chapter is to examine from a strictly practical perspective the problems facing British companies who wish to penetrate the Soviet market and to make some assessment of the effects of the changes taking place within the Soviet foreign trade system.

In comparison with the early 1970s, when it was the leading trading partner of the USSR, Britain has experienced a relative decline, taking it to ninth place in the early 1980s. Although there has been some improvement in the last three years, it still occupies sixth position.

A number of reasons can be offered for this lack of success. The political climate has frequently been presented as the major cause for this decline. There is a difference of opinion, however, on the significance of political factors. In evidence to the House of Commons Foreign Affairs Committee enquiry into UK–Soviet relations, Dr Norman Wooding of Courtaulds, for instance, claimed that his own company's business, and that of a number of firms with which he was well acquainted, were not adversely affected by the reactions of the West towards Soviet policy in Afghanistan.[1] On the other hand, another witness, Mr Ralph Land of Rank Xerox, considered that in a difficult political climate the total value of business did not grow and frequently declined. One concrete example which he used was the loss by Rank Xerox of a £2 million contract which was ready for signing within a week of the expulsion of 105 diplomats during 1971-72.[2]

Mr Anthony Hore[3] told the Foreign Affairs Committee that large capital business could be awarded to a country as a sign of political pleasure. Indeed, Khrushchev told a Western diplomat how in the early 1960s out of a total of 6 chemical plants, one each had been earmarked for Britain, France, Italy and the FRG, the other two being open to competitive tender. The proposition can be made that for very large capital projects the political climate and specific political events can play a role, but not usually in the case of other contracts. It is notable that political factors do not appear to have had a direct effect on the trade prospects of the other Western countries.

Other reasons, however, can be offered for the relative decline in Britain's trade with the USSR. It must be recognised that penetrating the Soviet market is a heavy commitment both in terms of the length of time involved and the resources required.

The rewards of entering the Soviet market are commensurate with the effort required to achieve a contract. In terms of credit rating, the Soviet Union's standing is excellent. Soviet organisations have never reneged on debts since 1919. Orders tend to be large in volume and the rate of repeat orders is high. But it must be recognised that the Soviet market is highly competitive and the USSR has the choice of suppliers throughout the world. In a speech in February 1986, Mr V.M. Ivanov, welcoming the growing interest of British companies in the Soviet market, warned: 'British companies must expect no special favours . . . we do not want yesterday's technology – only that of today.'[4] He stressed that considerable opportunities existed for British firms but they must be competitive in quality and price.

But in addition to presenting a competitive product, companies wishing to penetrate the Soviet market must be prepared to make a sustained commitment. Unlike their European competitors, some British companies have not regarded the USSR in the past as an important long-term strategic market but have only shown interest when there has been a downturn in other markets. 'Soviet buyers have long memories; they demand consistent service.'[5]

The pace of decision making in the Soviet industrial system, differences in business and social culture and the particular problems of making the right contacts in the Soviet foreign trade system all contribute to a long lead-in time to the market. Moreover, the tendency in the Soviet buying system of displaying a strong loyalty towards previous suppliers favours firms who have maintained frequent contact with Soviet foreign trade organisations. A consistent commitment towards the Soviet market is therefore necessary and a willingness to take a long-term view is required. There have been complaints from the Soviet side of a lack of British commitment, characterised by a tendency to drop in and out of the market. (The number of British firms which have been consistently involved in the market is in the region of 50.) Now, it must be admitted that there is a problem for companies. A firm has to be prepared to invest time and resources for at least 2 or 3 years without any signs of return and some firms decide that the effort is not worthwhile.

The demands of entering the Soviet market require an investment of time and resources which is more easily borne by the larger companies. The high professionalism of one of the most successful British firms in the Soviet market is reflected in their mini centralised trading company established for non-capitalist markets, the activities of which are designed to interact with the state foreign trade associations of the respective countries.[6]

The dominance of large British companies in the Soviet market does not, however, mean that it is an impossible market for medium-sized or smaller firms. The opportunities for smaller companies have been well exploited by West Germany and other Western countries. To achieve success, British firms must be prepared, therefore, to embark on a consistent and planned marketing strategy. Small companies, certainly, have particular problems in this respect, but it is important to make use of all available resources, even if it can be argued that these resources should be expanded, particularly when viewed in relation to those of other countries.

NEED FOR SPECIALISED KNOWLEDGE AND ASSISTANCE

There are a number of general sources of assistance and advice available to firms interested in exporting to the USSR. The Department of Trade and Industry (DTI) provides general market advice to exporters. In addition, the Fairs and Promotion Branch of the British Overseas Trade Board (BOTB) gives financial assistance for participation in a limited number of exhibitions and missions each year.

The East European Trade Council is an independent, grant-aided body responsible for stimulating British trade and industrial co-operation with COMECON countries. It is the BOTB's Area Advisory Group for Eastern Europe. It provides an excellent service of general information for exporters. Perhaps most important is the information it provides on the proceedings of the joint inter-governmental commission and the support and resources it gives to developing the joint working groups which report the Joint Commission. In 1985 Britain had only 4 operating groups – Machinery and Equipment, Agriculture, Electricity Supply, and Transmission and Automation Engineering Working Groups. The Medical, Machine Tool and Coal Industry Working Groups were revived in 1986 and two new groups, Oil and Gas and Energy Conservation, were being initiated. The development of such work is still at an early stage compared to that of the West Germans and the French, with 25 such groups, and the Italians with 12.[7]

The British–Soviet Chamber of Commerce, an independent organisation established in 1916, has a membership of around 600 firms. Over 50 Soviet organisations are also members. The Chamber publishes a journal and a most informative quarterly newsletter. It also organises four missions a year to the USSR. The work of the Chamber has been greatly enhanced by the opening of a representative office in Moscow which offers a wide range of facilities and services to members. The Chamber provides an efficient venue for seminars and exhibitions which, unlike Embassy premises, are accessible to the Soviets. By comparison with that of other countries, the Chamber's work is still at an early stage. Finland, Italy and France all have strong Chambers of Commerce in Moscow. The London Chamber of Commerce and Industry has an East European section which promotes information about trade with the USSR and sponsors seminars in London.

The functions of the British Embassy in Moscow in co-operation with the DTI and BOTB include giving market guidance and briefing, assisting established firms with a wide range of specific problems. It also maintains a dialogue with firms whose extended negotiations are taking place and helps firms whose Soviet dealings need setting within the context of government-to-government relationships. In the past a high number of companies have made use of Embassy facilities but in the event of a considerable growth of trade taking place, the small commercial department would be seriously overstretched. The abolition of the post of Scientific Counsellor has also affected its capacity to provide information. In comparison with other countries, Britain's commercial representation is small, especially in view of the fact that a British–Soviet Chamber of Commerce office has recently been established in Moscow.[8]

In general, therefore, our rather more successful West European counterparts tend to have a strong Embassy commercial representation and a Chamber of Commerce in Moscow. The major exception, however, is West Germany, which does not have a Chamber of Commerce in Moscow; instead, the services of such organisations to companies are provided either by banks or by specialist agencies.

The four British banks who have representation in Moscow readily provide assistance to firms. But perhaps most important of all in terms of specialist assistance is the Moscow Narodny Bank. This is a Soviet-owned but London-based bank which since its establishment in 1919 has been recognised as the leading specialist bank in the financing, support and promotion of East–West trade. It has considerable resources and in co-operation with other British banks has developed specialist assistance on the creation of joint ventures. The assistance available to firms from Soviet organisations will be examined later; their functions are being influenced by the changes which are taking place in the foreign trade system.

The first attempt in Britain to establish a specialist service to provide a comprehensive service to companies on an individual basis was made in Glasgow. The Trade Advisory Service is a publicly funded, non-profit making organisation established to assist companies wishing to trade with the Soviet Union by providing professional services on an individual basis on lines similar to the specialist agencies established in other European countries. Its services include market analysis, design of marketing packages suited to the requirements of the Soviet market, translations, making and sustaining contact with the appropriate trade organisations, organising trade missions and assisting participation in exhibitions, seminars and technical symposia in the USSR.

DEVELOPING A MARKETING STRATEGY

The development of a marketing strategy involves considerable time, effort and specialist knowledge. It is important that companies understand Soviet needs and priorities. This is particularly important at a time of such great change in the USSR and the second half of this chapter examines the implications of these changes. Once companies have established that there is a market for their product, it is worthwhile thinking in terms of planning a long-term coherent marketing policy.

In developing such a policy it is important to produce a detailed marketing package appropriate to the Soviet market. Many firms have unsuccessfully tried to use general marketing information without producing the material in a high-quality Russian translation. While the first line of Soviet officials who receive information about firms almost certainly know English, this is not necessarily the case with the technical specialists who may be asked to evaluate the product.

In relations with Soviet trade organisations it is vital to understand Soviet business culture and norms. Many British businessmen initially underestimate the calibre of foreign trade officials who have a high degree of education (usually to post-graduate level), are highly skilled negotiators and extremely knowledgeable about foreign markets. Soviet organisations tend to be highly specialised in their structure and it is therefore important to target precisely the correct division and officials. While the individual official will not have authority to take decisions alone, maintaining personal relationships is important. A consistent approach demands both constant support from board level of a firm and a person of high standing being responsible for the development of contacts with Soviet organisations as personal relationships are highly valued in the USSR.

The Soviet Union is a vastly different society and culture from our own. Doing business is very different from the norms of our society. One cannot simply 'cold call' on Soviet organisations. The preparation for visits has to be precise and organised well in advance. For the company new to the Soviet market, it is strongly advisable to join a trade mission for the first visit. Not only does it cost less than individual visits, but the participants frequently receive assistance in the Soviet Union with making appointments with organisations.[9] A number of organisations have recently been examining the advisability of continuing so-called 'horizontal missions', embracing a wide range of industries, rather than vertical or sectoral ones.

Having established the first contacts, it is important to maintain regular relations with organisations in the USSR. In this respect, constant, routine visits are useful.

A most important means of maintaining contact is through participation in exhibitions. Though taking part can be expensive, it is worthwhile, since failure to appear at an exhibition may be regarded by the Soviets as an indication that a company is not seriously interested in the Soviet market. Exhibitions are also an important means of contact with technical specialists, engineers and end-users, especially from outside Moscow. This is becoming even more important as end-users acquire increasing influence in purchasing decisions.

In general the level of British participation in exhibitions has been poor. For instance, at Inprodtorgmash (the Food and Catering Exhibition) in 1986, Britain had 17 companies represented (out of a total of 500 companies), whereas there were 60 Italian and 55 French firms. At the British Agricultural Exhibition in 1985, 30 firms were represented, while at the West German National Machine Tools Exhibition 227 companies participated.

When some interest has been expressed in a company's product, it is worthwhile promoting a technical presentation as a means of introducing technology to specialists and end-users. Such meetings can have a long-term effect on discussions concerning the technical specifications of equipment which will be purchased and decisions on the future allocation of hard currency in addition to stimulating interest in the product.

Such a policy of promoting one's product can be expensive, but if meticulously planned it can produce excellent results. Employing such methods of marketing will become increasingly important as more Soviet organisations become directly involved in decision making in foreign trade purchasing.

SOVIET FOREIGN TRADE REFORM AND ITS IMPLICATIONS FOR BRITISH COMPANIES

To assess the implications of the changes in the Soviet foreign trade system, it is necessary to examine the context of reforms.

It is important to look at the reform of the foreign trade system against the whole background of *perestroika*. Soviet observers have seen external economic policies and internal issues as being inextricably linked. The drive to increase radically the efficiency of Soviet industry through the improvement of the organisation of both production and labour and the modernisation of industrial plant and methods has led to an emphasis on the more rational use of resources and equipment and greater autonomy in decision making at enterprise level, the introduction of cost accounting and self-financing, and the development of 'economic' rather than 'administrative-command' methods of management.

Professor I.D. Ivanov has stressed the importance of the role of Soviet foreign trade in promoting these developments.[10] Foreign technology and methods of production could assist the acceleration of this process. But there was a clear need for change in the management of foreign trade and to develop new methods of co-operation with foreign partners so that Soviet foreign trade would play a more effective role in the development of the economy.

Considerable dissatisfaction has been expressed both with the export performance of Soviet industry and with the poor utilisation of imports. Energy products account for 80 per cent of exports to the developed capitalist states,[11] and many Soviet observers have pointed out the long-term dangers of dependence on the export of raw materials. They also stress the need to improve the poor export performance of manufactured goods: in 1985, for instance, machinery and equipment made up only 9 per cent of total exports to non-socialist countries.

This poor performance is partly related to the general deficiencies of Soviet industry. According to Nikolai Shmelyov, even by the most optimistic estimate only 17–18 per cent of the production of Soviet manufacturing industry meets world standards.[12] There have been many complaints of the poor quality of the goods exported, of the haphazard availability of manufactured goods and difficulties in the supply of spare parts, all making Soviet goods hard to market in the West. An article in *Izvestiia* complained that the West German firm Uni Ost was compelled to build its own repair shops, so bad was the condition of the tractors which it imported from the USSR.[13]

Moreover, many Soviet enterprises with great potential have shown little interest in exports. Many have long regarded exporting as a burden not worthy of the effort required. In addition, at ministerial and enterprise level there has been a considerable lack of enthusiasm and knowledge of foreign markets. Gorbachev himself noted the lack of interest at enterprise level: 'We must not put up with this any longer. It is important to actively stimulate work collectives, amalgamations and industries in general to increase the manufacture of export products.'[14]

While the inadequacies of Soviet export performances are well known, concern has also been expressed at the failure to make the best use of imports. Too many imports have been purchased to remedy short-term deficiencies. The USSR Minister of Foreign Trade, Boris Aristov, pointed out that many imported goods could have been produced at home. It was unjustifiable, for instance, to import quantities of rolled ferrous metals, pipes, paper and cotton. 'Imports should be increasingly orientated towards satisfying the requirements of the mechanical engineering and other priority industries.'[15] But even when new technology is imported, it is frequently not put to the best use. There are many reports of large quantities of imported machinery 'uninstalled, lying under the open sky' having been dispatched to unenthusiastic enterprises.[16]

In his report to the 27th Congress, Prime Minister Ryzhkov identified the problem. Maintaining that it was impossible to advance rapidly by traditional routes, the importance of orientating the ministries, associations and enterprises towards building up the country's export potential and involving them actively in the decision making in the purchase of imports was stressed.

The foreign economic relations agencies too should restructure their work in the spirit of the new demand . . . it is essential that these agencies should have closer contacts with the ministries and enterprises and that they should search for forms of co-ordinating their interests with the demands of the foreign market and be active participants rather than mere middlemen in carrying out national economic tasks.[17]

The new guidelines for Soviet foreign economic relations which came into force on 1 January 1987 were designed to meet these problems. Overall co-ordination and supervision of foreign economic policy were placed within the authority of the new State Foreign Economic Relations Commission under the chairmanship of the Deputy Prime Minister, Vladimir Kamentsev.

This was followed in January 1988 by the abolition of the Ministry of Foreign Trade and the establishment of the new Ministry of Foreign Economic Relations. K.F. Katushev was appointed Minister. The new Ministry will absorb the remaining functions of the State Committee for Foreign Economic Relations and the Ministry of Foreign Trade. It will assume a general policy-making and co-ordinating role and will be responsible for those aspects of foreign trade not devolved to industrial ministries or state committees.

It is, however, at this level of the management of direct foreign trade relations that the impact of the reforms will be greatest for British companies. In an attempt to overcome the problem of the production sphere being divorced from the foreign trade market and therefore bearing no responsibility for exports, direct foreign trade rights were given in January 1987 to 22 ministries and more than 70 enterprises, state committees and production associations. They account for about 26 per cent of the country's imports and 14 per cent of exports, including 65 of the exports in engineering products.[18] By the spring of 1988 a total of 26 ministries and 83 industrial enterprises had been given the right to trade directly with foreign countries. In December 1988 all Soviet enterprises which could compete on international markets were given the right to engage in export and import transactions as from April 1989. While this represents a considerable devolution of decision making (as previously over 90 per cent of foreign trade turnover of the USSR passed through Foreign Trade Organisations under the Ministry of Foreign Trade), it must be pointed out that the Ministry of Foreign Economic Relations still retains responsibility for trade in fuel, raw materials, food-stuffs and goods of strategic importance. Soviet officials, however, have stated that mechanisms are being developed to give key ministries (such as the Ministry of Oil and Gas) a limited measure of autonomy in decision making on purchases of foreign equipment. The Ministry will retain responsibility for decision making on larger turn-key projects and green field developments. The Foreign Trade Organisations left within the Ministry have been placed on a basis of cost-accounting and self-financing. The Ministry is to have responsibility for control over the observance of the state interests of the USSR in the foreign market, participating in planning strategy for the development of foreign economic relations and Soviet trade policy, the development of exporting and new forms of co-operation with foreign countries. The roles of the division dealing with economic work, planning and commodity administration have been enlarged. In addition to the loss of a number of Foreign Trade Organisations and the elimination of a number of functions, the apparatus of the Ministry of Foreign Trade and the State Committees for External Economic Relations has been reduced by 38 per cent.[19]

The Ministries and Departments with the right to trade directly with foreign partners are to have their own Foreign Trade Associations, based on the principles of self-financing and self-accounting. Amalgamations, enterprises and organisations with direct foreign trade rights will set up cost-accounting foreign trade firms.

All organisations and enterprises with foreign trade rights may maintain funds in convertible currency. In the past, central authorities were able to confiscate over-plan currency for grain imports – a new law forbids this. Convertible currency budgets can be used to acquire in world markets equipment and technology for the modernisation of production. The USSR Bank of Foreign Trade may grant loans in foreign currency for a period of up to four years for these organisations to set up and develop lines for export.

In general, the criteria for selecting enterprises, scientific institutions and associations for direct foreign trade rights are based on previous production and export records. Although many of them are large scale, it is by no means the major factor.[20] To the casual observer, a few of those listed may appear surprising. One such institution chosen may serve as a useful illustration of both the benefits derived from such rights and the evolution of such a policy. At the 1985 public health exhibition, the products of the Moscow Eye Microsurgery Research Institute amounted to 600,000 roubles, out of export contracts signed by Soviet Foreign Trade Organisations worth 800,000 roubles. The Ministry of Foreign Trade had made Licensintorg the sole exporter of the Institute's products in place of three Foreign Trade Organisations. One half of the Institute's own currency account at the Bank of Foreign Trade was set aside for the purchase of equipment and medicines. The importing of equipment, materials and instruments, previously undertaken by eleven different organisations, was now handled by one Foreign Trade Organisation – Tekhnabexport. Since then, the Institute's activities have expanded into the treatment of foreign patients for hard currency and the construction of a microsurgery centre which will be exported on a turn-key basis.[21] The advantages of Soviet organisations ultimately acquiring such rights could therefore be considerable in terms of their own development and efficiency.

In the long term the acquisition of direct rights by ministries and enterprises should be of benefit to British companies. There should be a greater opportunity for direct contacts with end-users and ministries who have direct responsibility for their products. Their involvement at an early stage of negotiations will undoubtedly be an advantage. The participation of the end-user in the decision-making process for purchasing will also be helpful. It will demand increased effort from British companies but it also presents opportunities, in particular for firms new to the Soviet market. However, the implications for firms in the short term are rather different. First, there will be a transitional period. It has already been noted that progress in the setting-up of new Foreign Trade Organisations has been variable to say the least. A number of companies have reported being obliged to attempt to maintain old contacts while at the same time developing new relationships with the new ministerial organisations. The problem has been enhanced by the fact that the Foreign Trade Organisations of the former Ministry of Foreign Trade have a vested interest in defending their position. One way in which they try to do this is to tell their business partners that their own power and influence are not affected. Foreign firms are then left to find out for themselves which new organisations are responsible for their product category and to establish direct contacts.

Personal contacts, which have always played such a significant role in developing trading links with the USSR, have been disrupted by the considerable turnover of personnel and the changes in the structure of the foreign trade bodies and the ministries. One marketing manager of a firm with long-standing trading ties in the USSR reported that the company's personal contacts were virtually wiped out overnight. The experience of companies has varied in this respect. 'If ministries and enterprises are to take key foreign trade decisions, contacts in Moscow will no longer be enough.'[22] The process of building contacts with new organisations will be time-consuming and will demand effort from firms.

From the communications point of view, the USSR is a difficult market in which to work at the best of times.[23] How efforts to build up contacts with new organisations will work in practice is uncertain. Many of the new enterprises are outside Moscow, some in regions without Intourist facilities and where foreigners are not normally permitted to travel. One Soviet official suggested to me that some of these enterprises may maintain branch offices in Moscow for the purpose of building contacts with foreign companies. For one company this may be an expensive process but the emphasis in foreign trade policy on encouraging participation of Republics at Council of Ministers and ministerial department level could be of assistance in creating representation for groups of organisations in Moscow. Regional authorities have started to make use of central locations to present local products to potential foreign buyers.[24]

The position of the Soviet Trade Delegation in the UK has been enhanced by the changes as individual members have been directly appointed to represent the interests of ministries and enterprises with direct foreign trade rights in Britain. This involves a considerable expansion of work in assisting these organisations directly in developing a position in the British market.

The functions of the USSR Chamber of Commerce and Industry have also been expanded. In the past the work of the Chamber has put a strong emphasis on assisting foreign companies in the USSR. The Chamber will now play a direct role in the setting of new Foreign Trade Organisations in Ministries and Enterprises through an Advisory Service. Having assessed the quality of products being produced, this Advisory Service will then assist in finding customers abroad. There will be an advertising service within the Chamber to help with promotional literature etc. This centre will be funded by the enterprises and ministries themselves. The Advisory Service will help enterprises to participate in exhibitions abroad and will arrange missions abroad for representatives of enterprises and ministries.

The Chairman of the State Foreign Economic Relations Commission, Vladimir Kamentsev, has admitted that the lack of qualified 'cadres' in foreign trade is a serious problem and that the only solution to the problem in the long term is to expand the training and development of specialists. According to Kamentsev the new specialists should possess a high degree of competence in the technical operation of the external market, be highly qualified in economics and fluent in foreign languages. While they should have a good specialist education, they must also have a sufficiently high degree of maturity to be able to take commercial risks. Varied forms of training are to include direct study in foreign banks and firms and the invitation of Western specialists to the USSR for consultation. The training of specialists for Foreign Trade Organisations and firms will be concentrated in the Academy of the National Economy and the All-Union Academy of Foreign Trade. The training of foreign economic relations at other levels of higher education will also be expanded in view of the needs of enterprises and organisations becoming involved in foreign trade.[25] The work of the Academy of Foreign Trade will be vastly expanded to provide a wider range of full-time, part-time and in-service courses. Emphasis will be placed upon the training of 'generalists', that is, people well versed in the operation of foreign trade and with knowledge of foreign countries rather than specialists in industrial production for the new foreign trade apparatus. There is considerable Soviet interest in developing relationships with management schools in British universities and polytechnics to construct training courses for the new 'cadres' as well as to help with advice on the expansion of institutions such as the Academy of Foreign Trade.

While new powers and responsibilities and methods of management are being defined in the USSR, British firms are likely in the short term to encounter a degree of uncertainty in relations and some inability on the part of the Soviets to take decisions. While such problems are of a temporary nature, the changes in the Soviet foreign trade system also have long-term implications for British companies.

Until the present time, over 50 per cent of Soviet imports have been consumables. This pattern cannot be expected to last much longer. It has been a clearly stated aim of the reform that there should be better planning and utilisation of imports. Kamentsev has pointed out the importance of working out on a national basis the import of foreign technology in areas such as automation, computing and microprocessing equipment and robotics. All the key branches of industry, along with individual regions and union republics, are to be involved in the planning of imports. It is therefore essential for British firms to understand the needs and priorities of economic development in the Soviet Union.

The days are past when British companies can think exclusively in terms of simply selling products on a straight cash basis. Firms will have to be much more flexible in their approach. They will have to be prepared to sell not simply products but the whole package of technology including proper training in its use. It will be necessary in many cases to consider licensing. Soviet officials have stressed to the Trade Advisory Service the importance of including 'Soviet participation' in future contracts. This may take a number of forms including the use of Soviet materials or Soviet labour or partial assembly in the Soviet Union.

Counter-trade will probably acquire a greater significance not only as a means of reducing the spending of hard currency but also of improving export performance. In the past, counter-trade has been unpopular with British firms, and Soviet organisations have also frequently lacked enthusiasm. To date, there has been no central planning responsibility for regulating counter-trade. Almost all counter-trade has taken place with the same Foreign Trade Organisation to which the British company made the sale. Without very high-level political co-ordination it has proved almost impossible to conduct counter-trade across Foreign Trade Organisations and Ministries. This has resulted in severe restrictions on the choice of goods available for counter-trade; it has therefore tended to revolve around raw materials and end products produced by plants built by Western firms in 'buy-back' arrangements. This limited choice has been aggravated by the tendency of Soviet organisations to hoard products rather than export them and by the poor quality of goods offered. In this respect, however, the situation is changing. Pressures will now be much greater against the hoarding of goods and in favour of promoting the production of high-quality goods for export. A number of products normally sold directly for hard currency have appeared in the Soviet lists as potential counter-trade items, including passenger cars, watches, microscopes and photographic equipment.[26] There is reason to think this list will continue to expand.

A co-ordinating commission on counter-trade has been set up to examine the major problems involved, in particular the difficulties in conducting counter-trade across Foreign Trade Organisations. The problems are complex and it may well be some time before we see any substantial changes.

Even firms selling high priority equipment to the Soviet Union have been offered payment in counter-trade, on several occasions in gas. Although for the smaller British company counter-trade might appear a daunting prospect, with the right kind of specialist assistance it can still offer a very profitable path to trading with the USSR.

JOINT VENTURES

For the first time since the concessions of the 1920s, foreign companies are now able to participate in true joint ventures in the USSR. Initially the basic arrangement was that the Soviet share of the authorised capital would be a majority one; foreign equity was limited to 49 per cent. At the beginning of 1989 this restriction was lifted, allowing the shares in the joint ventures to be fixed by agreement even if this means majority foreign holdings. The share of capital of the Western firm can be provided in the form of machinery, technology, licences and cash. The valuation of each side's contribution is to be based upon agreed prices which take account of world prices.

There are two levels of management with representation from both sides: the supervisory board which is meant to make strategic and policy decisions and the executive board which performs the routine management. While initially the Chairman of the Supervisory Board and the Director-General of the Executive Board had to be citizens of the USSR, as from January 1989 it is possible for them to be foreigners.

Joint ventures are not integrated into the Soviet planning system and are treated as foreign activities. No guarantees are given to them on sales. They are to act on the basis of cost-accounting and currency repayment and are to be self-financing.[27]

For the USSR, joint ventures offer considerable opportunity to acquire new technology at little cost. For British firms there are also advantages. The USSR offers a huge market with large labour resources. Foreign firms will be freed from payment of taxes for two years from the receipt of profits. Moreover, foreign participants in joint ventures are guaranteed the right to transfer abroad in foreign currency the sums that are due to them as a result of the distribution of profits coming from the work of the enterprise. It must be pointed out, however, that the operating premise of the joint venture is to market its products not only in the domestic market of the USSR, but also in the home market of the Western partner or, more probably, in a third market.

The agreement with the Italian combine FATA suggests that there is a Soviet desire to be reasonable and realistic in this regard. Of a total output from the FATA joint venture 80 per cent will be destined for the Soviet market and 20 per cent for export. At the present time, the full implications of the development of joint ventures are only beginning to be worked out. The conditions of joint ventures are far from immutable, as has been shown by the frequent changes in Soviet legislation in this area since 1987. Kamentsev, writing in late 1987, expected that the process of creating joint ventures would be simplified and that Ministries, Departments and Council of Ministers at republican level would be given the right to make such proposals.[28]

There is no doubt that the formation of joint ventures is a long-term process but, in comparison with firms from other countries, British firms have been slow to put forward proposals. By the end of October 1987 thirteen joint venture agreements had been signed – none with British firms. Perhaps the best-known agreement of Pepsico to open two Pizza Huts in Moscow is the most misleading. The more usual type of joint venture will be comparable to the agreement signed by the Italian firm Alnma Rose with the Uzbytplastik Production Amalgamation of Tashkent to produce household goods. The joint venture between Tairiku Trade of Japan and Irkutsk Lesprom will produce 9 million cubic metres of timber per year, of which 7 million cubic metres will be exported to Japan. The President of this company is Soviet, the Vice-President is Japanese and the supervisory board consists of four Soviet citizens and three Japanese.[29] At the end of 1988 there were ten joint venture agreements with Britain out of a total of 162 signed with Western companies. A considerable number of British firms are known to be engaged in discussions with the USSR concerning joint ventures.[30] British joint ventures involve small firms such as Gerald Computers (to form a company to manufacture educational software) as well as large ones such as John Brown (for the modernisation of two petrochemical plants) with a long history of Soviet contacts. Soviet officials have stressed that joint ventures are not intended to be the preserve of large companies. Indeed, particularly in the early stages, they would prefer to work in suitable medium-sized projects.

OUTLOOK

To assess the future prospects for British companies doing business in the Soviet Union inevitably involves speculation. A number of conclusions, however, can be drawn from the changes taking place in the USSR.

Despite the almost panic purchases of 1989–90, there will be a long-term decline in demand for imports in some traditional areas such as consumer goods. The long-term prospects, however, will remain bright for exporting in many areas of industry, particularly in high technology. British firms must not underestimate the extent of the foreign trade reforms nor the degree of change in the USSR in general. Ultimately, progress will depend on the development of *perestroika* but Soviet officials have indicated that further changes in the management of foreign trade are highly likely.

Looking to the future, it is probable that foreign trade rights will be extended to more organisations and enterprises, though it remains unlikely they will include ministries involved in strategic products. But if the reforms are successful, methods may well be devised to give such ministries some measure of formal participation in decision making in the foreign market.

In the drive to extend the rights to trade independently, increased participation at republican and regional level will be seen. Foreign Trade Organisations, directly responsible to the Republic Council of Ministers, have been created in the Union Republics to develop the export of the products of republican and local industries.[31]

In the transitional period, certainly at least for the next few years, exporting to the USSR will perhaps become more difficult for British firms. A greater degree of flexibility in attitudes and marketing policy, careful monitoring of the process of change in the USSR and a more professional approach to marketing will be required to overcome the kinds of problems outlined. Smaller firms in particular will need specialist assistance and resources. The Soviet Union has always been a worthwhile market for those British companies which have succeeded and it will continue to be so for those firms which can meet the challenges of the reforms brought about by *perestroika*.

NOTES

1. Dr Norman Wooding, Minutes of Evidence, *UK–Soviet Relations*, House of Commons, Foreign Affairs Committee, Session 1984–85, p. 14.
2. Mr Ralph Land, *ibid.*, p. 14.
3. Mr A.R.B. Hore MBE, *ibid.*, p. 15.
4. Speech by Mr V.M. Ivanov, Head of Trade Delegation of the USSR in the United Kingdom, Trade Advisory Service Seminar on Scottish–Soviet Trade, Glasgow, 18 February 1986.
5. Sir Bryan Cartledge, 'Business growth through industrial modernisation', USSR – Special feature, *British Business*, 5 September 1986.
6. Courtaulds is one of the finest examples of a firm maintaining a long tradition of trading contacts with Soviet organisations and developing marketing strategies and structures to meet specifically the needs of the Soviet market.
7. East European Trade Council, *British–Soviet Trade: An Assessment of the United Kingdom's Performance and Prospects*, p. 13.

8. East Europe Trade Council, *British-Soviet Trade*, p. 45.

9. Typically, trade missions include a considerable number of firms with extensive previous experience in the Soviet market, and new companies can derive benefit from the contact sustained with them during the mission. The provision of services for individual missions is variable but those organised by specialist agencies can offer full administrative and secretarial services which are most valuable in reducing the frustrations of doing business in the USSR to bearable level.

10. Address to CBI on Anglo-Soviet Trade, London, 2 March 1987.

11. V. Shastiko *et al.*, 'Round-table discussion on foreign trade', *Izvestiia*, 9 October 1987.

12. Nikolai Shmelyov, *Novyi mir*, June 1987.

13. V. Shastiko *et al.*, 'Round-table discussion on foreign trade'.

14. M.S. Gorbachev, Meeting of CPSU Central Committee, June 1985, *Selected Speeches and Articles* (Progress Publishers, 1986), p. 142.

15. Boris Aristov, 'Soviet foreign trade meets new tasks', *Vneshniaia Torgovlia*, 5 (1986), p. 3.

16. Vladimir Karavaev, 'Round-table discussion on foreign trade', *Izvestiia*, 9 October 1987.

17. N.I. Ryzhkov, *Guidelines for the Economic and Social Development of the USSR for 1988–1990 and for the Period ending in 2000* (Novosti Press, 1986), pp. 52–3.

18. *Ecotass Special*, (19 January 1987), p. 47.

19. V. Kamentsev: 'Problems of foreign trade activity', *Kommunist*, 15 (October 1987), p. 26.

20. The production combine based in Rostov-on-Don, Rostselmash, accounts for almost half of the output of agricultural machinery in the USSR.

21. A British firm has already purchased instruments and technology from this institute. The director of the clinic, Professor Fyodorov, is also President of the USSR–Great Britain Society.

22. *Business Eastern Europe*, 15 September 1986.

23. There have been some changes in this respect. The re-introduction of direct dialling to Moscow has been a great improvement. The absence, however, of modern fax, telex and reprographic facilities in many ministries, departments, institutes and enterprises, not to mention a general unavailability of telephone directories, can be a considerable hindrance to doing business in the USSR, particularly outside of Moscow.

24. *Izvestiia*, 10 May 1987. A presentation of diverse products was made, ranging from Kasli metal casting, Zlatoust steel engineering and decorative Urals stones to the Olimpisk children's bicycle. A proposal was made by Karelia Trade for the processing of timber waste. The Cheliabinsk tractor factory received a proposal for an order from the Finnish firm Harre for the joint manufacture of sanitary articles of stainless steel.

25. V. Kamentsev, 'Problems of foreign trade activity'.

26. *Business Eastern Europe*, 6 October 1986, p. 317.

27. *Ecotass*, p. 23.

28. V. Kamentsev, 'Problems of foreign trade activity'.

29. The state-owned Italian firm ENI hope to sign an agreement with the USSR Ministry of Oil Refining and Petrochemical Industry for the production of high-octane additives for oil products. These will be sold on the world market through ECO fuel. The initial capital of the joint venture will be 200–300 million dollars.

30. See chapter 11, p. 238 for more recent data.
31. V. Kamentsev, 'Problems of foreign trade activity'. Also reported in *Ecotass*: 'The Councils of Ministers of the Soviet constituent republics have each been given the right to form republican cost-accounting Foreign Trade associations which will perform foreign economic activities for the enterprises and organisations of the republican ministries and departments and for the production amalgamations, enterprises and organisations under their joint direction.'

11 Conclusions: Soviet–British relations under *perestroika*

ALEX PRAVDA AND PETER J. S. DUNCAN

The last decade has seen the worst and the best of times in post-war relations between the Soviet Union and Britain. In the first five years relations plumbed depths unequalled since the early Cold War period; in the last five they have reached new heights. Since late 1987 both sides have agreed that the bilateral relationship is better than at any time since the war.[1]

This dramatic shift in relations is evident, in varying degree, in all the dimensions of the bilateral relationship covered in the preceding chapters. Drawing on these chapters we shall focus on the thrust of change in the second half of the decade. As the chapter title suggests, we are interested in Soviet–British relations 'under *perestroika*' in two senses: the nature of changes which have occurred in the period associated with *perestroika*, and the extent to which such changes amount to a restructuring of the bilateral relationship. This involves considering the scope and depth of change in each of the major dimensions of relations; the factors shaping such change; and shifts in the overall configuration of relations. Assessing such issues may help us to evaluate the significance of recent and current changes. Are relations becoming less thin and fragile, less vulnerable to disruptive developments? It is as well to recall that previous upturns in relations, as in the mid-1970s, were hailed as remarkable improvements, only to be followed by a downward cycle. Do the changes of the last five years signal a departure from the historical pattern of oscillation highlighted by Curtis Keeble? To address these questions the following sections look at changing popular perceptions; the development of non-governmental and economic contacts; the course of political dialogue; diplomatic relations; and finally, the shifts in national elite images and perspectives that shape relations over the long term.

PUBLIC PERCEPTIONS AND CONTACTS

Of all the changes in relations over the last five years, perhaps the most visible and extensive have come in the sphere of public perceptions. For a Soviet population trying to absorb an overwhelming amount of new information about all aspects of the West, Britain appears as only a small part of a vast crowded canvas. What coverage the Soviet media do give the country depicts British society and politics, as Peter Duncan notes, in a more balanced and positive light. The policy of *glasnost'* has made other sources of information about the UK more readily available to the interested public. Since January 1987 an estimated audience of 18 million have been able to listen to the BBC without the interference of jamming.[2] More significantly, perhaps, Soviet viewers have been able to watch British politicians speak frankly about East–West relations and witness lively telebridge exchanges between Soviet and British groups. They have also apparently been impressed by the picture of daily life purveyed by commercials included in the screening of British programmes. Of course all the above sources have provided even more plentiful new information on the United States and the FRG which remain at the forefront of Soviet images of the West; the UK evokes a favourable yet still lukewarm response.[3] In one respect, however, Britain has scored higher than other states: the visibility of its leader. Mrs Thatcher made a greater impact on Soviet public opinion during her visit in spring 1987 than did Mr Kohl or even President Reagan in their subsequent stays in Moscow. In early 1989 she was voted the most popular woman by the readers of two leading Soviet weeklies and a public opinion poll revealed that a majority of Moscovites (52 per cent) trusted Mrs Thatcher while three out of four trusted the British,[4] a remarkable turnaround considering that a few years earlier the Soviet media had dubbed her the Iron Lady and one of the harshest critics of the USSR.

The marked improvement in Soviet public perceptions has been more than matched on the British side. While wariness of the authoritarian aspects of the Soviet system persists, the fear of a 'Soviet Threat' has diminished since the early 1980s and especially since the advent of *glasnost'* and *perestroika*. As Michael Clarke shows, the mid-1980s saw a major shift in the public image of the superpowers as international actors, with disapproval ratings for the Soviet Union coming to equal those for the US as people apparently became similarly cynical about the nature of superpowers. By 1987 the Soviet Union was thought far less likely than the United States to start a war; and according to one poll in late 1988, a substantial majority thought that Gorbachev had done most for world peace.[5] As far as the Soviet threat to Britain is concerned, recent years have also seen a sharp fall in public anxiety. The two-fifths who in 1981 saw Soviet policies as being harmful to Britain had more than halved by 1989.[6] Though public opinion is notoriously volatile, Michael Clarke suggests that these trends may not be susceptible to easy reversal. As he argues, the Soviet Union has now a far better image in Britain than at any time since the war.

In large part this better image is due to more favourable and far fuller media coverage of the Soviet Union and of *perestroika*. If, as Michael Clarke notes, editorial comment remains relatively sparse, radio and television have paid unprecedented attention to all aspects of Soviet life and given Soviet spokesmen far wider access to the British public. Moreover, the visibility of Soviet art, culture and sport has increased markedly. The announcement in 1988 of the first transfer of a Soviet footballer to a British team perhaps represented a more important token of 'normality' of the USSR for most people than the resumption of tours by Russian theatre and ballet troupes.

The growth in cultural exchanges has formed part of a wider resumption and reinvigoration of cultural, educational and scientific contacts largely frozen in the aftermath of the Afghanistan invasion. As John Morison shows, the Cultural Agreement of 1987 provided a framework for a higher level of exchanges; it was reinforced by the Memorandum of Understanding on co-operation in information, culture and education, hailed by Shevardnadze as an important step forward in bilateral relations.[7] A further fillip in this area came from the visit of the Secretary of State for Education and Science in October 1988 which produced the first bilateral agreement for exchanges between Soviet and British schools.[8] A cultural programme agreed in early 1989 expanded still further the scope for cultural and academic exchanges. In April 1989 Shevardnadze and Howe discussed plans for long-term co-operation agreements as well as the establishment of cultural centres in Moscow and London.[9] Prospects for the expansion of cultural and educational contacts between the two countries thus seem good. While the British Government has continued to place a generally low priority on cultural policy – the British Council spends only one-half of a per cent of its budget on the USSR – it did make additional funds available in 1988 for the expansion of facilities, including English-language centres.[10] On the Soviet side, efforts have been made to take advantage of greater opportunities for cultural contact, both to co-ordinate existing activities more effectively as well as develop direct exchanges. The British Council for its part also plans to use some of the additional funds to prime the pump for direct exchanges which, in conditions of *perestroika* and *glasnost'*, may well provide the fastest growing and most valuable element of informal contact between the two countries.

Perestroika has already made possible far larger flows of visitors between Britain and the Soviet Union: in 1988 an estimated 25,000 came from the Soviet Union and approximately 100,000 Britons travelled to the USSR.[11] The new environment has made it possible to extend existing contacts and create new ones. In many spheres established contacts have thickened and provided a basis for direct collaboration.[12] As well as expanding existing contacts, it has been possible to forge new ones on previously sensitive topics. For instance, Soviet lawyers were able to come to Britain in June 1988 to discuss ideas of judicial reform and a return visit is planned.[13] Whereas the numbers involved in specialist meetings may be relatively small, the contribution of broader contacts

234

to mutual understanding of each other's society, thinking and policy is considerable.

A similar broadening is evident in non-governmental contacts of a political nature, a tendency fostered on the British side by greater interest in the USSR and on the Soviet side by the higher priority assigned to building relations with a wider range of political opinion. The more relaxed and less narrowly ideological approach associated with 'new thinking' in Moscow has helped improve Soviet relations with the Left as well as with other segments of the British political spectrum. As Michael Bowker and Peter Shearman show, Soviet relations with reformist elements in the British Communist Party have eased. Less hidebound thinking in Moscow has also facilitated a more open approach to the British trade union movement, one that places less emphasis on labour issues and more on ones of peace. Contacts with the peace movements have been maintained, though here again stress has been increasingly placed on encouraging new popular elements, notably environmental groups.

The recent ascendancy of reform within the CPSU has accelerated a trend, noted by Bowker and Shearman, towards a more positive assessment of reformism within the Labour Party. (The policies of *perestroika* and *glasnost'* have in turn softened some of the critical views of the Soviet system within the Labour movement.) At a practical rather than theoretical level, the increasingly favourable Soviet attitudes to Labour also stem from the development by the party of a defence policy that has broken traditional British bipartisanship on security and fits in with Soviet objectives. While the shift from unilateralism to multilateralism initiated in 1988 may in a policy sense appear less favourable to Moscow, its enhancement of Labour's electoral appeal probably weighs more heavily in Moscow's calculations in improving relations with the party. Moscow appears to have taken Labour more seriously since 1988 in line with improvement in the party's performance and popular support. The Soviet authorities gave the Labour front bench team a high-level reception during its Moscow visit in early 1989 and Gorbachev when in London in April discussed a range of policy issues with the party's leader and his deputy.[14]

Relations with the organised Left in Britain have improved alongside rather than at the cost of contacts with other parts of the British political spectrum. The general growth of interest in the USSR and *perestroika* has made centre and conservative groups somewhat less suspicious of Soviet intentions and more amenable to meeting Soviet politicians and specialists both in Britain and in Moscow. Among the most important channels for a broader range of political contacts between the two countries have been parliamentary visits. Parliamentary contacts have grown in recent years, albeit slowly, and have benefited from the radical changes in political climate in Moscow. Members of the House of Commons Foreign Affairs Committee who visited the Soviet Union both in 1985 and in 1988 were very favourably impressed by the increased frankness of discussions. Soviet deputies, anticipating pioneering moves in creating a parliamentary system, have expressed considerable interest in discussing procedural and other issues with their British colleagues. As the new Soviet parliament assumes a far more important role in political life and foreign policy, so such contacts may well become a key strand of non-governmental political relations between the two countries.[15]

On the political as on the cultural and public front, *perestroika* has thus brought a more favourable climate for building better understanding and thicker contacts between the two countries. Public attitudes of course always remain sensitive to short-term political fluctuations and the maintenance of the improved atmosphere hinges on the continuation of reforms in the Soviet Union. None the less, greater information and the expansion of informal and direct exchanges and contacts, which has now started to get off the ground, offer a cushion against the inevitable ups and downs of government relations.

TRADE AND COMMERCIAL CONTACTS

Recent improvements in economic contacts provide another possible source of greater stability and solidity in overall bilateral relations. The last five years have certainly seen considerable public optimism from both sides about the potential for boosting trade. The 40 per cent figure set as a target for 1990 during Mr Gorbachev's December 1984 visit was echoed by Mrs Thatcher in Moscow in Spring 1987. According to Soviet statistics, overall trade turnover has increased steadily, from 1.8 bn roubles in 1986 to 2.1 bn in 1987 and 2.4 bn roubles in 1988, a rate of growth higher than that shown by trade with West Germany though lower than that of most other leading West European Soviet partners.[16] This would suggest that trade is on track to meet the 1990 target of 2.5 bn roubles turnover. However, British figures, calculated on a different basis, indicate a slight decline in 1987-88, due to a fall in imports from the Soviet Union. British officials see overall performance as disappointing.[17]

Behind these figures lie not only Soviet hard currency shortages, an important constraint on trade, but the perennial problems of doing business in the USSR noted by Michael Kaser and detailed by Anna Dyer. The reforms associated with *perestroika* may have changed the nature of the difficulties of penetrating the Soviet market rather than reduced their severity. The reforms, as Anna Dyer shows, have if anything made it more complicated for Western companies to trade. The extensive reorganisation of the Soviet foreign trade system, involving a high turnover of personnel and decentralisation, means that British companies have to make new contacts and find their way through a different and yet more extensive and confusing jungle than the one through which they had beaten their own paths for many years. In the short term, therefore, as Anna Dyer suggests, the reforms make improving trade performance more difficult and increase the need for support from business and government organisations.

In response to the new complexities as well as new opportunities of *perestroika*, there has been some growth in support services. In March 1987, the British–Soviet Chamber of Commerce opened an office in Moscow and plans exist to build a British–Soviet Trade Centre there in the near future. For its part the Government has responded with modest increases in support staff and a somewhat more active programme of trade-linked official visits to Moscow, though nothing on the West German scale. The Department of Trade and Industry has helped to form Soviet–British working groups covering thirteen sectors and areas of bilateral trade co-operation.[18] While maintaining its traditional insistence on adherence to strict commercial criteria in all measures concerning economic relations, the Government has made available considerable credits, on competitive terms, through the Export Credit Guarantees Department under an agreement signed in January 1987. The ECGD is also willing to provide cover for contracts that take advantage of the £1 bn credit support offered in principle by seven leading UK banks in October 1988.[19] However, more active support still is sought from the Government by major British exporters who want help to eliminate the perennial Soviet surplus and create a balanced bilateral trade in hard currency. Leading British companies underscore the national nature of competition for exports to the Soviet Union and point to the very high priority the Italians, French and especially West German Governments are giving to promoting trade links with the USSR.[20] Many on the British side, including the Foreign Affairs Committee, have urged that the government act to reduce the scope of COCOM restrictions 'to the minimum necessary for genuine military purposes'.[21] The Government has taken some steps in this direction by withdrawing additional restrictions on 'general exceptions' imposed in the wake of Afghanistan and successfully pressing the United States to follow suit.

On its part the Government has berated British businessmen for being 'too timid'[22] in taking advantage of new opportunities presented by *perestroika*. The Department of Trade and Industry underlines the need for companies to take a longer term view of their dealings with the Soviet Union and to show a greater flexibility in the kinds of contracts they offer.[23] As Anna Dyer argues, with hard currency being increasingly at a premium, Soviet firms will be even more favourably disposed than in the past towards deals based on counter-trade. Given the problems of finding goods that can be readily sold in the UK or in other hard currency markets, British firms will probably make greater use of consortia and other arrangements in order to compete effectively. At present French, Italian, West German and Japanese companies sometimes win contracts because they are more flexible and better attuned to the requirements of their Soviet partners, a point often stressed by Soviet officials.[24]

The relative caution and mixed success of British companies on the Soviet market emerges not just in trade but also in the area of joint ventures (JVs). Initially, British officials greeted the Soviet decision in January 1987 to allow JVs with considerable scepticism; the DTI saw this as a 'desperate throw'.[25] As Moscow amended legislation to meet early Western criticism, London, perhaps more slowly than other West European capitals, began to view JVs as a promising new form of commercial involvement with the USSR. After a sluggish start, British interest in JVs picked up through 1988. There were only ten JVs by the end of 1988 but a total of 27 by April 1989 with perhaps a further two score under discussion.[26] One half of the total foundation captial of 23m roubles at the end of 1988 was accounted for by one joint venture. The remainder were fairly small projects by comparison with those of Britain's leading competitors. At the end of 1988 Britain ranked twelfth in the Western league table of joint venture investment, just below Sweden and above Ireland[27] (compared with a ranking of sixth in trade turnover and eighth in exports).

For the Soviet Union, Britain, now as in the past, is a trading and commerical partner of middling importance, not among the critical few on which Soviet hopes of expanding contacts with the West rest, but among those advanced economies which offer reasonable potential for growing economic engagement. Soviet ministries and organisations involved in relations with Britain have sought to promote more active co-ordination of commercial with other ties[28] and seem to see the future in combining government contacts and direct enterprise links, a mixed strategy that testifies to the change in attitudes associated with *perestroika*. The last two years or so have also brought some changes in attitude on the British side which seems favourable to the growth of bilateral trade and commercial links with the Soviet Union. Assessments of the short-term prospects for bilateral trade remain circumspect and rightly so given Soviet hard currency shortages. It is not inconceivable, however, that this impediment might be reduced by British purchase of Soviet gas at some future date.[29] Members of the British corporate sector are showing a growing interest – if more slowly than some of their West European counterparts – in the possibilities of the Soviet market, an interest that reflects and may help to foster the warmer atmosphere in general political and diplomatic relations between the two countries.

POLITICAL DIALOGUE

High-level political dialogue pioneered the recovery of contact between the two countries in 1984 and has since remained at the cutting edge of the developing relationship. So prominently have leadership contacts figured in recent years that they have at times created an exaggerated impression of progress in overall political relations. Growth in traffic and communication at the top has outrun contacts lower down as well as headway made towards closer understanding on substantive issues. Movement in the political relationship has thus been rather top heavy and more impressive in form than substance.

Early signs of the resumption of political dialogue, after the freeze imposed as part of the British response to Soviet intervention in Afghanistan, appeared in 1983. Contacts began in earnest the following year with Mrs Thatcher attending Andropov's funeral in February 1984, Sir Geoffrey Howe visiting Moscow in July and Mr Gorbachev coming to London in December. Mr Gorbachev's visit as head of a parliamentary delegation was only his second official trip to the West and facilitated the improvement of contacts after he became General Secretary in March 1985. High level contacts multiplied with a visit by the Deputy Prime Minister, Lord Whitelaw, to Moscow and Foreign Minister Shevardnadze to London in the course of 1986. Thereafter working exchanges began to increase: 1987–88 saw half a dozen British ministerial visits, on political as well as trade issues, and nearly three times that number in the other direction, mainly on trade and commercial missions.[30] The pace of dialogue, however, has continued to be set by the two leaders. Mrs Thatcher paid a very successful visit to the Soviet Union in the spring of 1987, Mr Gorbachev stopped over at Brize Norton in December 1988 and came for a full, if rather brief, official visit in April 1989. On that occasion both sides agreed that such visits should become a permanent feature of relations and Mrs Thatcher agreed to go to Moscow in mid-1990 while the Queen accepted an invitation to visit the Soviet Union. As the first Royal state visit since the Revolution this would be an important symbol of more 'normal' relations between the two countries.

In terms of the frequency and intensity of dialogue Mrs Thatcher and Mr Gorbachev have set a remarkable record over the last five years: the two leaders have spent over thirty hours in direct talks.[31] The record is remarkable not just by contrast with an almost non-existent dialogue over the previous five years, but by comparison with other major West European states. French, Italian and West German dialogue with Moscow took longer to develop and still lacks at leadership level the intensity of the Gorbachev–Thatcher relationship. The factors that help to account for the special nature of this relationship also shed light on its uncertain foundations. Much hinges on personalities and political circumstance rather than fundamental shifts in the alignment of national interests. Temperamental rather than policy affinity has played an important part in making the dialogue intense and vigorous. Both Mr Gorbachev and Mrs Thatcher are self-confident combative politicians who enjoy hard-hitting discussions on fundamental, even philosophical issues. While their political philosophies differ in content, they have in common a critical attitude to conventional ways of doing things and a sense of mission. To some extent they are kindred political spirits, both maverick political reformers out to change the course of their countries' development.

As important as 'personal chemistry' and affinity may be in shaping the intensity of the dialogue, its origins and development have hinged more on political convenience and circumstance. The domestic and international circumstances in the mid-1980s happened to be conducive to an improvement in British–Soviet contacts. As before in the history of the relationship, Britain took the initiative to improve the climate of relations at a time when East–West tensions were running alarmingly high. Behind the initiative lay a combination of motives: concern to relieve destabilising tensions between East and West and a wish to raise Britain's international profile. Many in Whitehall perhaps felt by 1982–83 that East–West relations had deteriorated to an unnecessary and dangerous extent; some may have considered that matters were not helped by London matching Washington in ideological stridency. The political impact of such opinions was enhanced by Mrs Thatcher's inclination, after her second electoral victory, to take a more active and prominent role on the East–West scene. In any event, a review of policy towards the Soviet Union in 1983 resulted in a decision to try and achieve a 'higher level of political dialogue'.[32] Efforts were apparently made to persuade President Reagan to hold a summit with Andropov.[33] While Washington did not judge the time ripe for such a meeting, it presumably saw no harm in London despatching ministers to Moscow to sound out likely responses to upgrading contacts. Welcoming Mr Gorbachev's visit to London was part of Mrs Thatcher's strategy to take a more ambitious and less ideologically abrasive line on East–West relations. After meeting him she came out more positively than any other Western leader in favour of 'doing business' with Moscow.

The British initiative came at a time of political interregnum in Moscow and received a favourable if not particularly active response. The fact that Mr Gorbachev became General Secretary only a few months after his December 1984 visit to London clearly helped accelerate developments. More importantly, building dialogue with Britain fitted into his efforts to mend fences with all major Western powers. Britain, notwithstanding its record of cool relations with the Soviet Union, gained in attraction because of the scarcity of other Western interlocutors. Dialogue with the United States proceeded slowly even after the Geneva summit and the visit Mr Gorbachev paid to Paris in October 1985 failed to break through cool relations with France; those with West Germany showed little sign of significant improvement until early 1987. Britain also appeared as a worthwhile contact for more positive reasons. Mrs Thatcher was the longest established Western leader with unimpeachable hardline credentials which made any endorsement of *perestroika* and Soviet new thinking all the more valuable. Mr Gorbachev has since made clear that he much appreciated Mrs Thatcher's early enthusiastic recognition.[34] It is precisely the combination of hardline credentials and support for *perestroika* that has made Mrs Thatcher a useful sounding board for Mr Gorbachev's foreign policy initiatives and a proving ground for 'new thinking'. This helps to account for the debating nature of their exchanges and their concentration on contentious fundamental issues. Not only does Mr Gorbachev know that the Prime Minister will give him clear and frank answers,[35] he also knows that any headway made with her counts for a good deal in the eyes of other Western leaders.

To some extent Mrs Thatcher has been able to provide insights and exercise influence on Western thinking. While Soviet assessments of Britain's commitment to Europe remain uncertain, they recognise the growth of Europeanisation and, more importantly, the increasing weight that London carries in European Political Co-operation. Still more salient in Moscow's calculations of the value of dialogue with London are its close links with Washington. The special Atlantic relationship, which in Soviet eyes had lost some of its relevance in the 1960s and 70s, assumed renewed importance in the Thatcher–Reagan era. Mrs Thatcher's particularly close relationship with President Reagan made her a potentially useful force of moderating influence on US policy. While Soviet analysts have remained unclear about the exact nature of British influence over the United States, they have tended, as Margot Light notes, to upgrade their estimates at times of cool relations with Washington and improving contacts with London. This was especially the case in the pre-Reykjavik period (1984–86) during which Moscow made relatively little progress in relations with Washington while London seemed to be taking a somewhat more acceptable line on a number of defence and regional issues.[36] Since Reykjavik, and particularly since the INF Treaty and the rapid improvement of direct superpower relations it marked, the value to Moscow of Britain as a channel of information and influence on US policy has declined. Arguably, it is unlikely to recover in the post-Reagan era given the less intimate relationship likely to obtain between Mrs Thatcher and President Bush. The usefulness of political dialogue with London has also declined somewhat by virtue of the breakthrough in relations between Moscow and Bonn in 1987–88. Just as the scarcity of other Western interlocutors enhanced the importance of Britain as a partner in dialogue in 1984–86, so their readier availability since then has made it commensurately less critical. The cooler and tougher tone adopted by Mr Gorbachev at the meetings with Geoffrey Howe in February 1988 and with Mrs Thatcher in April 1989 might be viewed in this context. Both meetings highlighted the fact that however valuable the political dialogue as the leading front of improvement in Soviet–British relations, it has had a limited impact on substantive issues of differing policy interests.

POLICY ISSUES AND INTERESTS

Encounters between the leaders have been meetings of mind in a limited sense. They have aired differences rather than achieved important agreements. Dialogue has clarified rather than diminished differences in outlook and interest. Nonetheless, the process of clarification itself has helped to reduce tensions and further understanding if not consensus. As Mr Gorbachev remarked during his visit to London in April 1989: 'The fact that Madame Thatcher and I tell each other precisely what we mean to say builds a stable atmosphere of trust and enhances the predictability of our policies. At the same time our problems and differences assume clearer outlines. This alone makes it easier for us to tackle them.'[37]

The steps taken at the top towards greater transparency have been accompanied by efforts further down the government hierarchy to try and address some of the major problems that have traditionally beleaguered bilateral relations. The multiplication of governmental contacts took until 1987–88 to get underway and has only started to lay down 'a solid infrastructure' for a stable working relationship between the two countries.[38] In the 18 months between 1987 and early 1989 there were over a dozen meetings at foreign minister level and eighteen rounds of political consultations.[39] Steps were taken in 1988 to ensure more regular expert-level consultations on a wider range of issues including foreign policy planning, arms control, regional questions and human rights.[40] In terms of working contacts these developments place Britain somewhat ahead of Italy and France but still behind the United States and the FRG. The actual headway made in bilateral discussions as well as in multilateral fora perhaps places Soviet–British relations in a somewhat lower position, though the variations over issue areas make it difficult to generalise. Some issues such as human rights have seen limited progress. On regional matters exchanges have made headway and strengthened relations; security has remained a difficult and divisive area. A 'pacemaker' in establishing political contacts with Moscow in early stages of *perestroika*, London has increasingly appeared as a 'backmarker' in substantive negotiations with the Soviet Union, proceeding more cautiously and prudently than many Western states.

Prudence, caution and toughness have characterised Britain's 'backmarker' role on human rights, traditionally a sensitive area in relations with the Soviet Union. The remarkable shifts in Soviet policy on human rights since 1986, including the basic acceptance of human rights as a legitimate subject for international negotiation, have facilitated considerable progress in bilateral relations in this area. A list of outstanding bilateral cases of family reunifications was resolved in the course of 1987 and 1988 and a consultative framework established to tackle remaining issues.[41] Diplomatic sparring around the subject, however, continues and within multilateral fora, notably CSCE, Britain has still tended to take a very firm line on human rights.[42] The British response to Moscow's proposal to hold a CSCE conference on humanitarian issues in Moscow in 1991 is a case in point. Several West European governments took a 'yes if' position accepting the Soviet idea of holding such a conference and stipulated stringent conditions for its implementation. Britain, on the other hand, initially adopted a 'no but' stance, making any preliminary acceptance of the very principle of holding such a conference in Moscow conditional on prior improvement in the area of human rights. Only after consultation with Washington, which moved towards the 'yes if' position, did London agree to attend such a conference provided that certain improvements were in place by 1991.[43] While the course Britain took may be seen in tactical terms, it highlighted London's particularly firm line on human rights, one evident in Mrs Thatcher's linkage, in January 1989, of Moscow's human rights performance to the situation in Eastern Europe in general and Prague in particular.[44]

The Prime Minister's reference to Czechoslovakia in the human rights context points up a closer British focus over the last decade on Eastern Europe. Whereas London has traditionally shown a secondary interest in the region, Mrs Thatcher has ever since 1980–84 made a more vigorous relationship with selected East European countries part of her effort to activate Britain's role in East–West relations. Her own visits to Hungary in 1984 and Poland in 1988 symbolised a more active British interest in the reformist states evident in particular in support for Hungarian efforts to build closer ties with Western Europe. This growing engagement with Eastern Europe has extended the range of the Moscow–London European political agenda, even if the Eastern European item still figures less prominently than in discussions between Moscow on the one hand and Rome, Paris and especially Bonn on the other. Given Mr Gorbachev's overriding concern with stable evolution rather than ideological rectitude in Eastern Europe, Britain's support for Poland and Hungary is largely welcomed by Soviet reformers. It may also help to indicate London's growing appreciation of a wider Europe and Britain's role within it.

Under Mr Gorbachev Soviet policy has focused more closely on building better relations with all the major West European powers. Britain is therefore taken increasingly seriously in the European context; Mr Gorbachev has stressed Soviet–British relations should fit into the all-European process.[45] But this poses a greater problem than in the case of other West European states given persistent British anxieties about maintaining US links with Europe and consequent wariness of Soviet promotion of a Common European House that seems to exclude or at least marginalise the United States. So while European political issues have become more salient items on the Soviet–British agenda, they continue to bring out differences of interest rather than open up new common ground. London still views Moscow's concept of the Common European House with suspicion; Geoffrey Howe has drawn attention to the danger of such a notion resulting in a 'Soviet dominated common European dacha'.[46] The Soviet Union continues to see Britain as still largely Atlanticist in its European thinking and less amenable than Continental states to building political and economic entente.[47] The fact that Britain is less influential than the FRG on European issues and that London's interests coincide less with those of Moscow have made Britain a less important interlocutor for the Soviet Union, particularly since the improvement of relations beteen Moscow and Bonn in 1987–88. Symptomatic of this shift is the fact that while Gorbachev used the occasion of his December 1984 visit to London to introduce the notion of a common house in Europe, he omitted any such reference from his Guildhall speech in April 1989. Moscow rightly regards relations with West Germany as the ones that really matter for its European policy. According to Gorbachev 'two such nations as the USSR and the FRG largely determine all European weather and even more'.[48]

Beyond Europe, however, Britain has figured more prominently in Soviet calculations than the FRG or any other West European power. Gorbachev's determination to reduce the adverse effects of Soviet Third World policy on East–West relations has increased the value of Britain as an interlocutor on regional problems. For in addition to being experienced in Third World issues, a fact long appreciated by Moscow, Britain has been involved both directly and indirectly in some of the areas on which Gorbachev has concentrated diplomatic efforts. Afghanistan is a case in point. Involvement in arms supplies, plus Britain's considerable political knowledge and even influence in the region, have made London a useful interlocutor for Moscow. A source of friction between the Soviet Union and Britain, Afghanistan has nonetheless constituted a common concern and a subject for useful diplomatic exchange.[49]

Soviet concern under 'new thinking' to settle other outstanding regional conflicts by political means has enhanced the usefulness of talks with Britain on Central America, Southern Africa and the Middle East. In all these areas, particularly the last two, Britain has good contacts and an influential say in shaping West European policy. Moreover, there is growing Soviet recognition that while London has typically sided with Washington, it has adopted a more 'acceptable' position than the US in some regions, for instance the Middle East.[50] Regional issues have therefore provided the most fruitful area for what might be seen as an embryonic relationship of partnership between the two states. This relationship has evolved not so much within a bilateral but rather within a multilateral context, particularly within that of the United Nations.[51] The marked recent growth in Soviet interest in the UN in general and the Security Council in particular with regard to resolving regional conflicts, have placed an added premium from Moscow's standpoint on Britain's permanent membership of the Council. Britain in its turn has welcomed increased Soviet stress on collaboration within the UN framework even if it has not endorsed all of Mr Gorbachev's proposals for making the Security Council a more effective regional conflict manager.[52] Furthermore, Moscow's new willingness to co-operate with Western states on a whole range of global problems has made possible the growth of bilateral co-operation with Britain in several key areas. These include nuclear safety, environmental pollution and health. An agreement to work together to combat drug trafficking has produced co-operation between Soviet and British customs authorities. Police in both countries have exchanged information in efforts to counter terrorism and thus enhance international security.

SECURITY ISSUES

If the *perestroika* years have thus seen some movement towards co-operation and even embryonic partnership on regional and global problems to strengthen general international security, they have not witnessed comparable moves in the sphere of military security. Here we have seen only a moderation of the traditional adversarial nature of the relationship; interests and positions continue to differ in security more than in any other area. Under *perestroika* the Soviet Union has sought to reduce the salience of security in relations with Britain as with other states. Arms control and disarmament have made faster and more remarkable progress than in any other comparable period. From the British Government's standpoint, such progress has opened up potential scope for reducing the security differences with the Soviet Union. However, Soviet moves on the arms control front have created shifts that threaten to destabilise Western security structures and Britain's established role within them. The structural constraints on Britain's role within NATO, as Margot Light notes, still act as powerful impediments to a substantial improvement of relations with the Soviet Union in the security sphere. British anxiety about the Soviet security threat and its concern about problems of managing change in this area have made recent security relations between Moscow and London more difficult than those between Moscow and Bonn or Washington.

Continuing tensions over intelligence activities are perhaps symptomatic of such difficulties and unease, especially on the British side. A trickle of minor expulsions of Soviet representatives and tit-for-tat retaliations through the early 1980s culminated in a large-scale round in 1985.[53] Though this round involved over 30 being expelled on each side it did little to set back improving relations. Nor did it have much effect on the level of Soviet intelligence efforts in London. Having expressed concern publicly over continuing Soviet intelligence activities, the British Government took action in May 1989 to expel eleven Soviet representatives. This prompted traditional retaliation from Moscow and threats of additional measures to limit the number of Britons working in the capital.⁵⁴ While the timing of the initial action was not unconnected with the upcoming NATO summit, the episode pointed up the persistence of old-style responses in Moscow and the extent to which the British Government continues to perceive intelligence activities as symptomatic of the continuing danger the Soviet Union poses to British security.

At the core of the Soviet threat of course lie the military rather than intelligence capabilities of the USSR. It is the quantitative superiority and offensive posture of Soviet armed forces that continues to figure in British official evaluation of the threat and to underpin British security policy. However, it is the strategic and political dimensions of Soviet military power that determine how British and Soviet national security interests relate. This accounts for the fact that while the last decade has seen little real change in Soviet military capabilities, it has witnessed variations in the configuration of security interests between the two countries. Since security issues in the wider sense of the term remain central to general political relations, these variations have coincided with the changing contours of the overall relationship: high levels of conflict in 1979–83; a slight narrowing of the gap between security interests between 1984–86; and the emergence of new dimensions of old security problems since 1987.

In the years of the second Cold War, military factors and frictions figured particularly prominently on both sides. Britain's evaluations of the Soviet threat in the early 1980s laid special emphasis on the continuing offensive structure of Soviet forces and their increasing military build-up.⁵⁵ Moscow for its part saw London as the most active West European proponent of the deployment of cruise and Pershing missiles.⁵⁶ Towards the end of this period, as we have already noted, Britain sought to reduce the high level of tensions and help facilitate a resumption of East–West talks especially in the arms control field. Among the considerations that prompted London to seek dialogue with Moscow at this juncture were two sets of security concerns which subsequently played an important part in easing the improvement in Soviet–British relations, up to late 1986. The first was a fear that the behaviour of both superpowers might undermine the whole process of arms control and the framework built up in the 1970s. A concern to sustain the SALT regime provided some common ground between Britain and the Soviet Union. London displayed greater concern than the Reagan Administration to preserve the SALT II framework. London was also disconcerted by President Reagan's SDI vision on at least two scores. In the first place, SDI represented a line of thinking that could increase tendencies towards US isolationism and thereby threaten Britain's defence and security role in Western Europe. As importantly, a development of SDI would mean weakening and ultimately burying the ABM treaty. The upgrading of Moscow's ballistic missile defence system that this would make possible would in turn undermine the military rationale of Britain's nuclear deterrent. As Chris Bluth notes, London took a fairly critical stance on SDI extending beyond research. Moscow doubtless appreciated Geoffrey Howe's description of the SDI project in Maginot Line terms.[57] On SDI and the ABM treaty at least the gap between Soviet and British security interest showed some signs of narrowing.

With Reykjavik and the emergence of an INF deal between the superpowers the gap between Soviet and British interests widened once again. President Reagan's reported willingness to consider eliminating all ballistic missiles raised the spectre of the US at some future date signing away Britain's nuclear deterrent. US willingness at Reykjavik to contemplate deep cuts in strategic arsenals also lent credence to another source of danger to Britain's nuclear defence: Gorbachev's vision of eliminating nuclear weapons. The rapid, albeit fitful, progress made on START negotiations has reinforced such British concerns and Mrs Thatcher has repeatedly rejected any British participation in the START process until superpower arsenals have undergone very deep cuts. She has also stood out as a vociferous opponent of the Soviet denuclearisation campaign and the staunchest advocate of the principles of nuclear deterrence.

Disagreement between the Soviet Union and Britain over fundamental security issues has been compounded by growing friction over the major policy fruit of Reykjavik: the INF treaty. The double zero in Europe it involves has brought to the surface perennial British concerns about extended deterrence and NATO cohesion. Bonn may have presented the most immediate obstacle to the INF agreement, on the issue of Pershing 1-A missiles, yet the thrust of the agreement now seems compatible with West German security interests. Although officially London warmly welcomed the INF treaty, it considered the implications of the agreement as in many ways inimical to Western security interests in general and UK interests in particular. The government feared that it might weaken Flexible Response and 'decouple' the defence of Western Europe from American land-based nuclear weapons. Britain has therefore been in the forefront of efforts within NATO to 'compensate' for the loss of cruise and Pershing missiles by the introduction of air- and sea-based nuclear systems. Mrs Thatcher has also strenuously opposed the idea of a third zero, advocating instead the modernisation of tactical nuclear weapons. Denuclearisation of Europe would, so the British Government argues, leave Western Europe exposed to the 'intimidating power' of Soviet superiority in conventional arms.[58] Warnings of this kind have prompted Mr Gorbachev to label the Prime Minister a 'tocsin ringer' and have helped to bring about a cooling of relations.[59]

Insofar as Moscow has since 1988 moved towards accepting the need to reduce its conventional superiority and equalise the balance in Europe, British and Soviet interests should overlap at least in this area of security. Britain has welcomed the unilateral cuts announced in December 1988 and Soviet willingness to increase the security of both sides in Europe at lower levels.[60] At the same time, London has been more sceptical than have some of its NATO partners about the value of Moscow's unilateral reductions and of its longer term intentions to move towards a more defensive military posture. The Ministry of Defence has stressed that the Warsaw Pact has 'weapons to spare' while Geoffrey Howe has cautioned against Western opinion being carried away by Mr Gorbachev's Salome-like shedding of one or two of his 70 odd military 'veils'.[61] Furthermore, Britain has pointed out that given the relative density of forces and NATO's defence requirements, the Warsaw Pact might be able to retain the capacity to launch a surprise attack even after accepting deeper cuts than the West.[62]

Generally, then, the British have highlighted the pitfalls of conventional arms reduction. While welcoming Soviet acceptance of intrusive verification, London has laid greater stress than most of its allies on the problems encountered in testing military *glasnost'*.[63] Real though such problems may be, the basic reason for continued British–Soviet friction on security issues relates to the strategic and political implications of the substantial reductions in nuclear and conventional arms Gorbachev clearly wants. Britain is doubly apprehensive about proceeding in this direction. To start with, the very process of negotiating such cuts is likely to exacerbate differences within the Alliance. As Christoph Bluth notes, NATO lacks a consensus on its ultimate objectives towards the Soviet Union, particularly in relation to the 'de-nuclearisation' of Europe. Moreover, movement towards large cuts is particularly worrying for London since they would place in doubt its established defence role and ultimately its political standing within NATO and in Europe. Were Bonn and Washington to go along with Moscow's security objecives, London might find itself compelled to make a more active commitment to West European defence co-operation. Were Britain eventually to become a major force for West European defence integration, this might conceivably provide the basis for more stable security relations with the Soviet Union whose ultimate interests lie in having the UK balance the FRG to prevent any West German domination of a stronger West European defence. Under Mrs Thatcher, however, such a reorientation of British policy towards Europe is highly unlikely. Current differences on security are therefore likely to trouble Soviet–British relations for the foreseeable future.

However, the extent to which security differences set the tone of the relationship may be changing. While security issues have continued to figure centrally in relations over the last five years, the improvements in political dialogue and working relations have created somewhat stronger non-security strands. If security still constitutes the most important single element of the relationship, it may not be quite as dominant as when cultural, economic and political strands were thinner. Recent changes have begun to bring about a shift in the configuration of the relationship which could make it somewhat more stable. Whether it does stabilise and improve depends ultimately not just on movements in the larger East–West security environment but on the development of trust and understanding between the British and Soviet Governments. Some light may be shed on this question, as well as on the underlying tenor and direction of relations, by looking at the evolution of official attitudes on both sides.

CHANGING OFFICIAL VIEWS

The last five years have seen important modifications of stereotypes on both sides. The remarkable pace of change in the Soviet Union has made this process of modification a highly asymmetrical one, with Soviet elite views of the United Kingdom shifting only marginally and British images of the USSR experiencing considerable flux.

The improvements in British economic and political performance over the last ten years have become more readily apparent to Soviet officials especially as 'new thinking' has allowed for a more realistic picture of Western capitalist states as socially and politically resilient and economically prosperous. Soviet analysts have laid more stress on the UK's economic potential[64] and officials seem to have taken some account of recent growth in domestic performance and international investment. Politically, too, Britain is seen to have recovered self-confidence and raised its international stature. Though publicly criticised, the Falklands operation probably contributed to higher Soviet assessments of British capabilities and determination. Such determination is embodied by Mrs Thatcher, whose long term in office, political consistency and high international profile, plus her favourable attitude to *perestroika*, have also helped boost Soviet estimates of Britain's standing. William Waldegrave is probably right in his estimate that Moscow now sees Britain as 'one of the half-dozen countries that really matter'.[65] At the same time, it appears as a country reluctant to revise established policies and more cautious than other West European states in responding actively and positively to Soviet 'new thinking'. From a Soviet standpoint Britain has gained more in respect than in attraction as a key Western partner.

As far as bilateral relations are concerned, far more important changes have taken place in British perceptions of the Soviet Union. *Perestroika* in domestic and foreign policy has had disruptive, disquieting and confusing effects on the stereotypes of the Soviet Union in official circles. Disruptive because the changes have cast doubt on long-held beliefs about the nature of the Soviet Union;

disquieting because they have failed to provide alternative criteria by which to judge Soviet conduct; and confusing insofar as they have introduced contradictions within what was long a coherent view of the Soviet threat. *Perestroika* has brought about an uneven and even incoherent reassessment of the USSR, with far-reaching shifts in attitude towards Soviet domestic system, moderate changes in views of Soviet international conduct and only a modest change in the assessment of the overall nature of the Soviet threat and its implications for British policy.

Officials in Whitehall were perhaps prepared earlier than their Washington counterparts to acknowledge that domestic change in the Soviet Union stemmed predominantly from internal needs and weaknesses rather than external pressure. Yet both they and British politicians have been surprised by the speed and depth of economic and especially political reform since 1986. Many suspended judgment about the fundamental nature of *perestroika* until well into 1987, even 1988, lagging somewhat behind some of their West European colleagues. In a far-ranging reappraisal of Soviet developments in October 1988 Geoffrey Howe recognised the seriousness of Soviet towards a more pluralistic, law-governed and democratic society. For Howe as for Mrs Thatcher recognition of *perestroika* as a process bringing about fundamental change has posed certain problems. It sits uneasily with their image of the Soviet Union as a totalitarian system incapable of fundamental change except by revolution from below. As *perestroika* has come from the top it is difficult to fathom. Hence Mrs Thatcher's revealing references to it as a 'miracle', as something fragile and closely associated with the personality of Mr Gorbachev.

Reappraisal of changes in Soviet foreign policy has proceeded far more slowly than the reassessment of domestic shifts. While by 1987 greater stress was being laid on flexibility and pragmatism, the accent was still on the traditional view of the Soviet Union as an international actor different in kind by virtue of its expansionist ideology. Only after the withdrawal from Afghanistan and the practical operation of intrusive verification was recognition accorded to the claims by Moscow that the 'new thinking' signified a serious strategic shift, including moves towards the de-ideologisation of Soviet foreign policy.[66] The implications of such a change in Soviet foreign policy are of course far reaching. Indeed, Geoffrey Howe in October 1988 went as far as to state that the Soviet Union might be viewed 'less as an adversary and more as a potential partner'.[67]

This important shift in the image of the Soviet Union as an international actor has, however, been hedged around with various qualifications reflecting lingering doubts about the depth of de-ideologisation and the consequences of such a development for Britain policy. Marxism-Leninism is still seen as a significant factor in Soviet foreign policy. As Geoffrey Howe has put it: 'the tattered banner of Marxism-Leninism is nowadays flying at half mast wherever it is to be found. Even so Mr Gorbachev is not about to haul it down. It is important that we have no illusions on that score.'[68] Whatever the possible changes in Soviet intentions, it is argued that it would be dangerous to give them too much policy weight as long as Soviet military capabilities remain threatening.[69] Mrs Thatcher has been more reluctant than most of her Western colleagures to recognize that *perestroika* means the end of the Cold War. In her estimate the Cold War will end only when reforms have been successfully implemented in the Soviet Union; only then will it be possible fundamentally to revise British policy towards the USSR.[70] Meanwhile, the Soviet Union is seen as remaining separated from Britain by 'fundamental and immensely durable differences'. There is movement in the right direction but the Soviet Union still has a long way to go before it can be treated as a 'normal' state with which Britain could have a 'normal' relationship. The emphasis is thus firmly on the need to avoid euphoria and adhere to realistic and prudent policies.

Such British caution is a product not just of pragmatic concern to justify adhering to existing policies. It also reflects an underlying uncertainty about the depth and durability of *perestroika* and new thinking. There is also a somewhat schizophrenic element in attitudes towards the Soviet Union and Soviet policy, especially on Mrs Thatcher's part. On the one hand, she enthusiastically supports Mr Gorbachev's efforts and unhesitatingly trusts him as a leader; on the other, she apparently has lingering doubts about the residual hostile essence, the 'hard realities', of the Soviet system.[71] The stress placed on these doubts and 'realities' should also be seen within the context of domestic British politics and the determination of the Prime Minister to appear as the most dependable guardian of the national interest.

The views of the Soviet Union held by the Prime Minister and her government thus remain uncertain and in a process of transition. *Perestroika* has thrown old certainties into flux without substituting new ones. There is far less hostility yet still considerable wariness reflecting uncertainty. There is sufficient evidence of change to justify hopes of a less adversarial relationship and therefore less talk of the need for vigilance and more about realism and an open mind. On the other hand, sufficient doubts remain to warrant the caution and prudence in British policy which has permeated the whole relationship with the Soviet Union under *perestroika*.

Uncertain transition perhaps best captures the current state of overall relations between the Soviet Union and Britain. Transition towards a more substantial and less hostile relationship shaped somewhat less by security considerations and more by economic and political engagement. The higher level of political dialogue remains the most noticeable change in the relationship over the last five years and is highlighted as such in official assessments.[72] This may enable both sides to cope better with the differences which persist in most areas. On human rights and regional issues the gap between policy interests has narrowed; on security it remains formidable. Yet, as we have noted, the impact of security differences on overall relations may be diminishing as informal contacts, political engagement and economic links take on greater weight. Publics on both sides have become more favourably disposed to a relationship of greater trust. Although official opinion has changed far more cautiously it is moving in the same direction. The basis of a better working diplomatic relationship has been established. The potential exists for more extensive economic contacts. Even if we are a very long way indeed from the influence of Mammon outweighing that of Mars, the traditional overwhelming predominance in the relationship of military issues seems slowly to be waning. It is important to stress, however, that these embryonic shifts do not mark any breakthrough in the relationship and themselves remain highly susceptible to changes in East–West relations. It would be unrealistic to see the changes that have taken place in Soviet–British reations under *perestroika* as amounting to a restructuring of the relationship likely to break the historical pattern of oscillation as noted by Curtis Keeble. It would be more accurate to see the changes as facilitating a transtion from an aversarial, thin and oscillating relationship to a broader, more co-operative albeit still tense one whose course over the next few decades is likely to be marked by fluctuations less disruptive than those of the last seventy years.

NOTES

1. See *Tass*, 25 December 1987; *BBC Summary of World Broadcasts*, 29 December 1987; Howe, *Soviet Television*, 16 February 1988; Thatcher, *Izvestiia*, 6 April 1989, p. 2.
2. House of Commons Foreign Affairs Committee, *First Report*, Session 1988–89, *Eastern Europe and the Soviet Union* (HMSO, 1989), p. 275.
3. See V. Andreenkov, 'SSSR-Velikobritaniia: kakimi my vidim drug druga', *Vechernaia Moskva*, 6 April 1989. A poll of Moscow residents in early 1989 revealed that most respected Britain for its level of education and culture and lack of aggression; very few (13.5 per cent) felt very positively about the British; and one in three had no opinion at all about them.
4. *Ibid.*,
5. *The Observer*, 27 November 1988.
6. For a summary of MORI polls on this and other issues relating to the Soviet Union, see M. Evans, 'Gorbachev is seen by Britons as making the world safer', *The Times*, 5 April 1989.
7. Shevardnadze, *Pravda*, 16 February 1988; also see *Eastern Europe and the Soviet Union*, p. 11.
8. *The Independent*, 4 October 1988.
9. *Soviet News*, 12 April 1989, p. 119.
10. *Eastern Europe and the Soviet Union*, pp. xxxvii–xxxix, pp. 300–1.

11. 'The outlook for relations between the UK and the Soviet Union and the other countries of Eastern Europe', Memorandum submitted by the Foreign and Commonwealth Office to the Foreign affairs Committee; see *Eastern Europe and the Soviet Union*, p. 12.
12. For instance, the Royal Institute of International Affairs and the Institute of World Economy and International Relations, the co-organisers of the annual Anglo-Soviet Roundtable since 1975, were able in 1988 to undertake a collaborative project on international economic security and begin a further one on political security.
13. *Eastern Europe and the Soviet Union*, p. 288 (Memorandum of the GB–USSR Association).
14. *Soviet News*, 12 April 1989, p. 118.
15. *Eastern Europe and the Soviet Union*, p. xxxvii.
16. 'Soviet foreign trade January–December 1988', supplement to *Foreign Trade*, 3 (1989).
17. Kestor George, Head of the Soviet Section at the Department of Trade and Industry, in evidence to the Foreign Affairs Committee, see *Eastern Europe and the Soviet Union*, p. 193; 'UK Trade with the Soviet Union', Memorandum submitted by the Department of Trade and Industry, *ibid.*, p. 189.
18. 'UK Trade with the Soviet Union', *ibid.*, pp. 190–2.
19. *Financial Times*, 3 November 1988.
20. Letter submitted by the Chairman of Major British Exporters, *ibid.*, pp. 257–68.
21. *Ibid.*, pp. xxxv–xxxvi.
22. William Waldegrave in evidence to the Foreign Affairs Select Committee, *ibid.*, p. 33.
23. 'UK trade with the Soviet Union', pp. 185–6.
24. For instance, Yuri Chumakov, *Soviet News*, 29 March 1989, p. 102.
25. Kestor George in evidence to the Foreign Affairs Committee, see *Eastern Europe and the Soviet Union*, p. 194.
26. See *Pravda*, 16 April 1989, p. 4.
27. *Plan Econ Report*, 5: 10–12 (24 March 1989), p. 15, table 6 and L. Geron, *Joint Ventures in the USSR: Database* (RIIA, 1989), pp. 33–40.
28. 'Mezhvedomstvennoe soveshchanie v MID SSSR', *Vestnik Ministerstva inostrannykh del SSSR*, 24 (31 December 1988), p. 46.
29. See J. Stern, 'The potential for Soviet gas exports to the UK', Memorandum submitted to the House of Commons Energy Committee on UK/USSR Energy Relations (mimeo 1989).
30. See Annexe to 'UK trade with the Soviet Union', *Eastern Europe and the Soviet Union*, pp. 191–2.
31. Thirteen hours were notched up at the 1987 meeting in Moscow alone; see *The Times*, 2 April 1987.
32. Malcolm Rifkind in evidence to the Foreign Affairs Committee, House of Commons Foreign Affairs Committee, *Second Report*, Session 1985–86, *UK–Soviet Relations* (HMSO, 1986), p. 295.
33. According to Lord Pym who was then Foreign Secretary, *The Times*, 1 December 1984.
34. Speech at 10 Downing Street on 6 April 1989, *Soviet News*, 12 April 1989, p. 119.
35. V. Zagladin, *The Guardian*, 28 May 1986.
36. For a relatively realistic assessment of British–US relations which emphasises the differences in economic and political fields, see Alexander Lebedev, *Ocherki britanskoi vneshnei politiki* (Mezhdunarodnye otnosheniia, 1988), pp. 113–30.

37. Gorbachev's speech at Downing Street, 6 April 1989, *Soviet News*, 12 April 1989, p. 119.
38. See 'Sovetsko-britanskie peregovory', *Vestnik Ministerstva inostrannykh del SSR*, 5 (15 March 1988), p. 36.
39. According to Nikolai Uspensky, head of the Second European Department of the Soviet Ministry Foreign Affairs (in charge of relations with Britain), Moscow *Radio*, 22 March 1989, *Summary of World Broadcasts*, 23 March 1989, p. A1/1.
40. 'The outlook for relations between the UK and the Soviet Union'; see *Eastern Europe and the Soviet Union*, p. 10.
41. *Ibid.*, p. 11.
42. For instance, Mellor's speech, see *The Times*, 16 April 1988.
43. See *International Herald Tribune*, 17 November 1988; and *Eastern Europe and the Soviet Union*, p. xxxii.
44. *The Times*, 17 January 1989.
45. *Soviet News*, 12 April 1989, p. 119.
46. 'Soviet foreign policy under Gorbachev', *The World Today*, 45: 3 (March 1989), p. 44.
47. For one comment on Britain's greater coolness towards the Soviet Union by comparison with other West European states, see V. N. Zuev, *Angliia i obshchii rynok* (Nauka, 1988), p. 147.
48. Gorbachev's interview in *Der Spiegel*, *Soviet News*, 26 October 1988, p. 401.
49. See for example *Pravda*, 17 February 1988, p. 3.
50. See Gorbachev, *Soviet News*, 12 April 1989, p. 3.
51. See comments by Geoffrey Howe in evidence to the House of Commons Foreign Affairs Committee, *Eastern Europe and the Soviet Union*, p. 253; Lebedev, *Ocherki*, pp. 113, 116–17.
52. Geoffrey Howe, *Eastern Europe and the Soviet Union*, p. 259; and in his Cyril Foster lecture 27 October 1988, 'Soviet foreign policy', p. 43.
53. *Financial Times*, 24 April 1985.
54. *Financial Times*, 23 May 1989.
55. *Statement on the Defence Estimates 1981* (HMSO, 1981), p. 4; and *Statement on the Defence Estimates 1983* (HMSO, 1983), p. 20
56. See, for instance, A. V. Golubev, 'Sovetsko-angliiskie otnosheniia na rubezhe 70-80-kh godov', *Voprosy Istorii*, 7 (1984), p. 56.
57. Lebedev, p. 121; and also see A. Maslennikov, 'Staroe i novoe', *Pravda*, 22 January 1985.
58. *Statement on the Defence Estimates 1988* (HMSO, 1988), p. 2.
59. *Pravda*, 17 February 1988, p. 3.
60. *Statement on the Defence Estimates 1989* (HMSO, 1989), p. 1.
61. In evidence to the Foreign Affairs Committee, see *Eastern Europe and the Soviet Union*, p. 250.
62. *Statement on the Defence Estimates 1989*, p. 4.
63. Considerable umbrage was taken at the inadequate access given to British inspectors at the Shikhany chemical production facility in 1988; see Geoffrey Howe in evidence to the Foreign Affairs Committee, *Eastern Europe and the Soviet Union*, p. 250; and 'Soviet foreign policy', p. 43.
64. V. G. Trukhanovsky and N. K. Kapitonova, *Sovetsko-angliiskie otnosheniia 1945-78* (Mezhdunarodnye otnosheniia, 1979), p. 9.

65. *Eastern Europe and the Soviet Union*, p. 32.
66. 'Soviet foreign policy', p. 44.
67. Cyril Foster lecture, 27 October 1988, Central Office of Information transcript.
68. *Statement on the Defence Estimates, 1989*, pp. 1–2.
69. For instance, see *ibid*.
70. Mrs Thatcher on television as reported in *The Guardian*, 2 January 1989.
71. She interpreted the May 1989 Soviet tit-for-tat retaliation as showing that things had 'not changed very much at all', see *Financial Times*, 23 May 1989.
72. For instance, Gorbachev has stressed the 'new quality' of the dialogue and the fact that both sides have 'learned not to dramatise' their differences; see *Soviet News*, 12 April 1989, p. 119.

Index

For EU product safety concerns, contact us at Calle de José Abascal, 56–1°,
28003 Madrid, Spain or eugpsr@cambridge.org.

www.ingramcontent.com/pod-product-compliance
Ingram Content Group UK Ltd.
Pitfield, Milton Keynes, MK11 3LW, UK
UKHW010036140625
459647UK00012BA/1424